W9-CHE-954

education for safe living

Fourth Edition

education for safe living

Herbert J. Stack

Former Director of the Center for Safety Education New York University

J. Duke Elkow

Adjunct Professor of Education Center for Safety Education New York University; Associate Professor, Brooklyn College City University of New York

Prentice-Hall, Inc., *Englewood Cliffs, New Jersey*

Prentice-Hall, Inc.,
Englewood Cliffs, New Jersey

Library of Congress
Catalog Card No.: 66-11699

Printed in the United States of America
23919-C

preface

Safety education, accident prevention, and injury control have had a steady growth since the first edition of this text was published in 1942. The second and third editions of this book appeared in 1949 and 1957 and gave strong support to the dissemination of safe living practices and concepts highlighted in the 18th year book of the American Association of School Administrators, *Safety Education,* printed in 1940. Our elementary schools and the secondary schools have commendably accepted responsibilities for providing a safe school environment, efficient services and facilities, and appropriate instruction in safety for school youth.

Today, well over 500 colleges and universities offer courses in safety education, accident prevention, driver education for teachers, and related subjects. In recent years there have been substantial increases in the number of full time supervisors and many times that number of other personnel who devote many hours of assigned school time to keep accidents down to a minimum. The school safety coordinator is a valued member of the school's administrative staff. Standards for teacher certification in this field have been raised periodically and standard courses in driver education are now offered in well over 13,000 high schools by many thoroughly qualified teachers preparing youth for a motorized society. The effects of improved teachers' preparation, increased research activities in the safety field, and support to accident prevention by local and national agencies have helped to decrease the death and injury rates of children as well as among adults who have been exposed to the benefits of safety education programs.

This publication is designed for the use of teachers, supervisors, and administrators as well as students. It covers the broad areas of safety education and injury control from the elementary school through college and adult population. It includes a wide range of safety materials and programs, especially in the areas where hazards abound in a complex technological society.

This text represents a complete revision of the third edition, following a careful evaluation of the effectiveness of the text based on the judgement of many users of the publication. New chapters and two appendices have been added to meet the increasing demand for information, and to relate more fully the work of educational agencies to the forces at work behind the safety movement in the community.

It is believed that the concepts and principles contained within this text will provide futher stimulus to *Education for Safe Living.*

H.J.S.
J.D.E.

acknowledgements

The Center for Safety Education wishes first to express its appreciation to those who have prepared chapters for this new edition. This includes the following:

Contributors

Dr. Sidney Birnbach, Director of Health, Physical Education and Safety, Yonkers, New York. Paul Blaisdell, Director, Special Activities, Insurance Information Institute, New York. Dr. Leon Brody, Director of Research and Publications, Center for Safety Education, New York University. Dr. Walter A. Cutter, Director, Center for Safety Education, New York University. Philip Dykstra, Director, Home Safety, National Safety Council. Dr. J. Duke Elkow, Brooklyn College, City University of New York. Dr. Earl Hannaford, Safety Consultant, Bethpage, New York. Paul Hill, Assistant General Manager, National Safety Council. Dr. Victor G. Kane, Brooklyn College, City University of New York. Dr. Norman Key, Executive Secretary, National Commission on Safety Education, Washington, D.C. Professor John Kowalski, New York State University at Oswego. Dr. Herbert J. Stack, Center for Safety Education, New York University. Dr. William Tarrants, U.S. Department of Labor, Washington, D.C. Professor William J. Toth, Center for Safety Education, New York University.

Reviewers

In addition, we are grateful to the following reviewers:

Dr. James Aaron, Southern Illinois State University. Stanley Abercrombie, Assistant Executive Secretary, National Commission on Safety Education. Professor Homer Allen, Purdue University. Dr. Frank Bennett, Supervisor, Safety Education, Baltimore Public Schools, Baltimore, Maryland. Frank Cipriani, Assistant Dean, Evening Session, New York State University at Farmingdale. Norman Engelson, Director, First Aid and Water Safety, New York Chapter, American National Red Cross. Joseph Gibson, Supervisor, Pupil Transportation, Pinellas County, Florida. Dr. George J. Hoffman, Supervisor, Community Services, Board of Education, New York City. Dr. Frances Hoffman, Queens College, City University of New York. Dr. Irmagene Holloway, Division of Accident Prevention, U.S. Public Health Service, Washington, D.C. Leo Lechtanski, Building Manager, Warren Weaver Hall, New York University. Ray Martinez, Pupil Transportation, National Safety Council. Professor Samuel Messer, University of Miami, Coral Gables, Florida. Professor Marvin Mills, West Virginia State College, Institute, West Virginia. Dr. Francis McGlade, Safety Officer, U.S. Army General School, Indianapolis, Indiana. O. H. McKnelly, Supervisor, Pupil Transportation, State Department of Education, Springfield, Illinois, Dr. James

Nihan, Dean of Evening Sessions, New York State University, Farmingdale, New York. Professor Stanley Pechar, New York University, New York, New York. Howard Richardson, Supervisor, Driver Education, State Department of Education, Augusta, Maine. Dr. Harry N. Rosenfield, Director, Washington Office, National Safety Council, Washington, D.C. Dr. Nathaniel O. Schneider, New Jersey Safety Council, Newark, New Jersey. Professor Clinton Sparks, Westmar College, Iowa. Professor Ernest Shrot, Lock Haven State College, Pennsylvania. Professor Yustin Sirutis, City University of New York, City College. Dr. Tobias Wagner, Center for Safety Education, New York University, New York. Daniel Webster, Accident Prevention Division, U.S. Public Health Service, Washington, D.C. Edward Williamson, Consultant in Safety Education, State Department of Education, Tallahassee, Florida. Dr. Peter Yost, West Virginia State University, Morgantown, West Virginia.

Photograph Credit

Aetna Life Affiliated Companies, Hartford, Conn. Acheson, Topeka and Santa Fe Railroad, Chicago, Illinois, Don Erb, Photographer. American Red Cross, Washington, D.C. Center for Safety Education, New York University. Cunard Steamship Line, New York. Cypress Gardens Association, Florida. Detroit Public Schools, Detroit, Michigan. Elkow, J. Duke, City University of New York, Brooklyn College. Fire Department, Baltimore, Maryland. Greyhound Bus Lines, Cleveland, Ohio. International First Aid and Rescue Association, Alexandria, Virginia. International Harvester Co., Chicago, Illinois. Lehv, Maurice, Photographer, Brooklyn College, New York. Memphis State University, Memphis, Tenn. Molitor Photography, Ossining, N.Y. National Board of Fire Underwriters, New York City, N.Y. National Council Boy Scouts of America, New Brunswick, New Jersey. National Rifle Association, Washington, D.C. National Safety Council, Chicago, Illinois. New York State Department of Commerce, Albany, New York. New York State Ski Association, New York City. North Carolina Motor Vehicle Department, Bill Crowell, Photographer. Pellettieri, Luigi, New York University, New York. Perkins and Will, Architects-Engineers, Chicago, Illinois. Pinellas County Public Schools, Florida. Port of New York Authority, New York, N.Y. Savage, Stuart. Schnall, Ben, Photographer Hewlett Harbor, Long Island, New York. Seligson, Stanley, New York University, New York. Simmons, William R., New York University, New York. Southern Illinois State University, Carbondale, Illinois. Sozio, A. F., 130 West 42nd St., New York, New York. Standard Oil Company of New Jersey, New York, New York. Teaneck High School, Teaneck, New Jersey. Transworld Air Lines, New York, N.Y. United States Forest Service, Washington, D.C. United States Weather Bureau, Washington, D.C. University City Public Schools, Missouri, Helen Manley.

contents

1

concepts of safety—past and present

Living safely in a changing world presents one of the major and vital challenges which mankind faces, a challenge which will require all of man's ingenuity, perseverance and cooperative effort if it is to be met successfully. Although much progress has been made, people are just becoming aware of the human and physical barriers to safe living and the means of surmounting them.

In a world in which physical, technical and scientific accomplishments are speeding man far into outer space, to say nothing of providing him with electronic brains to help do his thinking, we are sadly lacking in comparable social achievements. Inability to live safely and enjoy the wonderful physical gains we have made brings to light the unconquered frontier in human behavior which stands between us and what we call safe living. Those who labor to provide tested solutions and know-how are indeed serving uniquely and significantly in man's ever-present struggle to better himself.

Mankind's need for safety and his efforts to provide it for himself and for those dear to him have been part of his living since the beginning of time. In the beginning, survival and safety were much the same thing. Although the hazards and the problems relating to survival have changed, as have the odds for and against survival, the fundamental problem is still the same. Since the time when primitive man sought shelter and developed crude weapons to protect himself from surrounding dangers, anticipating those dangers and meeting them skillfully and resolutely have been major keys to safety and survival.

The relationship between safety and survival prompts the question, "If the drive for survival is instinctive, why is action for safety not automatic?" In the answer to this simple question lie some of the fundamental concepts related to safe living. Without question, when man is faced with immediate threats to his life, he involuntarily fights off the danger or seeks ways to offset or eliminate it. As soon as the immediate danger disappears, man's involuntary drive ceases until he is again faced with a threat to his survival. This reaction is characteristic of all of man's physical drives, such as thirst and hunger. Once such a drive has been satisfied, the urge to act ceases.

In order to anticipate impending threats to his safety and to take safeguarding action in advance, man has to rid himself of concepts such as "accidents are bound to happen." Once he comes to the realization that he can protect himself, he can be motivated through safety education to overcome ignorance, carelessness and inefficiency, and thereby control accidents. The critical factor has been and probably always will be his ability to discipline himself and to respond voluntarily to disciplines imposed by society in order to achieve safety. Discipline is not just a matter of punishment and reward. It includes such things as strict and systematic education and training for obedience and skill, and a system of planning and orderly control of conduct. These are all ingredients of a safe pattern of behavior. Social scientists tell us that good personality is based upon self-discipline. Present-day concepts of safety call for developing and inspiring individual behavior consistent with safe living, for each individual, ultimately, must act on his own. Safety education and training provide the means for avoiding accidents.

The story of the safety movement chronicles man's victories in desperate battles, first with the relentless forces of nature and then with the hazards of machines of his own invention. In recent years, he has been faced with conquering the tragic toll of deaths and accidents on the highways. No matter what area of safety effort we view, man's self-discipline and ability to respond to and to live with necessary disciplinary controls remain the key factors. Engineering can provide safe tools and equipment. Enforcement of safe practices at work, at home and on the highways provides added controls. However, without the emotional conditioning gained through proper motivation, and the development of good safety attitudes through safety education, the ever-essential will-to-do is lacking. Without *education for safe living,* the battle to save lives and reduce injuries to a minimum can never be really successful and will only achieve a frustrating stalemate.

Today's Creed—Total Safety

Before reviewing the interesting history of safety's development in this country, it would be well to discuss today's concept of safety. With it in mind, we will have the perspective needed to assess each of the various developments and movements which produced it.

Safety education as we know it began in this country with the industrial safety movement of the early 1900's. The day when it was an 8 A.M.-to-5 P.M. matter has long since gone. Today's concept envisions safety for the whole person—safety around the clock—at work, at home, at play, on the highways—in fact, in all of our activities. Actually, the schools envisioned safety for the whole person before industry did, but industry is catching up rapidly through its off-the-job and home safety programs. Today's efforts make use of a multitude of agencies and organizations sponsored by schools, colleges, and branches of government, and dealing with highways, sports, recreation and a host of occupations outside the industrial field. These efforts reach into all our activities.

The total safety concept goes much further than merely including all of life's activities in its scope. The development of safe patterns of behavior requires individual participation and training in individual self-discipline and group behavior patterns without which actual performance is impossible.

Until the advance planning, and the establishment and enforcement of controls, of group- and self-discipline, which are components of today's safety education, became effective, advances in safety were sporadic and intermittent. An illustration of this non-direction is the fact that many safety concepts have come out of tragedy and disaster—for example, the great fire that swept through Chicago on the night of October 8, 1871. When shocked and grief-stricken citizens surveyed their 200 dead and the tremendous area of devastation, they knew that it was no act of God, but the result of their own negligence and lack of controls. Shocking conditions of disorder had existed in the city for a long time. Many buildings, of flimsy construction, were little better than shacks, and fires were a daily occurrence. Piles of refuse, boxes, straw and filth lay in the streets. Barns packed with hay and other flammables were attached to houses. Such necessary measures as building codes and fire control regulations were nonexistent or ignored. But Chicago learned a lesson and many other cities profited by it.

Thirty years later 602 persons were trampled to death in Chicago's Iroquois Theater fire. Again there was a national outcry, this time for rigid regulations in theaters, and they have since been put into effect. So with other disasters, such as the Johnstown flood, the sinking of the Titanic, the Triangle Factory fire in New York, the Morro Castle fire and the school-building explosion in New London, Texas. The Texas City disaster and the terrible loss of life in the LaSalle Hotel fire in Chicago and in the Winecoff fire in Atlanta also startled the American public. The collision of the *Stockholm* and the *Andrea Doria,* followed by the sinking of the latter, would have been a disaster if the seas had not been so calm at the time of the collision. Both vessels were modern and radar-equipped. That they collided was due to human error. Each such tragedy resulted in improved safeguards and greater public attention to the accident problem in general. If we could only view the daily national accident toll—in reality as great a disaster—with the same horror and determination to "do something about it," we would be a long way toward achieving our total safety aims and concepts.

Today's safety concepts call for the continuing, consistent application of measures through advance planning, engineering, enforcement and education. Anticipation and prevention go together.

History and Development of the Organized Safety Education Movement

Safety education is as old as man himself. Our ancestors sought protection from the dangers of their environment, and the young were given safety lessons to keep them from harm. The many studies conducted of primitive man show that in order to survive, children had to be protected from the dangers around them. They were taught safe living by their parents, other adults, and older children.

However, the organized safety education movement is of much more recent origin. It was in the eighteenth century that the terrible conditions that existed in the mines and factories in European countries finally brought national leaders to their senses, and organized efforts were made to improve factory working conditions. In the following discussion, we will first consider the development of safety in industry. This will be followed by a brief history of the school safety movement.

Industrial Safety

Public consciousness of the need for accident control was first awakened by the terrible conditions prevailing in the industrial centers of Europe during the eighteenth century. In England, where mechanized industry had its birth, the revolutionary changes in mining and manufacturing processes that began about 1750 brought men and women flocking from the farms to the cities in search of new employment. Many who had formerly plied their trades and crafts in their homes or in small shops now worked in factories under conditions so crowded and hazardous that accidents and disease took tremendous tolls.

Since labor was plentiful, employers were not concerned about the degraded conditions under which these unfortunate people lived and worked. Nor did the victims of accidents have any recourse to law. It was possible to sue an employer on grounds of negligence, but since the burden of proof was on the injured person, his case could easily be defeated if the employer could prove to the satisfaction of the court that the victim had contributed to the cause of the accident. Even when the code that we know as Employer's Liability came into existence and the employer was expected to provide reasonably safe working conditions, he still had various means of evading responsibility if he were sued for damages, and the injured workers found it almost impossible to recover.

Women and children were employed in large numbers during this period, and it was the unspeakable suffering and abuse to which they were subjected that finally aroused the English public to action. The enactment of laws to improve working conditions and shorten hours of labor began in 1802; governmental factory inspection was established in 1833; and eleven years later came Ashley's "Great Factory Act," requiring the protection of workers by guards applied to moving machinery. It was not until 1897, however, that England's first Compensation Act was passed and the workers began to get adequate redress for physical suffering and financial losses.

The United States experienced a corresponding industrial growth at a later period. Factories, mines and transportation systems developed rapidly. Living conditions of workers were better here than in England but accident conditions grew steadily worse. On the railroads, in the mines and in the steel mills, workers were killed by the thousands.

Insurance Employer's Liability Laws naturally prompted industrial organizations to seek insurance coverage against injuries to workers; and this development led to a reduction in the frequency of accidents. Insurance inspectors and engineers, to protect the interests of their companies, gave management valuable advice on reducing hazards in their plants. Before the industries began to develop their own safety activities, the insurance companies carried the major share of this responsibility. During recent years, both industries and insurance companies have greatly expanded their safety work to include education as well as engineering and enforcement. They have exerted a very important influence in the whole field of human conservation.

Workmen's Compensation Laws Great advancement in safety organization followed the enactment of Workmen's Compensation Laws which placed a definite responsibility upon the employer. These laws differ from Employer's Liability in that they require the employer to remunerate the injured employee whether or not negligence can be proved. As previously mentioned, Great Britain passed a Workmen's Compensation Act in 1897. Germany actually was the pioneer in 1884 with a compulsory compensation act covering sickness only. France and Italy passed similar laws in 1898; Russia in 1903. Maryland, in 1902, was the first state in this country to enact compensation legislation, but this law was inadequate and had little effect. New Jersey's law of 1911, a part of Woodrow Wilson's reform movement, is the oldest of such laws now in force in the United States.

Mechanical Safeguards Some safety devices were in operation before organized accident prevention was conceived. Those on the railroads, for example, included the locomotive steam whistle introduced in 1833, the Westinghouse air brake in 1868 and the automatic coupler in 1885. The first public exhibition of safety appliances was held in 1907 at the American Museum of Natural History in New York under the auspices of the American Institute of Social Science. Four years later the American Museum of Safety was organized in New York.

National Safety Council A safety committee of the Association of Iron and Steel Engineers arranged the first Cooperative Safety Congress in Milwaukee in 1912. Action taken at this meeting led to the organization of the National Safety Council in 1913, the first permanent body with a program devoted entirely to accident prevention. Its founders represented industrial corporations, government departments, insurance companies and other interests. First called the "National Council for Industrial Safety," the organization adopted its present name in 1914, as the scope of its activities was widened to include the field of public safety. Many influential leaders in American public life have served as its president.

The National Safety Council has become the most effective safety organization in the country and, in fact, in the world. In recent years, under the leadership of Presidents Ned Dearborn and Howard Pyle, it has expanded its efforts into all phases of safety and has been chartered by an Act of Congress as a noncommercial, nonprofit, cooperative organization. Its annual congress is attended by over 12,000 safety and management personnel from all the states and from many foreign countries. It is made up of a number of sectional organizations called "conferences" which aid the Council staff in developing their program. For illustration, the Industrial Conference includes representation from industries employing some 18 million people, and the School and College Conference includes representation from most of the national organizations interested in school and college safety. Reinforcing the work of the Council are more than 100 local safety councils affiliated with the National Council and several hundred others whose work is aided by the influence of the national organization.

Results in Industry Accident prevention in industry has justified the faith, the foresight and the persistent effort of these early pioneers. Deaths from work accidents throughout the nation have decreased steadily since 1912. Since 1930, the accident-severity rate in industry has decreased approximately 50 per cent, certainly a great achievement, because it means a saving of lives, a reduction of injuries, and a decrease in the loss of valuable property.

Today's Safety Concepts in Industry Today, industry demands five things of itself from a safety standpoint:

1. Management interest and backing, i.e., topflight leadership and planning.
2. Supervisory follow-through, i.e., firm, fair and friendly training in and enforcement of safe working practices.
3. Safe working environment, i.e., both physical and mental.
4. Employee participation, i.e., personal responsibility for and identification with safety.
5. A sound system of accident reporting and analysis, i.e., signposts to performance and action.

With these demands in mind, it is interesting to look at what industry would like the schools and colleges to do about safety. It would like to have graduates sent to it who:

1. Have good attitudes toward safety derived from actual training in and practice of safe living in their school and other activities.
2. Know and appreciate that safety will be expected of them when they take a job in industry in just the same way as they are expected to be proficient in the other skills they learned in school.
3. Have a record of good, safe accident-free performance in all school work and activities, including vocational and shop work.
4. Have had teachers whose sincere interest in knowledge of safety have caused them to integrate it into all phases of student work and activities.
5. Have learned self-discipline and have been taught to understand and live under authority.

The things that industry would like from the schools and colleges from a safety standpoint are inherent in the total safety concept previously discussed. The years we devote to our schooling are equal to about one-third of the time we spend in our working careers. Since a major portion of those attending schools and colleges go into industry, industry has a vital and compelling interest in school safety. With this present-day emphasis by industry on total safety in mind, the history and development of safety education in the schools covered in the next section becomes even more significant.

The Schools Join the Safety Movement

Before the child safety movement began, far more children died from accidents than do today. In 1925, preschool deaths totaled 9,100, and deaths among children of school age, 9,900. In recent years the number of fatalities for the preschool age has dropped to 8,380; for the school age to 6,000—in spite of a great increase in the child population. In fact, deaths for children under 15 in 1925 were greater than for workers in industry. It is no wonder that leaders in the safety movement began to direct their attention to finding ways to reduce this tragic, annual loss.

Industry had found that something more than engineering and enforcement was needed in the prevention of accidents, namely, the education of the employee in safe work habits and attitudes. Why not, then, apply this principle in a broader and more fundamental way? Why not include safety in the general program of education? Men of vision began raising this question soon after the organization of the National Safety Council, and brought it up recurrently at the annual congresses from 1913 to 1917.

The revolutionary change in transportation made attention to public safety especially important. With the greatly increased number of automobiles on streets and highways, traffic accidents were mounting to an alarming figure. Thousands of children were victims of these accidents every year, and the schools could no longer ignore this critical situation.

Two men, Albert W. Whitney and E. George Payne, were largely responsible for inspiring and guiding the earliest efforts to plan workable programs of instruction. Dr. Payne, at that time president of Harris Teachers' College in St. Louis, conducted an extensive study at Wyman School in that city to demonstrate that safety could be taught through correlation with practically every subject in the curriculum. Thus he successfully met the objection of many school administrators that additional teachers and money would be needed if safety programs were introduced. Teachers from all parts of the country visited Wyman School and returned to their communities convinced that the plan was practical. Further impetus was given by the publication in 1919 of Dr. Payne's book *Education in Accident Prevention,* of which more than 50,000 copies have been distributed.

A. W. Whitney, then associate general manager of the National Bureau of Casualty and Surety Underwriters, and formerly a professor at the University of California, was untiring in his efforts to launch the programs of instruction on a positive, constructive basis and to secure financial support for the development of materials and advisory service. His philosophy of "safety for more and better adventures" captured the imagination of educators, industrialists and businessmen alike; in fact it was largely responsible for the survival of this movement in the schools. Through his influence, the National Bureau of Casualty and Surety Underwriters from 1922 to 1938 provided approximately $500,000 to the National Safety Council to encourage child safety education. The accident-prevention work of this bureau was transferred in 1948 to the Association of Casualty and Surety Companies (now the American Insurance Association), which continued to support school safety activities, either directly through its accident-prevention department, or indirectly through annual grants to the Center for Safety Education at New York University.

In recent years the member companies of this Association have made financial grants to the Insurance Institute for Highway Safety which in turn provides for the support of the Center. This Insurance Institute is now supported by well over 500 companies including the stock, mutual and independent insurance companies.

The Detroit Program The results of a very comprehensive program initiated in the Detroit Public Schools in 1919 left little doubt as to the lifesaving values of safety education. A fourfold program was launched, stressing the following aspects:

1. A study of traffic accidents among children of school age.
2. Construction of a course of study for the elementary schools.
3. Instruction of a class at Detroit State Teachers College.
4. Cooperation with all civic agencies concerned with public safety.

Cooperative Plan in Kansas City Close cooperation between the board of education and the local safety council was the outstanding factor of a successful program organized in the early twenties in Kansas City, Missouri. Following conferences of the Safety Council Director with school officials, committees were set up to draft a program of classroom instruction and pupil activity. This material was printed in pamphlet form and distributed to every teacher in the system.

In all these initial stages, the Council acted simply in an advisory capacity and, once the classroom instruction was under way, concerned itself primarily with junior safety council organization. In 12 schools selected for experimental work, details of the plan—insignia, constitution and by-laws, teacher guidance, and the like—were studied by principals, teachers and Safety Council representatives. Eventually, a standard program was adopted that became a model for other schools throughout the country. Periodic home inspection campaigns, conducted by the pupils with their parents' help, resulted in a substantial decrease in hazards and in the city's fire loss.

Other Methods of Administration The administration of early safety programs naturally varied with the size of the community and with the type of local educational system. In Louisville, Kentucky, successful work was done under the director of health and safety. In Springfield, Massachusetts, the problem was handled as a regular part of the general program of education. In Pawtucket, Rhode Island, a teachers safety council met once a month to draw up plans, exchange ideas and prepare materials for stimulating the work throughout the schools. In Lynn and Worcester, Massachusetts, laboratory schools were set up as a means of justifying safety education.

At present, most school administrators consider safety education a responsibility of the schools. There are now over 600 members of the Safety Education Supervisors Section of the National Safety Council, while in 1925 there were but three cities that assigned responsibility to safety supervisors.

Program in the Secondary Schools Experimental work indicated that the high school student's interest in accident prevention was to a great extent the interest of an adult, and that the subject might best be introduced through such courses as civics, science, chemistry and home economics. Physical education and organized games and sports offered a good approach, particularly since studies showed that the largest percentage of school injuries took place in these activities. In general, the work in the high schools developed slowly until it received an impetus from the demand for programs of driver education.

According to *Safety Education,* the 18th Yearbook of the American Association of School Administrators, prepared in 1940 (1), approximately 600 schools then offered driver education courses. Amos E. Neyhart of Pennsylvania State College devised an early and highly successful program of road instruction that has since been widely promoted by the American Automobile Association. The National Bureau of Casualty and Surety Underwriters, whose educational director was Herbert J. Stack, also carried on a good deal of work in stimulating and coordinating the first efforts in this field.

The beginning of driver education not only was important in relation to the traffic problem; it also indicated that the modern high school was becoming concerned with safety in general. In 1935, the Education Division of the National Safety Council issued the first manual that attempted to outline methods of organizing programs of driver instruction. Shortly afterward, the National Bureau of Casualty and Surety Underwriters published a more comprehensive treatment of the subject, *Man and the Motor Car.* In 1954, the rights for the publication were given over to the Center for Safety Education and the fifth edition of the text was published by Prentice-Hall, Inc. In 1965, the name of the book, *Man and the Motor Car,* was changed to *Driver and Traffic Safety Education.*

The American Automobile Association text, *Sportsmanlike Driving* first appeared at about the same time as *Man and the Motor Car,* and is now in its fourth edition. Several other books on driver education have been published.

After World War II, driver education grew rapidly until 1952 when a plateau was reached. Since 1954, the number of schools offering courses has jumped from 8,000 to over 12,000. This growth was largely due to state financial support legislation which provides for the reimbursement of school districts on the basis of the number of students given instruction. More than half of the states now have legislation of this type, which will be discussed in a later chapter.

Influence of National Organizations The work of the National Safety Council in developing safety activities has already been discussed. The national and local councils have been strong influences in the encouragement of all phases of safety education. However, there are a number of other organizations that have had much to do with the promotion of school safety.

The American Automobile Association The automobile clubs affiliated with the American Automobile Association have been active for many years in providing lesson plans and posters to elementary schools, and in organizing school safety patrols. They have also made important contributions to the development of driver education in the high schools and colleges, primarily through training teachers and providing classroom materials.

The National Bureau of Casualty and Surety Underwriters The safety education work of this organization dates back to 1925 when its first grant of funds was made to the National Safety Council. The safety activities of the Bureau were subsequently transferred to the Association of Casualty and Surety Companies now the American Insurance Association which is supported by the stock insurance companies. This organization not only was active in industrial safety but made important contributions to school safety, primarily driver education. It aided colleges in the preparation of teachers and supplied schools with teaching materials. Its National High School Driver Education Award for states has had a notable influence on the extension and improvement of driver education. It also provided the basic grant to the Center for Safety Education from 1938 to 1959. During 1959 most of the traffic safety activities of the Association of Casualty and Surety Companies were transferred to the Insurance Institute for Highway Safety. This organization is now supported by over 500 stock, mutual and independent insurance companies.

The National Commission on Safety Education In 1944 this commission was established as a part of the National Education Association, following a grant from the Automotive Safety Foundation. Since it was organized it has done much to obtain wider acceptance of safety education by the schools. Many of its publications are on traffic safety and fire prevention, but it has also issued materials on other phases of safety in the elementary and secondary schools and in the colleges. It has co-sponsored four national conferences on driver education and several on pupil transportation. Recently it has been active in research, both carrying on research studies and publishing the findings of other studies. The publications of the National Commission deal with many areas of safety education and have made a valuable contribution to school safety.

Center for Safety Education Organized in 1938 at New York University, the Center has had much to do with the preparation of leaders in the safety field. Its activities cover the whole field of safety education, including well over 30 different courses. Some of these provide credit for advanced degrees; others are noncredit courses for industrial safety and traffic safety personnel. These courses are offered both on and off the campus. In addition, the Center has offered over 150 intensive courses for safety officers and civilian personnel of the U. S. Army, the Air Force and the Canadian Department of National Defense.

To make its program broadly effective, the Center awards assistantships and scholarships to educators from the various states; conducts research into problems of safety education; publishes research studies and other materials; assists states in preparing courses of study; and cooperates with many national organizations for the promotion of safety education.

Student Organizations

Mention should be made of certain student organizations such as school patrols and junior safety councils. As early as 1913 the American Museum of Safety advocated schoolboy patrols to protect children at crossings. In the same year in Tacoma, Washington, "Safety Scouts" were organized, and in the East the New Jersey Public Service Electric and Gas Company sponsored safety patrols. This movement has grown very rapidly, with several hundred thousand pupils participating each year. Standard rules for the operation of patrols were formulated in 1930 by a committee of the American Automobile Association, the National Safety Council, the National Congress of Parents and Teachers, the National Education Association and the United States Office of Education. Patrols have been most valuable in reducing accidents to children on the way to and from school. The first junior safety council was organized in Rochester, New York, in 1918. Councils are now found in hundreds of towns and cities.

Research

In the early years, development of research in safety education was very slow. The first doctoral study was completed by Henig at New York University in 1925. Following this, five doctoral studies on various safety subjects were completed under fellowships financed by the National Bureau of Casualty and Surety Underwriters. These studies appeared between 1927 and 1933 and were widely used in preparing courses of study. Since 1933, many research studies have been completed, over 70 on the doctoral level, and several hundred for the Masters degree. Some of these have been published as abstracts by the Center for Safety Education, others by the National Safety Council and the National Commission on Safety Education. In addition, many studies have been conducted by research agencies and organizations. In recent years funds for safety research have been made available by federal agencies such as the National Institute for Health and the U. S. Public Health Service. Many of these research studies have been used to prepare chapters in this text and are listed at the ends of chapters.

Teacher Education

Much of the instruction in safety education in the 1920's, although well intended, was of little value. Often the teachers relied on such superficial devices as safety rules, slogans, limericks and jingles. The first college courses in safety education were established in 1929. After that, opportunities for training in methods and subject-matter increased. Since World War II, however, there has been a rapid growth in teacher education; today more than 400 institutions of higher learning offer courses in driver education, general safety or other safety subjects. State requirements for the certification of teachers have also been raised. Although thousands complete these courses each year, the majority of teachers in the country have had little or no formal preparation to teach safety education.

The Philosophy of Safety

> Life is intrinsically dangerous. Life is partly routine, to be sure, but more fundamentally it is an experience of the unknown and hence based on adventure. . . . The prime quality in safety, therefore, is not the removal of danger but an improvement in the quality of adventure.
>
> *Safety for Greater Adventure:*
> *"The Contributions of Albert Wurts Whitney."*

What is the philosophy of safety? * How can its concepts enable man to live a life that is both satisfying and worthwhile? Through philosophy man attempts to discover the goals towards which he should direct his efforts. However, it is through science that he is able to obtain the knowledge, skills and techniques essential for the achievement or approximation of those objectives. As a result, we find philosophy and science complementing each other. Both are needed to help solve man's numerous and complex problems. In the field of safety, philosophy makes us aware of certain needs or shortcomings while science shows us how to remedy or overcome these needs. The experimental character of scientific investigation is the very basis of all research in the field of safety education.

From earliest times to the present, philosophy has always tried to formulate the objectives of a satisfactory existence and to determine the components of the good life. In safety, philosophy is so integrated with the life of an individual that it becomes his outlook upon life; it reveals whether he has found something in life worth pursuing. Civilized man constantly strives to improve his condition to enjoy a more plentiful life, and he can accomplish this only through persistent untiring efforts. The philosophy of safety humanizes science as it contributes to the life and welfare of mankind. According to Whitney, "The very most right thing about safety is that it leads to the more abundant life (11:42)."

The Philosophical Safety Concept For most persons, the word "safety" continues to be one-sided in character, carrying a negative or static connotation. It has come to have a one-sided character because of our desire to have it so. In the complete safety concept, not one but two questions arise. One must ask not merely "safety from what?" but also "safety for what?" The responses to these queries are clearly sufficient; no other is necessary to give a completely symmetrical character to the safety concept. In this symmetrical concept, "safety for what" is the positive aspect showing where one is going in the escape from an unpleasant situation.

Both safety and freedom seem one-sided because individuals are so absorbed in escaping from hazardous situations that they have neither the time nor the inclination to consider any activity beyond the escape. The negative aspect of the concept arises from viewing safety, or freedom, as an escape; the static element comes from one's willingness to accept release from threat without desiring to go anywhere in particular. This willingness to be satisfied with mere escape without going anywhere is

---

* Much of the material in this section is based upon the writings of a pioneer and leader of the safety movement, Albert W. Whitney. The quotations embracing his philosophical thinking were taken from *Safety for Greater Adventure* (11), edited by Herbert J. Stack.

deeply ingrained in human nature, with its involuntary physical drives. The immediate danger seems so pressing! Its removal will bring release. And there seem to be so many things that we shall want and need to do with the freedom that we shall gain. There seems to be so much leisure ahead in which one can make the necessary decisions. However, these decisions are best made at once because the removal of the disturbing condition creates a vacuum and something must be put in its place.

Safety Objectives in a Changing World In a world of constant change, objectives cannot be set for all time. New inventions, advanced techniques bring in their wake new values, new standards and new objectives. Constant change calls for new modes of adjustment, for re-appraisal of objectives. Man must not only adjust to his environment but must learn to control the new engines and innovations invented for the betterment and enrichment of life. He must make certain that the new knowledge and products are utilized for constructive, not destructive purposes. "The outstanding characteristic of our life today is the marvel-ous control which we now possess over physical forces and conditions. We have a host of powerful forces at our command. . . . A controlled world is now possible as never before (11:55)." In the early days of the

> It cannot be given to all of us to fight for freedom, but the fight for safety, the fight for real adventure, the fight for a life that shall be the measure of a purpose instead of the marred result of purposeless chance is within the right of all of us.
>
> *A. W. Whitney, in an address at the National Education Association Convention in 1919*

safety movement, many leaders thought the adoption of the slogan "Safety First" would have greater public appeal than the word "safety" alone. They had hoped its use would arouse general approval for the idea of safety as well as make the public safety conscious. But certain risks are an essential part of our highly dynamic industrialized civili-zation. Being guided entirely by a safety first slogan would not only impede progress but cause life to become dull and hardly worthwhile. Such a slogan would work well only in an unchanging order of society. Sound philosophical thinking says, "do what is needed but do it safely." Albert Whitney calls this to our attention when he states:

> In its development and growth, every movement has suffered from misconceptions and lack of definition and direction. Only recently has the safety movement begun to emerge from its confused state with somewhat definite patterns and implications. These are set forth . . . with a view toward indicating the trend of a growing philosophy of safety education with sociological background (11:39).

Safety is a Challenging Attitude Toward Life Herman H. Horne's philosophy of safety gives added perspective to the concept advanced by Whitney. He has said:

> Safety, in the broad sense of the term, is wholeness of life; in the narrow sense, wholeness of physical life, implying the avoidance of accidents. Safety education is the art of cultivating the knowledge, skills and attitudes that make for safety. Accidents do not just happen. They are caused (8:75).

The cause of most accidents can be attributed to the human element. An immature mind in a mature body, an emotional disturbance, a maladjustment that can be traced to a childhood experience, or an antisocial attitude bred by a deep-rooted resentment to society are among the factors responsible for accidents.

> Living perilously is a part of the price civilized man pays for his inventions and his mores. Man cannot surrender his inventions, but to reduce peril he can learn to live with them.
>
> *Herman Horne, "A Philosophy of Safety and Safety Education."*
> *Quoted in Safety for Greater Adventure, 1953*

Determinism is an unhealthy outlook upon life. Were we to accept such a philosophy, the teaching of safety would be rendered useless. If man is completely at the mercy of the elements and if whatever happens has been predetermined, it is useless to seek means of prolonging human life or of making life better. When an accident occurred, it would have to be accepted as something predestined. A determinist would say that if a person were injured or killed by an automobile, if was inevitable and could not have been prevented.

Living under such a philosophy would hardly require intelligence. Fortunately we have a more challenging attitude toward life. Although man can never become complete master of his destiny, in many ways he can influence the course of events to his own advantage. Determinism seems to repudiate the very possibility of education. If it is useless to resist the onslaughts of nature and the deadening forces around us, we might as well close our schools. Therefore, fatalism is an unacceptable philosophy of life. Self-determinism is better.

Safety Leads to More and Better Adventures Practicing safety precautions does not mean eliminating all activities that might be dangerous. The urge for adventure is in man's blood. It accounts for daring voyages, amazing discoveries, and attempts to solve the mysteries of nature. Certain dangers in life are intrinsic in our climb to a higher and nobler civilization. Those who have had the courage to face new experiences bravely, who have not considered safety the prime objective of life, have been instrumental in making man's life richer and fuller. It is thus obvious that adventure is a natural phenomenon with man. It is not only part of life but the law of life. Any attempt to chain man's adventurous spirit, to interfere with his effort to solve the riddles of nature and delve into the realm of the unknown, would be tantamount to arresting the progress of civilization.

Safety has no such absurd objectives. "Life at its best is taking risks for the things worth while. The good life is adventuring in the creation of values. Safety has its rightful place when no greater value is at stake for which a risk should be taken (8:21)." Safety enables us to choose between experiences that are unproductive, absurd and even stupid and those that enrich our life, make it interesting and worthwhile. Thus it is safety that informs man of the most proper choice possible; it is the driving force that makes the selection of the better experience imperative and devises the safest possible ways to achieve it. It makes for more and greater adventures by constantly increasing the number of possible good adventures. The highly interesting but potentially dangerous world of steam, electricity, automobiles, trains, airplanes and spaceships, has come about because we have been able to make life relatively safe.

A Personal Code for Safe Living Possessing power and imagination, man has succeeded in unlocking the secrets of the release of atomic energy and travel in space. As a result, more powerful and more marvelous machines will make their appearance. Obviously it is imperative that man learn to use them prudently. It is becoming more and more apparent that this is the task of education—education for progress, safety education.

Because of his unique abilities, man is able to make moral distinctions. This lends credence to the idea that improvement is possible. The questions naturally arise, "Does man always tend to make moral distinctions, does he always utilize his knowledge and power for constructive purposes?" According to Socrates, man's wickedness and wrongdoing are caused chiefly by lack of knowledge, by his inability to distinguish between what is right and what is wrong. Discipline—self-discipline—is the controlling factor in choosing and doing what is right not what is wrong. Psychologists have demonstrated that human nature is plastic and modifiable. It therefore follows that with proper education, man can learn to utilize his intelligence for constructive purposes, for making moral distinctions, for considering the welfare of others, for making life safer and better for all men. Human beings cannot become perfect any more than it is possible to make the world perfect. But through the application of philosophy to education, including safety education, man can learn to live at his best.

Man becomes the individual he is through interaction with his physical and social environment. By improving his attitude toward his fellows, he can be helped to achieve a more satisfying life. It is the function of education to help man satisfy his needs and thereby enable him to live more effectively. According to Briggs (2), the first duty of the school is to teach pupils to do better the things they are likely to do anyway. As most young people will be driving motor vehicles, is it not the function of the school to teach them how to be safe and good motorists? John Dewey points out that educational aims are founded on the activities and needs of pupils (5). Therefore highway safety, safety in athletics, occupational safety and the like should be included in the school curriculum. In this way our youth will be prepared to live, play and work safely.

If intelligence can be associated with the ability to adjust to new or novel situations, then the safety of the individual, his very survival, depends upon his use of intelligence. Safety education challenges man to use his intelligence to make satisfactory adaptations to the new and ever-changing environment. The worth of the individual, the preservation of his life, health and property are fundamental to a democratic society. Safety education has definite social implications and, of all phases of education, it is most harmonious with the democratic ideals of life, liberty and the pursuit of happiness. It has for its goal the prevention of accidents involving human life and property; it aims to keep the individual alive and free from accidental injury in order that he may continue to cultivate his own unique talents as well as contribute to the general welfare.

Whether voluntarily or involuntarily, each of us develops his personal safe-living code, incorporating some or all of the basic creative safety concepts, past and present. One's individual traits, natural endowments, ideals and personal will-to-do enter into shaping up a code for safe living. The precepts which follow are a summary of ideas to consider in settling upon a creative, active and personally satisfying code. Since all human behavior patterns and personalities must change and develop as life progresses, these precepts should be viewed as starting points for a zestful, rewarding and understanding way of life.

Dangers and hazards must be anticipated to prevent injury and death.

Problems must be faced up to resolutely and skillfully.

Advance planning and the establishment and enforcement of controls must be based on enlightened safety education.

Safety education must be sought and made use of.

Self-discipline and ability to live under authority are essential to safe behavior and personality.

Acceptance of individual, personal responsibility for one's safety is basic to safe living.

Safety is a way of life that applies to everything we do at all times—work, play, school, driving and community and family activities.

Safety is not just self-centered; it is oriented toward protecting others as well—a humanizing factor in all man's scientific and physical efforts.

Safety grows with and adapts to the needs of a changing world. More and better adventures are by-products of safety. Safety doesn't say "don't do it"; it says "do it safely."

It is not negative or static; it is not just an escape from danger; it is a freedom gained for doing worthwhile things in life. Safety creates opportunity, not a vacuum.

summary

Mankind's need for safety and his efforts to provide it for himself and his family have been a part of living since the beginning of time. The story of the safety movement chronicles man's victories over the relentless forces of nature. The Industrial Revolution resulted in a big increase in accidents, especially in the mines, in steel mills and on the railroads. In addition, terrible fires and other disasters convinced the American people that "something should be done about it." State Workmen's Compensation Laws were passed, industries were forced to seek insurance coverage and insurance inspectors and engineers aided in the development of safety programs.

The National Safety Council, organized in 1913, became the leading force in the safety movement. The accident rate for many kinds of accidents has decreased steadily in the last generation. The organized child safety movement was greatly influenced by the Council. In addition, the insurance and automobile industries, motor clubs and dozens of other agencies have been helpful in stimulating school safety. The same can be said for professional organizations of teachers such as the National Education Association. Programs for child safety have clearly demonstrated their value in saving lives and reducing injuries.

The child safety movement has been strongly influenced by certain basic principles or philosophies. Albert W. Whitney, the leading philosopher of the child safety movement, pointed out that the most important thing about safety is that it leads to a more abundant life. This idea developed into the concept of "safety for greater adventures." When danger is removed, hazards eliminated, there is greater freedom, happiness and growth.

However, life at its best is taking risks for the things worth while. Considering safety enables us to choose between experiences that are unproductive, absurd and even stupid and those that enrich our life, make it interesting and worthwhile. It is the function of education to teach pupils to do better the things they are likely to do anyway. Therefore the schools should teach children safety on the streets and highways, in athletics and recreation, in the homes and in all other activities. Safety education has for its goal the prevention of all types of accidents involving human life and property; it aims to keep the individual alive and free from injuries so that he may continue to cultivate his own unique talents as well as to contribute to the general welfare.

suggested projects and activities

1. Give illustrations to show that safety education is, in a certain sense, as old as mankind.
2. What were the industrial conditions in our country that gave rise to Workmen's Compensation Laws?

3. Trace the influence of great disasters upon the growth of the safety movement.
4. What were the primary steps in the early development of safety in the schools?
5. Show why self-discipline and ability to live under and understand authority are essential to safe living.
6. Defend the concept "safety first" as a phase of the philosophy of safety education. What dangers are inherent in this concept?
7. Defend the thesis that safety is both idealistic and pragmatic.
8. Compare the philosophies of safety as they have been expressed by Horne and Whitney.
9. Prepare and defend a philosophy of safety that you regard as adequate for today.
10. Prepare a personal code for safe living to fit your needs.

selected references

1. American Association of School Administrators, *Safety Education* (18th Yearbook). Washington, D. C.: National Education Association, 1940.
2. Briggs, Thomas H., *Secondary Education*. Washington, D. C.: U. S. Government Printing Office, 1919.
3. Center for Safety Education, New York University, *Twenty-Five Years of Research in Safety Education*. New York: The Center, 1951.
4. ________, *Research in Safety Education*. New York: The Center, 1956.
5. Dewey, John, *A Common Faith*. New Haven: Yale University Press, 1934.
6. Heinrich, H. W., *Industrial Accident Prevention,* (3rd ed.). New York: McGraw-Hill Book Company, 1950.
7. Holbrook, S., *Let Them Live!* New York: The Macmillan Company, 1938.
8. Horne, H. H., "A Philosophy of Safety and of Safety Education," *Safety Education Digest*. New York: Center for Safety Education, New York University, 1940.
9. National Safety Council, *Accident Facts*. Chicago: The Council (annual).
10. Soares, T. G., *Religious Education*. Chicago: The University of Chicago Press, 1928.
11. Stack, Herbert J., ed., *Safety for Greater Adventure: The Contributions of Albert Wurts Whitney*. New York: Center for Safety Education, New York University, 1953.

2

trends in accident occurrence

An understanding of the nature, size and scope of the accident problem is essential for effective work or study in the field of safety education, accident prevention and injury control. Accidents result from unsafe conditions and unsafe behavior. Research continues to reveal many causes of accidents. Programs for accident reduction which are based on such findings are playing an increasingly important role in reducing the tragic loss of life, limb and property. But it is obvious that a great deal more must be done to help mankind live safely, adventurously, and joyously in a complex technological society.

Basic Accident Facts

In the 20 years following 1945 accidents caused the death of nearly 2 million persons in this country. In the same period over 8 million persons became disabled and over 200 million received medical treatment for injuries that incapacitated them for more than one day (7). Each year over 45 million persons are injured in accidents, roughly one person in every four (7). Such accidents go on relentlessly with a death every five minutes of each day, 12 an hour, 277 each day, 1,800 in a week and over 101,000 in a year. Another measure of the enormity of loss lies in this fact: since accidental deaths kill a disproportionate number of young persons, over 3 million man-years of life are lost annually. Emphasis on deaths in accident prevention programs has often drawn attention from the terrible human toll in long-continued disability and suffering. For many of those disabled by accidents "the light went out even though the spark of life remained (6)."

During this century the death rate (deaths per 100,000 people) decreased steadily until 1961, at which point it began a slight rise. In 1961 the death rate was 50.4. In the five-year period ending in 1905 it averaged 88.9, in 1920 it was 71.2, in 1939 it was 70.8, in 1950 it was 60.3. In 1961 and 1962 it rose from 52.3 to 53.6. While the death rate has been reduced, it is apparent that there is still a great distance to go.

Significantly, all of the infectious diseases together now cause fewer deaths than do accidents. As a consequence, the medical profession, which has battled so effectively against infectious diseases, is continuing an all-out attack on accidents begun in the early '60's. In response to this pressing problem of accidents, the American Public Health Association in cooperation with the Public Health Service published *Accident Prevention: The Role of Physicians and Public Health Workers* (5). The World Health Organization has taken pains to alert the nations of the world to the tragic toll of human suffering and vast economic waste that stems from accidental causes.

Only three diseases cause more deaths than accidents. They are heart disease, cancer and vascular lesions, with death rates per 100,000 population of 370, 150 and 106 respectively (7). The accidental death rate is 52. The death rate for different types of accidents follows: motor vehicles, 22; falls, 10; fires, burns, 4; drowning, 3 and other, 13. Simply stated: accidents are the fourth leading cause of death. It is not surprising that the degenerative diseases have such high death rates but to find so many dying needlessly of accidents is tragic. Accidents kill many of the younger members of our society; they are the leading cause of death in the 1-to-35 age group. In fact, they cause more deaths than the total for many of the common diseases of childhood; of every five children who die between the ages of 5 and 14, two are killed in accidents. For young people aged 15 to 24, the picture is even more grim; more than half the deaths in this age group can be traced to accidental causes (10). The picture is not all grim. In the last decade, although the number of children and youth killed increased 15 per cent, the death rate dropped 10 per cent. Such a trend is cause for hope.

With marked changes in the make-up of our society evident in the near future a more accurate view of the problem will be given by death and injury rates than by numbers of persons involved. The projected trends in some areas of American life cited herein will make this statement clearer:

	1963	1970	
U.S. population	188.5 million	210.0 million	+11%
School age (5-17 years)	48.0 million	53.3 million	+11%
Elderly people (65+)	17.5 million	19.5 million	+11%
Motor vehicle mileage	800.0 billion	970.0 billion	+21%
Motor vehicle drivers	95.6 million	113.0 million	+18%
Weekly leisure time	72.0 hours	75.0 hours	+ 4%

Until recently, accidents claimed more lives during the working years of man (ages 20 to 65) than any other single cause. Recently heart disease has gone up slightly; the success of accident prevention programs has become evident in the slight decline of deaths of workers. In large industries today workers may be safer than in any area of human activity. Striking differences exist between the sexes in death rate: for men, the rate is 72; for women, 33. In nearly all areas of life's activities women have a markedly lower incidence of accident experience than do men.

Economics The cost of accidents in our society is enormous. In recent years the annual bill for accidents reached $16.1 billion in our nation. Ten years ago it was half this amount. This amount of damage includes property damage, costs of medical fees and hospital expenses, loss of wages, and the overhead cost of insurance (6). Against the tragic waste of human resources and the billions of dollars in economic waste, the funds now spent on accident prevention are woefully outweighed.

Property damage in motor vehicles alone has run over $2.6 billion while the total bill of vehicular accident costs exceeds $8 billion. Yet only $9 million is spent to lessen traffic accidents. Much more is needed. In the same period, work accidents cost $5 billion, while fire losses approached $1.4 billion. If the aggregate costs of accidents during any one year could be invested in housing facilities, a million homes could be built at a cost of 16.1 thousand dollars each, providing housing for more than 5 million persons.

The Accident Picture

To whom, where, when and how do accidents occur? Questions like these must be answered before satisfactory efforts can be made to understand and control accidents. The principal types of accidental deaths and injury are shown in Table 1 which summarizes the four major classifications of accidents, namely: motor vehicle, home, public (exclusive of work), and work.

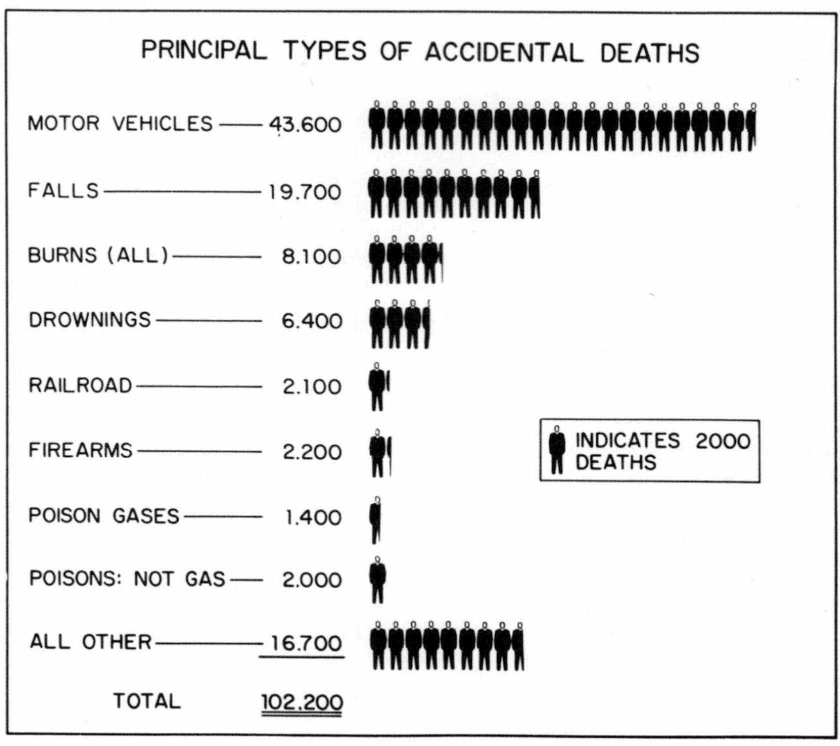

Figure 2:1, Principal Types of Accidental Deaths.

TABLE I

ACCIDENTS IN THE UNITED STATES DURING A TYPICAL YEAR

	Deaths	*Injuries (in millions)*	*Permanently Impaired (thousands)*	*Temporarily Disabled (millions)*
* Motor Vehicle	47.800	1.7	140	1.66
Home	28.500	4.3	120	4.2
Public (exclusive of motor vehicle)	18.000	2.3	50	2.3
Work	14.200	2.1	80	2.0
ALL ACCIDENTS	105.000*	10.4	380	10.1

* Note: The motor vehicle totals include some deaths also included in the work, home totals.

It is interesting to note that work accidents yield the fewest deaths, although the ratio of permanent impairments to deaths is higher than in the other three classifications. The fact that the industrial environment is controllable undoubtedly helps explain this lower death rate, particularly when it is realized that there are about 74 million full-time workers.

Variations in economic costs noted in Table 1 may be attributed largely to insurance claims. Caution is warranted, therefore, when estimating "average dollar losses per accident." Similarly, the costs attendant on deaths and injuires include workman's compensation, medical expenses and time lost, as well as insurance claims—especially in work and public accidents.

Unfortunately, there is no way of truly comparing these four classifications because exposure cannot be computed for home and public accidents, and degrees of hazard are also incalculable. These four classifications, then, should be considered in some detail.

Motor Vehicle Accidents

The earliest motor vehicle death in this nation occurred in 1895. Since then *more than 1.5 million persons have been killed* in traffic accidents in the United States. Over 55 million persons were injured and more than 13 million permanently disabled. One traffic death takes place every 13 minutes of the day. It is likely that one of every two persons living today will be involved in a serious motor vehicle accident during his lifetime, unless substantial gains are made in traffic safety in the future.

Annually the numbers of drivers, vehicles, miles driven and miles of roads continue to increase. The 82.7 million vehicles of 1963 will increase to 100 million by 1970 and the traffic mileage of 800 billion miles will go up 21 per cent (7). There will be 18 per cent more drivers including 22 per cent more young drivers with their higher accident potential. In the 12 months ending mid-year 1964 there were 46,220 traffic fatalities. These deaths occurred amidst the 12 million traffic accidents for which records were kept. The unrecorded accidents were many times that figure but were called minor mishaps. The cost of these recorded accidents exceeded 7.7 billion dollars in a recent year and will continue to mount annually due to rising repair and replacement costs for damaged vehicles, insurance costs and medical costs.

Seven out of ten deaths in a recent year occurred in rural areas. In urban areas, two-fifths of the victims were pedestrians; in rural areas most of the victims were occupants of vehicles. More than half of all deaths happened at night with the proportion somewhat higher in urban areas than in rural areas. The distribution for 43,600 fatalities was as follows: collision between motor vehicles 17,600; noncollision in roadway, overturning, running off roadway, 13,900; pedestrian accidents 8,200; collision with fixed objects 1,900; collision with railroad trains 1,340; collision with bicycles, 570; and other collisions 90. Figure 2 shows the annual motor vehicle deaths from 1930. Although mileage has mounted tremendously,

TABLE 2

MOTOR VEHICLE DEATHS AND INJURIES BY TYPE OF ACCIDENT DURING A TYPICAL YEAR*

Accident Type	*Deaths*			*Nonfatal Injuries*		
	Total	*Urban*	*Rural*	*Total*	*Urban*	*Rural*
Collision with:						
pedestrian	8,200	5,150	3,050	135,000	124,000	11,000
other motor vehicle	17,600	3,700	13,900	1,070,000	660,000	410,000
railroad train	1,340	470	870	5,000	3,000	2,000
street car	10	10	0	under 500	under 500	under 500
bicycle	570	270	300	30,000	25,000	5,000
animal, animal-drawn vehicle	80	0	80	4,000	under 500	4,000
fixed object	1,900	750	1,150	46,000	30,000	16,000
Noncollision	13,900	2,150	11,750	310,000	80,000	230,000
TOTAL	43,600	12,500	31,100	1,600,000*	920,000*	680,000*

* rounded

the rate of accidental deaths has decreased. Safety efforts have played a major role in this reduction.

More effective traffic accident prevention techniques of all kinds are needed if greater safety is to be achieved. The facts listed below indicate some of the conditions requiring particular attention.

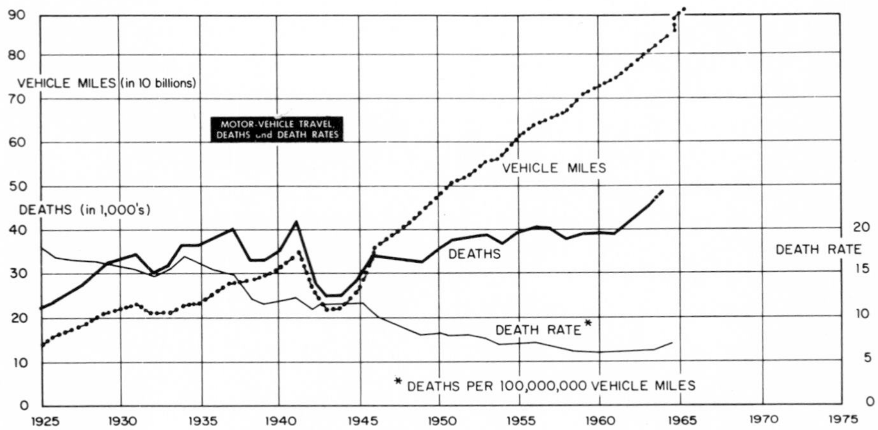

Figure 2:2, THE TRAFFIC PROBLEM.

Excessive speed is the outstanding driver violation in fatal accidents.

Seven out of every ten drivers in fatal accidents committed one or more violations at the time of the accident.

In one out of every three fatal accidents the driver or pedestrian had been drinking.

Death rates for night accidents are two-and-one-half times those for day accidents.

Improper driving contributes to 85 per cent of accidents. This includes: speed, failure to yield right of way, and following too closely.

On turnpikes, improper driving was evident 42 per cent of the time, bad driver condition 27 per cent, and vehicle defects 11 per cent.

Sunday, then Saturday, then Friday are the worst days of the week, in that order, for traffic mishaps.

Speed of motor vehicles on main rural roads has risen sharply; from 1946 to 1963 the average increase was: autos, 46 to 57 mph; buses, 48 to 58, trucks, 40 to 51.

Two-thirds of the drivers are male and they do nearly three-fourths of all the driving. No data yet compares their driving to the driving of females in the same setting.

The highest incidence of motor vehicle fatalities occurs in the age group 15 to 24.

Only if traffic safety programs can be devised to combat such conditions and thus alter the foundation of the estimates just cited will the current trends be changed. A vigorous program in traffic safety must provide for traffic supervision, engineering assistance, improvement of rural roads, reduction of defective vehicles, education of the public on road emergencies, strong support of traffic inventories, support for effective driver education programs, improved licensing and extensive driver improvement.

Home Accidents

In 1970 it is predicted that we will have 62 million households with a 210-million population. In the mid-sixties twice as many accidents and more than twice as many fatalities occurred in the home as at work. With more leisure time, more time to spend at home, more powered equipment, more backyard swimming pools, more play devices, more glass around the house, and more people, we may well expect that things will get worse.

About 4.4 million persons sustain disabling injuries and 120 thousand were permanently disabled at home, annually. Another 17 million are less seriously injured and 29 thousand persons die from accidents in the home. This means that one person in 43 in the United States is disabled for one or more days through a home mishap. The total cost of accidents at home was $1.2 billion in one recent year (7). This figure does not include any property damage, in which fire losses alone exceeded $450 million. It includes only lost wages, medical expenses and insurance costs.

Falls are the most frequent type of fatal home accident, followed by burns, suffocation, poisoning, and shooting. Their relative importance may be seen in Figure 3.

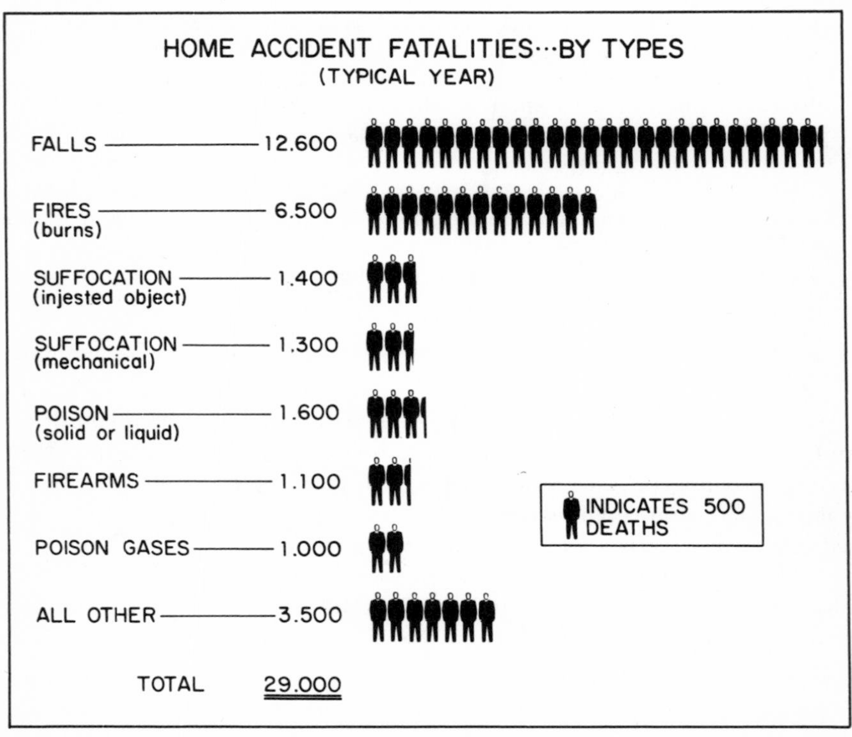

Figure 2:3, HOME ACCIDENT FATALITIES BY TYPES.

It is difficult to obtain reliable statistics concerning home accidents, first because of the privacy of the home, and second because there are no agencies primarily concerned with the home accident problem in the same way as, for example, the state motor vehicle bureaus are concerned with traffic accidents. However, an analysis of hospital data in home accidents indicates that there are two types of causes: mechanical and personal. The former type involve the use and care of equipment and the physical aspects of the home; the latter type spring from human relationships at home.

The mechanical causes most often producing injury are disorder, improper equipment, improper use of equipment, and need for repairs. Poor judgment, adult actions causing injury to children, physical frailty, hurry, and intoxication are rated in that order as personal causes of injury in home accidents.

Circumstances of 987 deaths from home accidents were tabulated by the Kansas Board of Health and by the Nassau County, New York, Health Department. This study revealed that one-fourth of all fatal accidents occurred in the bedroom. The yard and kitchen were next, but did not equal the total for the bedroom alone. The inside stairs, living room, outside stairs, and bathroom, in that order, followed kitchen and yard and equaled the total for both.

Two out of five accidental deaths occurred while the person was asleep. In three out of four deaths the activity being performed by the individual was of the simplest kind—walking on a level, standing, sleeping, sitting or reclining. Modern technology has developed hazards in glass doors, power tools, backyard swimming pools, rotary grass cutters, and overloaded electrical circuits, hazards that must be understood and coped with or eliminated if possible.

A study of the above type, although incomplete in sampling and quite localized in scope, evidences the need for research on home accidents that would attempt to determine the causative factors in urban and rural areas. When more complete evidence is available, it will be possible to reduce and/or eliminate the second largest class of accidents in the nation—those in the home. The home should be a haven of security for man in a troubled world. It can well become such when man organizes more effectively to eradicate the extensive hazards now found in and about his home.

Public Accidents

The problems in public safety are now more threatening than ever. About 17,500 persons lose their lives annually in drownings, falls, and other mishaps (exclusive of work and motor vehicle accidents) that occur in public places. Over 2.2 million persons are injured in public each year and of that number, 50 thousand receive permanent impairments.

Drowning is the most frequent type of fatal public accident. Drownings (4200) and falls (3900) constitute close to half the total number of fatalities. The relative frequency of the various types of public fatalities during a recent year is shown in Figure 4.

A number of facts relating to public accidents not caused by motor vehicles are of particular interest from an educational point of view:

An injury occurs every 14 seconds; a death every half-hour.
More than one-half of the drowning victims were under age 24.
One-half of the firearms deaths were of persons under age 24.
Three-fourths of deaths from falls were of persons over age 65.
Over one-half of the fire death victims were over age 45.

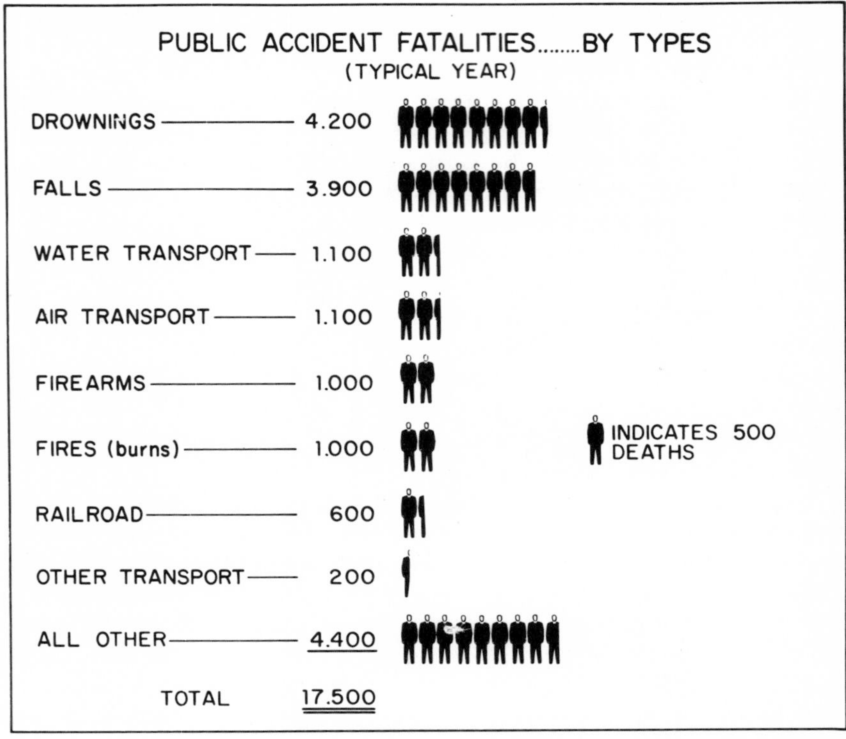

Figure 2:4, PUBLIC ACCIDENT FATALITIES BY TYPES

The "water-way jam" of 40 million boat owners necessitates boat safety training.

Private airplane use is mounting rapidly and safety controls are urgently needed.

Work Accidents

By 1970, 74 million persons will be at work in this nation. They will experience an accidental death rate of about 7.5 per 100,000. During the last decade work fatalities averaged about 14,000 annually, and non-fatal injuries around 2 million and cost us $5.0 billion. About 80 thousand workers became permanently impaired annually. Over 230 million man-days of work are lost each year in work accidents. Since 1913, when the National Safety Council was founded, work deaths have dropped from 21,000 annually to 14,000, and the work force has doubled in size and now produces five times as much in terms of our gross national product. This record reflects significantly the effective application of accident prevention procedures.

Workers suffer more accidental deaths and injuries off the job than they do on the job: seven out of ten deaths, and more than half of the injuries occur off the job—principally in motor vehicle accidents—and loss of production usually is greater from off-the-job than from on-the-job accidents. Although industrial leadership has done good work in curbing accidents within the plant, there is a need for modification of some aspects of the industrial safety program to meet these new conditions and to penetrate more deeply into the basic causes of work accidents. Industry will then be able to seek more effectively the reduction of off-the-job accidents, which are quite costly to management and seriously hamper personnel relations.

TABLE 3

DEATH AND INJURIES OF WORKERS*

	Deaths	*Death Rates* *	*Injuries*
At Work	14,200	21	2,000,000
Away from Work	31,700	48	2,350,000
Motor-Vehicle	19,100	29	650,000
Public non-motor-vehicle	6,600	12	800,000
Home	6,000	11	900,000
ALL ACCIDENTS	45,900	69	4,350,000

* Deaths per 100,000 workers

Research indicates that accidents result from a combination of causes, rather than from any single cause. An analysis of nearly 5,000 permanent disability and death cases indicated that two out of every three of the accidents had both personal and mechanical causes.

Although educators concerned with vocational shop safety must gather and utilize facts concerning school shop accidents, it is also essential that they know the basic facts of accidents in industry. Practices in school shops should reflect practices within the industries for which they are preparing the students.

Since they are concerned with the total welfare of the individual, schools have an excellent opportunity to offer well-rounded and well-integrated programs of safety education. Current figures show that school accidents occur least frequently to students in the lower grades, and most frequently to students in the ninth through twelfth grades. In activities that are under school jurisdiction, the accident rates increase gradually through the eighth grade, then jump sharply in the ninth grade and stay high through the twelfth grade; in activities not under the jurisdiction of the school, the rates are highest in the seventh and eighth grades, then taper off through the twelfth grade. A good safety program in the school thus will have the twofold effect of reducing school accidents and training students so that as adults they will be far safer workers.

TABLE 4

SCHOOL AGE ACCIDENTS*

ACCIDENTAL DEATHS OF CHILDREN AGE 5-14

Motor-vehicle	3,300
Pedestrian	1,450
Home	1,500
Public non-motor vehicle	2,200
Work	200
	7,200

DEATHS AND DEATH RATES FOR YOUNG PEOPLE

Years	*Deaths*	*Rate* *
1–4	5,052	30.5
5–9	3,570	18.1
10–14	3,181	18.0
15–19	7,245	48.9
20–24	7,312	63.1

* Per 100,000

Causes of Accidents

While much is known now about where, when and how accidents occur, little has been learned about the why factor. In the past, accident research dealt with the description of the physical factors present just prior to an accident and producing human injury and property damage. In more recent years careful study has attempted to identify the psychological factors that enter into accident causation. Other studies have noted the presence of biochemical, physiological and other human factors. Evidently, accidents are multi-causal. As Brody (2) has written:

1. Investigate any accident to determine its cause and it is inevitable that human factors of one kind or another—physiological, biochemical, psychological—will be found to have been involved.
2. These human factors are nevertheless meaningless, unreal, without reference to specific physical and social environments—that is to say, the nature of the work, the nature of the work organization, and "sheer" physical or chemical aspects of the environment.
3. Given the right combination of human factors and environmental conditions, an accident may ensue.
4. Chance has a great deal to do with the occurrence of the "effective" combination, and indeed with the consequence.

5. Because of the role of chance, the consequences need not be fatal, it need not be injurious, it need not even be property-damaging. But the potential therefor is always present.
6. As long as there is such potential, our primary concern lies with environmental conditions that are not right, and with human conditions that are not right, whether or not they evidence any statistical correlation with accident involvement.
7. Studying work accidents, therefore, is less profitable than studying work conditions—and near-accidents.
8. Within certain limits most of these conditions—human and environmental—are modifiable or compensable.
9. In this context there can hardly be accident-prone people, as such. Rather there are accident-disposing situations, in which *x* factors or forces interact to produce—or preclude—an "accidental" occurrence. Pursuing this line of reasoning leads inevitably to a concept of "multi-dimensional fields," phenomenally suggestive but genetically intricate.

Accidents may be due to three basic factors present at some time in some people in certain settings, namely: stress, an inadequate sense of responsibility, and chance. Through continued research on the accident phenomena and appropriate safety programming we shall become better able to understand accident causation factors and be capable of initiating appropriate intervention procedures.

Limitations of Accident Statistics

Altogether too frequently it is necessary to quote from isolated studies of accidents, in which information relating to specific accident problems may be highlighted. In many areas too little information is available for drawing valid cause-and-effect relationships dealing with accidental injuries and deaths.

Most of the facts that are available about accidents are purely physical, dealing with season, year, time of day or part of body injured; unfortunately very few relate to the underlying causes of accidents. If state agencies secured more accurate and more reliable data, it would be possible for researchers to delve more deeply into basic causes.

Educational Uses of Accident Facts

The nature, size and scope of the national accident situation has been presented briefly. Background information against which states and local communities may develop their own comparative surveys has been provided. Such surveys are necessary to determine what persons are not being reached by a given educational program with specific objectives, and in what ways they need to be reached to achieve those objectives. The goals of education as they relate to safety are discussed in detail elsewhere in this volume, and an elaboration has been made of the statistics needed for the formulation and execution of an educational program in each of the various phases of safety: street and highway, home, physical education and athletics, recreation and sports, school, public safety and work.

Accident information may be used for another purpose—to determine the effectiveness of a safety education program. This, however, is a long-term project and one wherein the issues are likely to become confused by the numerous geographical, political, sociological and technological factors that frequently contribute to the accident picture. Where it is possible to "control" these factors for purposes of investigation, the value of an education program may be determined by: (1) surveying the accident situation before the program is begun, (2) basing the program on the needs determined by the survey, (3) comparing the initial accident situation with that prevailing at intervals after the program has begun.

Finally, accident statistics, if adequately determined and maintained over a period of time, may serve as a basis for suggested revision of the educational program from time to time. Safety conditions in an area change for a multiplicity of reasons. Education must be geared to these changes. The value of inventories in education, as in business, depends upon their timeliness and appropriateness.

summary

Over 2 million persons have succumbed from accidental causes in the twentieth century in this nation; about 8 million have been disabled and more than 200 million individuals needed medical care for their injuries. Accidents are in fourth place among causes of death for people of all ages; for the young (1 to 35) they are the leading cause of death. The financial costs of accidents exceed $16 billion annually—the humanitarian costs have no measure.

Accidental injury and death occur in a wide variety of human activities: at home, at play, at work, in public places and in and around traffic. Accidents result from a combination of causes, rather than any single cause—and the majority of accidents may be attributed to the majority of the population. More sophisticated research than we have at present is needed to describe fully the accident problem. New procedures are needed to bring about a marked reduction in accident occurrence.

suggested projects and activities

1. Collect as many different charts as you can that identify clearly various phases of the accident problem. Assemble these in a folder for easy reference. Include a bibliographical listing of all materials available.

2. Analyze the pupil traffic problem in a moderate sized community. Prepare a complete report on the problem, including graphic presentations and recommendations for a solution.
3. Develop a series of graphic illustrations of the accident facts in any one of the major accident areas.
4. Make a comparison between accident statistics of the current year and the averages presented for the last decade. What conclusions may be drawn as to the causes of variations between the figures presented? Justify.
5. What problems exist in your community in securing, compiling, and reporting the accident facts? How may some of these problems be resolved?
6. Prepare a paper of 2,000 words on the causes of accidents. Include appropriate references and a bibliography.

selected references

1. Automobile Manufacturers Association, *Automobile Facts and Figures*. Detroit: The Association (annual).
2. Brody, Leon, "The Accident Phenomenon," *Personnel Administration,* Vol. 26, No. 6, November-December, 1963, 11-14.
3. Elkow, J. Duke, "Safe Living—A Prediction," *Journal of Health, Physical Education and Recreation,* Vol. 30, April, 1959, 21-22.
4. Florio, A. E. and G. T. Stafford, *Safety Education* (2nd ed.). New York: McGraw-Hill Book Company, 1962.
5. Halsey, Maxwell, ed., *Accident Prevention: The Role of Physicians and Public Health Workers*. New York: McGraw-Hill Book Company, 1961.
6. Keifer, Norvin C., "Some Problems of Accident Prevention." New York: Equitable Life Assurance Society of the United States, Sept. 20, 1962.
7. National Safety Council, *Accident Facts*. Chicago: The Council, 1963.
8. ________, *Report to the Nation 1964*. Chicago: The Council, 1964.
9. ________, *Transactions of the National Safety Congress and Exposition*. Chicago: The Council, (annual).
10. Spadafora, Jennie, "Accidents—The Number One Killer," *Safety Education*. Chicago: National Safety Council, May, 1963.
11. Strasser, Marland K., J. E. Aaron, R. C. Bohn and J. R. Eales, *Fundamentals of Safety Education*. New York: The Macmillan Company, 1964.
12. U.S. Department of Health, Education, and Welfare, *Accidental Death and Injury Statistics,* Publication #1111. Washington, D.C.: Public Health Service, Division of Accident Prevention, October, 1963.
13. ________, *Health Statistics,* Series B. No. 37. Washington, D.C.: Public Health Service, October, 1962.
14. ________, Public Health Service, *Vital Statistics of the United States*. National Office of Vital Statistics, 1937-1963.

3

psychology of safety education

Why are people involved in accidents? Why do some people have more than their share of accidents? There is no easy answer to these questions; they are highly complex problems. Research has shown that the answers are as broad and involved as the psychology of human behavior. One could say that accidents are due to the lack of knowledge about hazards and safe practices—people are poorly informed. In addition, they do not have the essential skills which they practice regularly. More recent studies, however, have shown that knowledge and skills are not enough, there are other factors to be considered, such as good attitudes. These attitudes are often closely tied to one's emotions and are highly important, even more important than knowledge and skills. Thus, the safe skier is not only well informed and has essential skills, but has good attitudes. In teaching safety, we not only must see to it that children are well informed and skillful, but most of all we must include lessons that will tend to improve attitudes. It will be noted that in this chapter much of the discussion will be concerned with attitudes and their improvement.

Psychological Causes of Accidents

At one time it was a common practice to ascribe accidents to one cause such as "carelessness," "recklessness," "inattention" or "thoughtlessness." However, recent studies such as those conducted by Bishop (2), McFarland (12) and Stiles (15) show that there can be many underlying causes that "set the stage" for the accident. Apparent causes are often the culmination of several underlying causes, some of which may be psychological.

Some accidents are due to lack of information about hazards; this is especially true among younger children. However, recent studies tend to show that in a great majority of accidents, individuals were well informed —they knew the hazards and they knew the regulations and safety practices, but failed to follow them. According to Gibson (8), this may be due in part to the failure to perceive hazards or failure to react in the face of perceived danger. While Gibson does not mention this, weaknesses in perception and slow reaction are common among older adults and may account for their large number of pedestrian accidents and falls.

There are also important skills that aid in safety—skills in driving, swimming, hunting, athletics, industrial arts and other activities. Athletes who lack the basic skills of competitive sports will tend to have accidents. The same is true of drivers and industrial workers.

Near-accidents occur with considerable frequency. When people experience these near-misses and ignore them, they tend to develop confidence that they will escape having an accident. Some even boast about these near-misses. When an accident does occur, they are surprised. However, there is a close relationship between unsafe practices or violations and accidents. Studies have shown that there is also a relationship between near-accidents and accidents.

Lack of knowledge and inadequate skills do contribute to many accidents. But according to McFarland (12) and Brody (7), both of whom have summarized several studies of the underlying causes of accidents, the principal causes lie deep in one's personality and are ordinarily referred to as faulty attitudes.

The Effect of Emotions

In recent years a number of studies have shown the importance of emotions as a cause of accidents. These emotions which come to the surface in the form of fear, anger, hatred, nervousness or anxiety are very powerful and have a strong influence on our behavior.

Lack of emotional stability has a tendency to contribute to accidents. Following are illustrations of persons in situations where accidents are likely to happen:

> The industrial worker who is worried because of debts and other money problems. The mother who is upset because of illness or intolerable conditions at home. The driver who loses his temper after being berated by a traffic officer. The non-swimmer who panics when thrown into the water as a boat capsizes. The person who is "scared to death" when a fire breaks out in the home. The child who is hurried and worried and runs across the street in the middle of the block. The driver who is extremely nervous when meeting an emergency situation.

The characteristic of emotional instability is highly important. It is often closely related to bad attitudes. According to Brody in *Basic Aspects and Applications of the Psychology of Safety* (7:7), "emotional instability is frequently reported among chronic offenders. When frustrated, they are apt to 'blow their tops.' It is hard for them to control their feelings." Two other research studies should be mentioned. According to Stiles (15), "unmet emotional needs of children and constant worry dispose them to have accidents." Dunbar (5) contends that "some accident-repeaters actually *will* to have accidents as an escape from an intolerable home or psychological situation in which they have become emotionally involved." When we are suddenly excited, our glands release adrenalin into the blood stream. This has an amazing effect on muscular fatigue and strength. We may attempt activities that are far too difficult or take chances that lead to an accident.

Ordinarily most drivers have fairly good control of their emotions. However, we know that in many instances alcoholic beverages interfere not only with coordination but also control of emotions. Lack of control lowers the inhibitions of drinkers; they may take unnecessary risks while driving, disobeying regulations or driving recklessly. This may account in part for the high incidence of accidents among drivers who have been drinking.

Nearly all people have periods in which they experience emotional stress. During these periods they will tend to be less alert and less attentive to what they are doing, and there will be a tendency to have accidents. The industrial worker who is "mad" because of difficulties with his supervisor; the mother who is upset because of a death in the family; the child who is disturbed because of a fight with a playmate—these are a few examples of persons upset by temporary emotional conditions.

Various emotions may contribute to accidents. Extreme fear, for example, sometimes results in panic and is an underlying cause of many deaths in fires. In fact, there is always a danger in the use of fear in teaching children, for dread of having an accident is just the frame of mind likely to cause one. According to life guards, many of the accidents that take place at beaches are caused by "showoffs," individuals who get satisfaction out of taking chances to get attention. Moreover, people who get upset over unimportant things are apt to act impulsively, which often results in accidents.

On the other hand, the "good" emotions such as love of one's associates and fellowmen tend to show up in the form of good sportsmanship, thoughtfulness, respect for laws, courtesy and fair play. These tend to contribute to greater safety.

Attitudes

Attitudes are highly important in safety education, in fact, many educators consider them more important than either knowledge or skills. How do attitudes or personality patterns come about? First of all, many influences reach man's mind without his being aware of them and they affect or mold him without his awareness. According to Levinson, "most of the reasons why we behave as we do stem from experiences we have had in the course of our growing up and of which we are no longer aware, especially those experiences very early in life." Attitudes have sometimes been called "emotionalized experiences." They are fundamental factors in safety—and they are the hardest to develop or modify for they are so deep-seated. Brody has the following explanation (7:10): "Just as eight-ninths of an iceberg lies below the surface of the water, so most of the factors or forces that shape an individual's personality are hidden in the background." Brody adds the following statement (7:12):

> Obviously, our problem is not simply the psychology of safe behavior . . . it is the psychology of human behavior generally. And needless to say, it is not the exclusive problem of driver educators and safety educators. It is the problem of educators generally . . . and of society. In effect, then, all educators are (or should be) part-time safety educators.
>
> How may we best tackle this difficult problem? What specific objectives may be formulated? What are some of the motivations that can be utilized in educational approaches? What educational techniques or processes are particularly promising?
>
> With at least a basic notion regarding the general nature of the attitudes and adjustments that are at the root of the problem, I believe we can state that the relatively specific "attitudes" that need to be developed are those that convince the individual that accidents are hardly accidental; that they are not an inevitable consequence of risks inherent in driving, working, or other activity; that they are, for the most part, personally caused; that they are therefore controllable; and finally, that every individual has a moral and social responsibility to prevent accidents to himself and to others, and to co-operate with others to this end.

Good attitudes are valuable in all fields of safety. These personal characteristics reveal themselves in the form of good sportsmanship, reliability, courtesy, dependability or the opposite. A youngster may be well-informed about the hazards of the water and be an excellent swimmer, but if he has poor attitudes, is reckless and takes chances, he will tend to have accidents. Similarly, a child may be well-informed about bicycle safety practices, but fail to follow them because of bad attitudes. Many traffic accidents which have physical causes such as "exceeding the speed limit" or "driving off the roadway" have bad attitudes as underlying causes.

Modifying Attitudes. The following methods have been extracted from Brody's suggestions for modifying attitudes. As is noted, some have questionable or limited value.

> *Logic.* The logical appeal in safety education puts everything on the basis of reason. In the light of our knowledge of the problem this is surely not enough.
>
> *Admonition and Exhortation.* It has been found that lecturing or preaching or warning will have little success.
>
> *Proficiency.* The natural desire of individuals to do things well or to be considered proficient has value up to a certain point; this is sound motivation.
>
> *Humor.* Humor has been a historic means of influencing people. It can stimulate interest, for people are receptive to humor. They often derive satisfaction from the mistakes of others; but this type of illustration must be handled tactfully.
>
> *Fear.* The so-called "fear approach" is still utilized to impress upon people the painful consequences of behavior. However, this is a negative method and dread of having an accident is just the frame of mind likely to cause one. The use of the fear approach should be limited.
>
> *Group Dynamics.* Group acceptance and group recognition motivate every individual. And as an inevitable consequence he subjects himself to the regulations of the group. Personal involvement of the individual members of the group is the key to this activity. Research conducted during the past two decades strongly supports the view that group processes may be the most effective means for developing or modifying attitudes and behavior. The purposes of group discussion are to stimulate group analysis of situations and to enable members to profit from their pooled experience or thinking. Subjects for discussion should be relatively real and specific. It is important that the leader be able to establish a friendly, informal atmosphere.*

* Further details regarding techniques will be found in *Basic Aspects and Applications of the Psychology of Safety* (7).

Wisely found that among bus drivers differences in temperment and emotions between repeaters and the accident-free were more marked than were differences in physical and sensory responses (19). Several other studies (12) now point in the same direction. Research carried on at the University of Colorado Medical School, in which many different tests and scales were used, showed that the instrument which best differentiated between "repeaters" and "accident-free" was the *Allport-Vernon Scale of Values.*

Thus, while earlier research studies tended to show that accident-repeaters were individuals with poor physical and sensory characteristics, more recent investigations emphasize that faulty attitudes, poor adjustment and lack of emotional stability are more important. Brody, in *Personnel Administration,* suggests a personality profile of accident-repeaters (3). They are apt to have:

1. Greater distractibility than "average."
2. A tendency to act impulsively.
3. A tendency to be asocial, nonconforming, aggressive, and intolerant of authority.
4. Emotional instability, including difficulty in tolerating tension and frustration.
5. An exaggerated notion of ability, unusual risk-taking, and an unhealthy need to "stand out."

Behavior Patterns

What takes place when an individual responds to his environment? Briefly, a stimulus impinges upon a sensitive part of the body called a sense organ. This impulse travels to the brain or other nervous center. It then proceeds to an effector or motor organ, which produces a response to the original stimulus. If the organ is a muscle, the response is a movement; if the organ is a gland, the response is a secretion. The following is an illustration: a child touches a hot radiator. This results in an impulse which travels from the nerve ending in the fingers to the nerve center. It then proceeds to a motor organ, the muscles in the hand or arm, and the hand is withdrawn. All of this requires less than a second. The child has had an experience that hot radiators burn and he should not touch them.

This is just one type of stimulus. Others affect our vision, our hearing, or our sense of smell. The stimulus may also be internal, as, for example, hunger or a toothache. Whether or not the response to a stimulus is to be a safe one depends on the quality and degree of sensitivity of the sense organ, on the "resistance" offered by the nerves, on the functioning speed and "motivation" of the brain, and on the limitations of the motor organization. Thus, alcohol and other narcotics will slow down the reaction; fatigue will have a similar effect. In attempting to identify the specific causal elements in an unsafe act, consideration must be given to each of these phases in the process of behavior. When stimulus is given to a group of children, individual reactions will be quite different.

Reaction and Coordination

The time lag that occurs between the instant that the eyes perceive a danger and the moment muscles go into action is called "reaction time." When faced with a situation that calls for simple action, the normal person may require one-quarter to one-half of a second. In a complex situation involving a choice of action, the time may exceed three-fourths of a second. The brain requires more time in which to make its decision.

Speed of reaction is an asset only if the response is a desirable one. For illustration, in some driving emergencies such as a skid, one should not slam on the brakes. This is the wrong reaction. As a matter of fact, some research studies have shown that the faster one's reaction time, the more likely is he to have a history of accidents. While a fast reaction time is valuable in avoiding accidents, there are other situations in which slow and discriminating reaction is better.

Attention Because concentration usually speeds up reaction time and perception, the factor of attention is important in safe behavior. When a person takes the "attention attitude" toward any part of a situation, he becomes more highly conscious of it than of any other part. Through the integrating action of the nervous system, the organism becomes oriented toward the "object of attention." It is not surprising, then, to note a research finding that, on the average, a driver is able to perceive an expected obstacle twice as far away as he can see an unexpected one. As would be expected, fatigue, distractions, or anything that interferes with attention tends to result in violations. Similarly, safety in any activity depends upon adequate attention to that activity.

Accident-Repeater and Accident-Prone An accident-repeater is a person who has had several accidents, or more than the average person. On the other hand, an accident-prone individual is someone with a *propensity* for accidents, at least temporarily. Thus a taxicab driver who covers 60,000 miles a year—six times the mileage of the average driver—may have several accidents in a year. He would be an accident-repeater but not necessarily accident-prone. It is important to understand the difference between these two terms for they are often used synonymously.

Several research studies have thrown light on this problem. Some have already been mentioned. Brody summarizes several studies (7:6) and indicates that "accident-repeaters and chronic violators are more distractible than the accident-free and other non-offenders." He also points out that studies show that "chronic offenders tend to show less personal restraint than do non-repeaters. They act impulsively; are inclined to take risks. Safety rules and regulations may therefore be regarded most casually." In addition, "many chronic offenders seem to be characterized by asocial or antisocial attitudes. They are aggressive, tend to be nonconforming, and intolerant. Aggressiveness has shown up in many group studies (7:7)."

On the other hand, knowledge of traffic laws, manipulative skills and psychophysical abilities such as reaction time, depth perception and glare recovery time *do not* per se differentiate unsafe people from others. However, individuals with very poor visual acuity or very slow reaction time would not be good driving risks.

The characteristics of accident-repeaters among junior high school pupils were studied by Birnbach (1). He found that the accident-free were better informed about safety and better adjusted to home and school conditions. They also tended to be more dependable and industrious, while repeaters tended to have greater crude strength and superior gymnastic skills. However, one reason why boys with greater crude strength and superior gymnastic skills were involved in more accidents is because they were usually in more kinds of physical education activities—their exposure was greater.

Perception Perception refers to the awareness of objects in one's environment. When used in connection with safety, it means the ability to recognize certain hazards. The driver on a city street, for example, sees dozens of objects ahead of him. Some of these are important because they are real or potential hazards. Drivers should be able to "spot" these dangers. The life guard has the important responsibility of observing swimmers and divers, noting dangers or bad practices and blowing his whistle or taking other steps to prevent accidents. Good industrial safety supervisors have become skilled in "perceiving" hazardous operations in shops. The expert skier recognizes certain hazards on the course and avoids them. One method that has been used to improve the perception of beginning drivers is to show motion pictures or lantern slides of hazardous conditions and having students practice in noting these hazards.

Individual Differences Individuals differ widely in physical and mental traits. This fact would seem to be related to the ability to avoid accidents. For example, it would appear that general intelligence would be an important factor. Yet studies have tended to show that intelligence, as measured by standard tests, is not important except in the lower levels of the I.Q. scale.

Youngsters who have superior coordination, agility and reaction time should be able to avoid mishaps. Athletes who are well trained and conditioned tend to have fewer accidents than those in poor physical shape. Fatigue and emotional instability also have a part to play. Children who are tired or emotionally disturbed are apt to have more accidents than those who are not. The same is true of drivers.

What about the effects of certain physical disabilities on accidents? It would appear the orthopedically disabled workers in industries would have more accidents than normal individuals, but according to Wagner (18) and others, this is not the case. If they are properly trained and placed, they have accident records as good as or better than those without handicaps. In addition, the Veterans Administration reports that the records of thousands of amputee and paraplegic veterans appear to be as good as that of the average driver. A study carried on by the Pennsylvania Motor Vehicle Department also showed that drivers with hearing disabilities have a better accident record than those with normal hearing. It would appear that the loss of an arm or leg and partial deafness are not serious disabilities as far as accident records are concerned. Many industries now employ disabled persons and find that their accident records are satisfactory. Apparently, individuals who have a disability, and know about it, are so pleased to be gainfully employed that they take every precaution to avoid being injured.

Motivation and Interest Creating and maintaining interest must be the concern of every teacher of safety if his pupils are to derive the maximum benefit from instruction. In general, interest may be motivated and maintained through an appeal to one or more of the basic motives of individuals. Those of special value in teaching safety are the following:

1. Self-preservation. Perhaps the most important of all personal drives is that for self-preservation, the desire of the individual to be free from danger and from personal injury. In instruction, emphasis should be placed upon the injury to the individual rather than upon the accident as such. Posters, notices, and similar materials emphasizing the consequences of accidents may be utilized. However, unless extreme care is exercised, undue emphasis on the negative phases of accident prevention will result, and excessive fear and alarm may be developed. The purpose of safety education is to develop not fear of injury but rather an appreciation of the need for caution in everyday situations.
2. Personal gain or reward. The desire for reward for work well done is an important incentive. Election to a safety committee or a safety patrol urges the pupil to continue interest and activity in safety. However, one must guard against the danger of overemphasizing reward instead of the true values to be derived from the safety program.
3. Group membership or loyalty. Pupils want the approval of their group or their class. For that reason they are likely to cooperate in whatever the group may do, being particularly careful to follow the code or rules set up by the group for membership. This desire may be utilized in teaching safety through the safety club, the safety patrol, the junior drivers club, and so on. School loyalty may be generated through an appeal for greater safety in order to win the safety banner for the school.
4. Responsibility. Most pupils will accept the responsibility connected with the activities in which they engage; in fact most pupils desire such responsibility and for that reason are quite willing to serve as members of the safety council or safety patrol, as the safety inspector of the home-

room, and so on. The alert teacher and school administrator will delegate to pupils as much responsibility as they are capable of assuming.

5. Pride. Both children and adults take pride in their work. The display of craftsmanship in the preparation of a poster or exhibit will appeal to all.
6. Rivalry. Both individual and group interest may be generated and maintained through friendly competition. For example, in a given school the various homerooms may compete for the right to retain the school safety flag for each of the six-week periods during the school term. Under careful guidance friendly competition of this sort may well be used to develop greater safety in and among the various safety groups in the school.
7. Leadership. The desire for leadership is strong in many students and may be used to advantage in safety work. Students possessing the qualities that make for good leadership should be selected as members of the safety council, the safety patrol or the student safety court. In the homerooms, opportunities for expressing such leadership can be found in the jobs of safety monitor, cloakroom monitor, or chairman of the safety program committee. Students who speak fluently before groups should have the opportunity to represent their schools on the city-wide safety council or be permitted to bring the cause of safety before adult groups.

Applications in teaching The group-discussion method is considered one of the best methods of improving attitudes. However, there are other methods that can be used, but little research has been conducted relative to these methods. They *may* have some value.

1. *Travel and excursions* provide vivid, firsthand experiences that may be made the basis for the development of worthwhile attitudes.
2. *School assemblies and homeroom activities* may help direct the growth of desirable attitudes.
3. *An individual with a strong personality* who provides vivid experiences and also indicates his attitudes on issues is likely to affect the attitudes of his listeners.
4. *Prestige and expert opinion* tend to influence the modification of attitudes. Pupils tend to be influenced by recognized leaders.
5. *Appeals* may help bring about changes in attitudes in connection with Fire Prevention Week, Clean-Up Day or other special campaigns.
6. *Lectures* may be helpful in changing attitudes if the personality of the speaker and pupil interest are also favorable. However, they should rarely be used in the elementary schools unless supplemented by other teaching methods such as visual aids.
7. *Newspapers, radio and television* might have some value. On the other hand, certain types of programs might have the opposite effect.
8. *Motion pictures* that are carefully selected and followed by discussions should have value.
9. *Cocurricular activities* such as safety councils, school patrols, and student self-government should be helpful, if properly conducted and supervised.
10. *Role playing* may have some value, but little attention has been given to its use in safety education.

Instruction in the Schools

The problem of modifying behavior to reduce the number of unsafe acts and violations is a very important one. While the home can do a considerable amount, teaching safety education is largely the responsibility of the schools and colleges. In most schools, safety will be integrated with other subjects; in others, the direct method of teaching will be used or there will be a combination of both methods. Instruction should begin in the kindergarten and extend through the secondary schools. Much of the instruction involves knowledge, skills and attitudes. Children must learn about the dangers of the street, develop skills in crossing the street, and good attitudes so they will not make errors. Similarly, high school students must learn about safe practices, rules and regulations, and acquire basic skills. But most of all, they should develop good attitudes. It can readily be seen that education for safe living requires expert teaching.

Teachers will use the traditional methods that are discussed in texts in educational psychology for much of this instruction. They will make use of laws of learning—use, disuse, effect, primacy, recency and vividness. But as pointed out in this chapter, the improvement of attitudes and control of the emotions are very important in safe behavior. There are certain motivations that can be used in getting at attitudes. Logical appeals, admonitions and exhortations are not of great value. The desire for proficiency, the use of humor and the "fear approach" under certain conditions can have more value. Many of the attitudes that make for safety are the same as make for proficiency and good performance in other fields. These include characteristics such as fair play, cooperation, reliability, good sportsmanship, self-control and thoughtfulness. These are good objectives for the kindergarten and the grades as well as the high school course in driver education. It has been found that one of the best ways of improving these attitudes is by group discussion. Teachers in the elementary school will recognize this as good teaching. It takes far more time than the traditional question-and-answer methods but is more effective.

Sawers in *Group Discussion Techniques in Driver Education* (13) proposed a complete program for the utilization of this technique in driver education courses. Several research studies have shown that this method has been quite effective in other fields of safety.

The following are general techniques for use in conducting group discussions:

1. The group should not be too large; the typical class size is satisfactory.
2. The discussion leader should be just that, not a lecturer.
3. Efforts should be made to secure maximum participation.

4. When questions are raised, they should be referred to the group.
5. Members of the group should relate items of personal experience.
6. The final result should be a group acceptance of desirable practices.

summary

Research has shown that the reasons why people are involved in accidents are as broad and involved as the psychology of human behavior. While knowledge and skills in safety are of some importance in safe behavior, attitudes are of greater importance, chiefly because they are tied up to emotions and are powerful influences. Many accidents have underlying causes, and in order to control accidents we must get at these underlying causes.

Studies of accident-repeaters and accident-free persons show that the so-called psychophysical characteristics do not differentiate unsafe people from others. Personality characteristics, such as impulsiveness, aggressiveness, emotional instability, insecurity and tension are much more important.

Teachers of safety education should apply the laws of learning: the laws of use, disuse, effect, primacy, recency and vividness. Since good attitudes are so important in safe behavior, types of lessons should be stressed that will tend to improve attitudes. There are certain motivations that can be used in getting at attitudes. Logical appeals, admonition and exhortation are not of great value. The desire for proficiency, the use of humor and the "fear approach" under certain conditions can have more value. Undoubtedly one of the best approaches is through group discussion. This method requires considerable time which may account for the fact that it has not been used extensively in the schools.

suggested projects and activities

1. Make a list of the personal characteristics that best differentiate accident-repeaters from the accident-free.
2. Prepare in outline form illustrations of the use of the laws of learning in teaching safety.
3. Make a list of the personal desires or incentives that may be used to motivate learning. Give illustrations in the field of safety education.
4. Prepare an outline that could be used for a study of the underlying causes of accidents in a camp.
5. It has been found that the characteristics of accident-prone persons resemble closely those of juvenile delinquents. What are some of these characteristics?
6. Prepare a self-rating scale (10 items) that might be used for rating the safety practices of bicyclists.
7. Altogether too little time is available for classroom instruction in driver education (30 clock hours). What suggestions can you make for some use of the group-discussion technique even though but little time is available?

selected references

1. Birnbach, S. B., "A Comparative Study of Accident-Repeater and Accident-Free Pupils." Unpublished Ed. D. document, New York University, 1948.
2. Bishop, Richard W., *One-Car Accidents and the Young Driver*. Abstract of a doctoral thesis, New York University. Detroit: Automobile Club of Michigan, 1963.
3. Brody, Leon, "The Accident Phenomenon," *Personnel Administration*, Nov.-Dec., 1963.
4. Crow, Lester D., *Educational Psychology*. New York: American Book Company, 1958.
5. Dunbar, Flanders, *Mind and Body: Psychosomatic Medicine*. New York: Random House, 1947.
6. ————, *Emotions and Bodily Change*. New York: Columbia University Press, 1954.
7. ————, and Leon Brody, *Basic Aspects and Applications of the Psychology of Safety*. New York: Center for Safety Education, 1959.
8. Gibson, James V., "The Contribution of Experimental Psychology to the Formulation of the Problem of Safety," in *Behavioral Approaches to Accident Prevention*. New York: Association for the Aid of Crippled Children, 1962.
9. Haddon, W., *et al., Accident Research*. New York: Harper & Row, Publishers, 1964.
10. Likes, Norman R., *Psychological Approach to Accidents*. New York: Vantage Press Incorporated, 1954.
11. Malfetti, James L., "Scare Techniques and Traffic Safety," *Traffic Quarterly*, April, 1961.
12. McFarland, R. A., *et al., Human Variables in Motor Vehicle Accidents: A Review of the Literature*. Boston: Harvard School of Public Health, 1955.
13. Sawers, Kenneth, *Group Discussion Techniques in Driver Education*. New York: Center for Safety Education, New York University, 1962.
14. Selling, M. S., "Psychiatric Findings of 500 Traffic Offenders and Accident-Prone Drivers," *American Journal of Psychiatry*, XCVII (1940), 68–79.
15. Stiles, G. E., "Relationships of Unmet Emotional Needs to Accident Repeating Tendencies in Children." Unpublished Ph.D. thesis, New York University, 1957.
16. Stratemeyer, C., *Accident Research for Better Safety Teaching*. Washington, D. C.: National Commission on Safety Education, 1964.
17. Vaughn, J., *Positive versus Negative Instruction*. New York: National Conservation Bureau, 1928.
18. Wagner, Tobias, *Selective Job Placement*. New York: Association of Casualty and Surety Companies, 1946.
19. Wisely, H. M., "Personal Characteristics of Commercial Bus Drivers Related to Accident Proneness." Unpublished Ph.D. thesis, Northwestern University, 1947.

4

traffic safety education

Experts are virtually unanimous in assigning the key role in traffic safety to education. While engineering and enforcement are largely identified as "external" or environmental influences upon behavior, education works from "within" to affect individual attitudes, customs and behavior patterns. The human factor is recognized as the ultimate means of affecting traffic understandings and desired behavior.

Today, a myriad of organizations in our nation are expending countless educational efforts in acknowledgement of the potential of education in coping with human factors. Traffic authorities recommend that the full impact of our nation's educational effort be brought to bear on this problem; some propose a "cradle-to-grave" education effort which would extend from childhood through adult life.

In this chapter we will discuss two phases of traffic safety education: (1) pedestrian and bicycle and (2) driver education. Traffic safety for adults has been included in the chapter on transportation safety.

Pedestrian Safety

The yearly pedestrian death total has dropped steadily in the past 20 years from approximately 10,000 to 7,900 in spite of the increase in population. However, pedestrian deaths still account for nearly 45 per cent of the motor vehicle deaths in urban areas.

How can we account for this reduction in spite of the increase in population and the number of motor vehicles? There are various reasons given. Painted crossing lanes and one-way streets have been of value as have improved traffic signals and "walk" lights. Traffic control by police officers and crossing guards has helped as has the control of pedestrian traffic by school safety patrols. Moreover, the slowing down of vehicular traffic in some cities has tended to increase safety.

In addition, an important contribution has come from traffic safety education programs, especially in the schools. In many cities pedestrian obedience to signals is high; one rarely sees "jay-walkers" or other offenders. Children have been taught that the safest place to cross streets is at the crosswalks. We still have a problem of children playing in the street, but as more playgrounds are built, fewer children will play on streets.

The School Program

Pedestrian safety is one of the most important safety subjects in the elementary schools. In a recent year, according to *Accident Facts* (14), more than 1,500 children in the 5 to 14 age level were killed and 55,000 injured. There is a marked variation in the causes of accidents between the urban and rural areas as is indicated by the following table:

TABLE 5

PEDESTRIAN ACTIONS RESULTING IN ACCIDENTS—SCHOOL AGE

	Urban *Per cent*	*Rural* *Per cent*
Crossing		
(a) at intersections	38	17
(b) between intersections	45	46
Walking in roadway	6	15
Playing in roadway	5	8
Other in roadway	2	3
Standing in roadway	1	2
Getting on or off vehicles	1	1
ALL OTHERS	2	8
Total	100	100

Teaching safe pedestrian practices Since pedestrian safety is so important, it should be included in all of the grades. The following are some of the important practices that should be included:

1. Before crossing the street at intersections, look in all directions, especially for turning vehicles. Walk, do not run.
2. Cross only at crosswalks (these walks should be marked).
3. Cross only when traffic light is green.
4. When intersections have special signals, cross only when "walk" signals are on.
5. When there are alternative routes to schools, use those streets where traffic is not heavy.
6. Do not play in the street. Use playgrounds, parks, or vacant lots.
7. Cross at intersections, not in the middle of the block.
8. Do not step out from behind parked cars into the lane of moving traffic.
9. When getting into or out of a car, always use the side nearest the curb.
10. Always obey traffic officers, crossing guards, and safety patrols.
11. Never hitch rides on vehicles.
12. When walking on highways where there are no sidewalks, use the left side, facing traffic.

The following are suggested lessons:

1. Secure pedestrian safety posters and arrange for a display either in the classroom or on the school bulletin board.
2. Construct a series of safety signs such as are used in the community.
3. List all of the devices or engineering features that help reduce pedestrian accidents.
4. Make a list of the street crossings that are especially dangerous.
5. Prepare a talk on "Good Pedestrian Practices."
6. Prepare posters that show recommended safe practices.
7. Using a miniature camera, make a series of 2″ x 2″ color slides showing good pedestrian practices. Arrange for the class to see these.
8. Make a list of the bad practices of drivers that endanger or annoy pedestrians.
9. Prepare a radio or television skit to explain safe practices.
10. Work with the principal to arrange for an assembly to demonstrate good practices. A motion picture film could be used for a part of this program.
11. Have the captain of the safety patrol talk to your class or to a larger group.
12. Have children visit a busy intersection, and record the number of common violations in a 15-minute period.
13. Show motion picture films that emphasize pedestrian safety.
14. Have children make a list of the discourteous, unsafe pedestrian acts that they observe during a school day.

School Safety Patrols School safety patrols are the most familiar safety organizations. They are found in most elementary and junior high schools. Accidents to children on the way to and from school have shown a downward trend in the last decade. While patrols work in close cooperation with the police, it should be borne in mind that they should be under the supervision of the schools. They assist pupils in crossing the streets, but do not attempt to regulate traffic (except in a few instances).

Figure 4:1, PATROLS HAVE HELPED REDUCE ACCIDENTS GOING TO AND FROM SCHOOL

Standard rules have been prepared by the National Safety Council, the American Automobile Association, the National Commission on Safety Education, the National Congress of Parents and Teachers, the International Association of Chiefs of Police and the United States Office of Education.

Liability and Legality Accidents involving members of patrols are exceedingly rare. However, from time to time, questions have arisen regarding liability and legality. Members of the patrol are a part of the safety education program of the schools; the police usually serve in an advisory capacity.

As a general rule, most state legal authorities believe that school districts may organize patrols to guide pupils across the street, provided that members are not allowed to control motor vehicle traffic. If a member of a patrol is injured performing his approved duty, the school board may not be liable. This interpretation differs in the various states.

Bus Patrols These may or may not be a part of the regular school patrol. In general their duties are as follows:

a. Check attendance.
b. Maintain order.
c. Supervise the safe and orderly loading and unloading of the bus.
d. See to it that children are seated in a proper and safe manner.
e. Assist in arranging books, lunch kits, and other parcels in their proper places.
f. Assist children in crossing the street or highway upon the signal of the driver.
g. Be familiar with the operation of the emergency door and be prepared to assist the driver in emergencies.

The patrol should always be the last to board the bus and the first to alight. In the case of a two-member patrol, one should enter first to maintain order while the other is assisting in the loading. He should remain in the rear of the bus in transit and be the last to leave.

Hall and playground patrols Many schools also use indoor patrols for the control of traffic in halls and cafeterias. Some schools use patrols on playgrounds and in the gymnasium. Sometimes patrol members have charge of bicycle racks. In other instances they are on duty at school functions such as field days and parents' nights. This work not only provides protection for the pupils, but also is good training for the members of the patrol.

School safety courts The school safety court is used frequently as an auxiliary to the general student safety organization. It is found in some elementary schools but more often in secondary schools—especially the junior highs. In general the purpose of the court is twofold: (1) to provide a procedure for enforcing traffic regulations and (2) to provide a medium for educating pupils in the appreciation and observance of law. Careful planning is necessary if the court is to function well. The principal or faculty adviser should be present at all sessions to ensure fair dealing and orderly procedure.

Adult crossing guards In recent years, it has become difficult for patrols to function at congested intersections without aid. Pupils cannot control vehicular traffic when few breaks occur in the traffic. The number of intersections is steadily increasing, and there are not enough traffic officers available. For this reason, many communities are using adult crossing guards. Sometimes janitors or retired police officers are employed, but the general tendency today is to use women.

According to reports of communities, adult guards are working out satisfactorily. They are assigned where traffic surveys show the greatest need. Guards usually have some training given by the police department.

Bicycle Safety

According to *Accident Facts* (14), in a recent year 500 bicyclists lost their lives in traffic accidents. Of this number, about 300 were children of school age. Studies of accidents show that two out of three who were killed or injured were violating a traffic law or safe practice.

It is reported that one out of five bicycles involved in accidents were defective; the correction of defects will make for safer cycling.

The following were some of the most common violations:

Improper turns.
Disregarded traffic signals.
Carried extra rider.
Ran into opened car door.
Did not have the right of way.
Weaving and cutting in.
Ran into parked car.

There has been a great increase in the use of bicycles in the last two decades, especially among children of school age. It is estimated that the total of bicyclists in the United States is well over 20,000,000. Some of the attitudes, knowledge and skills that contribute to safe cycling are much the same as those used in operating a motor cycle or scooter, and are related to those required by automobile drivers. The bicycle is recognized by state laws as a vehicle and riders should follow the appropriate state motor vehicle regulations, such as keeping to the right, using signals, obeying traffic lights and stopping at stop signs.

Bicycle control in the community Publications on bicycle safety have been issued by the National Safety Council, the American Automobile Association, the National Commission on Safety Education, the Bicycle Institute of America and other organizations. The three booklets listed below, which can be obtained from the Bicycle Institute of America, include most of the essential information:

Bike Regulations in the Community
Bike Safety Programs
Bicycle Safety Tests

The first of these deals largely with the development of a model municipal ordinance. While this is not the responsibility of the schools, copies of the ordinance can be given to the mayor, a member of the council or the chief of police. A local ordinance aids greatly in insuring the success of the safety program.

Among other features, the model ordinance provides for the registration and licensing of bicycles together with testing and inspection. The schools are interested chiefly in the latter and the classroom instruction that should accompany the program. In most cases the tests are given on school grounds or on municipal playgrounds, but in some instances streets are closed to traffic and used for testing.

In a citywide program a committee is appointed consisting of representatives of the schools, the police, bicycle dealers, service clubs and in some cases Parent-Teachers Associations, veterans organizations, and others.

Steps in the Inspection and Testing Program

1. The model municipal ordinance is passed (if not already in effect).
2. A committee is appointed to organize the program.
3. Materials are ordered from the Bicycle Institute of America (or some other agency).
4. Publicity is sent out and the program announced in all schools, both public and parochial.
5. Since the superintendent of schools or his representative is a member of the committee, the program is given official approval by the schools.
6. A schedule is sent out giving the time and the place for inspection and testing.
7. Teams are appointed to be assigned to each area.
8. Registration and testing forms are delivered to each testing area.
9. The personnel for a team generally consists of representatives of the schools, the police, a bicycle repair store and a service club, with two older Boy Scouts or safety patrol members as recorders.

Inspection and tests It is best to conduct inspections before the tests are given. This is generally done by a bicycle repairman or a police officer. Details of the inspection and testing are described in *Bicycle Safety Tests* (4). The first step is an inspection and fitting test; the second, inspection for mechanical condition. If a cyclist fails on an inspection, defects should be corrected before he is assigned to further testing.

The following are the types of activities suggested for the schools:

1. Demonstrations of bicycle safety equipment.
2. Demonstrations of proper riding practices. (Since this requires considerable space, it can be done in the auditorium, in the gymnasium or on the playground.)
3. Preparation of written reports or compositions dealing with safe cycling.
4. Development of a safe practice code for cyclists.
5. Building of a storage rack at the school.
6. Preparation of a bicycle safety program for the school assembly or a Parent-Teacher meeting.

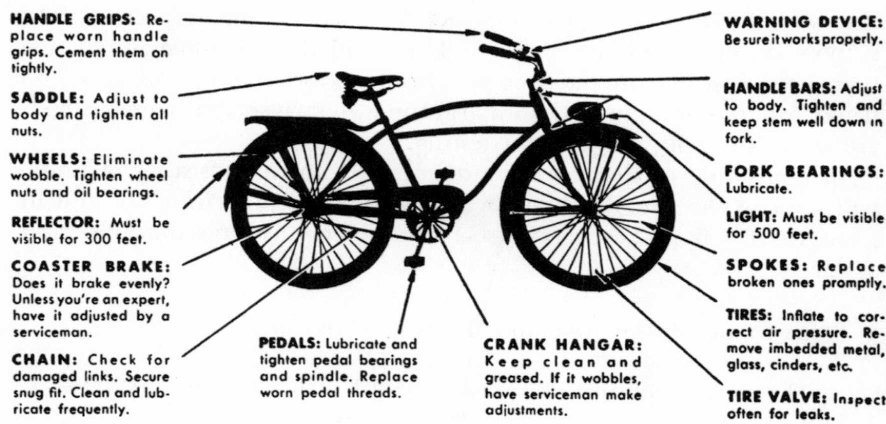

Figure 4:2.

Adult Pedestrians

According to *Accident Facts* (14), the death rate for adult pedestrians is high, much higher than the rate for children of school age. This is especially true for the over-65 age group. There are various reasons for this. First of all the older adult's reactions, hearing and vision may be defective. When he gets into a difficult situation, his reactions are slow. While there are not too many facts on this, there is also evidence of many instances in cities where the pedestrian had been drinking or was under the influence of medicines. These often decrease alertness and reaction time. It is also claimed that older adults fail to understand the limitations of the driver in stopping a car. They walk slowly and are not used to high-speed traffic.

All of these combine to make the older adult pedestrian a serious problem both in the cities and in rural areas. Traffic lights and officers, together with "walk" lights help, but deaths and non-fatal accidents are still too high. Since the adult population in the country is steadily increasing, educational programs of community organizations should pay more attention to strengthening the pedestrian safety program.

High School Driver Education

Although the high school driver education movement started in the thirties, its beginning is generally associated with the years following the second World War. During that decade it became the fastest growing subject in the high school curriculum. Today, over 1.25 million high school students receive the benefit of some type of course each year; this represents approximately half of those eligible for such a program. A number of circumstances have contributed to the rapid growth of this course. The record of the youthful driver on our highways has been substantially poorer than that of most other age groups. The driver education course reaches the young new driver. Since the beginning of the program, a number of research studies have indicated that such courses reduce traffic accidents and violations; consequently it has been advocated by many agencies in and out of school.

Today, driver education is recognized as a phase of general education which meets a pressing social need. It is only natural that high school youth be prepared to drive safely in a society which depends on the motor vehicle so extensively. This formal course provides the best means by which high school students can acquire the desired basic concepts, habits and skills needed by the modern traffic citizen. The high school is the best equipped agency for reaching the greatest number of new drivers at an age when they are highly motivated for the learning.

The Goals and Principles

The highway safety action program of the President's Committee for Traffic Safety has stated that the ultimate goal should be the requirement that every beginning driver complete an approved course in driver education. The goals of driver education are not unlike those of general secondary education. The student who develops the concepts, habits and skills needed for good traffic behavior acquires the self-discipline so important to effective citizenship. American secondary education subscribes to seven cardinal principles. They are (1) health, (2) command of fundamental processes, (3) worthy home membership, (4) vocation, (5) citizenship, (6) worthy use of leisure time and (7) development of ethical character. The foregoing principles are closely associated with the benefits and activities of classroom and practice driving experiences in driver education.

> It is doubtful to me that any form of education can more eloquently be justified from an humanitarian point of view and from an economic point of view than eradicating the pending incompetency that wells up out of the youth of America because they are not taught as they should be taught. This whole business of how to manage a motor vehicle . . . has become increasingly complex by the minute. Driver Education is an essential function in the master plan for coping with today's traffic problem. . . .
>
> *Howard Pyle in "Action for Safety," 1964*

The course deals directly with current needs of students, involving each of the seven principles. The driver education student is solving real problems affecting his life and is obliged to employ the knowledge and processes learned in other courses, as well as those acquired in driver education. Thus, the course is inter-disciplinary in nature and permits the student to integrate theory into the solution of living problems.

Objectives of High School Driver Education

In 1949 the First National Conference on Driver Education was called by the National Education Association, National Commission on Safety Education to establish national policies. The fourth such conference, held in 1963, defined traffic and driver education as "those learning experiences provided by the school for the purpose of helping students to become good traffic citizens and to use the motor vehicle safely and efficiently."

The statement of objectives, originally developed at the 1949 conference, remains the same:

1. To develop in young people a *strong sense of personal and social responsibility* for the common welfare, particularly as it is affected by and involved in the operation of motor vehicles.

The learner is involved in the development of a realistic philosophy which will enable him to make a responsible addition to the traffic society.

2. To develop *pride in maintaining high standards of performance,* particularly in the operation of motor vehicles.

The phrase "high standards of performance" requires expression in terms of behavior; the learner must cultivate a high value for the behavior identified when high standards are spelled out in performance.

3. To promote the *safe, efficient, and enjoyable use* of equipment and environment, especially of motor vehicles and highways.

While this goal is the subject of study in the classroom, driving and laboratory activities provide a learning-by-doing experience to literally fulfill the stated goals.

4. To promote *effective habits of cooperation* in meeting problems of the common welfare, especially those concerned with the use of motor vehicles and highways.

Every citizen and driver can lend support to those movements aimed at improving the traffic welfare by his participation in positive action programs; this distinguishes him from those who limit themselves to passing comments regarding "what should be done" to improve existing conditions.

5. To prepare young people *for socially useful vocations* suited to their individual abilities, particularly those that involve the use of motor vehicles.

Through experiences in vocational exploration, the student becomes aware of career possibilities in the motor vehicle and related fields. Effective placement of personnel in the thousands of motor-vehicle-related fields will result in more efficient adjustment of society to the technological and economic environment which has been so influenced by the motor vehicle.

Like other movements, driver education also suffers from certain misconceptions about its objectives; according to one of these the high school course is an experience designed to prepare youthful drivers to pass a driver licensing examination; actually, this is only an accrued benefit of the program.

The objectives listed above are intended to serve as guides for planning a program of study for the local situation. They imply that the acquisition of knowledge alone is not enough to meet the stated goals; knowledge must be combined with skills and the development of attitudes which enable the student to function efficiently in traffic.

National Conference Recommendations

The reports of the National Conferences have set guidelines for the sound expansion and conduct of state and local driver education programs. Conference recommendations on organization and administration of programs, planning instruction, teaching staff, state leadership, and the like, serve as basis for evaluating and goals for upgrading public school programs.

Organization and Administration

The National Conferences place upon officers of state and local school systems the responsibility for effective leadership in organization and administration of driver education programs. This leadership is exercised by developing policies concerning program financing, instruction, teacher preparation and use of materials and resources, and by assigning to qualified persons responsibilities for carrying out such policies.

Financing and Legislation for Driver Education Funds for driver education should come from the same source as other public school programs; however, when local and state funds are not adequate to provide the minimum complete driver education course, it is recommended that the state provide the additional funds through special appropriation.

Programs in public schools should result from decisions of state and local boards of education. State laws should be limited to authorizing the course, or to providing for the expenditure of public funds. The National Conferences further state that there should be no legislation requiring schools to provide the course or to specify matters of an instructional nature.

At the present time about one-half of all states have passed legislation dealing with financial support. In most cases, the intent has been to stimulate enrollment in courses. It is of interest to note that according to the National High School Driver Education Achievement Program (8), in states having such legislation, 54 per cent of the eligible students are enrolled, while in states without such legislation the enrollment is only 28 per cent.

General Program Characteristics A complete program of driver education includes both classroom and driving experiences; both phases are necessary to achieve all of the objectives. Classroom instruction should be given concurrently with practice driving, or at least should precede driving. The subject should be offered on the same basis as other electives, preferably for one full semester. National Conference reports indicate that the aims of the course are not fully met when it is included only as a part of other subject areas.

Since the student is at the height of his motivation for driver education just before reaching the legal driving age, the subject should be offered at the grade level where most students are closely approaching this age. The course should also carry credit toward graduation.

Many schools are unable to provide instruction for all students for the complete course. Under these circumstances it is recommended that classroom instruction be provided for all. The selection of students for the complete program should be made on the basis of their nearness to driving age, personal needs and nearness to leaving school.

Minimum instructional time should range from 45 to 60 clock hours. This time should include at least 30 hours of classroom instruction and six hours of practice driving, exclusive of time in the car as observer.

Criteria for Selection of Learning Experiences The 1960 National Conference specifies that, for any type or level of instruction in driver education, the learning experiences should:

1. Contribute to the general objectives of education.
2. Contribute to the basic purposes of driver education.
3. Originate in problems that are vital to the students.
4. Be consistent with the developmental level of the students in terms of age, knowledge, experience, insight and manipulative ability.
5. Recognize individual as well as group needs and interests.
6. Be balanced with respect to all phases of the programs.
7. Stress positive rather than negative aspects of learning.
8. Harmonize with the local setting in which the learning takes place.

9. Motivate and focus student effort toward continued self-improvement long after termination of the instruction.
10. Emphasize self-directed student activity.
11. Provide for student acquisition of positive and wholesome attitudes both in the classroom and in practice driving.

The element of competition which pits the skill of young drivers against each other cannot be reconciled with the purpose of driver education. *Emphasis should be on developing a voluntary cooperative attitude on the part of students.*

Methods of Instruction

The driver education teacher must vary teaching methods according to student needs, group size, available facilities, school program organization and other local conditions. Methods should be selected to provide learning experiences in as realistic a setting as possible. The teacher's challenge is to obtain, regardless of the methods, direct involvement and participation of the student. The teacher must be skilled in a variety of methods, including:

1. Teacher presentations.
2. Directed group discussions, often involving action commitments.
3. Classroom forums or panels.
4. Visiting specialists and resource persons.
5. Skill-developing exercises.
6. Drills, in meaningful settings, to strengthen desirable habit patterns.
7. Demonstrations, such as of skills for use in emergencies.
8. Dramatizations and role-playing.
9. Cooperative problem-solving tasks.
10. Projects involving student use of survey, interview and observation techniques and opinion polls.
11. Psychophysical equipment, driving simulators, models and mock-ups, and comparable aids to supplement basic instruction.
12. Filmstrips, motion pictures and other audio-visual resources.
13. Field trips to traffic courts, highway departments, driver licensing bureaus and motor vehicle inspection stations.
14. Student participation with adults in community and statewide safety conferences.
15. Evaluation designed to aid both teacher and students in measuring progress and in setting new goals.

Nature and Scope of Instruction

As stated earlier, the complete course must provide both classroom and practice driving instruction in order to meet objectives. Details of actual courses of study for both phases of driver education are relatively uniform in programs across the nation.

Classroom Instruction Various courses of study in classroom instruction differ little. The following are the units recommended by the National Commission on Safety Education:

1. Motor vehicle transportation in American life.
2. Human capabilities and limitations for driving and walking.
3. Characteristics of streets and highways.
4. Laws governing the use of motor vehicles, and penalties for non-observance.
5. The motor vehicle as a mechanical device.
6. Consumer values in automobile ownership and operation.
7. How to operate a motor vehicle.
8. Relationship of drivers to non-motor vehicle traffic.
9. Driver examining and licensing.
10. Traffic accidents—national, state and local.
11. Controls over vehicles, streets, highways and their users.
12. Outlook for the future.

Driving and Laboratory Experience

Although the classroom phases of most driver education programs are similar, differing plans have been used in schools to provide adequate driving experiences.

Since the beginning of the driver education movement, the most popular plan for practice driving has been the *dual-control* car plan. Groups of pupils, up to four, practice in a conventional automobile with an instructor. After instructor demonstrations, pupils practice manipulating the car under close supervision, completing a succession of lessons according to prescribed procedures.

The Multiple-Car or Range Program More recent plans have been developed to increase the pupil-teacher ratio, thus lowering the cost of providing driving experiences. The *multiple-car* plan, unlike the dual-control plan, requires an off-street driving area on which a street layout is provided. All driving is done on this special area which reproduces typical physical conditions found on the street. The area is equipped with from six to twelve vehicles. First, step-by-step instruction is given to students in a dual-controlled vehicle. Subsequently, students proceed to solo operation of cars under supervision of the instructor at a control point on the driving range. At first pupils move cars in the same direction; in the latter stages of instruction a normal traffic pattern is simulated. A recent report indicates that 398 schools in 19 states are using ranges (8).

Figure 4:3, THE RANGE AT MUNFORD HIGH SCHOOL IN DETROIT

Note the various traffic situations and the 10 cars being used. Ranges are widely used in the Michigan program. If 12 cars are used, up to 600 students a year can be given instruction on this range. In addition, 600 adults can be instructed in after-school and evening hours.

Simulators

Another plan used to provide driving-type experiences under laboratory conditions involves the use of driving simulators. Students "drive" a dummy car in accordance with instructions and with motion picture films. These films are designed to provide typical experiences encountered in driving, such as in the area of emergency and advanced driving skills, without the hazards of actual driving. The transfer of training from simulators to actual driving by students reduces actual learning time in the vehicle. Most schools give 12 periods on the simulator and 3 on practice driving. A recent report shows that 399 schools in 34 states were using simulators (8).

Content of Practice Driving Instruction

Regardless of the plan used to provide practice instruction, the general goals are the same—to teach safe, efficient, economical operation of motor vehicles. This is accomplished through a series of planned, sequential learning experiences, under supervision of a qualified teacher.

Following is a typical list of units for practice driving instruction:

1. The driver's compartment:
    a. Safety aids
    b. Gauges
    c. Starting devices
    d. Controls.
2. Predriving procedures.
3. Starting and stopping the engine:
    a. Automatic transmission cars
    b. Gearshift cars.
4. Gearshift and selector positions.
5. Putting the car in motion, stopping.
6. Shifting and downshifting.
7. Backing the car.
8. Right and left turns.
9. Turning around:
    a. At intersections
    b. At driveways
    c. U Turns
    d. On narrow streets.
10. Parking:
    a. Angle
    b. Parallel
    c. Upgrade, with and without curb
    d. Downgrade, with and without curb.
11. Starting on an upgrade:
    a. Automatic transmission cars
    b. Gearshift cars.
12. City driving.
13. Highway driving.
14. Freeway driving.
15. Skill exercises.
16. Road test in traffic.

The topics above may be modified to meet local needs. In some areas special emphasis may be placed upon winter driving or skills under other adverse conditions and on emergencies.

Organizations Which Support Driver Education

At least 80 different national organizations have endorsed driver education. Well over ten of these have been very active in the movement. In the early years the American Automobile Association and the casualty and surety insurance industry were strong supporters. The Automobile Association still continues its aid and the principal insurance support now comes from the Insurance Institute for Highway Safety, which is made up of over 500 insurance companies. Most insurance companies provide reduced insurance premiums for drivers who have completed courses. In some states this reduction is from 10 to 15 per cent. The reduction is good from the time a student is covered by insurance until he is 25. In some states, this would be for eight years; the total savings to the family or the individual would amount to several times the cost of the high school course.

Among the other agencies that have aided the program are the following:

Professional The American Driver and Traffic Safety Education Association is a department of the National Education Association. It represents professional educators in the safety education movement. It works toward the improvement and extension of driver and safety education in schools and colleges by conducting conferences for the improvement of teaching, by sponsoring programs with cooperating colleges for teacher education, through dissemination of materials designed to improve safety instruction and by other means.

The counterpart of this group on the state level is the association of professional driver and safety education teachers. Nearly every state has its association of driver educators. Many state associations are affiliated with ADTSEA.

The American Association for Health, Physical Education and Recreation, also a department of the National Education Association, has established a division to support and encourage safety education programs in schools.

Quasi-public The National Safety Council and local councils have always been strong supporters. The National Commission on Safety Education has also been a strong influence in raising standards.

Government Agencies The President's Committee for Traffic Safety has also been helpful in securing national support.

State motor vehicle departments and state and local police have made important contributions to driver education. In addition other state departments, including education and highway departments have been helpful.

Other Agencies The automobile and petroleum industries have been of great aid to the schools, especially by the loan of automobiles, and the publication of teaching aids. Parent-Teachers Associations have also been strong supporters as have farm organizations and service, civic and fraternal clubs. These are just a few of the organizations that have aided in the development of driver education.

summary

Traffic accidents are the leading cause of death among children of school age. Pedestrian and bicycle safety should therefore be stressed, especially in elementary and junior high schools. The practices and attitudes that children develop in the schools tend to be followed in adult life. Children not only need to be well informed about traffic safety but should also develop the skills and attitudes that will make them safer pedestrians and bicyclists. By giving actual experiences in desirable pedestrian and bicycle practices, the schools will improve these skills and attitudes.

School safety patrols have been found to be very effective in reducing accidents of children on the way to and from school. While patrols are a responsibility of the schools and should be under the direction of a teacher, in many instances police officers aid in supervision and training. Patrols should always follow the standards that have been developed by national organizations.

While bicycle safety instruction should be given in the schools, many communities have also organized bicycle licensing and testing programs designed to improve cycling practices.

Driver education during the decade following World War II was the fastest growing subject in the high school curriculum. During the past five years, an average of 1.2 million students have completed courses in over 12,000 high schools. The seven cardinal principles of secondary education are closely associated with the benefits and values of driver education. In addition, National Conferences on Driver Education have established five specific objectives. More than one-half of the states have some type of financial support for driver education. This has resulted in a steady increase in course registration.

A complete program of driver education includes both classroom and driving experiences with minimum instruction time ranging from 45 to 60 clock hours. The so-called standard course has 30 classroom periods and 6 of practice driving, the remainder being devoted to observation in the car. In recent years, the multiple-car plan has shown significant growth in certain states. The same can be said of the use of simulators. Both of these methods are valuable in increasing production.

Driver education has had the public support of over 80 national organizations—educational, civic, fraternal, industrial, commercial and governmental. At least ten of these organizations have been very active in stimulating programs through publications, field staff, scholarship grants to teachers and in other ways. There is every reason to believe that driver education will continue to grow as it has in the past decade.

suggested projects and activities

1. Prepare a complete program of bicycle safety to be used in an elementary school.

2. Describe the methods used to reduce pedestrian accidents in your community.
3. Organize a program that could be used in September for a school assembly devoted to the installation of new safety patrols.
4. Secure from the police department a record of the causes of child pedestrian accidents. Compare these with the records included in this chapter.
5. Prepare the outline of a talk that you could give to a newly organized school patrol.
6. Using a miniature camera, take a series of pictures to illustrate traffic safety in an elementary school. Arrange to give this talk before one of the classes or at an assembly.
7. List the advantages that the simulator program of driver education has over the dual-control plan.
8. Make a sketch of a range or multiple-car area showing the various traffic facilities.
9. Make a list of the methods that could be used to improve the quality of driver education in the schools.
10. Prepare a plan that could be followed to hold driver education in the schools in a situation in which school authorities are considering dropping it.
11. Prepare a program that could be used in a city of 100,000 population for an attack on pedestrian accidents.

selected references

1. American Automobile Association, *Policies and Practices for School Safety Patrols.* Washington, D.C.: The Association, 1958.
2. ________, *Adult Crossing Guards.* Washington, D.C.: The Association, 1958.
3. ________, *Model Pedestrian Protection Program.* Washington, D.C.: The Association, 1954.
4. Bicycle Institute of America, *Bicycle Safety Tests.* New York: The Institute, 1955.
5. ________, *Bike Regulations in the Community.* New York: The Institute, 1955.
6. Brody, Leon and Herbert J. Stack, *Highway Safety and Driver Education.* Englewood Cliffs, N.J.: Prentice-Hall, Inc., 1962.
7. Florio, A. E. and G. T. Stafford, *Safety Education* (2nd ed.). New York: McGraw-Hill Book Company, 1962.
8. Insurance Institute for Highway Safety, *National High School Driver Education Achievement Program.* Washington, D.C.: The Institute (annual).
9. National Commission on Safety Education, *Bicycle Safety in Action.* Washington, D.C.: The Commission, 1950.

10. ________, *Policies and Practices for Driver and Traffic Safety Education.* Washington, D.C.: The Commission, 1964.

11. ________, *Driver Education and Driver Simulators.* Washington, D.C.: The Commission, 1960.

12. National Safety Council, *Pedestrian Safety*. Chicago: The Council, 1957.

13. ________, *Safety Education Data Sheets,* Nos. 6, 29, 84. Chicago: The Council (n.d.).

14. ________, *Accident Facts.* Chicago: The Council (annual).

15. ________, and Automotive Safety Foundation, *Youth and Traffic Safety.* Chicago: The Council, 1964.

16. President's Committee for Traffic Safety, *Education*. Washington, D.C.: The Committee, 1960.

5

home and farm

Mention the word "safety" to the average man on the street, and chances are the conversation will immediately turn to highway or airplane accidents. Such events are dramatic and therefore "news." Unfortunately, emphasis on traffic accidents is not confined solely to the lay public but too frequently to those responsible for safety programs as well. It has not been until very recently that constructive efforts have been directed toward the problem of home and farm safety. This neglect and apathy may be attributed to at least two factors. The first is the concept that a man's home as his castle is immune from the eyes of the public; home is not subject to inspection, nor is the homemaker required to eliminate hazards. It is through persuasion that the home must be made safe. The second, and perhaps the more important factor, is the inadequacy until recent years of data on home accidents and the resulting lack of recognition of the seriousness and magnitude of the problem. To be sure, information on fatalities associated with home accidents has been available since the late '20's, but even today, except for selected areas, we still have little more than estimates and projections as to the extent and detail regarding the nonfatal injuries experienced in American homes.

Likewise, information regarding the nature and scope of farm accidents on a national scale is comparatively meager. A few states have conducted detailed studies of such accidents, but, again, what little information we have is primarily confined to fatalities. However limited such information may be, it does indicate that home and farm accidents are problems of great magnitude. We are living in a changing era and the many advances in technology certainly affect living safely in the home. It is a pushbutton era and with each new labor-saving device, additional hazards are encountered. Today, we have a mobile population; on an average, two out of five families move every two years. These changes involve tensions and adjustments to new communities which in turn may cause accidents.

> To many persons it is astonishing that accidents, in the home kill nearly twice as many persons as do work accidents—and that nearly three times as many disability injuries occur at home as on the road.
> *National Safety Council, "The Fight for Life."*

The urbanization of America and the population explosion have resulted in people living close together. Apartment living involves sharing; an unsafe act of one person may involve many families. Transportation is a problem of present-day living; children are often driven to schools and playgrounds, which makes it necessary for the traffic safety program to be a part of the home program. In many communities, the purchaser must carry the groceries; this involves a knowledge of how to lift, handle and carry packages. More women are working outside the home, which makes it necessary for children to be more self-sufficient and knowledgeable about safe practices in the home.

The Accident Situation

Home Fatalities Accidents in the home and immediate surroundings are a major cause of death and disability in the United States. During the past decade an average of over 28,000 persons lost their lives each year due to accidents in the home. More lives were lost from this one cause alone than from the combined tolls of tuberculosis, diphtheria, polio, syphilis, rheumatic fever and murder. For those who are statistically minded, deaths from home accidents average one every 19 minutes, or three per hour. However disheartening these figures may be, it is encouraging to note that the death rate from home accidents has steadily declined during the past ten years from 19.6 to 14.5. The distribution of home fatalities by type and age for a typical year is shown in Table 6. In the nation, nearly half of all accidental home deaths result from falls. Deaths from fires are next in importance, amounting to about one in

TABLE 6

DEATHS FROM HOME ACCIDENTS BY TYPE AND AGE

Type of Accident	*ALL AGES*	*0–4 Years*	*5–14 Years*	*15–24 Years*	*25–44 Years*	*45–64 Years*	*65–74 Years*	*75 Years and Over*
Falls	12,200	450	80	20	200	950	2,100	8,400
Fires, burns, and deaths associated with fires	6,100	1,400	700	200	900	1,250	600	1,050
Suffocation—ingested object	1,700	1,300	30	20	80	100	70	100
Suffocation—mechanical	1,500	1,400	20	10	20	20	10	20
Poisons, solid or liquid	1,400	400	30	90	350	400	80	50
Firearms	1,200	60	330	180	250	250	90	40
Poison gases	800	40	60	110	200	230	80	80
Other	2,600	1,050	150	170	200	200	270	560
Total	27,500	6,100	1,400	800	2,200	3,400	3,300	10,300

Source: Estimates by National Safety Council, based on data from the National Office of Vital Statistics and state health departments.

five. The importance of falls and fires, as well as of the other types of accidents, varies from one part of the country to another. It is also noteworthy that nearly half of all victims of falls and fires are over 65 years of age. During the year for which the figures in Table 7 were selected, 10,500 of the 12,200 fatal falls occurred to persons in the 65 and over age group.

Home Accidents

From 1935 to a recent year, the death rate from home accidents declined from 26.0 to approximately 14.5. The population increased, especially in the age groups most susceptible to fatal accidents—children under four years and adults over 65.

National Safety Council, "Accident Facts."

Farm fatalities Farming leads all occupations in total accidental work deaths (followed by service and construction), and ranks third in rate per 100,000 workers (behind mining and construction). Annually, about 8,500 farm residents die and 800,000 sustain disabling injuries in work, home, recreation, and traffic accidents. Traffic is the chief killer (35%), followed by work (25%), traffic deaths while pursuing farming occupation (5%), home (25%), and public non-motor-vehicle (10%). Most states now have voluntary organizations promoting farm safety. In states with particularly active farm safety committees or councils, full-time farm safety specialists and aggressive accident prevention programs reaching farm families, the decrease in fatal farm work accidents has been substantial, often remarkable.

Permanent and Temporary Injuries Since the reporting of home and farm accidents to any central agency is not required by law, information concerning permanent and temporary injuries is somewhat limited and at best relies on an educated estimate. However, from several local and regional surveys projections can be made as to the extent of nonfatal injuries due to accidents in the home and on the farm. In recent years, an average of more than 100,000 persons have suffered some degree of permanent injury from home injuries—an amputated finger, a permanently stiffened joint, and, in many cases, even more serious impairment. During these same years, over 4 million Americans were temporarily injured (disabled for over 24 hours) each year through home accidents. This compares with approximately 1.4 million disabling injuries due to motor vehicles; 1.9 million due to work accidents; and 2.1 million caused by accidents during recreation or in other public places. Thus, it can be readily seen that accidents in the home account for nearly half of the total injuries suffered in this nation in any given year.

Economic Loss Recent estimates indicate that home accidents, fatal and nonfatal, conservatively, result in an economic loss of approximately $1,050,000,000 annually. Economic loss from farm work accidents places an additional burden of $550,000,000 on American pocket books.

Types of Home Accidents

Human errors account for the great majority of accidents in the home and on the farm, as is the case in industry and other areas. It is useful, therefore, to analyze accidents by type and location in order to devise an effective prevention program.

Accidents by type

Falls, burns, asphyxiations and suffocations, poisonings and gunshot wounds are the main classifications. In addition, a large percentage of home and farm accidents are not readily categorized and are termed "miscellaneous."

Falls Of all types of accidents, falls are the most common, accounting for about half of all home fatalities. They occur most frequently on stairs that are cluttered, poorly lighted or in need of repair. People also fall from high places—porches, balconies, windows, ladders and trees—as well as on smooth, slippery surfaces—bathtubs, improperly polished floors, wet or greasy linoleum, icy walks and steps and in the yard. Even a short fall of only three to four feet may prove fatal, especially to the aged. They often have poor vision, are infirm and lack coordination.

Falling on stairs may be prevented by keeping the staircase free of misplaced articles, well lighted and in good repair. All stairways should be equipped with handrails, stair treads should be in good repair, and treads and risers should be properly proportioned. The bottom step of basement and outer hall stairs should be painted white to prevent falls

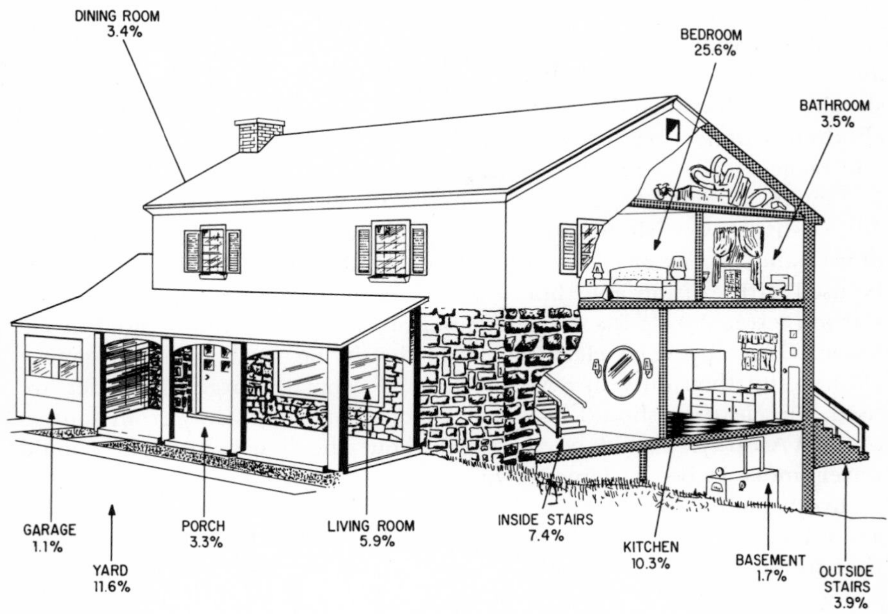

Figure 5:1.

occasioned when persons mistakenly believe they have reached the floor or landing. Outside, attic, and basement steps should not be too steep and should not be used to store canned goods, brooms, mops, garbage and the like. Scatter rugs should be anchored. Anchoring scatter rugs with nonskid materials and arranging furniture to clear space for passing will help to prevent falls; windows should be screened; and only a sturdy stepladder or stepstool should be used to reach inaccessible shelves or to hang pictures and curtains. Rubber mats and handrails prevent falls in bathtubs; ashes, sand or salt may be used on icy walks and steps, and snow should be removed immediately. Keeping things in their specified places will prevent many falls in the home, in the yard, and in farm buildings.

Burns and Scalds Burns and scalds usually occur during cooking and laundry operations, sometimes from contact with exposed electric wires, open fires, cook stoves, utensils filled with hot liquids, or hot objects such as toasters and irons. Fuels, gases, and cleaning fluids also are sources of burns, as are matches, open hearth fires and refuse fires.

The prevention of burns and scaldings involves many safety precautions. Matches should be kept in metal containers out of reach of children. Open hearth fires, bonfires, and refuse fires should be well screened. Special care must be taken when using kettles and containers with long handles to prevent the handles from catching in one's clothes and to prevent children from upsetting them. Electrical appliances should be disconnected when not in use, and placed out of reach of children. Connecting cords should be in good condition; discard frayed and ragged cords to prevent shock and burns in handling. Light switches and chains should be placed at some distance from bathtubs, wash basins and washtubs. One should *never* touch a light switch or chain with wet or moist hands; shock or electrocution may result. Flammable liquids should be used with caution and should be stored in plainly marked containers. Carbon tetrachloride is a dangerous poison, and should not be used in the home. Only approved cleaning fluids should be used for dry cleaning clothes and then only in a well-ventilated room. If large quantities are used, the cleaning should be done out of doors, well away from sources of fire. Ashtrays should be provided about the house, and one should never smoke in bed or lying down.

Every family should have a safe fire exit plan for the home, and a second way to get out if the normal exits are on fire. Simple precautions that should be adopted include sleeping with the bedroom door closed; hot gases rise rapidly and it is only two minutes to survival if a fire starts on the first floor if the door is open. If the door is closed the time differential is much greater, for this involves from 5 to 11 minutes. The door holds back smoke and toxic gases. A wise family has a predetermined place to meet if a fire does occur.

Asphyxiation and Suffocation Asphyxiation by gases is one of the serious causes of home accidents. Such gases may come from leaky gas pipes, defective gas appliances, coal stoves, furnaces, oil stoves and burners and the exhaust from automobiles. If carbon monoxide gas is breathed into the lungs and the victim is exposed too long, he loses consciousness and may die unless removed to fresh air and resuscitated at once.

To avoid asphyxiation, garages and all rooms in which engines are running should be well ventilated; gas appliances should be inspected by a qualified workman; and furnaces should be properly banked at night. All rooms in which coal and gas stoves are burning should be well ventilated. If an unconscious person is found in a gas-filled room, he should be carried into fresh air, artificial respiration should be started, and a doctor should be called immediately.

Suffocation is caused by a lack of air or oxygen in the lungs and may result from immersion in water or other liquid, exposure to dense smoke or, rarely, in the case of infants, smothering under bedclothes. Resuscitation must be begun immediately in each case. Special care should be taken in arranging bedclothes so that infants will not become entangled in them. The room itself should be kept warm so that the covers need not

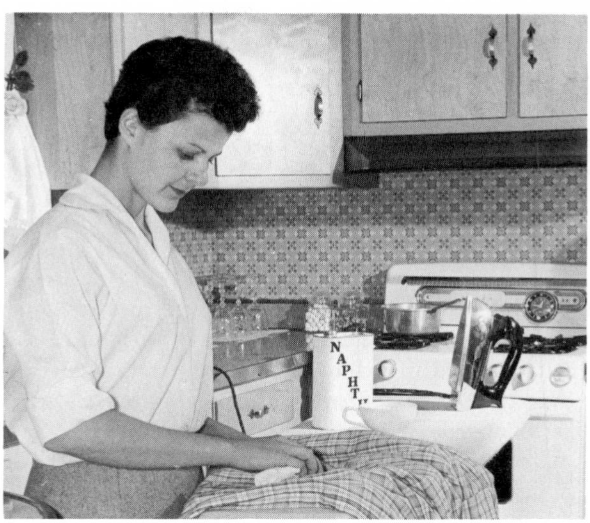

Figure 5:2, NAPHTHA IS MORE EXPLOSIVE THAN GASOLINE AND SHOULD NEVER BE USED FOR HOME DRY-CLEANING.

be heavy. All children should be taught not to place small objects such as marbles or pieces of rubber in their mouths, for these may cause strangulation or serious lung impairment. Children should not be allowed to play with plastic bags, because these also could cause suffocation.

Poisoning Careless use or storage of poisons frequently leads to fatalities.

> Beware of "Harmless" Poisons
>
> Every year 600,000 children ingest potentially poisonous substances—everything from the foulest-tasting household chemicals to chocolate covered pills. Keep *all* household chemicals, medicines, insecticides, polish, kerosene, vitamins, disinfectants, deodorizers, lye, corrosins and laxatives where children cannot reach them.
>
> *National Safety Council, "Family Safety," Spring,* 1964

Through curiosity and from observing adults, children often taste the contents of bottles and small containers. Not infrequently adults mistake poison for medicine. To guard against such possibilities, poisons and medicines should be kept in well marked bottles, each in a place of its own. Bottles containing poisons should have distinctive identifying characteristics, such as a pin or tack in the cork, and should be placed out of the reach of children. Insect powders should be kept away from foods. To avoid food poisoning, all cans, jars and other containers should be thoroughly sterilized. All members of the family should be taught to recognize the poisonous snakes, berries, and plants native to the home area.

The ingestion of poisonous substances by children, over 600,000 each year, has resulted in the establishment of over 400 poison control centers. These are found in every state. Over 500 children die annually as the result of taking some poison. These children are not drinking arsenic or cyanide—they are poisoned by candy flavored "baby aspirin," the regular aspirin, insecticides, kerosene, detergents, bleaches, or polish placed within their reach.

Gunshot Wounds Forgetting a shell in a gun, carrying the gun incorrectly, pointing it at a person, and accidentally discharging it while walking through brush or crawling under fences—these are some of the actions which lead to accidental deaths and serious injuries. Safety precautions require that all shells be removed before the gun is put aside, that the gun be inspected immediately when it is picked up, that firearms not be pointed toward persons, and that users of firearms be instructed in the proper technique for carrying, cleaning and firing them. A large percentage of gunshot accidents take place in the home.

> Of the deaths occurring inside the house, over half happen in the bedroom, with the living and dining rooms, kitchen, stairs, and bathroom next in that order. The principal accident type in each of these locations is falls; fire is next.
>
> For each of the four most important types of accidents occurring inside the house—falls, fires, poisoning and suffiocation—the principal place of occurrence was the bedroom. The living-dining-room area was the next most frequent location of falls and suffocations while the kitchen was the next most frequent location of fires and poisonings.
>
> Outside of the dwelling, the order of importance of places of fatal accidents is: yard, porch, garage, walks and roof. Falls were the leading type of accidents in all of these places except the garage.
>
> Non-fatal home accidents present a slightly different pattern as far as location is concerned. According to a rather intensive study of 1,620 injuries occurring to San Francisco area residents during 1954 and 1955, approximately three-fourths of the nonfatal injuries occurred inside the dwelling unit and one-fourth somewhere outside the home but on the home premises. There were more accidents in the kitchen than in any other location—accounting for over one-fourth of all reported injuries. Females had more than three times as many accidents in the kitchen as they had in either of the two next most frequent locations.
>
> Once again, the cause of the accident varied by location. As might be expected, injuries under the broad accident type of "struck by dropped, dislodged or overturned object" occurred most frequently in the kitchen. Almost all of the "struck by knife while using" accidents occurred in the kitchen, whereas this type of accident involving a hand tool tended to occur in either the basement or yard.
>
> "Struck by object thrown by or in the hand of another person" occurred considerably more often outside than inside the home. "Falls due to slipping or tripping on floor" were reported to have occurred most frequently in the kitchen, bedroom or the living room. "Falling from furniture" happened

most often in a bedroom, with the kitchen as the second most frequent location.

"Ingesting medicine" occurred most often in a bedroom, with the kitchen and the bathroom being the next most frequent location, in that order. "Ingesting insecticide or rodenticide" took place most frequently in the kitchen and the basement respectively, while "ingesting household cleaning substance" accidents were about evenly divided between kitchen and basement.

Thus it becomes apparent that all areas and rooms contribute to some extent to the accident toll in the home, and that the most dangerous areas are those in which most members of the family gather for the greatest length of time or in which most work is done.

The Do-It-Yourself Movement

In recent years, there has been a very rapid increase in the repairs and improvements home owners are making about their own homes (15). They include finishing rooms in attics or basements, painting and wall-papering, installing electrical fixtures, building concrete driveways and swimming pools and dozens of other activities. It is a surprising fact that "every fourth home has some type of home workshop and that two-thirds of all the paint sold is applied by Mr. and Mrs. Homeowner and that almost three billion dollars annually are spent for lumber and other building materials (15)."

As would be expected, a large percentage of the millions of home owners who are working in and about their homes to improve conditions have had relatively little training or experience in the use of various kinds of tools and equipment. Consequently, there has been an increase in accidents in recent years. Many of the activities that contribute to these accidents have been discussed in this chapter. However, there are certain general principles that could be applied (15).

Attitudes. Besides saving money, "do-it-yourself" activities can provide an enjoyable means of relaxation from the cares of everyday life. The "safe way" is synonymous with better living; therefore, one should try to develop a positive attitude toward safety that would serve as a guide to safe behavior and satisfying home activity.

Planning the Job. A good attitude needs to be supplemented with "know-how." If the "know-how" is beyond your skill and equipment, the work should be done by licensed tradesmen. If the job is not familiar, study the processes involved before attempting to perform them. This may be done by consulting a good repair guidebook.

Plan Work Facilities. An unplanned workshop area that "grew like Topsy" can present many hazards and prove more inefficient as it is enlarged. Establish a basic plan that takes into consideration the safety factors of adequate floor and bench space, lighting, ventilation, heating, storage facilities, and appropriate tools or equipment for anticipated activities.

Hand Tools. Enough hand tools should be procured to perform anticipated operations properly. It should not be necessary to use a tool for operations it was not designed to do. The selection and use of quality tools permits safer work. For example, a better tool will hold a cutting edge and not give way under stresses within the limits of its design; sharp tools are safer to use than dull ones. Always provide a permanent storage place for tools, preferably on a tool board or rack.

Power Tools. Generally speaking, the safest power equipment obtainable is that from a reputable, established concern, experienced in the manufacture of that particular type of machine. Authorities agree that single-unit stationary equipment generally is safer than a multiple-type machine driven by one motor. Stationary equipment should be wired to a separate circuit that may be switched off and locked when not in use. All power equipment should be operated strictly in accordance with the manufacturer's instructions, with all guards in place. When operating portable power tools, particular attention should be given to footing, grip, freedom of movement in operation, and to proper grounding of the static wire. Special care needs to be used in the operation of power lawn mowers, especially the electrical and rotary types.

Personal Clothing, Equipment. By anticipating the hazards and exposures connected with a job, the proper dress and equipment may be determined. Particular attention should be given to protection from flying particles, falls, respiratory hazards, and getting caught in power driven equipment. The safe worker is careful to wear tough-soled shoes when walking among sharp projections or crepe soles on slippery surfaces.

Ladders, Supports. The high incidence and the severity of falls in the home present a major safety problem. Many of these falls occur in connection with home repair activities. Consequently, special attention should be given to proper selection and use of ladders and supports. Many falls occur from improper placement of ladders and from overextending the reasonable limits of a ladder. The base of the ladder should be placed at about one-third of its length away from the building.

Work Safely. The safe home worker has developed the habit of perceiving hazards and he takes the time and effort to eliminate or minimize them. He takes measures to control the movement of children around hazards. Knowing that hurrying tends to encourage accidents, he allots adequate time for the job and he avoids doing alone those handling or lifting operations that require more than one person. He also is a good housekeeper.

Safety Practices on Farms

Modern farmers do many kinds of work requiring various skills for safe performance. They deal with machinery, chemicals, electricity, vehicles, tools, livestock, farm structures, weather and nature. With such diversity, farming safely requires planning, alertness and knowledge of basic safety practices.

Figure 5:3, FARM WORK CAN BE HAZARDOUS. THE GANG PLOW IS ONE OF THE SAFER MACHINES.

Tractor and machinery accidents are common. Modern farm equipment is fast, complex and often ineptly operated. Machinery must be handled carefully, provided with adequate guards and regularly inspected and maintained for maximum efficiency and safety. Instruction manuals should be read and the directions followed. Only persons able and skilled should operate tractors and machinery.

Tractors, if improperly hitched or turned sharply at speed, encountering rocks or holes or operating on slopes and hills, can tip over or flip backwards. This is one of the most serious accident situations. Unshielded power take-off shafts are deadly, as thousands of farm families have learned; the PTO must never be operated unless shields are in place. Suitable clothing should be worn, as loose or tattered apparel can catch on moving shafts, gears, belts, and the like. Before unclogging or servicing machinery in the field, shut off the power. Thousands of hands, arms and lives have been lost in corn pickers, balers and the like when unclogging attempts were made with the power on.

Such equipment should be refueled only after engines have been stopped and allowed to cool for a few minutes. Fire extinguishers and first aid kits should be carried on tractors and self-propelled equipment. Equipment being transported on roads should be properly and visibly marked and lighted, and extreme courtesy should be practiced. Children should never be permitted to ride on tractors and equipment.

Chemicals are widely used in today's farming to increase production and quality. The following rules are paramount for safe use of farm chemicals: read and obey all labels; apply as directed; store chemicals in original containers inaccessible to children and animals; never put chemicals in pop bottles or leave portions or empty containers around where children can get to them; safely dispose of unused portions and empty containers.

Farm falls kill and injure thousands annually, especially older people. To help prevent falls, good housekeeping and proper maintenance is fundamental. Remove all unnecessary obstacles, objects and unused artifacts from all areas and routes where people work, play or move about. Keep ladders, steps, flooring and walkways in good repair. Never use makeshifts for climbing. Good lighting is essential. Haste, carrying too much, and carelessness while working in high places contribute to falls.

Farm animals can be dangerous if improperly handled. Bulls should be safely confined and led only by strong staffs fastened to nose rings. Boars, stallions and rams must be handled carefully and with respect. Animals with young often turn vicious and require care in handling. Children must be kept away and protected. Never startle or frighten animals. Horseback riding requires proper instruction and skill.

Here are several other important safety suggestions. Guns and ammunition should be safely stored away from children. Farm driveways should be cleared of obstructions. Ponds, stock watering tanks and cisterns should be protected to prevent child drownings. Lightning rods and aerials should be checked for proper grounding. Regularly inspect electrical wiring and equipment for defects, to prevent fire and shock. Keep tools in good condition and put away after use. Store gasoline and kerosene out of the house in well-marked, approved containers. When running engines or using chemicals in barns or sheds, keep doors and windows open. Fuel storage should be at least 40 feet away from the nearest building. Watch smoking habits.

Preventing Home and Farm Accidents

Two types of factors contribute to home and farm accidents—personal and environmental. A study of 500 home accidents disclosed that the personal element was a factor in 99 per cent of the cases in that a person did something unsafe, used poor judgment, did something to cause an injury of a child, was physically incapacitated or was in a hurry. Among the environmental factors which are known to contribute to such accidents are (1) building features, such as structural design, floor plans, and mechanical installations; (2) equipment and materials, such as housekeeping aids, appliances, utensils, tools, machinery and farm animals, and (3) housekeeping conditions which relate to the use and care of equipment and building features in the house or farm buildings or on the premises. With the exception of animals and wholly unsafe equipment, these features are dangerous not in themselves, but only when they are improperly used. Hence the problem of environmental factors resolves itself into a matter of adequate control through the proper use and repair of farm and home equipment and appliances.

Nearly every accident in the home is due to two causes: (1) a dangerous thing, and (2) a careless person. A potentially dangerous thing may be gasoline, a kitchen knife, leaking gas, or a force such as electricity. But not all things in the home are equally dangerous; in fact, most of them are harmless and become causes of accidents only through personal carelessness. However, a few things like electricity, gasoline, and sharp-edged tools are dangerous, needing only the slightest amount of carelessness to produce serious damage or injury. This carelessness may be reflected in the condition of the mechanical aspects of home and buildings or in some personal action of the individual. It is therefore necessary to educate the individual to recognize those materials, equipment features and personal actions which may become "danger spots" leading to home accidents.

The Role of the Individual in Home and Farm Accident Prevention

It is the individual who pays the price exacted by accidents. It is he who has the accident, who receives the injury, who suffers the pain, who pays the costs. Therefore, it is his responsibility and his family's to recognize that he may avoid accidents by knowing what to do.

In the first place, it is the obligation of the family to assign tasks and responsibilities to its members *that each can perform*. Too frequently this is overlooked, and the inevitable results. In the second instance, the members of the family must learn that certain practices are hazardous and in need of modification or elimination, and that other practices and habits are definitely safe. These desirable practices include the following (10):

1. Take sufficient time to do all things regardless of the need for hurrying.
2. Plan all daily activities, making allowances for possible interruptions.
3. Recognize fatigue and its relation to one's ability to perform.
4. Recognize one's physical condition and the advantages of working within the possibilities of achievement.
5. Undertake only those activities which can be performed easily in a day.
6. Realize that a period of recuperation is necessary after a period of disability.
7. Cultivate the habit of emotional control.
8. Change slowly from inactivity to activity.
9. Think through every problem before engaging in the activity.
10. Understand and follow carefully all directions.
11. Recognize the fact that one's reactions slow down as age increases and that one's ability to discern moving objects decreases with age.
12. Plan for the safety needs of the younger members of the family by (a) fitting the house to the child, (b) educating the child to live safely in the home and on the farm, and (c) providing situations in which correct habits will be formed, wholesome attitudes will be developed and adequate skills will be mastered.

Finally, the safety of the home can be increased through the planning and construction of buildings and premises that embody maximum safety features. Just as industrial accidents have been reduced by planning factories with every possible safety feature, so home and farm accidents may be reduced through the use of accepted safety standards in the location, construction and remodeling of home and farm buildings and equipment.

Among the practices which should govern are the following:

1. Buildings should be located so as to reduce the hazards created by moving machines, traffic and the like.
2. Buildings should be constructed with adequate lighting facilities and with due regard for the health and well-being of the individual.
3. Stairways should be well lighted and supplied with handrails and banisters. Avoid steep stairs, which increase hazards to safety.
4. Stair steps should be uniform, regulation size; the edge of each step should be painted with a bright color to serve as a guide to the walker.
5. Light switches, gas petcocks, and fuel supplies should be located at convenient but safe places.
6. Furniture and portable machines (sewing machines, cream separators and the like) should be arranged in an orderly way where they will not create hazardous situations.
7. Broken furniture or machinery and unsafe areas of buildings should be repaired immediately or withdrawn from use until they can be repaired or replaced.
8. Lightning rods and fire extinguishers or water supply tanks should be installed to protect buildings against fire.
9. Machinery used infrequently or only during special seasons should be stored in sheds located on a far side of the yard lot.
10. Special pens and quarters should be constructed for such animals as bulls and boars.
11. Adequate storage space should be provided for utensils, tools, and small farm implements.

Home and Farm Safety and the Community

Functional home safety requires that the educational program reach all groups, the adult as well as the child. To some extent, the adult may be reached through school children. However, this method leaves his education pretty much to chance. A concerted effort must be made through the cooperative endeavor of many community groups and agencies. Through the radio, television, magazines and newspapers, the problem of home and farm safety can be brought to the attention of the general public. Special programs, exhibits, demonstrations, and movies stressing home and farm safety may be sponsored by such community groups and departments as the American Red Cross, the Safety Council, the fire, health, and police departments, youth groups such as the Boy and Girl Scouts, and social and service clubs. The National Congress of Parents and Teachers has as one of its goals the prevention of home accidents and lists in its manual a series of activities which may be undertaken in cooperation with other groups interested in the problem of home safety. Many instances can be cited where through a carefully and cooperatively planned program, utilizing the resources of the community, a marked reduction in home and farm accidents has been attained.

The Instructional Program

At present relatively few schools (either elementary or secondary) offer safety instruction as a separate and distinct course. Instruction is provided through correlation or integration with existing courses, or (on the secondary level) through a distinct unit within a given course. The following sample units indicate how home safety may be offered at different levels (11):

UNIT—SAFETY AT HOME

The Primary Grades (1–3)

Objective To help children become safety conscious in the home as well as in the school.

Subject Matter Falls: Toys scattered about. Playing on stairs, banisters, furniture and small rugs. Climbing sills, trees, unlighted cellar steps, boxes and the like. Disposal of fruit peels.

Burns: Playing with matches. Playing near stoves, bonfires, open fireplaces and utensils containing hot liquids. Tipping pans and kettles to see what is in them. Carelessly turning on the hot water faucet. Not reporting a burn to an adult at once.

Christmas safety: Guiding children to ask for safe toys. Care in use of electric toys. Safety around the Christmas tree—sturdy tree, safe electric lights, noninflammable trimmings. Disposal of tree.

Activities (1) Paint tin containers for matches. (2) Collect pictures of "safe" toys. Make posters using pictures of safe toys. (3) Let children decorate schoolroom tree. Have them see that standard is heavy, and will not tip. Show the children safe decorations. Have committee dispose of tree. (4) Bring cork stoppers to guard the sharp points of scissors and other tools used in schoolroom.

The Intermediate Grades (4–6)

Objective To develop an appreciation of the causes and prevention of home accidents and one's ability to aid in their prevention.

Subject Matter Construction and location of home: Away from major street and traffic hazards. Safe driveway. Role of city ordinances.

Furnishing the home: Making the home attractive and safe. Placement of furniture. Hanging pictures, drapes, awnings. Placing and anchoring loose or scattered rugs. Dangers of slippery floors. Lighted stairways. Proper screening of windows and doors. Closet hazards—accumulation of rubbish, use of matches.

Heating and lighting the home: Use and care of heating plant. Hazards of overheating; stove polish explosions; defective chimneys and flues; asphyxiation. Disposal of hot ashes. Approved lighting fixtures. Kerosene lamps and lanterns. Gas fixtures and appliances.

Providing food for the family: Care of food. Preparation of food—hot liquids, hot grease, handling utensils, handling electrical appliances, loose clothing around open fires. Needs for ventilation, sanitation.

Good housekeeping: Cleaning windows. Disposal of rubbish. Storage of oily rags, mops and the like. Hazards of extreme varnishing of floors and highly polished floors. Dangers of hot liquids, acids, lyes, poisons; carelessly leaving things lying and standing around; hurrying up and down stairs.

Personal cleanliness: Skin soaps. Celluloid combs and toilet equipment. Bathroom hazards—slippery rugs, wet floors, use of electrical fixtures with wet hands. Disposal of old razor blades.

Recreation and leisure: Electric toys and dangers. Care of toys. Hazards of playing with matches; testing unknown substances and liquids; playing with stove. Precautions for children's parties and games; skating; coasting.

Tools and repairs: Use of tools. Dangers of neglected repairs; handling and lifting heavy objects: falling from roof or ladder when painting or repairing; falling over misplaced objects in cellar, stairs, attic, sheds.

Activities (1) Report a real home accident you read of in the newspaper or which occurred to you or a friend. (2) Tell a story of heroism in which someone avoided or prevented a home accident. (3) Show slides, motion pictures, or other pictures pertinent to the subject of home accidents. (4) Give a book report on *The Little Lame Prince*. (5) List ways in which toys may prove a source of danger. (6) Discuss with parents the value of fire extinguishers in the home. (7) Collect clippings from newspapers telling of home accidents.

Junior High School Grades (7–9)

Objective To develop an appreciation of the family's dependence on each of its members if all of them are to be safe at home.

Subject matter Types of home accidents: Statistical summary. Causes—personal factors, such as lack of skill, poor judgment, fatigue, hurry, handicaps, intoxication. Place—stairs, yard, kitchen, living and dining room, porch, bedroom, basement, bathroom, others. Types—falls, burns including conflagratións and explosions), poisonings (drinking poisonous liquids, overdoses of medicine, food poisoning, carbon monoxide gas), firearms and fireworks, mechanical suffocation (preschool children).

Activities (1) Collect newspaper clippings illustrating types of home accidents—fatal and nonfatal—and consider why less publicity is given to home accidents than to motor vehicle accidents. (2) Make a chart for home inspection. Conduct the survey and list three danger points for correction (3) Show a medicine chest properly equipped to guard against mistakes. (4) Plan a safe home; all members of the class may join in this project or committees may be used. (5) Invite the city electrician to demonstrate the dangers of heavy loaded and improperly replaced fuses. (6) Make a survey of gifts improper for young children.

Senior High School (10–12)

Objectives To develop a feeling of responsibility for keeping the home safe. To give an understanding of the principal causes and methods of prevention of accidents at home. To eliminate preventable accidents. To develop habits of safe home living.

Subject Matter Falls: Floors–slippery floors, loose linoleum and carpets, scatter rugs. Stairways—loose step covering, poorly lighted stairs, no handrails, toys and materials on stairs. Ladders—use of unstable ladders or chairs, boxes, and the like. Bath tubs—rubber mat, handrail; soap on floor, standing in tub, pulling light chain while hands are wet. Windows—insecurely fastened screens, sitting on window ledge, cleaning. Porches—poor construction, insecurely fastened swings, inadequate railing, cluttered appearance. Walks—ice and snow, wet leaves, scattered toys and objects. Chairs—tilting, use as ladders, needing repairs. Tools—need for storage of hand and garden tools, should be properly repaired and sharpened. Climbing—trees and buildings. Wells and cisterns—should be covered, regularly inspected, properly curbed.

Burns: Matches. Stoves, fireplaces, steam pipes and radiators. Dry cleaning. Gas fixtures and lamps. Electric equipment and appliances. Pot handles. Hot liquids. Clothing and toilet articles.

Electric shocks: Proper installation by expert. Proper use and care of electric cords on radiators, steam pipes and under rugs. Handling fallen electric wire. Pulling switches. Lights and appliances in kitchen, dining room, laundry. Radio installation. Electric toys.

Poisoning: Storage of medicines and poisons. Labeling. Food poisoning. Plants (ivy, oak, sumac), animals, reptiles, insects. Household poisons—disinfectants, paint, lye.

Gas injuries and suffocation: Asphyxiation. Drowning. Carbon monoxide.

Fires: Building construction. Matches and smoking. Open fires, stoves, furnaces, heaters, lamps. Rubbish and waste. Gasoline, kerosene, and other petroleum products. Spontaneous combustion. Incendiarism. Hot grease. Fire extinguishers.

Cuts, scratches, bruises: Sharp objects. Broken glass, saws, axes. Lifting heavy objects.

Miscellaneous: Firearms. Fireworks. Candles. Home movies. Toilet articles. Christmas hazards.

Activities (1) Locate, analyze, and report to the class the latest statistics concerning home and farm accidents. (2) Survey your own home to find strong and weak points of protection, using the home inspection blank. Determine which of the hazards may be eliminated in (a) a week's time, (b) without causing any expense to your family. (3) Determine the cost of an accident to any member of your family during the past five years; compare this cost with that of removing the cause of the accident.

Full instruction in the prevention of farm accidents will be limited to schools serving rural and farm areas, but it might not be amiss to bring into all programs a brief treatment of farm safety. The following unit indicates the areas which should receive consideration in educating for farm safety.

UNIT—FARM SAFETY

Machinery: A major cause of accidental death and injury on the farm. Inspection and repair of machinery. Safe operation of tractors in the field, on the road. Riding and standing in hazardous positions. Extra riders on tractors and equipment. Unclogging, cleaning or servicing machinery in the field; shutting off power before doing these. Age and ability of tractor operators, especially youths. Dangers of exposed power shafts, chain drives, gears. Properly shielding power-take-off shafts. Danger from tattered or loose clothing, gloves, improper or worn shoes. Special precautions in using tractors, corn-pickers, combines, balers, other harvesting equipment, belt-driven machines, tillage implements and electrically powered equipment.

Falls: A serious accident problem. Stumbling over junk, implements, ropes, broken flooring and walkways, hidden obstacles. Falls from ladders due to improper usage or poor repair. Falls on steps and stairways due to clutter, haste, poor lighting, carrying too much, no handrails or poor repair. Slips on ice, wet surfaces, spills or from muddy shoes. Falling from equipment, horses, hayloft, while picking fruit or pruning trees. Falling in holes or uncovered wells. Falls while carrying heavy objects. Good housekeeping, good repair, and removing obstacles help prevent falls.

Vehicular: Leading killer of farm people. Hazards in traffic while driving cars, farm trucks and tractors on roadways. Proper marking and lighting of slow-moving farm vehicles. Good maintenance. Hayrides. Crossing the highway. Walking along highway or riding bicycles. Making turns off roads into driveways or field entrances. Clearing driveways of sight obstacles. Pulling onto highways. Special hazards of driving in bad weather, on snow and ice, at night. Stopping distances at various speeds. Compensating for reduced accelerating and stopping abilities of heavily-loaded farm trucks. Common sense and courtesy on the road.

Farm chemicals: Proper handling, application and storage of farm chemicals. Disposing of unused containers. Dangers of storing chemicals in containers other than original, for example, in pop or milk bottles. Protecting small children. What to do in case of ingestion or contact. Importance of always reading and obeying labels.

Fires: Defective flues, chimneys, stoves and furnaces. Worn or overloaded electrical wiring. Kitchen fires, grease fires, electrical fires, kerosene and gasoline fires, barn fires, rubbish fires. Matches. Fire extinguishers in home, barn, on tractors and trucks. Family fire-escape plans, home fire drills, getting help. Proper handling and storage of flammable liquids and chemicals. Good housekeeping to remove clutter, paper, rags, etc. Regular inspection for fire hazards.

Lightning: Lightning rods and ground connections. Grounding telephone, radio and TV antennas. Safe and unsafe places to be during electrical storm. Unsafe to be near fence, under tree, on high ground in open, working in hayloft with hayfork, and other implements.

Firearms: Proper handling, care, use, and storage of guns and ammunition. Hunting and target shooting. First aid.

Drowning: Farm ponds, nearby unsupervised "swimming holes" in rural creeks, rivers and small lakes. Swimming, life-saving and resuscitation. Necessary equipment for safe swimming or boating in large farm ponds. Protecting small children from drowning in stock watering tanks, ponds and receptacles to collect rain water.

Exposure: Sunstroke. Overheating. Exposing body unduly for suntan or when working in hot weather. Frostbite and freezing. Cold, wet weather. Proper clothing for all conditions. First aid.

Hand tools: Tool house, farm shop. Axes, hammers, shovels, saws, picks, hoes, chisels and rakes. Pitchforks, hayforks, scythes and sickles, corn and hedge knives. Good housekeeping and good repair. Cutting tools kept sharp are safer.

Power tools: Portable chain saws, power mowers, electric drills, shears, buzz and band saws, grinders, etc. Maintenance and special precautions for safe operation.

Livestock: Care of brood animals, animals giving birth. Handling work and riding horses. Special precautions in keeping and handling herd sires—bulls, boars, stallions and rams. Use of pens and stalls.

summary

Accidents in the home, farm and ranch are a major cause of accidental death, ranking second to those in traffic. Nonfatal injuries, however, are several times greater than those caused by motor vehicles. The most important causes are falls, burns and scalds, suffocation, internal poisons, firearms and poison gases. Nearly one-half of the fatalities are from falls, most of which involve persons over 65 years of age.

It has been difficult to organize successful campaigns against home accidents. The three E's—engineering, enforcement and education—can be used in the attack on traffic and industrial accidents, but for the most part home safety campaigns have to depend on one E—education. A home is a man's "castle" and is not subject to many controls.

Approximately three-fourths of the accidents occur inside the dwelling;

the remainder outside. In nearly all cases, the person injured was committing some unsafe act.

There are several ways in which it is possible to get results in home safety. The first is through home safety instruction in the elementary and secondary schools. A second is through work by organizations such as Parent-Teacher Associations, women's clubs, farm organizations and health departments. In addition, the various media such as radio, television, newspapers and motion pictures can be used.

In recent years, there has been a rapid increase in the number of repairs and improvements that home owners are making in and about their own homes, called the "do-it-yourself" movement. There has been a significant increase in accidents in these activities.

Farming leads all occupations in the number of accidental work deaths and ranks third in the death rate (per 100,000 workers). Farm organizations such as the Grange and the 4H Clubs, community extension departments and the manufacturers of farm equipment are working with the National Safety Council to reduce accidents. The education program has been quite effective.

suggested projects and activities

1. Keep a record of home accidents happening to members of the class or their families.
2. Plan a home safety campaign to be conducted in the autumn at your school. Utilize community agencies with which you are familiar and indicate the contribution that each can make.
3. Prepare materials for a dramatization or skit to be used at the school assembly or for a radio program.
4. Make a collection of newspaper clippings of home and farm accidents. Prepare a class exhibit of these materials.
5. Develop a home and farm safety exhibit and make arrangements for a display of this in a store window.
6. Make a list of the types of "do-it-yourself" activities in the average home. Underline the activities that may be especially hazardous.
7. Make a list of the community agencies that can be helpful in carrying on a home, farm and ranch safety program.

selected references

1. California State Department of Public Health, *Home Safety Project, Final Report, 1953-1957*. Berkeley, Cal.: The Department, 1957.
2. *Extension Service Review, Farm and Home Safety,* Vol. 34, No. 3, (March 1963). Washington 25, D.C.: U.S. Government Printing Office.
3. Future Farmers of America, *FFA at Work for Safety—A Handbook for Teachers of Vocational Agriculture*. Washington 25, D.C.: Office of Education, Department of Health, Education, and Welfare (n.d.).

4. Gadalla, Saad M., *Selected Environmental Factors Associated with Farm and Farm Home Accidents in Missouri.* Columbia, Mo.: Rural Health Series Publication 16, University of Missouri, College of Agriculture, 1962.
5. Halsey, Maxwell, ed., *Accident Prevention: The Role of Physicians and Public Health Workers,* Chapters 4, 5, 7, and 9. New York: McGraw-Hill Book Company, 1961.
6. National 4-H Service Committee, *4-H Leaders Handbook on Safety.* Chicago: The Committee (n.d.).
7. National Safety Council, *Accident Facts.* Chicago: The Council, 1963.
8. ________, *Congress Transactions,* Volumes on Farm and Home Safety Sessions. Chicago: The Council, 1953-1963.
9. ________, *Safety Education,* Chicago: The Council, A Magazine for teachers and administrators.
10. Nevins, Irmagene G., "Home Accidents and Their Prevention." Unpublished doctor's thesis, New York University, 1941.
11. Office of State Superintendent of Schools, *Safety Curriculum Guide,* Curriculum Bulletin No. 27, March 1960. Madison, Wis.: Office of the Superintendent.
12. Office of the Superintendent of Public Instruction, Illinois, *The Challenge of Safety Education, An Elementary and Junior High School Safety Guide for Teachers and Administrators.* Springfield, Ill.: Office of the Superintendent, 1959.
13. Pennsylvania Department of Health, *A Study of Accidents to Pennsylvania Farm People.* Harrisburg, Penna.: Department of Health, 1951.
14. Rochester Safety Council, *Where They Get Hurt.* Rochester, New York: The Council, 1961.
15. Stack, H. J. and Leon Brody, ed., *Tips to the Handyman-Hobbyist and How to Do it Safely.* New York: The Home Insurance Company, 1941.
16. Tennessee Department of Public Health, *Action Programs for Accident Prevention in Tennessee.* Nashville, Tenn.: The Department, 1963.
17. U. S. Department of Labor, *Proceedings of the President's Conference on Occupational Safety.* Bulletin 243. Washington, D. C.: The Department (n.d.)
18. ________, *Farmwork, Safety, and You.* Washington, D. C.: The Department, 1962.
19. U. S. Public Health Service, *Home Accident Prevention Text for Use by Local Health Departments.* Washington, D. C.: U. S. Government Printing Office, 1957.

6

recreation and outdoor life

The American people in increasing numbers seek adventure, excitement, thrills, status and enjoyment in recreation and sports. More hours of leisure are becoming available in our economy than ever before. Americans swim, fish, water ski, skydive, golf, hunt, bowl, hike, drive cars and camp, to list but a few of the sports that engage their interests. That we are an active nation is evident. Nearly 100 million swim annually, 40 million use boats, 34 million fish, 30 million fire weapons, 20 million hunt, 28 million camp, and 6 million golf. By 1970, over 100 million Americans will swim or play in the water, 50 million will be boating and some 15 million will be water skiing. Obviously many persons will engage in three or more sports each year.

Over 20 billions of dollars will be spent annually on sports and recreational activities. Annually, boat enthusiasts now spend over $3 billion, hunters $1 billion, archers $35 million and the bowling industry alone contributes over $1.5 billion to the gross national product. How much all of our sports activities contribute to our national economy has not yet been computed. Yet a significant portion of our $16 plus billion annual cost of accidents arises from mishaps within sports and recreational activities.

Among the many positive outcomes of sports experiences are improved physical, social and emotional health. These results are possible whenever man participates in such activities safely. When man selects a sport, he desires to enjoy it for years to come. He may try to learn its hazards and the measures needed to overcome them. He frequently needs instruction in the techniques of the sport or comparable activity and in the safety procedures known to be effective in reducing misadventure and permitting safe play to continue.

> Recreational accidents, like those on the highway, in the home, and in industry, *can be prevented.* To this end our public safety programs must be designed to help people get the most out of their leisure by learning to play safely.
> *Howard Pyle in "Family Recreation and Safety"* (2).

Today many of the individual sports and recreational activities which adults enjoy are taught in physical education programs in schools. This is especially true in areas where physical education has provided school youth with large-muscle movement activities that will carry over into their adult years as well as contribute to their developmental growth. However, even when physical education programs have specific safeguards, careful supervision, and excellent facilities, those engaged in recreation find fewer restrictions placed upon them, and are often left to their own resources and self-discipline to cope with the hazards present.

The types of activities used for recreation are many and varied. The sites for such are almost endless. Men play in all kinds of places from the highly organized recreational areas of commercial resorts to completely unorganized areas like the sea, or the virgin forest explored by hikers.

It is the intent of this chapter to describe some of the safe practices that are to be used in sports and recreation that will enable man to gain enjoyment, rest, relaxation, and renewal from his participation in them. It is well known that those who know how to recreate gain much out of life, live longer and bring greater happiness to themselves and their families. An urgent plea is made here that the reader study with great care the nature of the sport, recreation or outdoor activities in which he will participate so that he may enjoy them and secure the benefits they may give without paying a penalty for inexpertness or for impetuous action.

Since hazards exist even in organized parks, fields, and recreational areas, and are naturally present in mountain lakes and streams, man must learn simple rules that will guide him safely through experiences in outdoor life and sport. When he understands the hazards in a sports activity, when he compensates for those dangers he cannot remove, when he creates no new hazards, he will be able to continue with that sport for many years. When his knowledge, skills, or attitudes about safe practices fail him, he will not care to continue or will be unable to do so.

It will be apparent that certain principles of safety that pertain to boating, for example, may at times also be related to fishing, hiking or camping. Very often the adventure within a sport is increased when many different types of activities are included. To illustrate, camping out where hunting, fishing, swimming, boating, and skin and scuba diving may be enjoyed is vastly different from camping out in the back yard of one's home. It is absurd to study camp safety rules without giving consideration to safety in the related activities that that kind of camping will make possible. While it may be impossible to learn every single isolated fact about an activity in order to prevent an accident, it is usually possible to follow proven patterns of prevention of accident causes that may lead to human injury and property damage.

General Sports Safety Principles

All individuals who plan to participate in sports, recreation or outdoor living activities, whether occasionally or frequently, should consider the following basic principles for the prevention of accidents:

Be physically and emotionally fit when recreating.

Verify your capabilities for vigorous participation by means of an annual or seasonal medical examination.

Know the limitations of your equipment.

Participate in activities only when properly equipped.

Use equipment only for the purpose for which it is intended.

Know the hazards of the sport in which you plan to engage.

Secure effective instruction from qualified personnel.

Learn how to cope with or remove hazards that are present.

Avoid creating any unnecessary hazards.

Keep others informed of what, where and when you are going to act, when hazards are inherent in the activity.

Know in advance when and where to send for help.

Take time to plan the activity in which you will engage.

Allow for ample periods of rest and relaxation. Pace yourself.

Know and act your age.

Use progression in training; go from basic to advanced skills.

Through practice, build in a response system that will be ready and able to cope with hazards when they occur.

The sports indicated below are discussed in this chapter primarily for the safety considerations that should be explored, identified and used:

archery
camping
fishing
golf
hunting
swimming and water safety
skiing

If activities of interest to the reader are not covered in this text, he may apply the principles of hazard control (see p. 115) to those activities he chooses to gain a fuller enjoyment of life. It becomes an important lesson in human behavior to prepare oneself fully for safety in sports. For it is in the realm of human behavior that accident causation primarily lies. Perhaps 70 per cent of our sports and recreational accidents can be eliminated if we provide ourselves with sufficient knowledge, effective skills, and desirable attitudes. Self-discipline, personal responsibility, and self-enforcement are valuable aids to living safely in our complex environment.

Safety in Selected Sports

Archery

It is a thrill to release an arrow and see it strike its mark, be it the bull's eye of a target or the heart of a deer. Man once sought game with bow and arrow out of necessity. Today it is a sport. In recreation some men seek game in the role of an archer. Each year tens of thousands of hunting licenses are issued to men who hunt with bow and arrow. Over 7.5 million archers of varying skill pursue archery as a sport in the United States.

As a weapon, a bow has tremendous power. A hunting arrow released from a hunter's bow will penetrate three feet into a sand box compared to the one and one-half foot penetration of the bullet from a Garand rifle. That this activity has been controlled in school physical education programs is apparent from the low incidence of accidents in archery in the schools. That considerable danger exists in recreational hunting is obvious when one notes the frequency with which archers who hunt ask for hunting areas restricted to them and free from hunters with firearms. Considerable stealth is essential when stalking game with bow and arrow, and such guarded movements have often caused riflemen to mistake archers for "legal game."

To enjoy the thrill and adventure of archery, learn the following rules:

1. Use only good quality bows and arrows.
2. Provide adequate protection behind all targets and approaches.
3. Never draw bow with the arrow pointing toward another person or persons.
4. Nock arrows only when it is safe to shoot.
5. Do not draw an unnocked bow near a person.
6. Obey starting and stopping signals when shooting with others.
7. Never leave bows and arrows about unguarded where young or careless persons might misuse them.

8. Remember always that bows and arrows are not toys, but weapons capable of inflicting serious injury or death.
9. Practice the skills of archery progressively from the simple to the more difficult.
10. Use proper personal protection (arm guards and finger tabs).

Camping

In quest of adventure, 28 million persons participate in camping. Throughout our nation one finds auto camps, adult camps, overnight camps, children's camps, day camps, school camps, family camps, and many other specialized types of camp settings. In recent years the camp has become an adjunct to the regular school program in many areas. This movement is called "outdoor living education." The schools purchase or lease camp sites and send pupils there for varying periods of time during the regular school terms to study campcraft, nature, outdoor sports, folk dancing and other activities in a well-rounded program of outdoor life education. Such measures instill an appreciation of the out-of-doors in youth and introduce them, in their formative years, to the values of camping and outdoor living.

Auto Camping It is now possible to travel across the country more than a dozen times by auto while carrying camping equipment and to stay at a different state or national campsite each night without ever staying in the same park twice. This sport of auto-camping is increasing in popularity in our country. It is not costly, nor is the hazard high when one understands good camping practices. Some of the recommended procedures for this sport include:

1. Plan travel time between camp sites carefully to avoid fatigue and worry.
2. Follow the rules and regulations of each camping area carefully.
3. Camp only in designated areas.
4. Use fire with a purpose, to warm or to cook. Put out all fires when not needed to prevent forest fire.
5. Keep young children supervised within the camp area to prevent their being lost.
6. Adapt to animal and plant life. Neither tease nor feed animals. Observe posted regulations. Be aware of kinds of hazards present like snakes, poison ivy, and many other dangers of outdoor life.
7. Use only approved drinking water.
8. Swim only in safe areas, observing rules and regulations for safe swimming. (see page 99)
9. Maintain first aid equipment in top condition.
10. Secure needed immunizations in advance of camping trip (tetanus, typhoid, etc.).

11. Treat all injuries promptly. The threat of tetanus from soil-contaminated wounds is always present.
12. Use axes and knives only for the purposes for which they were intended.
13. Secure advice from qualified persons in areas where you do not possess adequate skills or knowledge.

Organized Camping Each year over 5 million youngsters attend some 10,000 organized camps for five days or longer. A large core of specialists and general camp counselors direct this vast camping venture, realizing their responsibilities for the safety of all campers. Although there are no records to reveal whether there are more injuries at home or in summer vacation areas, it may be expected that youngsters in an entirely strange environment would be more liable to have accidents unless a thorough educational and preventive program were conducted.

An early study by Sanders indicates that about two-thirds of injuries occur to the skin, the remaining third consisting of muscle injuries, bruises, strains, sprains, and bone injuries. Falls account for 32 per cent of the accidents among boys and 28 per cent among girls, and 20 per cent of the boys' accidents and 31 per cent of the girls' happen when they are walking or running on camp paths. Sanders contended that 25 per cent of the accidents could have been prevented if the sites had been well selected and if proper care and equipment had been used. It was also reported that 27 per cent might have been eliminated by disposing of poison ivy, by supervision in the use of axes and knives and in horseback riding, and by the wearing of proper footwear (12:45).

Although safety standards are high in the better camps, many hazards still remain. Among these are rough pathways, broken glass, boards with protruding nails, snakes, insects, poisonous plants, and participation in such unfamiliar activities as horseback riding and rifle shooting.

To provide greater safety in the camp, living and play conditions must be improved. Those who feel that camping means freedom from all the restraints found at home must be carefully supervised. The hazards of activities such as swimming, axe-throwing, arts and crafts and campfire games must be understood by all if accidents are to be avoided.

All the safety measures essential for aquatics should be vigorously enforced for water activities in camp. Areas should be set off for nonswimmers, beginners and advanced swimmers. Correct use of boats and canoes, and life-saving procedures should be a part of the education of every camper. Activities such as overnight hikes should not be attempted before the following items have been checked: water and food, nearness to phone, first aid equipment, physical condition and equipment of hikers and any special instructions needed by campers.

Equipment and facilities found in some camps present many serious dangers. These include candles and lanterns, art-craft tools, inflammable material used for theatricals, and camp shop tools. Pathways should be free from exposed roots and rocks, and steps and railings should be in good condition. Adequate illumination should be provided, and fire extinguishers should be in proper condition and regularly checked throughout the summer. Poison oak, poison ivy and all tin cans and glass should be removed from the grounds and swimming area.

Finally, each camp should develop and strictly enforce a specific safety code covering the various activities common among its campers. The American Camping Association has established standards for the safe conduct of camps. With the proper precautions, camping can be a rich educational experience in safe living.

Fishing

Thirty-four million people in the United States fish each year. The sum spent annually on fishing equipment exceeds 2.5 billion dollars. As a sport, fishing is engaged in by more people than any other, with the exception of activities like swimming and wading.

Injuries and drownings occur while fishing, although it is not known how many. Each fisherman has several mishaps every year. Among these are the bites and stings of animals, fish and insects; poisoning by plants and reptiles; cuts and lacerations from fishing, boating and camping gear; falls from high places or on rough terrain; burns from sun, fire, cookstoves or lanterns; and last, weather and water hazards. In one recent year, 54 per cent of the fatal boating accidents were associated with fishing (13:292).

Fish hooks can be dangerous. In bait, fly or surf casting, in still fishing, spinning fishing, or in trolling there is a constant danger of being hooked. Not only do puncture wounds result but even frequent lacerations. Hooks are not sterile and frequently cause serious infection when they pierce the skin.

Some basic safety precautions for the fisherman include:

1. Learn to swim before taking up fishing.
2. Know what is behind you before attempting to cast.
3. Keep a safe distance away from anyone who is casting.
4. Wear a wide-brim hat as partial protection from flying hooks.
5. Learn how to remove the hook from a fish without hooking yourself.
6. Avoid careless use of hook and line when others are nearby.
7. Render large fish harmless before attempting to remove hooks.
8. Watch the weather. If in a boat when a storm threatens, seek safe harbor.
9. Do not overcrowd a boat.
10. Know the hazards of the stream, lake, or waters you fish (drop-offs, rapids, etc.).
11. Carry a first aid kit to treat any injuries that might occur while fishing.

Golf

Well over 6 million people play golf each year, and countless others frequent driving ranges and miniature golf areas. Golf has been said to be America's safest sport. It has always been a "gentleman's" game, and the rules of etiquette are for the most part rules of safety.

The two hazards in golfing are being hit by a ball or being hit by a club. Neither of these occurs on well-regulated courses or where normal rules of golf etiquette are followed.

Accidents are most apt to happen to beginners. It is recommended that each golfer have 100 square feet of room when swinging a club. In a gymnasium measuring 80 by 40 feet, only 32 students would be able to swing clubs at the same time. Since the instructor requires room to demonstrate, to move about and supervise the activity and to effectively stage his lesson, it would be unwise to have more than 25 students in such a room. A class should be so organized that four golfing activities are carried on concurrently rather than all students swinging simultaneously.

Specific safety suggestions for golf are:

1. Learn the rules of golf. Observe golf etiquette.
2. Use proper warm-up, especially on cold days.
3. Always make certain no one is close before starting any swing with any club.
4. Set aside steel-shafted clubs and umbrellas during electrical storms since they attract lightning.
5. If hands blister easily, wear golf gloves.
6. Avoid playing too long early in the season. Fatigue predisposes one to accidents on the course.
7. Call "fore" before swinging into a hard hit ball.

Hunting

Nearly 14 million hunting licenses are purchased annually by 19 million persons who hunt and shoot. Over 30 million Americans own and use guns. No firearm licenses are necessary for the 3 million additional participants in trap, skeet and target shooting. The firearms in use range from BB guns to high caliber rifles. Although firearms can be dangerous weapons, very few states require more than a small fee and evidence of legal age for licensing. Some states require hunters to pass a firearms course or test prior to being licensed.

Nearly 2,200 accidental deaths occur each year from firearms. About one-half of these are attributed to hunting accidents, and the rest occur at home, either preparing for or cleaning up after hunting or firing. Most firearm casualties are men, only 10 per cent are women. The 15-to-24 age

Figure 6:1, A SAFE PRACTICE IN THE USE OF GUNS.

group experiences the most accidental deaths, accounting for 550 deaths (7:8). The 25-to-44 age group ranks second with approximately 500, less than 50 per cent of which are due to hunting accidents (the rest to home accidents). Essentials of safe hunting, stated by the National Rifle Association of America, follow:

1. Know your gun.
   a. Be sure the gun and ammunition are in good condition.
   b. Sight-in gun before hunting with it.
   c. Learn to be a good shot.
2. Handle your gun properly.
   a. Treat every gun as if it were loaded.
   b. Always point the muzzle in a safe direction.
   c. Be sure of your target.
   d. Keep your finger out of the trigger guard until ready to fire.
   e. Practice self-control.
   f. Open the action and unload any gun which is not in use.
   g. Store hunting guns in a safe place.
3. Fulfill your responsibilities as a safe hunter.
   a. Follow the rules of safe hunting.
   b. Learn to identify game.
   c. Know and observe the game laws.
   d. Be courteous and promote friendly hunter-farmer relations.
   e. Insist that your companions be safe hunters.

Swimming and Water Safety

One hundred million persons are active annually in the United States, recreation in or on the water. Nearly half of our citizens boat, fish, swim, sail, skin dive, water ski or enjoy other aquatic sports for extended periods of time. Each year enjoyment is marred for a small percentage of those who seek fun in or on the water. Annually 4,400 persons drown while at play. Another 2,000 drown in homes or from boats. In 86 per cent of the cases victims of drowning are males (13:289). We have never had an accurate accounting of the numbers who receive serious injury while having fun in water sports. Yet some records of near-drowning are being developed along with the causes and means of prevention (1). It is a tribute to those engaged in water safety work that the fatalities are low. Through water safety education, a continued reduction in drownings and injuries in and on the water is possible.

Backyard swimming pools are in great demand. Over 300,000 are now in use in our nation. In a few years that number will double. Swimming in the backyard is usually a family affair, sometimes a neighborhood event. Since trained lifeguards are seldom present, a great need exists for the dissemination of safety precautions in the use of the home swimming pool. Its supervision is the responsibility of the home owner. That he has not met fully his responsibility is evident in the frequent proposals of legislation to fence off, cover over, or install safety alarms in his pool.

Since many water accidents are caused by a person's being thrown suddenly into the water (by a boat capsizing, a car dropping into water, slipping off a bridge), it is necessary to know how to swim under adverse conditions. Therefore, those persons who cannot swim well, yet wish to engage in water sports, should be made aware of the added hazard created by their limited swimming abilities and must learn to swim better.

If safety instruction is made an integral part of an individual's training in water sports, drownings will be reduced. Agencies and youth groups like the American Red Cross, the Boy Scouts of America, the Girl Scouts of America, and the schools will initiate much of this training. The National Safety Council recently advocated a national program for teaching swimming to all youngsters at the 4th-grade level. It is called "Operation Waterproof 4th Grade." Some years ago, several campaigns to "drownproof" Americans were initiated. All of these efforts are concerned with teaching youth effective swimming skills at an early age so that good watermanship skills will be begun in youth and retained for years to come.

Specific rules for the prevention of water accidents include:

1. Swim only in supervised areas.
2. Never swim alone.
3. Swim only when you are in good physical condition.
4. Do not use flotation equipment where you would be unsafe if it failed.
5. Avoid deep water swimming until sufficiently skilled for it.
6. In diving from boards:
   a. Avoid collisions with persons in area of board.

b. Avoid bouncing board out of control.
c. Leave area in range of board promptly after diving in.
d. Use progression in developing skills needed for advanced dives.
e. Be certain that water depth meets safety standards.
f. Avoid horseplay in and around water.

Research on Drownings Drownings happen in unusual places: bathtubs, wells, cattle watering troughs, sewers, slop buckets and rain barrels. Victims of accidents studied by Gabrielson (4), were engaged in 27 different activities at the time of the mishap: fishing, boating, horseback riding, ice skating, hunting golf balls, water skiing and canoeing. Other findings of his study were:

Highest incidence of deaths were in June, July, August.

Greatest frequency occurred on Sundays.

Peak periods of drownings was at 4:00 P.M.

One of ten victims was under the influence of alcohol.

Drownings occurred at a ratio of six men to one woman.

One in four deaths were of non-swimmers from upset boats.

One in four drownings happened to recreational swimmers.

Nearly one in five were drownings of children under five, who were left unattended by parents for a few minutes.

Education in water safety should have the following objectives for each individual:

To understand the hazards of water sports and how to minimize and prevent the occurrence of accidents by avoiding common errors, such as swimming alone.

To swim and dive skillfully.

To use boats correctly.

To have knowledge and skills necessary to perform life-saving activities near water and to render first aid, including resuscitation.

To appreciate that water safety is both an individual and a group problem, and to accept individual responsibility for the promotion of safe conduct in all water activities.

Boating and Sailing

Boats of many types are used by millions of people for pleasure and business. In boating, the hazards of the water are always present. In principle, all persons who use boats or work or play on or near the water, should be able to swim. Nonswimmers who boat must wear life-jackets and remain with the boat should it swamp or overturn.

The largest yachting and pleasure boat organization is the United States Power Squadrons, established fifty years ago. Its membership exceeds 60,000 in 25 districts in the nation. They have a genuine interest in teaching and spreading the idea of safe boat handling. The Coast

Figure 6:2, A LIFE PRESERVER FOR EACH PASSENGER.

Guard Auxiliary has provided instruction in safe boat handling for over 25 years through 17 Coast Guard Districts (14). The American National Red Cross covers boat safety as a phase of its program. It is inexcusable for a boating enthusiast to fail to secure effective instruction in safe boat handling before he takes to the water. With so many free and valuable courses available, the boating public can, if it wills to do so, become safer on the water.

Rules for safe boating follow:

1. Know your boat and its limitations.
2. Don't overload a boat. Seats do not indicate capacity.
3. Distribute the weight evenly in a boat—from side to side and bow to stern.
4. Keep low. Step in the center when boarding or shifting seats.
5. Watch the weather. Head for shore *before* a storm breaks.
6. Head *into* waves. Approach high waves at an angle at low speed.
7. Use the right sized motor for the boat. (Too much power can damage a boat or even swamp it)!
8. Watch where you are going at all times.
9. Keep speeds that are reasonable for conditions present.
10. License your boat and follow all regulations in effect in the area.

Skin and Scuba Diving

Underwater diving and swimming is a thrilling sport. It also has educational, commercial and military uses. Nearly 7 million persons dive into the water in quest of adventure, fortune or fun annually. Of this number, more than a million use underwater breathing apparatus. The skin diver breathes surface air and with the aid of snorkel, face-mask, flippers, and at times, insulated suits and weapons, explore below the surface of the sea and fresh water areas. He marks his diving area off with a skin-diver's flag on a float (red flag with a white diagonal stripe on it).

Figure 6:3, AIDING A BEGINNER IN SCUBA DIVING.

The scuba (self-contained underwater breathing apparatus) diver uses the equipment of a skin diver and, in addition, has tanks of air, oxygen and, at times, other gases to increase the period of time under the water as well as the depth to which he may descend. He may also use motorized carts and other underwater devices such as depth gauges, waterproof watches, cameras and emergency flotation devices.

The widespread growth of the sport of scuba diving requires setting up a number of safety precautions, such as:

1. Before making a first dive, secure expert instruction.
2. Be so boringly familiar with your equipment and its limitations that you can do the right thing at the right time without thinking about it. (13:23)
3. Use standard and approved properly fitted equipment.

4. Never dive alone. Teamwork is essential for safety.
5. Know your limitations and abilities. Study the underwater environment for plant and animal life, tides, currents, temperature and the like.
6. Do not dive when ear, throat or respiratory infections are present. Have a thorough medical examination for this sport before beginning and periodically thereafter.
7. Display special diver's flag; it indicates diver is down and requests 100 feet of clearance.
8. Know the dangers of inhaling air under pressure, of oxygen poisoning, of air embolism and of diet before diving.

Water Skiing

Water skiing was originated on Lake Washington in Seattle by Don Ibsen, an ardent snow skier. Since then the sport has grown rapidly and over 6 million persons ski on water, over 70 per cent of them women. And one out of every five boats purchased today is used almost exclusively for water skiing. National contests in this sport began in 1930 with scheduled competition in three events—slalom, jumping and trick riding.

Figure 6:4, FUN IN RECREATION—WHEN CONDITIONS ARE SAFE! FAILURE TO CHECK SAFETY FACTORS MAY RESULT IN SORROW!

Accidents in water skiing, a fairly safe sport, stem from being struck by the towing boat or another boat, striking debris or a fixed object, hitting the water with force or by being entangled in the tow rope. About 4.5 per cent of the fatal boat accidents a few years ago were the result of water skiing mishaps. To increase safety in this engaging activity the following rules are suggested:

1. Avoid excessive speed or skiing in shallow water.
2. Watch the water ahead of you. Do not depend on the driver to keep you away from dangerous objects and rough water.
3. Learn and use proper hand signals.
4. On falling, recover the skis, as they will keep you afloat.
5. Two persons must be in the boat that pulls the skier.
6. Should the skier fall, the driver must cut speed and determine if the skier is entangled in the rope.
7. Stop the motor when taking a skier aboard a boat.
8. Do not pull skiers in swimming areas.
9. Wear a flotation device for your own protection.

Skiing

Skiing is a sport enjoyed by more than 5 million persons and is a more than billion-dollar business in America today. Television coverage of skiing events has added greatly to the public's interest in taking up this activity. As a competitive sport skiing is carried on in four main categories: *downhill,* the most dangerous; *slalom,* the most graceful; *cross country,* the most grueling; and *jumping,* the most spectacular, mastered by only a few.

Figure 6:5, SKIING SAFETY IS POSSIBLE WHEN ONE IS PROPERLY EQUIPPED, EFFECTIVELY CONDITIONED, ADEQUATELY TRAINED, AND DETERMINED NOT TO TAKE UNREASONABLE RISKS.

Skiing can be one of our most hazardous sports, especially when the performers are not properly trained. Skiing requires an unusually high degree of developed skill, excellent physical condition, courage and good judgment. Accidents frequently occur when the skier: is not in good physical condition; is going too fast for the conditions or his ability; is fatigued; is careless or reckless, or has improper attitudes; has not mastered the fundamental skills; or is skiing on faulty trails or in bad weather or bad snow conditions.

Four strategies may be employed in reducing the occurrence of skiing injuries and mitigating their consequences. These four are: a) better training, and use of gentler slopes by the unqualified; b) development of more effective release bindings and other protective devices; c) provision of the best possible emergency orthopedic and general medical care; and, d) provision of the best continuing medical care and rehabilitation (16:10).

Basic suggestions for safe skiing are:

1. Secure medical approval prior to taking up skiing.
2. Wear proper equipment, particularly boots and bindings.
3. Use warm windproof clothing, proper sunglasses.
4. Never ski alone in remote or rugged areas.
5. Secure instruction from a qualified instructor prior to skiing.
6. Learn and observe the rules of the trail.
7. Do not go down slopes until you have been pronounced ready to do so.
8. Safety releasable binding should be used by all beginners.
9. Recognize your limitations and do not attempt feats beyond your ability and control.

summary

No attempt has been made herein to describe the newer types of recreational activities of man as well as some of the older ones that he has long enjoyed. It is obvious that persons who go surfing, sky-diving, drag-racing, flying, sports car racing, or bob-sledding, and enjoy a wide variety of activities do so for adventure, in quest of excitement, as self-testing activities, as danger-inviting and hazard-overcoming feats. Their acceptance of risk may be at a high level at certain times in their lives. So long as they are free of injury they often attribute their injury-free success to their skill when in fact it may be due to just chance or a peculiar combination of events that they escaped injury. Essentially, however, it is each man's basic responsibility to develop an awareness of the requirements for safe participation in a sport and to live up to such knowledge through acquisition of skills and attitudes that will make the sport recreationally enjoyable and satisfying because it is free of injury to one's self and to others.

Since the sports and recreational activities man selects during his leisure time have many hazards, it is important that proper safety attitudes be instilled in his early years by teachers, friends, sports experts, parents and youth group leaders. Where basic skills and knowledge have not been imparted, it is to be hoped that experienced persons will give these sports participants good instruction and that sports and recreation leaders will disseminate, through the press, radio, and television, information pertinent to the hazards present, how they may be removed or compensation made for them, and how no new hazards need be created. With the cooperation of organized sports groups and recreation specialists, man can learn to recreate safely through a long and healthy life. In truth, if man remains free of accidental injury his recreational participation through sports should continue to enrich his life and should add more years to it.

suggested projects and activities

1. Submit an essay to your instructor of not more than 1,500 words indicating how safety procedures make it possible for an individual to gain greater enjoyment from recreation and sports.
2. Develop a lesson outline to be used in teaching about recreational activities. Underline all items that stress safety considerations.
3. Prepare an assembly program for a junior or senior high school audience on the topic "Safety in Sports." Indicate what film or films you might use, the value they have, and what exhibition or student group activity you would use to round out an interesting, hour-long assembly.
4. Apply the principles of safe sports participation to activities not covered in this chapter, horseback riding, drag-racing or sports car rallying, surfing, sky-diving, or any other activities. List in detail and describe the elements of safe play in the sport selected.
5. Develop a plan for securing more accurate reporting of recreational and sports accidents in your community. Apply the plan for a three-month period and report your findings to the proper authorities. What follow-up would you recommend for this study?
6. Identify several areas for research which would be designed to study more fully the causal factors of sports accidents and prescribe measures for intervention to lessen injury.
7. Conduct a survey of the sports activities in and around your school. Identify the hazards that are known to exist and ones that have not been carefully ascertained by school authorities. Develop recommendations for overcoming the hazards and submit them to the school safety director.

selected references

1. Brown, Richard L., "New Facts on Near-Drownings," *Journal* of the American Association for Health, Physical Education and Recreation, September, 1963.
2. Center for Safety Education, New York University, *Family Recreation and Safety*. New York: The Center, 1961.

3. Elkow, J. Duke, "Fitness and Safety," in *Family Recreation and Safety*. New York: New York University. 1961.
4. Gabrielsen, Bramwell W., *Facts on Drowning Accidents*. Athens, Ga.: University of Georgia Printing Department, 1956.
5. Halsey, Maxwell, ed., *Accident Prevention,* New York: McGraw-Hill Book Company, 1961.
6. "Hazards of Water Sports," *What's New,* Abbott Laboratories, #225, August-September, 1961.
7. National Safety Council, *Accident Facts,* Chicago: The Council, 1964. See also annual issues.
8. ________, *Family Safety*. Chicago: The Council (quarterly).
9. ________, *Public Safety Newsletter*. Chicago: The Council (monthly).
10. ________, *Safety Education*. Chicago: The Council.
11. Ryan, Allan J., *Medical Care of the Athlete*. New York: Blakiston Division, McGraw-Hill Book Company, 1962.
12. Sanders, J. Edward, *Safety and Health in Organized Camps*. New York: National Conservation Bureau, 1933.
13. Strasser, Marland K. *et al., Fundamentals of Safety Education*. New York: The Macmillan Company, 1964.
14. U. S. Coast Guard, *Pleasure Craft*. Washington, D.C.: U. S. Government Printing Office, 1962.
15. U. S. Navy, Diving Manual. Washington, D.C.: U. S. Government Printing Office.
16. United States Public Health Service, "Skiing Injuries," in *Public Health Reports,* Vol. 77, No. 11, November, 1962.

7

sports and physical education

Sports and physical education have been established in the schools for developing, maintaining and improving the students' physical, mental, social and emotional health, now and in their future, through vigorous movement activities. To achieve the objectives of total fitness through such activity programs, effective safety techniques must be used. Accidents connected with school athletics and physical education activities often receive unfavorable publicity, frequently ill-conceived and improperly assessing the situation. Too often such accidents result in emotional demands or recommendations that these activities be abolished rather than in a more desirable policy of adopting measures to increase the safety of participants and thereby to retain the many values that may be derived from such vigorous activities.

In recent years many measures have been taken to make physical education and athletics relatively safe. The professional literature in these areas evidences constant concern with safety. Elements of sports safety have received significant attention in the American Medical Association's six national conferences on the Medical Aspects of Sports (2) as well as in other conferences co-sponsored by the Association. The first National Conference on Accident Prevention in Physical Education and Athletics was sponsored in 1963 by the American Association for Health, Physical Education and Recreation. Its conference report (1) merits careful study by school administrators, physical educators and safety specialists.

This chapter is concerned with the development and application of principles of safe participation in physical education and athletic activities so that hazards will be minimized and maximal physical social, and emotional benefits will be attained.

The Need for Safety in Physical Education and Athletics

Two factors point to the need for greater safety precautions in the field: (1) the increasing number of participants, and (2) the accident experience in all of these activities.

Increased Participation

Millions of persons in this country engage, to varying degrees, in physical education, athletics and sports. In the schools, participation in physical education is almost universally required. In later life, vast numbers of our people are active in sports. If a good foundation has been established, pleasure from movement activities will be experienced. If an effective base for safe participation has been formed, years of enjoyment may ensue from sports activities unmarred by accident.

A survey of research findings reveals that physical education and athletic activities continue to account for the greater portion of school accidents (10). To some degree this is to be expected. Vigorous movement activities involve certain risks and hazards that seldom occur in other school activities. Participation in such pursuits is decidedly more dangerous than sitting in the home or in school, yet it is this element of danger which seems to transform them into stimulating, even thrilling, adventures. However, with proper precautions these elements of danger may be reduced to permit the maximum enjoyment of threefold benefits:

1. *Physical:* the values of physical vigor, strength, skill, and endurance.
2. *Social:* the elements of teamwork; team play, the ability to follow, and leadership; privileges and responsibility, including, in a democracy, the responsibility of keeping oneself physically fit and working towards total fitness.
3. *Emotional:* satisfying desires for adventure, for release from tension and stress, for the development of emotional control, and for relief from the failures or disappointments of everyday living.

The Accident Situation

It is difficult to compare the relative dangers of various physical education and recreational activities. However, many experts contend that athletic pursuits tend to have a low incidence of accidents when contrasted with the routine activities of daily living.

In recent years the accident-reporting system used by the National Safety Council has provided a fairly accurate summary of school accidents. A careful review of an annual issue of *Accident Facts,* the section on school-age accidents, will quickly show the reader that the physical education and athletic fields are the settings for most school accidents. For boys, about half of all school accidents occur in the area of the physical education department's responsibility; for girls about 45 per cent occur in the same area. A recent issue (7) shows that basketball is the most dangerous activity in grades 10 through 12, with football almost as dangerous. Significantly, accident rate for boys in the physical education program rises rapidly in the higher grades in school: in the kindergarten a rate of .5 is noted; in grades 1–3, 1.0; in grades 4–6, 2.8; grades 7–9, 8.4; and grades 10–12, 10.7. The average for all grades is 4.6 per 100,000 student days. (A rate of .1 is equivalent to 8,000 accidents). By comparison, the rates for girls in school are: kindergarten, .4; grades 1–3, .7; grades 4–6, 2.0; grades 7–9, 4.6; grades 10–12, 4.1; and the total for all, 2.4. Girls do not have either the frequency or the severity of accidental injury that boys experience. Research dealing with variations in accident experience and the sex of the persons involved would be valuable.

The accident experience of junior and senior high school students reported by Pechar (10) was concerned with 1,408 accidents to students over a one-year period in 96 selected schools in one state. Of interest in this study is the ranking of accidents in terms of four variables abstracted from the original thesis (see Table 7).

The greatest number of accidents occurred during the months of October and September with the fewest in June. Most occurred during the late afternoon and morning. Eighty-two per cent occurred to those in the 15-to-17 age group. Most occurred on the athletic field with the gymnasium ranking second. Sprains were the most frequent type of injury with the leg and foot most often involved.

College Sports Accidents

Sports and physical education participation in our colleges is at a new peak because of mounting enrollment, a renewed national emphasis on physical fitness for youth, a need for adequate conditioning for military service, and a gradually unfolding realization that sports and exercise con-

TABLE 7

RANK ORDER OF SPORTS ACCIDENTS

Activity	*Number of accidents:*	*Incidence: per 1,000 exposure*	*Days lost: gross*	*Severity: days lost per 1,000*
Football	1	2	1	2
Basketball	2	7.5	2	7
Wrestling	3	5	5	6
Soccer	4	6	4	5
Track & field	5	10	7	11
Heavy apparatus	6	14	3	9
Baseball	7	7.5	8	10
Touch-flag football	8	9	6	8
Lacrosse	9	4	10	4
Softball	10	12.5	12	14
Volleyball	11	11	11	13
Games and relays	12	18	9	17
Tumbling	13	16	13	15
Swimming & diving	14.5	15	16	16
Ice hockey	14.5	3	15	3
Six-man football	18	1	14	1
Badminton	22	12.5	18	12
Tennis	22	17	19	18
Calisthenics	22	19	17	19

tribute to the good life. Yet in quest for more adventure, greater recognition, achievement, personal pride, improved vigor and added health, a number of our students will meet with accidental injury. While many sports accidents do occur we note that our national acceptance of the risks of sports is higher than it should be.

In our colleges touch football is played annually by over 350,000 students. Every year about 5,000 are injured to the extent of requiring medical treatment and there is one death. Uncounted numbers experience injuries that some years later are painful and recurrent reminders of the vigorous activities of the good old days of one's youth. In a study at Michigan State University (4) the rates of injuries per 1,000 students were listed for the physical education program as follows: wrestling, 26; doubles tumbling, 22; boxing, 19; paddleball and squash, 15; apparatus, 12; individual tumbling, 10; handball, 9; ice skating and hockey, each 9; soccer, 8. In the intramural program, ice hockey, wrestling, touch football and boxing, in that order, were the leading hazardous activities. Touch football was cited, but not as one of the most hazardous sports.

Intramural activities have the following injury rate per 1,000 participants in the above cited Michigan State study: ice hockey, 24.5; wrestling, 15.9; touch football, 13.4; boxing, 9.7; swimming, 8.6; fencing, 5.3; gymnastics, 5.11; softball, 4.8; volleyball, 2.6. Data on college accidents is very

THE BILL OF RIGHTS FOR THE COLLEGE ATHLETE

Participation in college athletics is a privilege involving both responsibilities and rights. The athlete has the responsibility to play fair, to give his best, to keep in training, to conduct himself with credit to his sport and his school. In turn he has the right to optimal protection against injury as this may be assured through technical instruction, proper regulation and conditions of play, and adequate supervision. Included are:

Good Coaching. The importance of good coaching in protecting the health and safety of athletes cannot be minimized. Technical instruction leading to skillful performance is a significant factor in lowering the incidence and decreasing the severity of injuries. Also, good coaching includes the discouragement of tactics, outside either the rules or the spirit of the rules, which may increase the hazard and thus the incidence of injuries.

Good Officiating. The rules and regulations governing athletic competition are made to protect players as well as to promote enjoyment of the game. To serve these ends effectively the rules of the game must be thoroughly understood by players as well as coaches and be properly interpreted and enforced by impartial and technically qualified officials.

Good Equipment and Facilities. There can be no question about the protection afforded by proper equipment and right facilities. Good equipment is now available and is being improved continually; the problem lies in the false economy of using cheap, worn out, outmoded, or ill-fitting gear. Provision of proper areas for play and their careful maintenance are equally important.

Good Medical Care. . . Including:

First. . . a thorough preseason history and physical examination. Many of the sports tragedies which occur each year are due to unrecognized health problems. Medical contraindictions to participation in contact sports must be respected.

Second. . . a physician present at all contests and readily available during practice sessions. It is unfair to leave to a trainer or coach decisions as to whether an athlete should return to play or be removed from the game following injury. In serious injuries the availability of a physician may make the difference in preventing disability or even death.

Third. . . medical control of the health aspects of athletics. In medical matters, the physician's authority should be absolute and unquestioned. Today's coaches and trainers are happy to leave medical decisions to the medical profession. They also assist in interpreting this principle to students and the public.

American Medical Association
Committee on Injury in Sports
(2)

limited. In the future it is to be hoped that colleges will pool their data on accidents to college men and develop more effective intervention media to lessen the hazards of college sports activities so that fun and adventure will be more attainable.

Causes of Athletic Injury

Accidents are seldom due to a single cause. A wide variety of causes usually occurs concurrently and an accident resulting in injury may happen on such an occasion. A witness, for example, may state the cause to have been simply falling, yet more careful analysis may show that some of the following conditions led up to that nonreversable moment when the fall produced injury: personal physical weakness, being pushed when off balance, having been improperly selected for the activity, inadequate coaching, being too highly emotional or just pure chance.

In the study by Pechar (10) the factors that contributed to accidents in physical education and athletics were categorized as falling into two areas: (1) *personal factors,* made up of physical factors and mental-emotional factors, and, (2) *administrative factors.* It was recorded that 62 per cent of the accidents were due to personal factors and 38 per cent to administrative factors. Physical factors relate to bodily condition and performance, such as fatigue, muscular weakness and skill. For the accidents that were studied, poor skill, fatigue, and poor condition ranked in the order mentioned as causes. The sports for which physical causal factors were recorded were in order of rank: football, apparatus, wrestling, track and field.

Several mental-emotional factors were reported as causes of accidents and ranked as follows: disregarding instructions, taking unnecessary chances, and acting before thinking. Such behavioral faults caused sports accidents in the following fields, in rank order: apparatus, football, wrestling, and baseball.

When nearly seven out of ten sports injuries studied in one state's school athletic program stem from physical and mental-emotional factors we might well ask if we are meeting the needs of youth for good instruction, proper player selection and close observation of the condition or fatigue of the performers. Good coaching demands full awareness of the players' personal and emotional characteristics and ready recall of any combination of conditions that might set the stage for a sudden tragic mishap.

Administrative factors that contributed to sports accidents included the following: equipment, facility, leadership and program. More than one-half of the accidents related to equipment were due to inadequate and faulty protective equipment (51 per cent) with inadequate or faulty personal equipment causing somewhat fewer (30 per cent). Inadequate or faulty activity equipment caused one accident in ten and a failure to store equipment or to provide adequate storage space for it caused nearly the same number of accidental injuries.

Facility factors causing accidents include poor surfacing, especially in football; obstructions in playing surface, noticeably in basketball, and limited size of the area in which the accident occurred. Accidents resulting from leadership factors stem from an inadequate amount of instruction, poor officiating, and inadequate amount of supervision. Some of the program factors producing injury to performers were: too many participants in the activity, noticeable in football, basketball and wrestling; a level of performance demanded by the activity that students could not meet for varying reasons; and a high ratio of participants to teachers. Experienced coaches, physical educators and administrators are aware of the accident potential that stems from program and leadership inadequacies. However, from time to time it is essential that they be reminded of the variables that result in recurrent mishaps and maintain high standards of administration in sports. The stresses and tensions brought on by unreasonable demands of local sports enthusiasts, including parents and youth, must be parried by unexcelled professional judgment sustained by strong personal integrity.

Personal safety rules Since many accidents are due to the failure of the individual to exercise reasonable personal controls, it would be helpful if teachers and coaches would stress the importance of developing a personal philosophy of safety. Rules for personal safety, suggested some years ago by Lloyd, Deaver and Eastwood are still valuable:

1. Never continue playing a game when fatigued.
2. Do not attempt a hazardous new skill except under the direction of a qualified person.
3. When jumping, see that the landing surface is sufficiently soft for the height of the fall, and that there are no obstructions or uneven surfaces.
4. Proper personal equipment should be worn at all times for protection.
5. Refuse to play the game if the equipment is improperly erected, or if the floor or field is slippery, rough, or has obstacles that may lead to injury.
6. When participating in an activity, always keep in a position away from flying equipment such as a bat, discus, shot, javelin.
7. Never enter the water unless a supervisor is present.
8. See that all injuries receive immediate and adequate attention.
9. Never try any stunts beyond your range of ability.
10. Select activities that are within the range of your physical capabilities.
11. Avoid taking part in activities in overcrowded space.
12. Never take advice or instruction from an unqualified person.
13. Demand a physical examination before entering physical education activities, and a recheck before going out for any arduous sport.

14. "Warming-up" before participating in strenuous activities is a wise precaution against strains and sprains.
15. It is desirable that those participating in sports be protected by insurance against the cost of serious injuries.

Principles of Safe Participation

When reviewing the principles of safe participation, certain factors should be considered. First, safety in sports, recreation and physical education depends to a great extent upon the skill with which the activity is performed. The skilled athlete uses his body more efficiently than the unskilled. Second, attitudes are extremely important in the prevention of accidents. The emotionally charged athlete may disregard his skill or knowledge of safe practices in the stress of a situation and precipitate an accident. Therefore, the emotional climate of a vigorous movement activity situation must be carefully watched by the teacher, coach and administrator. Third, knowledge of rules and observance of them will tend to curb athletic or recreational accidents. Rules specify acceptable behavior and are designed to control the game. Finally, fourth, careful organization and administration are necessary for carrying out an effective safety program. A low accident rate does not just happen; it is planned through good leadership, administration, equipment, skill and condition controls.

When leadership controls fail, negligence suits may be instituted against the school and in some instances, its staff members. Awards have reached unusual sums in recent years. Perhaps the highest was for $1,215,140 awarded to a youth who was paralyzed from the neck down after he suffered a broken vertebra in the neck. On an appeal the award was reduced to $356,000. He had leaped from a springboard over an obstacle and ended in a forward tumble. His instructor had left the gymnasium to seek aid for a student who had received a rope burn (10).

The well-prepared teacher of physical education and the coach usually have a fairly good conception of the principles underlying safe participation in their areas. Simply stated, these call for:

1. An understanding of the hazards involved in each activity.
2. The removal of unnecessary hazards.
3. Compensating for those hazards that cannot be removed.
4. Creating no unnecessary hazards.

Understanding the Hazards A thorough understanding of the hazards involved in any activity necessitates a comprehension of the nature of the activity, the equipment being used, leadership responsibilities, the place of skill in the activity, and the need for adequate classification and good physical condition of the participants.

Removing Unnecessary Hazards Understanding the hazards connected with an activity does not imply that the activity must be avoided.

Rather, it should induce one to remove the hazards. This may be done by two means: (1) correcting or supplying a mechanical feature as in planning adequate play areas, leveling play areas, treating floors with a slip-proof compound, providing well-lighted, well-ventilated locker rooms and adequate first aid facilities; and (2) emphasizing the human element, particularly good leadership, which recognizes and removes equipment or mechanical hazards, equalizes competition, and trains and conditions pupils to be safe.

Compensating for Hazards Which Cannot Be Removed Even though all hazards possible to eliminate are recognized and removed, some activities by their very nature cannot be completely freed from danger. Swimming, for example, obviously is more dangerous than walking, but the individual who understands the hazards entailed in water activities and has developed adequate skills can participate in them with a minimum of danger. Here again good leadership becomes an important factor: Teaching correct procedures, suitable progression, and adequate skills will compensate for many hazards. Constant vigilance is necessary to keep the overambitious from attempting activities beyond their skill and capabilities. Not only the leader, but the pupil as well, must be responsible for guarding against this possibility.

Creating No Unnecessary Hazards Activities present hazards when competition is not equal. For example, contact games become highly hazardous when students are poorly classified as to their ability and capacity. Keeping schedules down to a reasonable number of contests within the season may reduce hazards such as those found when football is played too late in the fall. Since poor and inadequate equipment creates additional hazards, only the best protective devices should be used.

Early in the relationship of instructor and student the student should be lead to understand thoroughly that he must assume his share of responsibility for his own safety and for the safety of others. Players must realize that it is foolish to conceal an injury from the coach; such action may threaten the team's success as well as aggravate the original injury. In order that safety consciousness developed through athletic activities may carry over into the student's behavior at home and on the streets and highways, the desirability of a life free from accidents must be stressed. When the student learns that safety is a means of furthering his enjoyment of sports, it is relatively easy for him to appreciate the necessity of the same type of correct safe behavior in the other activities of daily life.

The four basic principles that have been cited can be applied in any field or activity with excellent results. While effective in the teaching of safety in sports their application to traffic, home, public, or industrial safety will be helpful in developing a fuller understanding of the problem area.

Many principles of safety and accident prevention have been reported in the literature in health and physical education. They were reviewed and revised as a part of a doctoral study completed by Pechar (10). Some of the more pertinent principles for safety and accident prevention are abstracted and reported here:

Within the required program:

A medical examination should be required for each student, and the physician's statement as to whether the student may or may not participate.

An accident-reporting system should be instituted to provide uniform records of all injuries and accidents . . . to determine cause . . . to institute preventive measures.

Plan program activities appropriate for sex, age, ability and condition of the students.

Safety instruction should be an integral part of the physical education and athletics program.

Program participants should be protected by health and accident insurance.

Employ only qualified and certified teachers.

Interschool Program:

Contestants and teams should be as equally matched as possible.

Athletes should be under medical supervision throughout all seasons and physicians must be present at all combat sports contests.

Provide safe transportation for all athletic teams.

Limitations should be placed on athletic contests, number of practice periods, number of events, etc.

Principles concerning Facilities:

Provide safe playing surfaces.

Check facilities seasonally as well as prior to each use . . . to identify and remove unsafe conditions.

Avoid overlapping play areas.

Provide adequate illumination for each activity.

Keep play areas and surroundings free of obstructions.

Principles Concerning Participants:

Safety of a participant relates to the proper development of his skill, proper conditioning, effective warming up and adequate strength development.

Pupils should progress from simple athletic skills to the more advanced.

Participants should know, respect, and obey the rules and regulations of all sports activities in which they engage.

The participant should think before he acts in physical education activities.

Participate in activities only when wearing the personal protective equipment commonly prescribed.

Principles Concerning Equipment:

All personal equipment (including protective equipment) is to be adequate, properly fitted and constructed, clean and properly used.

Frequent inspection and correction of defects must be provided.

Movable equipment must be safely stored when not in use.

Safety rules and regulations regarding the use of equipment should be established and enforced.

Only safe equipment may be used; this implies that it be durable, constructed by reliable manufacturers of high quality materials under high manufacturing standards.

Principles Concerning Leadership:

Supervision of all activity areas should be performed by qualified and certified teachers.

Effective officiating must be provided for all contests.

First aid, as well as proper follow-up treatment, must be provided for all injuries.

Primary concern should be given to the well-being of participants in the conduct of physical education activities rather than to the outcome of games or contests.

Pupils who are injured may not return to the activity without the consent of the designated physician.

Teachers must begin activities at an easy pace and build up skill and endurance as the season progresses.

The teacher should teach pupils to feel responsible for their own safety and that of fellow participants without by-passing the teacher's responsibility.

The preceding principles can be used to reduce injuries in most of the sports and in physical education activities. In some instances it is admittedly difficult to set up sufficient controls to take care of all possible situations. However, the principles already given may be applied as indicated in the sections of this chapter that follow.

Baseball and Softball

Our national sport, despite its popularity, has been largely replaced in the schools by softball. In fact, the College Physical Education Association recommends that hard ball be discontinued in physical education classes. Since the safety precautions are similar, the two are considered simultaneously here.

Softball has more players and more spectators than any other sport in the world. It is listed as a hazardous sport for high school boys, low in degree of hazard for college men, and a little higher for college women.

Hazards More than 10 per cent of the injuries occur to the arm and hand, leg and foot, and the head and neck. Almost all injuries to the head and neck are caused by careless throwing of the bat and collisions between the base runner and baseman. Most of the leg injuries are caused by uneven playing surfaces and base sliding. Hazards may be reduced if the following practices are applied:

1. Plastic skull caps when at bat.
2. Smooth-seam softball (14″ for grade school, 12″ for high school)
3. Bats with nonslip grips of tape, cork or other material.
4. Smooth playing surfaces.
5. No spikes (except for advanced players in competition).
6. Playing areas and "on deck" areas marked.
7. Protected players' bench for those not playing.
8. Bats gripped firmly with dry hands to prevent slipping.
9. Masks, chest protectors for catchers.
10. A player should call for a fly ball to avoid collision.
11. Head first slide prohibited (except for those with "bad" knees).
12. When sliding is permitted, players must wear sliding pads.

Basketball

The safety procedures advocated for basketball are applicable to other court games of a similar type. Conditioning exercises for the feet, ankles, and knees should be practiced for at least three weeks before one engages in actual game activities. Good condition is essential for effective basketball play. Effective playing skills will allow the participant to delay the onset of fatigue. Practice sessions should not be too long for youngsters nor should a schedule be too heavy or long. Frequent substitutions help avoid overstrain to players. The sport is so strenuous that all injured players should be excluded from participation until their injuries have healed completely or a physician permits their return to play.

Poor officiating has been responsible for many accidents in sports contests. The alert official checks the playing surfaces for hazards, seeks to correct improper or unsafe player equipment, and does not hesitate to call the coach's attention to a player who is attempting to hide an injury. Competent officials should be employed to provide close supervision of all contests.

The players' equipment should be the best. Shoes should fit and should be of good quality and construction. If glasses are worn, they should have unbreakable lenses, or, if prescribed by an oculist, contact lenses may assist the player in overcoming refractive errors of the eyes. The playing surfaces should be properly treated. Obstructions to play must not exist and at the ends of the courts there must be ample room left to prevent collision between players coming down the floor at a speed that carries them beyond the playing area.

The weights of all players should be checked regularly. All weights should be stable by the end of the second week. The player of normal weight should have shown a progressive though slight gain, and the overweight boy should approximate the ideal weight, height, and build for his age.

Boxing

The desirability of including boxing in the school physical education program is debatable. Although various studies indicate the accident incidence to be low, some physicians claim "hidden" injuries impair brain tissue. Most states now prohibit interschool boxing by law. The President of the National Safety Council, Howard Pyle, wrote an article "Let's Abolish Boxing" to express his hope that "the citizens of this country will become angry enough to end this shoddy sport before others are maimed and killed (11)."

For those who promote boxing, who wish to make it safer and more popular, the following safety suggestions are made:

1. Promote boxing only when good leadership and adequate equipment are available.
2. Observe established rules for each age group.
3. Suitable mat, standard ring, proper weight gloves must be used.
4. Protective devices must be used during workouts.
5. Boxing gloves should not be used to settle a grudge.
6. Blindfold boxing, group elimination, or other dangerous mass-boxing events should not be allowed.
7. Conform to all accepted procedures for sports participation, *i.e.* medical examination before and during the season.
8. If any injury occurs, secure immediate medical attention.

Field Hockey

At one time many persons felt that field hockey was too rough a sport for men. Yet today it has been adapted to the women's sport program and is now a popular activity. It is played almost exclusively by girls and is an ideal sport where speed, accuracy of action, and endurance are factors.

The most serious accidents are due to poor fielding surfaces, inadequate protection, unnecessary roughness, lack of training and old injuries. All of these dangers may be prevented. Controls that may help reduce accidents in this sport follow:

1. The playing field should be of grass and in good condition.
2. Shin guards are to be worn.
3. The goalie should wear special pads and shoes.
4. Balls should be kept well painted for visibility.
5. Goal space should be covered with net, not wire.
6. When fielding the ball with the hand, the fingers should be toward the ground.
7. The ball, not the opponent, should be played.

8. When stick is not in play, it should be carried across the body.
9. Good officials will lessen rough and hazardous play.
10. Use only rated officials in interschool matches.

Football

Good leadership and adequate facilities and equipment can prevent at least half of high school football injuries. The young adolescent is too frequently swayed by his desire to emulate the college star, and often allows his enthusiasm to warp his better judgment. Hence, sane leadership is essential to guide the player safely through the football season. The fundamentals of the game should be carefully taught, and contact activities, such as tackling and blocking, should not be permitted until players have been well conditioned. For some players this will mean one week; for others it may mean longer. When tackling is taught, dummies should be used. Tackling is the skill engaged in most frequently when injury occurs (10:84).

Practice periods should not be continued to the point where fatigue

Figure 7:1, Equipment Designed to Protect Vital Points of Contact.

reduces skill. No scrimmage should be held before the players have warmed up sufficiently or after fatigue has reduced their skills. The careful coach will not allow his boys to be "cannon fodder" for a much superior team; neither will he permit injured or fatigued players to practice or to continue in the game. All injuries should be carefully treated and followed up.

Competent officiating is a prime requirement. In addition, each player must know and obey the rules of the game. He should be provided with proper protective equipment and should thoroughly understand its purpose. Furthermore, all players should warm up properly before the start of each half of the game to prevent injuries. These occur most frequently to the knee and ankle, head and shoulder, arm and hand, pelvis, thigh, chest, and back. The commonest type of injury is the sprain; next is some type of bone injury.

The playing field should be level with a good stand of grass, and free of holes and ruts, stones, broken glass, and other dangerous objects. All field lines should be made with slaked lime, with yard markers of flexible material placed outside the playing area. Players' benches should be set off and to the side of the playing area. The article "Is Your Boy's Football Helmet Safe?", was written to alert parents to basic requirements of proper helmet design and selection (9).

Gymnasium

Safety in gymnasium activities may be increased through competent instruction designed to instill safe work habits and a feeling of responsibility for one's safety as well as for that of members of the group; and through the use of high quality apparatus and through regular inspections. The floor surface should be level and treated to prevent slipping; protective equipment such as safety belts should be used until the instructor gives permission to discard such devices; all uprights and other projections that cannot be removed should be thoroughly padded. All stairs leading from the gymnasium should be well illuminated, and all doors should open outward. Locker rooms should be well lighted. Emphasis should be placed on keeping locker doors closed when they are not in actual use, and any form of "horseplay" should be ruled out immediately. Showers should be controlled by a mixing valve to prevent hot water burns, and shower floors should be of the nonskid type.

Gymnastics and Tumbling The use of heavy apparatus for gymnastics has been decreasing steadily during the last two decades. To some extent, expensive equipment, lack of trained instructors, and an unfavorable accident record have been responsible. When safety procedures were virtually nonexistent in this sport, injuries were quite prevalent. Yet under proper leadership gymnastics can be reasonably safe. The introduction of new-type equipment and a greater variety of devices for gymnastics such as trampolines for rebound tumbling will require more careful control of these devices. Failure to comply may result in legislation to restrict activities which are fine when properly done but dangerous when not effectively supervised.

Suggestions for safeguarding these activities follow:

1. Sufficient mats, carefully placed, are essential for apparatus and tumbling stunts.
2. Hand and ceiling safety belts should be used when dangerous stunts are being learned.
3. Maintain safe spacing between apparatus and tumbling lines.
4. Proper spotting at all times will curb accidents.
5. Handguards and gymnastic chalk should be available to protect performers' hands (and, therefore, grip) at all times.
6. Hazardous equipment must be locked up when not under proper supervision.
7. Proper warm-up and good condition are essential prior to attempting difficult maneuvers.
8. Stop "horseplay." When concentration wanders, accidents rise.

Playground

Careful planning and proper zoning of play areas will prevent many accidents. Equipment of the best quality, carefully inspected and properly used, will reduce the possibility of accidents. Since the improper use of playground apparatus is dangerous, pupils should be carefully instructed in its correct use. For example, pupils should be impressed with the fact that it is better to sit than stand when on a swing. All apparatus and jumping and game pits should be placed along the sides of the playground and as far away from the game area as possible. In short, the playground should be so arranged that the activities of one age group will not interfere with those of another (3).

All the play surface should be smooth and free of stones or other dangerous objects. Bicycles must not be ridden on playfields; riders should dismount before entering and place bicycles in a rack at the entrance or just inside. In spite of all precautions, some children will violate safety rules, thereby causing accidents and injuries. Hence, eternal vigilance and constant supervision must be exercised. Simple rules of conduct should be posted and called to the attention of all children (3:41–43).

If activities are carefully scheduled, if sufficient apparatus and personal equipment is utilized to keep children occupied, and if children are classified according to age or ability in order that they may participate in activities suitable to their interests and needs, the possibilities of accidents will be greatly reduced. To assure the proper treatment of playground injuries, well-stocked first aid kits should be available. Finally, all accidents should be reported and studied and steps should be taken to prevent others.

Track and Field

The activities in the sport of track and field are of low hazard, excluding weight events, which are considered dangerous. Nearly all track and field injuries occur to the leg and foot or arm and hand. Head and neck injuries are more frequent in high schools, and thigh injuries in college.

Suggestions for safe participation in track and field follow:

1. Number of competitors in any race should be governed by the safe capacity of the track.
2. Lanes should be provided for short races run on curves.
3. During meets track and field must be kept clear of spectators, coaches and competitors (except when they are competing or warming up).
4. Rope off dangerous areas to prevent collision and injury from participants and equipment.
5. Implements for weight events should be checked out and used only under supervision in designated and protected areas.
6. A runner should not jump, lunge or throw up his arms at the finish.
7. Cross-country runners should have their ankles taped.
8. Mass hurdling should not be permitted.
9. Adequate mats or pits must always be used (indoors and outdoors).

Volleyball

Volleyball is probably the least understood sport in the school curriculum. While it is a comparatively safe game, it is seldom played or taught effectively. Yet it is a game of speed and force when played properly. Since well over 7 million persons participate in this sport annually, a few suggestions are made:

1. Make all posts and connections fast.
2. Play only six men (eight girls) on a side.
3. Have competent officials to enforce all regulations.
4. Teach players that they must stay in their own zones.
5. Proper warm-up and use of fingers will prevent most injuries to hands and fingers.
6. A thorough warm-up including jumping should be used by all spikers.
7. Expert spikers should use caution when playing with inexperienced players to avoid injuring them.

First Aid

The principles of first aid should be understood by all who participate in physical education, recreation, athletics and wrestling. This means that one should know what procedure to follow in case of injury and be prepared to render aid immediately. The usual procedure includes having at least one teacher present who has had first aid training; calling physicians; notifying parents; arranging for the hospitalization of serious cases; transporting the injured persons; guiding the parents to the best sources of treatment, after-care, and other details that arise as the result of an accident. The up-to-date school will have readily available the name and telephone number of the family physician or an alternate. Accident records should be kept in order to be able to: (1) identify hazardous situations, (2) procure data for subject matter in the safety program, (3) have facts available when there is a question of liability, and (4) help prevent further accidents of a similar nature. First aid is discussed more fully in Chapter 12.

Some state athletic associations have sponsored or aided schools in developing accident insurance plans to meet the cost of athletic injuries by participants and to establish desirable methods for the prevention of future accidents. These plans have proved valuable also in having so-called "minor" accidents brought to the attention of the doctor for proper diagnosis. The fact that it is necessary to report the accident offers an excellent educational experience in proper care of injuries.

summary

If each student is taught the hazards connected with the activity; if all possible hazards are removed; if the student compensates for those hazards that cannot be removed; and if he acts in a way that does not create unnecessary hazards, there should be a minimum of accidents in physical education and athletics. Constant stressing of these principles should lead to patterns of behavior that will eventually result in better safety practices on the part of older adults as well. Students must be made to understand and practice the correct procedures in these activities so that safe performance will be carried on with or without guidance. Furthermore, each participant must be made to realize that there is one best method of performing any activity—the correct method. In this way these principles can be utilized to provide maximum enjoyment and the healthful benefits of physical education and athletic activities when they are performed safely.

suggested projects and activities

1. List sports commonly played in your school and develop a list of safety principles for each sport, using the four guiding principles presented on page 115.

2. Formulate a checklist for safe participation in several of the physical education activities.
3. List common injuries that result from participation in sports, and outline first aid procedures for each.
4. Review a number of films on athletics and physical education and select for an assembly program those which offer the best examples of safe practices. Submit an annotated bibliography of ten outstanding films in this area.
5. Formulate a safety code which will cover in a general way all of the physical education activities used in elementary and secondary schools.
6. Write an essay, suitable for publication, of not more than 2,000 words, showing how safety procedures make it possible for one to enjoy recreation and sports more fully.
7. Devise an accident-reporting form that will be used to report accidents in all physical education activities.
8. Prepare a lesson outline on safety in one of the following activities: baseball, football, field hockey, basketball, boxing, gymnastics and tumbling, soccer, tennis, or softball.

selected references

1. American Association of Health, Physical Education and Recreation, *Suggested School Safety Policies.* Washington, D.C.: The Association, 1964.
2. American Medical Association, *First National Conference on Medical Aspects of Sports.* Chicago: The Association, 1959. A similar conference has been held in each succeeding year, and a report published on each.
3. Center for Safety Education, "Safety for Recreation Areas and Playgrounds," in *Safety Education Digest,* ed. J. Duke Elkow. New York: The Center, 1955. Out of print.
4. Dzenowagis, Joseph G., "College Sports—Accidents, Injuries," *Safety Education,* March, 1962, p. 3–5.
5. Florio, A. E., and G. T. Stafford, *Safety Education* (2nd ed.). New York: McGraw-Hill Book Company, 1962.
6. Forsythe, C. E., *The Administration of High School Athletics* (4th ed.). Englewood Cliffs, N.J.: Prentice-Hall, Inc., 1962.
7. National Safety Council, *Accident Facts.* Chicago: The Council, 1964.
8. ———, "Safety Education Data Sheets," "Safety in the Gymnasium," "Play Areas," "Playground Apparatus," "Safety in Sports—Baseball," "Safety in Football," from issues of *Safety Education.* Chicago: The Council, 1950-1956.
9. ———, "Is Your Boy's Football Helmet Safe?" *Family Safety,* The Council, Fall, 1963, pp. 28–30.
10. Pechar, Stanley F., "A Study of the Nature, Frequency and Related Person and Administrative Factors of Physical Education Accidents Among Boys in the Junior and Senior High Schools of New York State." Unpublished Ed.D. dissertation, New York University, 1961.

11. Pyle, Howard, "Let's Abolish Boxing," *Family Safety,* National Safety Council Chicago, Fall, 1962.
12. Seaton, Don Cash, *Safety in Sports*. Englewood Cliffs, N.J.: Prentice-Hall, Inc., 1948. Out of print.
13. Strasser, Marland K. *et al., Fundamentals of Safety Education*. New York: The Macmillan Company, 1964.

8

occupational safety

Recent statistics indicate that the number of wage earners in the United States is well over 70 million and is increasing yearly. By far the largest percentage of these workers are employed in industry, but there are many millions in other occupations—teachers, nurses, policemen, firemen, and dozens of other non-industrial workers. Naturally, when unemployment is high the number in such source occupations decreases.

National Safety Council estimates indicate that the total cost of accidents involving workers in a recent year exceeded $5 billion dollars (12). Of this amount, $1.3 billion was for visible costs such as insurance overhead, medical and hospital costs and wage losses. Other costs include the money value of damaged equipment, production delays and time losses of other workers.

In the last two decades there has been a steady downward trend in both the number of deaths and the death rate in industrial accidents. In fact, since 1912 the rate has decreased 67 per cent.* There is a wide range in the accident frequency rates of various industries, for example, from over 35.0 in mining down to as low as 1.52 in aircraft manufacturing and .98 in communications. The

* U.S. Department of Labor figures will differ.

average for all industries is approximately 6.2. All workers should be given instruction in safe practices, depending upon the nature of their occupation. In addition, since a large percentage of the young people now in the schools will sooner or later be employed in industries, they should be given safety instruction.

There is another compelling reason for safety instruction. Millions of men and women are engaged in "do-it-yourself" activities in their homes. They are amateur carpenters, electricians, auto mechanics, painters and gardeners. In fact, it would be difficult for most owners to maintain their homes unless they were able to make repairs and do much of their own work. Under certain conditions, these "do-it-yourself" jobs may be hazardous, especially those that men do. The basic training that they received in industrial arts and vocational education should aid in developing safe practices that will help reduce accidents. For this reason all students should have some experience in industrial arts for, even though many become white collar workers, a large percentage will do work around their own homes.

Moreover, according to *Accident Prevention Can Be Learned,* "Dynamic forces are now at work changing our society. They bring vitality and excitement which can easily be used in motivating students to learn accident prevention. They also bring problems. We cannot know in advance what implications today's changes will have for safety. In some respects, life will undoubtedly become less hazardous, in others more so."

Deaths from Work Accidents

From 1937 to 1963 deaths from work accidents declined from over 18,000 to 13,700, certainly good evidence of the value of industrial safety activities.
National Safety Council, "Accident Facts."

Hundreds of poisonous chemicals have been developed in the last two decades; the explorations of outer space have raised new problems; many new industries have sprung up; off-the-job accidents have been steadily increasing. In fact, there are dozens of other problems that require the strengthening of safety programs.

In this chapter we will consider two areas: (1) industrial arts and vocational education, and (2) safety in industry.

Industrial Arts and Vocational Education

Industrial arts education is elementary instruction given in the basic industrial skills. Some of this may take place in the grade schools, but it is more often found in the junior and senior high schools. The most common subjects included are woodworking, electrical shop, auto me-

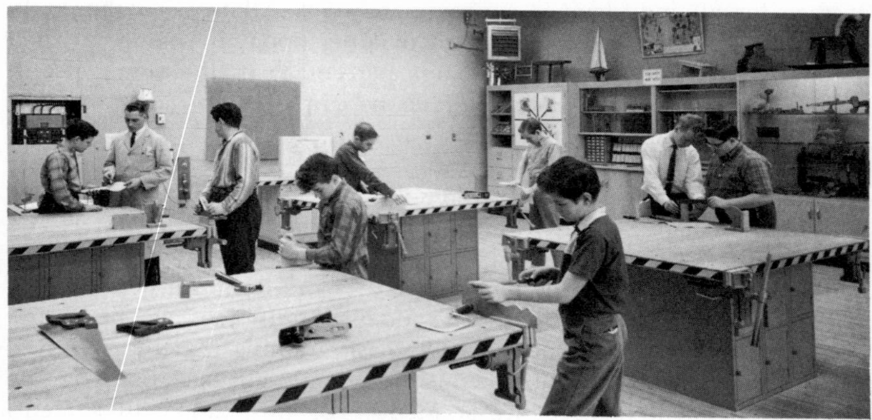

Figure 8:1, SAFETY IS AN IMPORTANT PART OF THE INDUSTRIAL ARTS PROGRAM.

chanics, metal working, and sometimes printing and agriculture. Students usually spend several weeks in each shop, although in many schools the instruction is given in what is called a general shop. Safety is obviously important in each of these subjects.

Vocational education is aimed at the acquisition of specific skills in one subject through which the individual may be expected to earn his livelihood. It ordinarily is offered in vocational high schools, but may be offered in general or technical high schools. The student may spend several years specializing in one field, or work part-time in an industry.

Serious accidents in school shops and laboratories are relatively rare but, as might be expected, there are some minor accidents from time to time. According to *Accident Facts* (12), the accident rate for high school boys in school shops per student enrolled is 2.0 as compared to 13.6 for physical education and 8.8 for interscholastic sports. For junior high students, the rate is lower. The rate for girls in homemaking and industrial arts is still lower. In the past two decades there has been a decided improvement in school shop safety. The question now is what should be included in a good safety program.

Environmental Controls In the design of school buildings, consideration should be given to all the factors that make for safety in the shops. This includes adequate lighting; heating and ventilation; proper floor surfaces; isolation of hazardous areas and processes; and adequate personal facilities. In addition, machinery, tools and other materials should meet the standards of recognized national agencies. Proper protective equipment should be available and used.

The Shop as a Laboratory Consideration should be given to:

Illumination. Proper over-all lighting along with special lighting at the point of each work station and activity is essential.

Ventilation. The ventilation should be adequate in terms of both purity and temperature of the air. Special controls should be provided where activities such as welding, sanding, buffing, spraying, painting and grinding are conducted.

Color standards. Color dynamics should be applied to room surfaces, machinery, switches and controls; to the identification of work-process and assembly areas; and to the identification of hot, cold, acid, caustic and hazardous materials.

Personal facilities. Items such as drinking fountains, water supply, lavatory and toilet facilities, first aid facilities, and clothing and project storage lockers are especially important.

Noise control. Every effort should be made to control noise at its source and to locate shops away from classrooms.

Radiant energy control. Control of radiant energy is necessary for activities such as casting in foundry operations, preheating in plastics forming, and flashes from electrical and welding operations. Protective equipment and clothing should be available both for students and instructors, and inspection should be given on their use.

Hand tools A large share of the accidents are due to faulty use of hand tools such as planes, screwdrivers, chisels and saws. Accordingly, it is important for instructors to see to it that students use the proper tools for the particular job. Using chisels for screwdrivers or the reverse often results in injuries. Sharp tools are safer than dull.

Machine and Power-driven Tools These must be properly installed from both a mechanical and an electrical point of view. Proper guards should be installed and used. Floor receptacles should be recessed and master and individual switch controls on each machine should be located within convenient reach of the student. Moreover, capacities of each machine should be posted on or near each piece of equipment.

Floor, Ramps and Walkways Floors should be treated to reduce the possibility of slipping. The same is true for ramps and walkways. Nonskid waxes are now available for wood and tile floors. In many cases, machines are installed in concrete or wood blocks where there is less danger of slipping.

Operation Controls In both industrial arts and vocational education, procedures should be posted for each piece of equipment and process. In addition, instruction regarding each of these should be given to all students before they begin work. The proper use of hand tools is especially important with beginners. Some schools require students to take safe practice tests in shops in which they are working. These are of value in themselves, and are also useful in case of liability suits against the school district or the instructor.

Regulations A schedule should be established for the maintenance of hand tools, machines and other pieces of power-driven equipment. There should be daily inspections of certain machines and periodic inspections of motors, electrical connections, furnaces, and other apparatus. Some of the daily inspections can be conducted by an appointed student safety inspector under the supervision of the teacher. Regulations regarding the use of machines should be posted and included in instructions and tests.

Housekeeping *School Shop: Learn Safe Work Habits Here* (8), a publication of the United States Department of Labor, points out that "good housekeeping is one of the most important factors in accident prevention. Orderliness and good housekeeping are fundamentals of good management."

Aisles and walkways should be unobstructed; materials and equipment properly stored; refuse should be stored and removed regularly; and provision should be made for the proper storing of projects—both those in progress and those completed.

Personal Protective Equipment In industrial arts the amount of protective equipment required is limited, but in vocational education it is essential to have equipment equivalent to that in many industries. Goggles should be used by persons working on grinders, hand saws, milling machines, and other machines. Hoods are essential for work with acids and certain other chemicals; helmets with goggles should be used in welding operations. In addition, loose clothing should not be allowed for persons working around machinery. Ties and rings should be removed and loose or flapping sleeves rolled back or secured.

Job Training and Safety The correct manner of performance should be taught with the pupils' first introduction to the activity, and continued through each subsequent experience. Only in this manner can safe habits and attitudes be integrated with school activities.

The job or operation should be broken down into its various steps, and each of the steps examined in terms of the hazards that may be associated with it. The instructor finally determines the controls that will assure safe and efficient operation.

Education for Safety Through the School Shop (4) includes descriptions of the use of tools and machines, with the safety precautions for each emphasized by being set in boldface type. An example is the following description of the use of the electric drill in auto mechanics:

> *Electric drill.* The portable electric drill has many uses, such as drilling, driving a hone, sanding or buffing disc or wire brush to remove carbon. In some cases it is mounted on a stand and used instead of a small drill press. Hold drill firmly and be prepared for it to cut through by reducing pressure. Use a small electric drill for light work and larger drill for heavy work. Do not overload drill, causing it to overheat. When drill is used to drive a hone it should be well supported and operator should be prepared for a heavy torque.
>
> **Always inspect extension cord for defects. Defective cords should be replaced or repaired at once. Be sure cord is not in a position to trip anyone or be run over by cars, jacks, or creepers. Protect eyes by wearing goggles**

while drilling. Leave drill in safe position when not in use. The drill casing should be grounded, preferably by means of a 3-wire conductor.

In preparing such descriptions it is a good policy to emphasize the safety precautions.

Pupil Organization Many schools use students as safety foremen or supervisors. They conduct inspections, check tools in and out, aid other students in selecting tools and equipment, and help them in their work. According to *School Shop: Learn Safe Work Habits Here* (8), when students take the initiative and participate, real learning takes place—students can provide aid in:

Program planning
Safety leadership
Inspections
Hazard hunts
Accident reporting
Analysis of accidents
Correcting physical hazards
Promoting safeguards
Promoting safe attitudes
Developing safe practice lists
Reports on safety topics
Preparation for emergencies
Role playing
Audio-visual aids
Student self-understanding

Safety Instruction Few parts of the school curriculum lend themselves to teaching safe practices as do industrial arts and vocational education. Safety instruction should be integrated into each of the activities. As the instructor explains the operation and demonstrates it, he should point out the hazards and the students should practice the operation under his supervision. Thus safety instruction is woven into the operation of all projects in the various shops.

Teachers should follow a regular pattern: (1) preparation, (2) explanation, (3) demonstration, (4) practice, (5) evaluation, and (6) review. Courses of study should include these steps, and should emphasize safe practices.

Evaluation of student achievement in terms of safety performance should be based largely on observation. However, it is difficult for the instructor to keep his eyes on 25 or more students. Other methods of evaluation may include tests of knowledge concerning tools and machine parts, skills and attitudes, progress reports, and the quality of projects completed.

Safety in Industry

Successful safety programs may differ considerably in emphasis among various companies. Some place great importance on mechanical guarding and safety engineering; others stress safe work practices through compliance with safety regulations; still others depend to a large extent on emotional appeals to workers and place their emphasis on human relations and positive personal motivation. Greatest success can be achieved from a personalized safety program designed and developed to meet the immediate and long-term needs of a particular industrial organization. Limited success will be achieved and much effort wasted if an attempt is made to adopt accident countermeasures indiscriminately without first identifying the specific current accident problem areas.

Figure 8:2, ORDERLY ARRANGEMENT OF MACHINERY AND GOOD HOUSEKEEPING REDUCES ACCIDENT EXPOSURE.

There can be no question about the value of an industrial safety program. From a financial standpoint alone safety efforts are beneficial. For smaller organizations operating with low profit margins, rate differentials for workmen's compensation insurance may mean the difference between operating at a profit or a loss. Other financial benefits include reduced medical costs, reduced operating costs because of less damage to equipment and produce, and increased production resulting where men can work without fear of personal injury. Less tangible benefits include higher employee morale, conservation of skills, maintenance of production capability, and improved public relations. The humanitarian aspects of personal injury prevention are also important.

Elements of a Safety Program

A well-organized safety program encompasses all phases of the environment and operations of an establishment and is basic to the prevention of industrial accidents. The kind of program and the emphasis placed on

BASIC ELEMENTS OF AN INDUSTRIAL SAFETY PROGRAM

1. Management Leadership. Top management must take an active and interested part in the development and operation of the safety program. Management's assumption of responsibility and declaration of policy are essential for continued success.

2. Assignment of responsibility. Management must definitely assign responsibility for various aspects of the safety program to the supervisors, workers, and the safety engineer. In particular the direct safety responsibilities of the first line supervisor must be emphasized.

3. Maintenance of safe working conditions. Plant layout, machine guarding, safe tools and equipment, materials handling, human factors engineering of man-machine-environment systems, and purchasing all contribute to a safe physical plant.

4. Employee selection, training, and placement. The qualifications of the man must match the demands of the job. Proper selection, training, and placement are essential to this objective.

5. Accident reporting and analysis. Accidents must be reported and analyzed so that contributing causal factors can be identified.

6. Selection and application of corrective actions. Actions required for eliminating the causal factors or minimizing the severity of their results must be selected and applied.

7. Measurement of safety performance. Measurement techniques must be applied to appraise the quality and effectiveness of accident prevention efforts and to serve as a basis for their ultimate prediction and control.

8. Adjustment and Reappraisal. Adjustments in programming components must be made based on the measured results.

each of its aspects will vary widely from plant to plant, depending on such factors as size, management interest, and the nature of the hazards inherent in the operations performed. Regardless of the type of operation, however, certain basic elements are incorporated into most safety programs. These elements are shown on p. 135.

Top management leadership All successful safety programs have one thing in common—active, aggressive leadership exercised by the top level of management. A climate of sincerity in accident prevention must exist at the top and be communicated downward through various levels of supervision until it reaches the man at the machine or workplace. The areas where direct management action is necessary include the following:

1. *Establishment of Policy.* Management must establish and publish an accident prevention policy. The policy should clearly state management's thoughts on safety and spell out how the safety program will operate. The policy should cover such items as: (1) the relationship of safety to production operations; (2) management's intent to provide a safe physical plant; (3) requirements for compliance with safety rules, including the use of personal protective equipment; (4) the organization of the staff safety activity; (5) the role of supervision in accident prevention; and other pertinent policy matters depending upon local conditions.
2. *Delegation of Authority.* The responsibility for the plant safety program should be placed as near the top as possible. In larger plants it is customary to delegate the actual administration of the safety program to a staff member who devotes his full time to it. In smaller plants, safety program administration may be a collateral duty carried on by someone with several primary assignments.
3. *The Safety Organization.* The safety director should function in a staff capacity as an advisor to management on matters pertaining to safety. He has no direct authority over line functions and "manages" no one except his own office staff. His authority is derived from his knowledge and his ability to perceive problems which others without his specialized orientation may not detect. He should be able to advise the operating officials and heads of operating departments on safety matters of interest to them. There should be a distinct separation between the line organization and the staff safety activity in the organization structure of the plant.
4. *Duties of The Safety Director.* The safety director's duties vary. The larger the plant, the more extensive is the program and the more numerous are the administrative duties delegated to him. Some of the safety director's tasks may include:
   a. Making periodic inspections of the plant and suggesting corrective measures to eliminate physical hazards.
   b. Assisting the first-line supervisor in his conduct of accident investigations.
   c. Studying work methods and analyzing jobs to detect potential accident problems.
   d. Prescribing safe work practices and assisting the first-line supervisor in training the employees to follow safe procedures.
   e. Maintaining records of accidents and analyzing the recorded information for accident causation.

f. Establishing a system of measurement for use in accident prediction and control.

g. Prescribing corrective action to be taken by line managers and supervisors in carrying out their responsibilities for accident prevention.

h. Appraising the results of the accident prevention program.

i. Establishing safety training programs for first-line supervisors.

j. Making periodic reports to top management and other line levels on the progress being made.

5. *Supervisor's Responsibility.* There is little doubt that the first-line supervisor is the key man in every safety program. The safety director *does not stop accidents.* Responsibility for accident prevention must go hand-in-hand with responsibility for production quantity and quality and for meeting production schedules. Safety cannot be thought of as something separate and apart from production. Both are the responsibility of line supervision. The supervisor may look to the safety director for detailed technical knowledge of *how* to prevent accidents but he cannot delegate to others the responsibility for seeing that the physical hazards in his department are eliminated, that safe work practices are used, or that the workers are properly supervised. The first-line supervisor is the keystone that supports the entire structure on which industrial safety is built.

6. *Determining the Results from Safety Measures.* Knowing the results of the efforts made to provide safe working conditions and to train workers in safe practices is important. Analysis of accident reports to determine the principal sources of injuries is one of the uses of accident records. However, information from accident records can be only as reliable as the reports on which the records are based. Most companies require the supervisor to report the details of accidental injuries and it is to his advantage that the reports be accurate and complete.

The over-all accident problem in a department may be gauged by comparison with past injury experience in the same department. A standard for use as a reference or guidline can be obtained by making a comparison with the injury experience of similar operations in other plants.

A standard method of measuring the accident experience of a department or plant has been established by the American Standards Association and is generally used by companies throughout the United States (1, 2). The standard system eliminates the problem of variations in amount of exposure to potential accident-producing situations by means of simple indexes called the frequency rate and the severity rate.

The frequency rate is defined as the number of disabling injuries per 1,000,000 man-hours worked. The number of man-hours is simply the total number of hours worked by all employees in a department or plant during a month, a year, or other period of time. The method of computing the frequency rate is shown in the following equation.

$$\text{Frequency rate} = \frac{\text{number of disabling injuries} \times 1{,}000{,}000}{\text{number of man-hours worked during the period}}$$

The frequency rate, it should be noted, measures only the occurrence of work injuries and does not take into account their severity. The time charge, expressed in days, is the basis for measuring the severity of injuries and it varies according to the type of disability, such as temporary total disability, permanent injuries, and death. The time charge for a temporary total disability is the number of calendar days of inability to work. A fixed schedule of charges is used for the permanent injuries and deaths since the actual time away from work does not provide a complete measure of their severity.

The severity rate is defined as the number of days charged for disabling injuries per 1,000,000 man-hours worked and is figured in a manner similar to the frequency rate.

$$\text{Severity rate} = \frac{\text{number of days charged} \times 1{,}000{,}000}{\text{number of man-hours worked during the period}}$$

Frequency and severity rates are computed for successive time periods and their upward or downward trends are used as indicators of accident prevention effectiveness.

Other indexes of safety performance include number of lost-time accidents, accident costs, number of no-injury accidents, frequency of vehicle accidents per standard number of miles driven, and the percentage of time a worker is involved in unsafe behavior.

Research has revealed new techniques which have improved our ability to measure safety performance. Our new measurement system is known as the critical incident technique. The critical incident technique was evaluated by Tarrants (20) to determine its usefulness as a method for identifying industrial accident causal factors. In applying this technique an interviewer questions a number of persons who have used a particular machine, performed a particular job, operated a particular piece of equipment, or worked in a particular environment, and asks them to recall within a specified time period errors they have made or observed and/or unsafe conditions they have observed in performing the operations concerned. The objective of the technique is to discover causal factors which are critical, that is, which have contributed to an accident. A collection of critical incidents is used to define problem areas for further accident prevention use. Often hazardous situations or frequently occurring unsafe acts can be detected and corrected before an actual major or minor injury occurs.

It has been shown that the critical incident technique dependably reveals causal factors in terms of errors and/or unsafe conditions which lead to accidents, identifies causal factors in both injurious and noninjurious accidents, reveals more information about accident causes than previously available methods of accident study, and provides a more sensitive measure of total accident performance.

Another technique for measuring noninjurious accidents (the so-called "near-misses") has been examined by Shreiber (18), Rockwell (17) and others. These experiments have applied the industrial engineering technique of work or activity sampling to the detection of unsafe behavior.

In one study (17) it was found that a group of eight workers was engaged in unsafe behavior 21 per cent of the time. When the safety engineer made an inspection of the area, the proportion of unsafe acts went down to three per cent. After the inspector left, the unsafe acts increased to the previous 21 per cent level within a few days. The effect of publicity campaigns, training programs, supervisor's safety talks, etc. on unsafe behavior might also be measured by this means.

Designing and Maintaining a Safe Environment

Since a safe and healthful place to work is of fundamental importance in the safety program, the mechanical, physical and environmental conditions should be given first consideration. This necessitates a thorough analysis of the plant layout, machinery, tools and equipment, materials handling facilities, housekeeping, maintenance operations, buildings and other structures work, environments, and materials used in manufacturing processes to determine where hazards may exist. Following this initial survey, a complete list should be made of all physical changes necessary either to eliminate the hazards or minimize the severity of their consequences. It is important that problems be detected in advance of injury or property damage losses insofar as possible.

Layout of the workplace The layout of a plant should be such that materials will flow through the various departments with a minimum of delay and backtracking. The more efficient the layout of machines and processes, the less movement of materials is involved and the less the likelihood of injury. The layout should provide adequate space around each machine so that materials being processed can be handled easily and safely. Adequate light and ventilation, sufficient room for maintenance operations, and provisions for anticipated expansion are also important factors.

Machine safeguarding Machine safeguarding involves the elimination of hazards from the transmission of power and from the point of operation where work is performed. Belts, pulleys, gears, clutches, couplings, shafts and flywheels are examples of items requiring guards. Points of operation include rotating mechanisms, cutting or shearing mechanisms, rotating mechanisms with in-running nip points, screw or worm mechanisms, and forming or bending mechanisms.

Safeguarding may be done in a number of ways—by fixed or barrier guards, by interlocking controls, by automatic feeding devices, by remote controls, and by sweep or pull-back devices. Methods best suited to the condition should be used. Much information is available on machine guarding in state safety codes and through nationally recognized sources such as the Association of Casualty and Surety Companies, the U. S. Department of Labor, and the National Safety Council (3, 7, 14).

Tools and equipment It is important that hand tools and equipment be maintained in a safe condition. Where tools are issued by the employer, safe tools can be assured by a system of tool inspection and maintenance by the toolroom operator. Tools owned and maintained by the workers should be inspected periodically by the supervisor. Examples of unsafe condition are mushroomed chisel heads, split hammer handles, sprung jaws, poorly sharpened or poorly set cutting heads, broken insulation, and lack of proper grounding facilities.

Materials handling facilities Injuries frequently occur in materials handling operations. Injuries from this source can be controlled by:

1. Substituting mechanical handling for manual handling.
2. Careful training of personnel in materials handling methods.

3. Strict adherence to established standards of height when stacking material, of aisle width, of power truck operation, etc.

Information about modern methods of materials handling can be found in several sources listed in the bibliography at the end of this Chapter (3, 5, 7, 10, 13, 19).

Housekeeping Housekeeping is concerned with the arrangement of materials in the stockroom and in the plant. It involves the disposal of scrap, the orderly flow of materials in process, and the physical condition of the workplace. Good housekeeping practices will lead to orderly production, reduce excessive materials handling, make the work more efficient, and generally contribute to accident reduction. Good housekeeping can best be accomplished by establishing standards and procedures for maintaining the physical environment in good order and by instituting positive control measures to assure that the standards are maintained.

Maintenance Maintenance in industry is primarily keeping production facilities in good operating condition and making repairs after breakdowns occur. Preventive maintenance goes a step further by requiring a periodic inspection of important parts of machines and equipment to detect wear and to make replacements when needed or to replace parts according to a predetermined life-cycle schedule. Both regular and preventive maintenance are important factors in sustaining safe environments.

Work areas Falls are one of the major contributors to industrial injuries. Usually falls occur as a result of unsafe working surfaces. The condition of floors, stairs, scaffolds, working platforms, ladders, etc. is of prime importance in maintaining a safe workplace. Falls on a level may be due to a slippery floor, unevenness of the floor surface, holes or depressions, obstacles in aisles, poor construction, or defective lighting. Falls from one level to another may result from inadequately guarded floor openings, unsafe ladders, unsafe scaffolds, or unsafe work practices.

> Accidents and Productivity
>
> There can be few more effective ways of improving productivity than by cutting down accidents at work. This can only be achieved by sustained and unremitting efforts by all concerned—management, supervisors, workers, trade unions.
>
> *John Mare, Minister of Labour, Great Britain*

Environmental Hazards

The control of health hazards in the work environment is an important part of providing a safe workplace. Health hazards often result from the nature of the work and the environment in which the work is performed. For example, work involving metal fabrication may be exceptionally noisy, and some operations may involve temperature extremes, while others may produce toxic dusts, gases, vapors, or fumes.

Many health hazards are more difficult to recognize and control than those involving only mechanical operations. It may be desirable to secure opinion on possible health hazards from specialists in occupational health or environmental hygiene. Information on occupational health problems is available from state labor departments, state departments of health, state industrial commissions, and from the Public Health Service of the U. S. Department of Health, Education and Welfare. Many states have safety and health codes covering industrial lighting, removal of air contaminants, sanitary facilities, and special activities such as spray painting.

Flammable materials and strong oxidizing agents present a problem of fire and explosion. Fire control methods are largely based on the idea of preventing the outbreak of fire, providing for its early detection, preventing its spread, and providing for prompt extinguishment. Vapors of some solvents are toxic in addition to being fire hazards. Even when the concentration of vapors is kept well under the lower limits at which they will explode, they may be too high for health. The lower explosive limit should not be used as a criterion for health hazards.

Limits have been established by the American Conference of Governmental Industrial Hygienists for the concentrations in air of the more frequently found industrial poisons. These are based on an assumed exposure of workers for a period of approximately eight hours per day for an indefinite period and are known as "threshold limits" or "maximum allowable concentrations" (MAC). Threshold limit values are useful as a guide for determining conditions which may be hazardous and which may require improved control measures (16, 19).

Human Factors Engineering

> Accidents are so varied in the circumstances attending them, with as many factors (including chance) contributing to their occurrence, *that no one factor can be expected to be prominent statistically.* In addition, it is necessary to reaffirm the importance of following up the results of laboratory investigations of accident type behavior by relevant exploration of the actual settings in which accidents occur.
>
> *Leon Brody in "Human Factors Research in Occupational Accident Prevention"*

A high percentage of accidents result from a combination of unsafe acts and conditions, seldom solely from either one. Many so-called "operator errors" have been touched off by faulty design or construction, operating practices that create hazards, or a lack of standardization and identification which so confuses the operator that he cannot avoid making mistakes. Accident investigators are often quick to classify accidents erroneously as having resulted solely from poor work practices, lack of judgment, inattention, or carelessness. A closer look at the causal factors will often reveal ways in which engineering can be applied to reduce both the frequency and the severity of operator errors. One approach to the development of safe working conditions has been given the title "human factors engineering."

Human factors engineering may be defined as "The application of the principles, laws, and quantitative relationships which govern man's response to external stress to the analysis and design of machines and other engineering structures, so that the operator of such equipment will not be stressed beyond his proper limit of capabilities (21)." The human factors engineering approach to the accident problem is to build machines and working areas around the operator, rather than place him in a setting without regard for his physiological and psychological requirements and capabilities.

In examining man-machine environment systems, primary attention is given to the human and how he interacts with equipment, machinery and environment. In broad terms, the goals of human factors engineering are human economy and efficiency. If this point of view were carried out in practice, fewer accidents should result, training costs would be reduced, and the necessity for extensive redesign of equipment after it is put into use should be eliminated.

Extensive research in this field is now being conducted under the sponsorship of both the federal government and private organizations. The results of much of this research may be found in the publication *Human Engineering Guide to Equipment Design* by Morgan, Cook, Chapanis and Lund (11). The application of human factors engineering techniques to industrial accident prevention is described in detail in a special report by Tarrants entitled "The Role of Human Factors Engineering in the Control of Industrial Accidents" which appeared in the *Journal of the American Society of Safety Engineers* (21).

Off-the-Job Accidents

The off-the-job accident problem deserves considerable attention by industrial managers, safety specialists, supervisors and key workers. At the present time, accidents occurring while the worker is away from the plant result in a greater loss of industrial manpower in the United States than do accidents occurring during working hours. For example, the National Safety Council reports that in a recent year there were 30,000 fatal injuries to workers off the job compared with 13,700 fatal injuries arising during or out of the course of employment in industry. For the same period, 2,250,000 nonfatal injuries occurred off the job as compared with 2,000,000 nonfatal injuries on the job (12).

These huge accident losses present a direct challenge to industrial managers to extend their accident prevention programs to off-the-job activities engaged in by their employees. Ideally, the influence of a plant safety program should not stop when the worker leaves the plant gate, but should extend throughout the time he is "on his own," whether he is driving his automobile, working in his own workshop, or engaging in recreational activities. Managements are beginning to realize that it costs just as much to hire and train a replacement for a worker injured off the job as it does for one injured at work.

One reason managers in general have been slow to adopt effective off-the-job accident prevention measures is that the costs of these accidents are largely indirect and thus are not reflected in premiums paid for workmen's compensation insurance. Other measures of accident results should be applied so that full consideration can be given to all identifiable loss sources. These losses may appear as the result of absenteeism, scrap loss, impaired employee efficiency because of injury, rework costs, production lags, disruption of work schedules, etc. All of these factors are deserving of consideration by the employer.

Off-the-Job Accidents

Noteworthy reductions in traffic accidents have been recorded for employees and their families by off-the-job safety programs. Many companies have found that off-the-job accidents outnumber on-job accidents by 10-1, 20-1, or even higher ratios. Traffic accidents account for over 60 per cent of the off-the-job deaths and 20 per cent of the injuries.

National Association of Independent Insurers,
the Insurance Information Institute, "Steps to Traffic Safety."

Consideration should be given to include off-the-job accident prevention as a part of the over-all plant safety program. The fundamental principles of safety are the same regardless of the setting in which they are applied. Good results are often achieved by joining with other local industries, community organizations, newspapers, radio and television stations, schools, etc. in developing a safety program to reach the employee through a number of different channels of communication. It is also important to recognize that activities which will help reduce accidents outside the plant may also contribute to their reduction inside the plant. The primary need at the present time is for every supervisor to orient his thinking to include off-the-job safety as one of his accident prevention concerns.

summary

The number of wage earners in the United States is well over 70 million and increasing year by year. The largest percentage of these are in industry, but there are also many millions in nonindustrial occupations. In the last two decades, while there has been a steady downward trend in deaths in industrial accidents, the total cost of accidents in a recent year exceeded $5 billion dollars.

The industrial arts and vocational education program of the public schools and colleges builds a safety foundation in certain basic activities such as woodworking, electrical shop, auto mechanics, metal work and, in rural areas, agriculture and ranching. The schools have taken advantage of the controls and safe practices developed in industry. As a result, serious accidents are comparatively rare.

A well-organized safety program encompasses all phases of the environment and operations of an establishment and is basic to the prevention of industrial accidents. Such a program requires top management leadership; delegation of authority; a safety organization; maintenance of safe working conditions; employee selection, training and placement; accident reporting and analysis; corrective action; and measurement of safety performance.

Human factors engineering has become highly important since it has been found that such a large percentage of accidents are due to errors on the part of the worker.

In addition, off-the-job accident prevention is being given more and more attention by industries. It has been found that several times as many accidental deaths occur off the job as on the job. Many industries have had unusual success in reducing these accidents.

suggested projects and activities

1. Outline a comprehensive accident prevention program designed to control accident losses within an industrial company. Indicate how a safety program should be integrated into management functions.
2. Discuss the role of the safety engineer or safety specialist in a large manufacturing plant. In what ways might this role change in a small plant? What changes in the safety engineer's role do you envision might occur as a result of technological advances in industry?
3. What role does the first-line supervisor play in the prevention of industrial accidents? What contributions to a safe industrial climate should be made by top and middle-level managers?
4. What methods are currently used to measure accident performance in industry? Discuss the merits and limitations of each method. Suggest improved techniques for identifying accident problems and measuring the effectiveness of accident prevention efforts.
5. Discuss a procedure for designing and maintaining a safe work environment. Develop a safety inspection check-list for use by the supervisor as a means of systematically reviewing his potential accident problems.
6. Discuss the role of human factors engineering in the control of industrial accidents.
7. Arrange for a field trip to an industry in the area and observe the precautions taken to protect employees. Make a comparison between the safety practices in this industry and in school shops.

8. Prepare a job sheet which includes the recommended safe practices.
9. Develop a series of safe practices that could be used with one machine such as a handsaw, a lathe or a grinder.
10. What are some of the safety characteristics that industries would like to see in prospective employees graduating from a high school?

selected references

1. American Standards Association, *Standard Method of Recording and Measuring Work Injuries,* Z 16.1-1954, R. 1959. New York: The Association, 1959.
2. ________, *Classifying Accident Causes,* Z 16.2-1963. New York: The Association, 1963.
3. Association of Casualty and Surety Companies, *Handbook of Industrial Safety Standards,* 10th Rev. New York: The Association, 1962.
4. ________, and New York University, Center for Safety Education, *Education for Safety through the School Shop.* New York: The Association, 1952.
5. Blake, R. P., *Industrial Safety* (3rd ed.). Englewood Cliffs, N.J.: Prentice-Hall, Inc., 1963.
6. Blum, Milton I., *Industrial Psychology and Social Foundations.* New York: Harper & Row, Publishers, 1956.
7. Bureau of Labor Standards, U. S. Department of Labor, *Safety in Industry Series:*
   Bulletin 216: *Control of Electrical Shock Hazards,* 1960.
   Bulletin 219: *Mechanical Handling of Materials,* 1960.
   Bulletin 231: *Personal Protective Equipment,* 1961.
   Bulletin 232: *Fire Protection for the Safety Man,* 1961.
   Bulletin 239: *Mechanics for the Safety Man,* 1962.
   Bulletin 246: *Maintenance and Safety,* 1962.
   Bulletin 207: *Controlling Noise Hazards,* 1959.
   Bulletin 222: *Chemistry for the Safety Man,* 1960.
   Bulletin 226: *Respiratory Protective Equipment,* 1961.
   Bulletin 211: *Control of the Physical Environment,* 1960.
   Bulletin 223: *The Consultative Approach to Safety,* 1960.
   Bulletin 247: *The Fundamentals of Accident Prevention,* 1962.
   Washington D.C.: U. S. Government Printing Office.
8. Bureau of Labor Standards, U. S. Department of Labor, and the U. S. Department of Health, Education, and Welfare, *School Shop: Learn Safe Work Habits Here.* Washington, D.C.: U. S. Government Printing Office, 1958.
9. DeReamer, R., *Modern Safety Practices.* New York: John Wiley & Sons, Inc., 1958.
10. Heinrich, H. W., *Industrial Accident Prevention* (4th ed.). New York: McGraw-Hill Book Company, 1959.
11. Morgan, C. T., J. S. Cook, A. Chapanis, and M. W. Lund, *Human Engineering Guide to Equipment Design.* New York: McGraw-Hill Book Company, 1963.

12. National Safety Council, *Accident Facts.* Chicago: The Council, 1963.
13. ———, *Accident Prevention Manual for Industrial Operations* (5th ed.). Chicago: The Council, 1964.
14. ———, *Safety Data Sheets:* No. 50: *Safety In the General Metals Shops,* 1951. No. 53: *Safety in the Machine Shop,* 1951. No. 6: *Cutting Implements,* 1952. No. 79: *Coordinating Safety in Industrial and Vocational Education Programs,* 1957. No. 87: *Safety in the Electrical Shop,* 1958. Chicago: The Council.
15. ———, *Supervisor's Safety Manual* (2nd ed.). Chicago: The Council, 1960.
16. Patty, F. A., *et al., Industrial Hygiene and Toxicology,* Vol. I. New York: Interscience Publishers, Inc., 1958.
17. Rockwell, T. H., "Safety Performance Measurement," *Journal of Industrial Engineering,* Vol. 10 (Jan.-Feb., 1959) 12–16.
18. Schreiber, R. J., "The Development of Procedures for the Evaluation of Educational Methods Used in Accident Prevention." Unpublished doctor's dissertation, Columbia University, 1957.
19. Simonds, R. H. and Grimaldi, J. V., *Safety Management* (Rev. ed.). Homewood, Ill.: Richard D. Irwin, Inc., 1963.
20. Tarrants, W. E., "An Evaluation of the Critical Incident Technique as a Method for Identifying Industrial Accident Causal Factors." Unpublished doctor's dissertation, New York University, 1963.
21. ———, "The Role of Human Factors Engineering in the Control of Industrial Accidents," *Journal of the American Society of Safety Engineers,* Vol. VIII, No. 2 (Feb., 1963), 9–26.
22. ———, "Engineering as a Foundation for Optimum Safety Success," *Journal of the American Society of Safety Engineers,* Vol. VI, No. 4 (Oct., 1961), 23–28.

9

fire prevention and protection

Fire has been of great service to man. In one form or another, it heats our homes and cooks our food; it powers our industries, railroads, steamships and motor cars. From fire, electricity is produced that operates the appliances and devices used in our homes, in industry and in commerce. It speeds our jets across the country and thrusts our missiles into orbit. It enters into practically everything we do and is an important source of energy. *Fire is one of our greatest servants.*

On the other hand, uncontrolled fire kills over 11,000 persons each year in the United States besides injuring several hundred thousand; it devastates hundreds of thousands of acres of forest and grazing lands; it burns hundreds of thousands of homes and farm buildings; it damages countless automobiles, motor boats, and aircraft. Fire out of control may ruin many blocks of buildings in a city. In a single year, it destroys over a billion dollars worth of property. *Uncontrolled fire is a bad master.*

Nature of the Fire Problem

> Increases in Fire Losses
>
> According to the National Board of Fire Underwriters, fire losses have increased steadily since 1940.
>
> During that year the loss was $286 million, but in a recent year it was four times greater, more than $1,200 million.

Over a period of years, according to the National Board of Fire Underwriters, the annual property loss from fire in the United States has averaged over $700 million. Moreover, there are many indirect losses. In industry, fire may deprive management of a part of its physical plant and its earning power, while the worker loses wages. The destruction of buildings decreases the sources of tax revenue. The devastation of forests burns up valuable timber, and often affects the water supply. Moreover, the cost of operating and maintaining fire departments alone is over a billion dollars a year. There are also the insurance costs which amount to hundreds of millions of dollars.

What percentage of fires is preventable? This is a difficult question to answer. Leading authorities estimate that it might be more than 80 per cent. But this is a high percentage and such prevention would not be possible unless every force in the community stepped up its fire-prevention and protection activities. One of the necessary elements for reaching this objective is a knowledge and understanding of the situations from which fires arise. In this chapter some of these situations will be considered; for a more detailed treatment, the references at the end of the chapter should be consulted.

The Chemistry of Fire

Three things must be present for a fire to occur: (1) fuel, (2) oxygen, and (3) heat or a source of ignition. We are familiar with the burning of materials like paper, matches, oil, and grease. But many other substances, such as metals, will also burn under the right conditions. For example, the oxyacetylene blowtorch will burn through a steel beam. Many of the common metals such as aluminum, lead, and tin will burn at high temperatures, especially when the oxygen is concentrated. That is why liquid oxygen is used with certain types of fuels in rockets and missile boosters. However, *oxygen* alone cannot cause a fire. There must be *fuel,* and *heat* or *ignition.* Substances left in the open air will not burn until a kindling temperature is reached. This kindling temperature may be brought about in various ways: by chemical action, friction, sparks, flames, electricity, the sun's rays, or by lightning. Many substances, such as alcohol, gasoline and benzine vaporize and their flashpoints are much lower than their kindling temperatures.

Ordinary burning is one form of oxidization. Another form is so rapid that an explosion occurs as in the case of gunpowder and dynamite. Another illustration is the explosion of the mixture of gasoline and air in the cylinder of the automobile engine. A third type of oxidation is very slow, sometimes resulting in spontaneous combustion. Fermentation is a form of oxidation, and produces heat. When this heat reaches a certain temperature, the hay may start to smoke and may burst into flames. Similar chemical action will produce heat in rags that are soaked with linseed and soybean oil or grease. Dairy foods, grains and fodder are also subject to spontaneous combustion when stored without adequate ventilation. Even on a cold winter day when the surface of a pile of sawdust is frozen, if one digs several feet into the pile he will find the sawdust warm or even hot; the sawdust is fermenting. Piles of soft coal and charcoal are subject to the same action. Hay should not be stored in a barn unless it is dry. Farmers sometimes throw salt on damp hay to reduce oxidation and the dangers of fire. Each year millions of dollars worth of property is destroyed as a result of spontaneous combustion.

Combustion Products Highly Dangerous

The products of combustion include a variety of gases, depending on the nature of the substance which is burning and the flow of oxygen. Three of these products are carbon dioxide, carbon monoxide, and water vapor. The second of these is a deadly poison and is given off extensively when combustion is incomplete because of insufficient oxygen. There are, however, several other poisonous fumes that are also dangerous. According to Paul W. Kearney in an article in *Family Safety,* (6), "a surprising fact is that very, very few of our 12,000 annual fire victims actually 'burn to death.' In the opinion of case-hardened firemen, most of them die without knowing there is a fire; their bodies often don't have a mark on them. . . ."

Two things happen in a fire:

1. The products of combustion, being lighter than air, rise and are swept throughout the building by convection.
2. The products of distillation, being heavy, sink to the lowest level.

One of the products of distillation which hugs the floor is hydrocyanic gas, a deadly poison. Kearney urges that in case of fire, rather than crawling out of a building because the air near the floor is the coolest, it would be better to *crouch* and run out of the room. However, the National Safety Council still favors covering the nose and mouth with a wet handkerchief and crawling.

It is a striking fact that in the LaSalle Hotel fire, superheated air which originated on the first floor suffocated persons on the upper floors. On the 17th floor, rooms with open transoms were gutted, while on the same floor, rooms with closed transoms were unharmed. All 61 victims of the disaster were asphyxiated by combustion gases while approximately 80 per cent of the bodies were untouched by flames.

Regarding fires in the home, Kearney makes several suggestions:

1. Don't open a door when there is a fire until you first feel it with the palm of your hand. If the wood is hot, don't open that door.
2. Always plan a home so that there are several methods of getting out in case of fire.
3. Be sure to have a method of escape from every room in the house, especially the attic.
4. Don't sleep with the bedroom doors open, but be sure a window is open.

Causes of Fire

In a recent year, according to facts provided by the National Fire Prevention Association (17), there were 890,000 building fires. The total fire loss was over 1.1 billion dollars. The following were the most common causes:

Smoking and matches.
Defective heating equipment.
Electricity.
Open flames and sparks.
Flammable liquid and explosions.
Defective and overhead chimneys.
Rubbish.
Children and matches.
Spontaneous ignition.

In addition to fires in buildings, there were over 103,000 forest fires. Fires also involved 229,000 motor vehicles, 160 aircraft, and 21,900 miscellaneous locations. The total number of fires was 1.2 million with a property loss of $1.5 billion. Residential fires were by far the most numerous of the building fires with a total of 627,000, followed by storage (including barns), 111,000; industrial, 47,000; mercantile, 48,000; public buildings 31,500; and miscellaneous, 21,000. In the last decade, the trend in the number of fires and the losses has been upward.

Matches and Smoking It is surprising that so many fires are caused by the careless use of matches and smoking. Each week almost every local newspaper will carry one or more stories about fires of this type. The following is an illustration:

Four Members of a Family Meet Death When Home Burns

Four members of the family of J. B. Williams of Washington Avenue, in St. Paul, were burned to death on October 12 when their home was destroyed by fire. This included Mrs. Williams and her three children, the father being out of town on business. It appears that the fire started in the living room from a cigarette thrown into a wastebasket. It spread rapidly through the house enveloping the stairway and the second floor. Apparently, Mrs. Williams and the children met death through smoke inhalation.

Many fires occur when people fall asleep while smoking in bed. Others are started because of carelessness with matches. Dangers can be minimized if the following precautions are observed:

1. Never smoke in bed or when relaxing on a couch or chair and apt to fall asleep.
2. Never throw away a burning match. Be certain that the match is out and break it in two.
3. Keep matches in metal or earthenware containers and out of the reach of children.
4. Never carry loose matches in the pocket. Do not strike them in closets or fuel storage bins.
5. Always strike a match away from yourself. If it breaks, or the head flies off, it will not be likely to set your clothing on fire.
6. Never try to locate gas leaks or examine tanks with a lighted match. Use a flashlight.

Electricity and Appliances Many fires have electrical origins. For the most part the causes are defective wiring, bad insulation, poor switches, overloading and amateur wiring. Other fires are caused by lack of care in using appliances such as irons, toasters and hot plates. Only approved cords, switches and other fixtures should be used. Under no circumstances should blown fuses (15 ampere) be replaced with coins or other substitutes. A blown fuse indicates either a short or an overloaded circuit; to replace it with anything but a new 15 ampere fuse would cause an already overheated wire to become hot enough to cause a fire. In recent years, circuit breakers have been installed in many homes in place of fuses. Irons and other appliances should be equipped with automatic shutoffs to prevent overheating, and they should be disconnected when not in use.

In many instances houses built a generation ago have inadequate wiring. Electric clothes driers, washing machines, irons, air conditioners and stoves require additional electric current. It is usually best to modernize a home by having new wiring installed. The possibilities of fires from electrical causes will be reduced if only electrical equipment bearing the Underwriters Laboratories label of approval is used, and wiring is installed by qualified electricians.

Lightning When we think of the number of thunderstorms that occur annually in the country, the area which they cover, and the number of times lightning strikes the earth, they do not appear to be very dangerous. During a year, about 600 persons are killed and 1,500 injured by lightning. Nine out of ten of the victims are sportsmen, vacationers or farmers. It is said that lightning will strike a given point only once in 100 years, unless it is a tall structure like a skyscraper or a radio tower, a tall tree, or other object which is higher than its surroundings. A tall steel structure may be struck many times during a year. Lightning is one of the evidences of the tremendous forces of nature; a single bolt may contain millions of volts and up to 200,000 amperes.

Lightning is highly destructive, costing more than $50 million yearly besides the losses from forest fires. It can be rendered nearly harmless to wooden buildings by the installation of lightning rods. Radio or television antennae do not have heavy enough wire to act as lightning rods and should always be grounded. Danger spots for people out of doors include such places as under a tree, near a wire fence, in the water or on a high elevation. Two of the safest places to be are in a steel skyscraper or in a house equipped with lightning rods.

Radio and Television Many recent developments such as radio and television have created new fire hazards for the home. Some fires are caused by lightning striking the aerial; others by overheated sets. Still others are caused by power lines coming in contact with antennae, usually during heavy storms. Outside antennae should never be located near power lines. In addition, an approved lead-in wire should be used and a well-grounded, approved lightning arrester should be installed. It should also be remembered that a television set, even when disconnected, has a high voltage charge. Before attempting to make repairs this voltage should be discharged, for it is enough to cause a severe shock.

Flammable Materials There are a number of new materials that are of a flammable nature. This includes those made of a pyroxylin compound and those made of cotton, camphor, and certain acids. Some of these ignite if heated above the boiling point of water. Combs, hairpins, toys, knife and fork handles, baskets, trays, and the like which are made of celluloid pyralin, fibuloid or French ivory should be kept away from fires and hot substances. The same could be said for regular nitrate motion-picture film. Such film, when ignited, burns rapidly and gives off stifling fumes. Safety or acetate film, which is no more combustible than ordinary paper, should always be used by amateurs, and in other than regulation booths. It is urged that Christmas trees and materials used in decorations or displays be made fire-resistant by dipping or spraying with fireproofing liquids.

Rubbish and Open Fires Many buildings have accumulations of waste materials, which are ideal sources of fire. Broken furniture, old newspapers, boxes, clothing, oil, wax and other combustibles should be stored in places where heat from a furnace or chimney, a spark from a cigarette, or spontaneous ignition will not set them aflame. Attics, closets and basements should be cleaned regularly. Many school building fires originate in basements where combustibles are stored. In a recent typical year, over 60,000 rubbish fires occurred. Many fires are also caused through improper screening of open fireplaces and by failure to extinguish camp and picnic fires. Fireplace screens are a *must* if fireplaces are to be used.

Another common cause of fires in homes and barns is the burning of brush, leaves, and dead grass. Hundreds of homes and farm buildings are destroyed each year from this cause. If there is a heavy wind, fires of this kind often get out of control. It is always best to have fire control equipment present when burning brush or grass. Several years ago, hundreds of beautiful shore residences were destroyed when forest fires got out of control in Bar Harbor, Maine. Other forest fires have destroyed valuable property in California, at New Jersey shore resorts and in Staten Island, New York.

Fires in Schools Over a period of years, more than 1,000 deaths have occurred in some 90 school fires. In fact, it is estimated that each year 3,400 fires occur which endanger the lives of pupils and teachers (16). In many cases these are in dormitories or wooden residences that lack proper safeguards and where no regular fire exit drills are held. Many of these fires originate from improper heating and ventilating equipment, electric wiring and appliances, or gas piping and appliances. Others start in school shops, laboratories, lunchrooms and storage areas.

One of the worst school fires was the New London, Texas, explosion of gas which resulted in the death of 294 persons. A recent school disaster occurred in Chicago when the Lady of Angels School burned, with a loss of 94 lives.

Heating Units Serious fires may result when stoves and furnaces are improperly installed, overheated, or defective. Stoves and furnaces should be kept away from woodwork, and nearby flammable surfaces should be protected by asbestos or metal sheathing. Floors under furnaces should be made of concrete, brick, or tile. The furnace pipe and furnace should be inspected frequently. This applies to furnaces burning gas, coal or oil. Where the pipes pass through floors or walls, double-walled metal thimbles of at least three-inch radial thickness should be used.

The use of oil and gas stoves and furnaces presents fire hazards requiring additional care. The burners of oil stoves should be cleaned regularly and boiled occasionally in a strong solution of lye or washing soda and water. It is also best to fill oil supply tanks during daylight hours and never near an open fire or light. Oil fuel should be stored in an outer shed or in underground tanks some distance away from buildings. Special precautions should be used in the handling of portable oil heaters since they may be easily overturned or the handle may give way while they are being moved.

Each year the fire loss from overheated or defective chimneys runs well over $30,000,000. The deficiencies are largely due to improper construction. Chimneys should be built solidly with a stable foundation on concrete laid in the ground. The flue should be lined with tile, fire clay, or other approved material. Where chimneys pass through the roof or floor they should be surrounded with at least two inches on all sides with loose cinders, plaster, or mortar.

Chimneys should be inspected regularly for cracks, rust spots or overheating. Soot accumulates where soft coal or wood is burned, but gas and oil fuels leave little residue. Salt, sand or ashes should be used to extinguish chimney fires.

Petroleum Products, Gases, Fats, Polishes Many fires result from the burning of flammable oils and gases, especially petroleum products such as gasoline and kerosene. In fact, nearly all of the fires in motor boats and automobiles involve gasoline. Petroleum products should be stored in tanks or cans to prevent their coming in contact with air, sparks, or flames. Gasoline, for example, has a flashpoint of —45 degrees Fahrenheit, which means that it vaporizes at a temperature as low as 45 degrees below zero.

Gasoline vapor is heavier than air, and it seeks the lowest level avail-

Figure 9:1, INSPECTOR REVEALS FIRE HAZARDS.

able, often getting far from its source. Sometimes leaks from tanks at filling stations run into sewer lines and explosions may occur 100 or more feet from the tank. Because of the highly explosive nature of gasoline vapors, extreme care should be used in handling the liquid. At one time service stations used to clean floors with gasoline. Regulations now prohibit this, and nonflammable cleaning mixtures are used instead. When gasoline is used about the home, it should be stored either in underground tanks or in small quantities in safety containers approved by the Underwriters Laboratories.

Fires in motor boats are due to several causes. Some result from leaks in the gas tank, the gasoline vapor being ignited by a match or a spark. Others occur when the boat is being refueled. Gasoline vapor sinks down to the bottom of the boat where it may be ignited. It is essential that there be good ventilation when the boat is taking on fuel. Other fires result from backfires. Because of the serious dangers of fire, all motor boats should carry at least one fire extinguisher. This should be not the carbon tetrachloride type, but preferably the foam or carbon dioxide type.

Kerosene is considerably less dangerous than gasoline, but under certain conditions can cause severe damage. When poured on live coals or wood embers, it has sometimes resulted in serious explosions. When it is used as a fuel oil in heaters, stoves and lamps, it should be poured well away from open flames and fire.

Other Fuels Gases, both natural and manufactured, are widely used for cooking and heating. Since some of these gases are odorless, they normally are treated to give off a smell that will reveal their presence. To guard against asphyxiation and explosions, only odorized gas should be used, and good ventilation should be provided. Appliances and equipment should be checked periodically for leaks and loose connections. In case of doubt, the gas company or the fire department should be called.

Cooking Oils and Grease Many fires are caused by the spilling of oils or grease over a fire. Since these substances burn easily, care must be exercised in frying and broiling foods. If oils or fats ignite, flames may be extinguished with sand, baking soda, salt or a metal cover. Never use water, because it spreads the flaming grease and increases the possibility of damage.

Aircraft A study of accidents in transport and military aircraft, reveals that many of the deaths are caused by fires. Most of these are crash fires which result when the aircraft, out of control, strikes the ground. The gasoline or jet fuel is ignited and the occupants burn to death. A much smaller number of fires occur when the aircraft is in flight.

There are many different causes of aircraft fires, including overheated motors, electrical short circuits, lightning, backfires, leaking fuel, frictional heat developed when nose-wheel strut skids along the concrete runway following a crash landing, and electrostatic sparks.

Atomic Explosions When ordinary munitions such as nitroglycerine or dynamite explode, high temperatures result. But these temperatures do not compare with those of an atomic explosion which may reach millions of degrees Fahrenheit. At the bombing of Hiroshima, glass, metals, concrete, in fact practically everything turned into a vapor, because of the tremendous heat. Scientists, however, have found ways in which the speed of nuclear fission can be reduced so that reactors can be used in electric power plants, submarines and steamships. Special precautions must be taken in fighting fires resulting from nuclear action.

Fire Protection

Building Construction and Inspection

Faulty construction and inspection of buildings results in many fires. For this reason the National Board of Fire Underwriters has spent a great deal of time on the development of standards for all types of construction, including schools, churches, factories, grain elevators and dozens of other kinds of structures. The National Fire Protection Association has also been active in the development of standards; their publication, *Fire Prevention Handbook,* lists over 100 national fire codes covering every conceivable kind of operation in industries, in homes, on farms and in transportation. As a result of these standards, the various states and cities

Figure 9:2, Fire Destroys Thousands of Homes Each Year.

Figure 9:3, Industrial Fires Result in a Loss of Hundreds of Millions of Dollars Each Year. Sparks From a Conveyer Belt Resulted in the Total Loss of This Mill.

have also developed building codes. For illustration, when a builder constructs an apartment house there are certain standards he must meet regarding electric wiring, incinerators, water supply, fire extinguishers, roof coverings, ventilation, chimneys, heating plants, air conditioning, exits, and the like. It is the responsibility of the building inspector to see that the builder follows the specifications of the codes.

However, while carefully built concrete and steel structures may be fireproof, the furnishings in such a building, furniture, carpets, drapes, bedding and the like are flammable and can burn just as easily as in a frame building. Fortunately, many school buildings have desks, chairs and other equipment made of metal, so that the danger of fire is reduced. The same is true of new industrial plants. In most towns and cities, when dwelling houses are constructed inspectors make certain that the various codes are followed. The codes may set standards for electrical installation, fire walls, heaters, fuel tanks, gas installation, and the like. Fire protection standards and inspection have done much to reduce the dangers of fire.

Fire Alarm and Sprinkler Systems

Many buildings, especially in industries, use automatic fire detection equipment. It could be used in schools and apartment houses especially in boiler and storage rooms. Many buildings have installed sprinkler systems. These are especially useful in industries, warehouses, farms, stores and boiler rooms in apartment houses, and could be used in homes. In the sprinkler system, heat from a fire melts a metal fuse, allowing water to spray over the area. Many fires are extinguished by sprinkler systems before the fire department arrives.

Fire Fighting

Fire departments today are greatly improved over those of a generation ago. Apparatus is much more efficient and fire-fighting techniques have been greatly improved. Training programs for both volunteer and paid firemen have resulted in more efficient operations.

Figure 9:4,
BALTIMORE FIREMEN DEMONSTRATE DIFFERENT TYPES OF EXTINGUISHERS.

It is essential that everyone knows what to do in case of fire. If the fire is in a home, the first thing to do is to get all members of the family out of the house and call the fire department. In case a fire is reported at a fire alarm box, the person making the report should wait to direct the firemen to the fire.

Fire departments use different types of extinguishers. For small fires they will depend on CO_2 or foam types. For the larger fires, they will generally use water. In buildings supplied with running water, fire-fighting equipment such as standpipes, water towers, and automatic sprinklers will be used. In rural homes and communities not served by running water, such simple precautions as placing pails filled with water or sand at strategic places should be taken. Moreover, if there is water pressure in the farm house and barn, hose connections should be available. In boys' and girls' camps, the usual practice is to have pails of water or sand attached to a hook outside each cabin.

All vehicles used for public transportation should carry fire extinguishers, and every passenger car and motor boat should have at least one. The types of extinguishers are shown in figure 9:5.

Fire Drills

Exit drills are an integral part of the schools' fire safety programs. "The principal should establish in the minds of pupils an awareness of the need for rapid and efficient exit drills," according to *School Fires—Prevention, Control, Protection* (19). He should also point out that fires are not always discovered immediately, thus leaving little time for evacuation. Normally, it takes one minute to evacuate each floor of a school building, or three minutes to empty a three-story building.

The exit drill should be a learning experience and should be planned to meet various situations. One situation might be with all students in the auditorium. Another might be the sounding of the fire alarm when students are passing from one class to another. Many states require at least one fire drill a month. The principal should make certain that all school personnel know where each alarm station is located.

The plan for the school, according to *School Fires* (19) should do the following:

Designate normal evacuation from all areas of the building and establish alternate routes in case the ordinary routes cannot be used.

Provide blocked exit drills.

Insure rapid, orderly evacuation of all occupants.

Permit two teachers in adjacent rooms to combine their groups so that one teacher can lead the children and the other maintain order along the line for the two groups.

Train pupils to leave the building in an orderly fashion without teacher supervision if necessary.

Insure adequate care of handicapped pupils and teachers.

Specify definite outside assembly areas or stopping points at least 50 feet from fire hydrants for each group as well as rapid roll call after evacuation.

Designate staff members to check toilets and other areas for pupils who may not be at their regular stations at the time of evacuation.

Instruct students in physical education classes as to desirable procedures concerning street clothes.

Provide for window and door closure, and for turning off motors, burners and gas valves.

Caution against retrieval of personal belongings.

Give explicit instructions as to line of authority.

Instruct the children concerning future school activities in case the building must be abandoned temporarily.

Designate key personnel (not students) to re-enter the building, if feasible, to do first aid fire fighting.

Provide instruction to students and teachers for crossing streets or highways in case positions become untenable on school grounds.

	WATER TYPE			
	STORED PRESSURE	CARTRIDGE OPERATED	WATER PUMP TANK	SODA ACID
CLASS A FIRES wood, paper trash-having glowing embers	YES	YES	YES	YES
CLASS B FIRES flamable liquids, gasoline, oil, paints, grease, etc.	NO	NO	NO	NO
CLASS C FIRES electrical equipment	NO	NO	NO	NO
USUAL OPERATION	Squeeze handle or turn valve	Turn upside down and bump	Pump handle	Turn upside down
RANGE	30'-40'	30'-40'	30'-40'	30'-40'
SERVICE BY	Check air pressure	Weigh gas cartridge add water if required	Discharge and fill with water annually	Discharge annually -recharge

Figure 9:5.

1. The common hand extinguisher, the soda-acid type, is a 2½-gallon container filled with a solution of bicarbonate of soda and water, above which is suspended a small bottle of sulphuric acid. When the extinguisher is inverted, the acid is released to mix with the soda solution, forming carbon dioxide gas, which forces the water solution from the container. This type of extinguisher is suitable for ordinary wood, rubbish, and brush fires.

2. The foam extinguisher, from which the extinguishing agent is expelled, operates on the same principle as the soda-acid type, but devolops a thick foam that may be used to smother brush, rubbish, and particularly oil fires.

3. Carbon tetrachloride extinguishers contain a liquid which, when

	FOAM	CARBON DIOXIDE	DRY CHEMICAL
	FOAM	CO2	DRY CHEMICAL
CLASS A FIRES wood, paper trash-having glowing embers	NO (but will control small fires)	NO (but will control small surface fires)	NO (but will control small surface fires)
CLASS B FIRES flamable liquids, gasoline, oil, paints, grease, etc.	YES	YES	YES
CLASS C FIRES electrical equipment	NO	YES	YES
USUAL OPERATION	Turn upside down	Rupture cartridge-squeeze release	Rupture cartridge-squeeze release
RANGE	30'-35'	2'-4'	6'-12'
SERVICE BY	Discharge annually -recharge	Weigh semi-annually	Weigh gas cartridge-check condition of dry powder

heated, turns into gas to form a blanket over the fire, thereby shutting off the oxygen supply. This type of extinguisher should be used for electrical, grease, and chemical fires, but should not be relied upon to put out serious fires.

4. The carbon dioxide extinguisher has proven to be effective in blanketing and smothering all classes of fires. Since it is a nonconductor of electricity, it is quite effective on Class C fires—fires involving electrical equipment.

5. The dry chemical type, in which a talc type powder is expelled by compressed gas, is becoming more and more popular. Like carbon dioxide, it can be used on all classes of fire, but it is most effective on flammable liquids and electrical fires.

Forest Fires

Millions of acres of valuable forest and grazing land are destroyed each year by fire. One great fire in Idaho in the early 1900's burned over 30 million acres and resulted in the loss of 85 lives. Forest fires not only result in the loss of valuable timber and by-products, but also affect the flow of streams in the area and may result in floods. It is very important to protect the great forests at the headwaters of our rivers. Fires also kill animal and vegetable life and the heat may be so great that it burns up the soil humus so that it is years before young trees will grow again. They also destroy our natural scenery, as anyone who has seen the results of a fire will attest. Who can estimate the loss when a total forest area as great as one of our large states is burned?

According to Davis in *Forest Fire—Control and Use* (5) "There are about 125,000 forest fires annually in the United States. Of these approximately 92 per cent are caused by man. The rest are started by lightning for which no effective means of prevention have yet been devised." According to the U. S. Forest Service the most important causes of forest fires are: campfires, burning debris, incendiarism, lightning, lumbering, railroads, matches and smoking. Nearly 90 per cent of those caused by lightning occur in the Rocky Mountain and Pacific states.

Various methods are being used to prevent fires. Since so many are caused by man efforts are being made to educate people in fire prevention. In addition to the work being done by the schools, the scouting organizations and farm groups have active programs in forest conservation. National and state forest services are using signs, posters, exhibits and other devices. Articles appear in newspapers, magazines and pamphlets, while radio, motion pictures and television are also being used. Many of these media feature "Smokey the Bear."

The Forest and Conservation Services have developed many techniques for locating and fighting fires. Thousands of rangers have been assigned to state and national forests. Aircraft are being used to locate fires and, when possible, to land rangers to extinguish them before they get out of control. It is not possible to include in this brief discussion the many interesting methods that have been devised for fighting fires. Those who are interested may consult the references at the end of this chapter.

Instruction

Most schools arrange some type of program for Fire Prevention Week, which is designated in October of each year by the President. During recent years there has been an effort to include fire prevention lessons at various seasons during the year. It is important that this instruction fit the grade level of the pupils. Fire safety should be taught as needed on a school-year basis. It should begin in the kindergarten and extend through the senior high school.

The following suggestions appear in the New York State bulletin on Fire Prevention Education (18):

> *Fire Prevention Education* should continue to be included in the total pattern of experiences offered by the school as has been done in the past. This aspect of education is a continuous one, woven into the school and the community experiences of boys and girls.
>
> *The Choice and Sequence of Topics* rests with the school itself. The outline of suggested learnings that follows lists those contained in various subject-matter areas of the total curriculum. They are highlighted here in order to emphasize the fire prevention education program.
>
> *The Needs* of individual children for fire safety instruction differ from community to community, as well as from child to child. Consequently, the suggestions given here will need adaptation by local schools.
>
> *The Positive Approach,* what to do rather than what not to do, is the most effective way to children's learnings. Nonetheless, in matters dealing with health and safety, a knowledge of what not to do cannot always be left entirely to chance.
>
> *The Goals* of fire prevention education should be attained without arousing unnecessary fears. The approach to this entire program might well be to secure fire safety through developing skill, knowledge and respect for fire.
>
> *The Correlation of This Program* with other parts of the curriculum is recommended whenever the opportunity presents itself for natural integration. The suggested learnings will serve as a guide to areas for emphasis.

The bulletin recommends that the following materials on fire prevention be taught in senior high school classes:

A. Citizenship Education:
   1. Fire prevention as a part of civil defense
   2. Protecting forests and other natural resources

B. Health Education and General Science:
   1. Fire prevention in the home
   2. Responsibility of different family members in preventing destructive fires
      (a) Protection of young children
   3. Periodic inspection and removal of fire hazards in the home
   4. Dangers of misuse of fire
   5. Fire-fighting equipment for the home and automobile
   6. Responsibility in emergencies
   7. First aid:
      (a) Treatment and causes of burns and scalding
         (1) Differentiate between various degrees of burn. The seriousness of the burn is related to its extent on the body.
      (b) Care for electric shock and for asphyxiation
         (1) Symptoms of fainting, gas poisoning and electric shock
      (c) Recommended procedures for moving injured people
   8. Responsibilities in emergencies such as atomic bomb attack

C. Biology:
   1. Forest fire prevention and protection
   2. Conservation of natural resources
   3. Fires caused by lightning

D. Physics:
   1. Prevention of electrical fires with particular reference to proper installation and upkeep of electrical wiring and apparatus
   2. Friction as related to fire prevention

E. Chemistry:
   1. Danger of use of flammable liquids
   2. Safety precautions applicable to the laboratory
   3. Flameproofing and fireproofing
   4. Chemical fire extinguishers

F. Homemaking:
   1. Safe and efficient use of household equipment and supplies
   2. Fire prevention in the home

G. Industrial and Vocational Education:
   1. Safe practice in the use of torches and various heating devices
   2. Fire prevention and fire extinguishing in the shop

According to *The Challenge of Safety Education,* a publication of the Illinois Department of Public Instruction, the following material on fire prevention should be stressed in the elementary schools:

A. What is fire?

1. Relation of elementary sciences to fire prevention
   a. Why fire burns
   b. Heating
   c. Ventilating
   d. Lighting, etc.
2. Most common causes of fire
3. Three classes of fire
   a. Class A—wood, paper textiles.
   b. Class B—oils, greases, and paints
   c. Class C—electric equipment

C. In case of fire:

1. Know how to report a fire.
2. Know how to evacuate the building.
3. Know how to evacuate a smoke-filled room.
4. Know how to use a fire extinguisher (upper grades).
5. Know how to put out clothing fires.
6. Know how to stay out of the path of fire apparatus and away from hydrant and equipment being used.

B. Role of the fire department in the community:

1. Fire fighting
2. Inspection to discover hazards
3. Enforcement of fire code
4. Inhalator squad
5. Other duties in the community

D. Fire prevention:

1. Know the meaning of "flammable," "inflammable," "nonflammable," "toxic," "explosive," etc.
2. Know the safe behavior around bonfires, stoves, open fireplaces, etc.
3. Know how to detect fire hazards.
4. Know the proper use of electric toys, appliances, etc.
5. Know why a person should break a match, tear a cigarette apart, douse a fire, etc.
6. Know the heating qualities of TV tubes and the proper placement of the set in the home.
7. Know how safe your home is.
8. Know why matches should be stored in a metal container.
9. Know why you should buy electric equipment with the Underwriters Label.

Community Responsibility

Fire prevention is primarily a problem of the individual. But it is also a community problem and should receive the support of every civic-minded group and organization. Fire departments, insurance underwriters, chambers of commerce, social service and civic groups, schools and youth organizations should cooperate in a fire prevention program. This is especially true during Fire Prevention Week when these activities are coordinated and publicity is provided through the press, radio, television, motion pictures, posters, exhibits and the distribution of fire prevention literature. Many cities arrange for fire departments to demonstrate fire prevention at schools. Others have appointed firemen with full-time responsibility to give talks and show motion pictures in schools and before civic organizations.

Many state, national and local organizations are engaged in the prevention and control of fires. Most states and the federal government have rangers and fire wardens who patrol forests to locate fires and supervise their extinguishment. Almost every state has a fire mashal who is responsible for the investigation of fires of suspicious origin. There are also several private agencies that have taken a leading role in fire prevention. One of these is the National Board of Fire Underwriters which is now a part of the American Insurance Association. Another is the National Fire Protection Association which emphasizes the educational aspects of fire prevention. A third is the Underwriters Laboratories, which conducts experiments to test devices, materials and apparatus of all kinds that might affect fire hazards. When one sees an Underwriters Laboratories label on an item, it indicates that it is safe and reliable for the purpose designed.

While it is true that in the last decade there has been an upward trend in the losses due to fires, it must be remembered that during this period the number of homes and the property values have also increased. There is clear evidence that fire prevention and protection activities have kept fire losses from increasing unduly.

summary

Fire is one of our greatest servants but it can also be a bad master. It causes the death and injury of thousands of people each year besides destroying over a billion dollars worth of property. It is estimated that over 80 per cent of all fires could be prevented if all forces in the community would step up their fire prevention and protection activities.

Smoking and matches, defective heating equipment, electricity, open flames

FIRE-PREVENTION TIPS

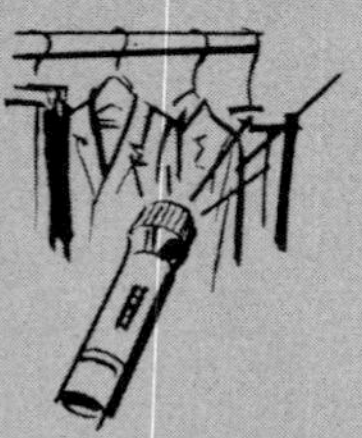

Use only flashlights or other electric lights in your storage closets.

If you suspect a gas leak, call your gas company.

Dry clothes adjacent to heating surfaces, not directly above them.

Inspect your chimney and furnace annually for defects and improvements.

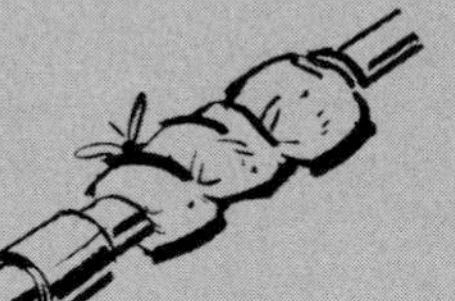

Thaw frozen pipes with heating tape, electrical heater, or hot towels.

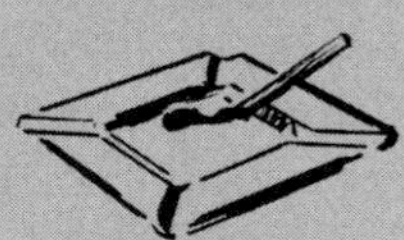

Place burned matches and cigarettes into fireproof ashtrays or receptacle.

Protect your fireplace area with a fire screen to prevent sparks from flying.

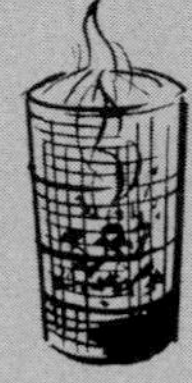

Always burn leaves or trash safely in enclosed metal containers.

When melting paraffin or wax on a stove, always use a double boiler.

Store hot ashes from furnace or stove in a metal container in safe place.

Use closed metal cans for storage of flammable liquids and fuels.

Hang lantern on a metal bracket to keep the heat away from the wall.

When placing curtains near a stove, hang them high above the source of heat or flame to prevent fire.

Before discarding lighted matches, break them in two to make certain they are out to avoid fires.

Keep the telephone number of your fire department near your telephone.

Figure 9:6,
FIFTEEN SAFE PRACTICES TO HELP PREVENT AND FIGHT FIRES.

and sparks, flammable liquids, defective chimneys, accumulations of rubbish, and spontaneous ignition are the chief causes of fires. All of these are subject to control through programs of education, fire prevention regulations and enforcement. It is estimated that over 3,000 fires occur each year in school buildings; many of these endanger the lives of pupils and teachers. All schools should be of fire-resistant construction, should have adequate exits, safe heating and ventilation plants and fire extinguishers. Regular fire drills should be held in all schools.

Every community should have a program of fire protection including fire extinguishment. All buildings should be constructed in accordance with national standards or building codes. They should be inspected regularly, and hazardous conditions corrected. A well-organized fire department should have adequate equipment and well-trained personnel. In addition, all homes, industries and other buildings should have fire extinguishers and, in some cases, fire alarm and sprinkler systems.

Millions of acres of valuable forest and grazing land are destroyed by fire each year. A large percentage of these fires is cause by man. National and state forest services have developed programs for both fire prevention and fire fighting. Otherwise the loss would be far greater than it is.

Fire prevention education should be included in all schools. In both the elementary and secondary schools it can be integrated with other subjects or be taught by correlation. While October is Fire Prevention Month, there is an effort to include fire prevention instruction as is needed at various seasons during the year.

suggested projects and activities

1. Prepare a series of demonstrations on the causes and prevention of fires that could be given in the upper elementary grades.
2. Prepare a chart which could be used to show the causes and origins of fires.
3. Develop an outline of the methods used by fire departments in fighting fires in homes.
4. Prepare a list of instructions that should be given to all teachers regarding procedures in fire drills.
5. Prepare an outline of methods that can be used in fighting forest fires.
6. Prepare plans for an assembly program on fire prevention that could be given at an elementary school.
7. Develop an outline of a 15-minute radio program on fire safety.
8. Arrange with the fire department to conduct a demonstration of the methods used in fighting various types of fires with fire extinguishers.

selected references

1. American Insurance Association, *Fire-Safe School Buildings.* New York: The Association, 1965.

FIRE PREVENTION TEST FOR THE ELEMENTARY SCHOOLS

		TRUE	FALSE
1.	A penny or any piece of metal should be used in place of a fuse.	T	F
2.	Frayed or cracked lamp cords can be used when run under rugs.	T	F
3.	Air, flammable material, and heat are necessary to start a fire.	T	F
4.	Gasoline used for dry cleaning can be stored in any part of the house.	T	F
5.	When looking for something in a dark closet, do not use matches or candles as a light.	T	F
6.	Oily rags or mops can never start a fire.	T	F
7.	The attic or the basement is the safest place for storing waste papers.	T	F
8.	Home fires can be prevented by the exercise of good housekeeping rules.	T	F
9.	When the furnace is in use during cold weather, it is good practice to inspect the pipes periodically.	T	F
10.	It is a good plan to use flameproof material for decorations in the house.	T	F
11.	A good way to put out a campfire is to cover it with earth.	T	F
12.	Spontaneous combustion can occur when steel or other metals are stored in a dry place.	T	F
13.	It is a good conservation practice to burn leaves rather than to pile them on a compost heap.	T	F
14.	It is important to notify an adult whenever a fire breaks out.	T	F
15.	Fire drills should emphasize exits and fire escapes.	T	F

2. ________, *Your Farm and Fire Safety*. New York: The Association, 1965.
3. ________, *Your Fire Safe Home*. New York: The Association, 1965.
4. ________, *Inspection Blanks for Schools*. New York: The Association, 1965.
5. ________, Davis, Kenneth F., *Forest Fire—Control and Use*. New York: McGraw-Hill Book Company, 1959.
6. Kearney, Paul W., "Smoke, the Real Killer in a Fire," *Family Safety*, Spring edition. Chicago: National Safety Council, 1962.
7. National Commission on Safety Education, *Fire Safety for Senior High Schools*. Washington: The Commission, 1951.
8. ________, *Fire Safety for Junior High Schools*. Washington: The Commission, 1950.
9. ________, *Safety Guides for You*. Washington: The Commission, 1961.
10. ________, *The Teacher Fireman*. Washington: The Commission, 1953.
11. National Fire Protection Association, *Automotive Fire Alarm Systems for Private Dwellings*. Boston: The Association, 1950.
12. ________, *There is No Place Like Home for Fire*. Boston: The Association, 1950.
13. ________, *When Fire Strikes You*. Boston: The Association, 1951.
14. ________, *School Fires*. Boston: The Association, 1946.
15. ________, *The Quarterly*, July. Boston: The Association, 1960.
16. National Safety Council, *Accident Facts*. Chicago: The Council, 1963.
17. ________, "Estimated Losses in Building Fires by Causes and Occupations." *Accident Facts*. Chicago: The Council, 1962.
18. New York State Education Department, *Fire Prevention Education*. Albany: The Department, 1961.
19. United States Department of Health, Education and Welfare, *School Fires—Prevention, Control, Protection*. Washington: The Department, 1962.

10

transportation

Transportation of people and goods, whether by sea, land or air, has long been an important factor in the growth and expansion of civilizations. Phoenicians in 1000 B.C. were seasoned merchants of the seas, sailing hundreds of miles from home to trade with other peoples. The Romans built an extensive road system to facilitate free movement of people and goods. Today, Americans are utilizing the air, in addition to roadways and merchant fleets, to expand their horizons from coast to coast and around the world. Mobility is inseparable from our way of life.

Yet with this tremendous transportation system that can deliver our smallest need to our doorstep or circle the earth with thousands of pounds of goods in a matter of hours, there comes a staggering loss in human lives and property damage that challenges the imagination. Accidents in the various modes of transport kill over 50,000 people, injure another 3 million and cost over $7 billion annually (13).

There has been a steady increase in highway fatalities since World War II and, with the present trend continuing, these figures will increase to even greater numbers. Our transportation system, even though it has provided an outstanding service for

Figure 10:1,
PUBLIC TRANSPORTATION. BOTH RAIL AND WATER TRANSPORTATION ARE STEADILY DECREASING, WHILE AIR AND BUS TRAVEL ARE GROWING RAPIDLY.

our people and is the life line of our country, has claimed the lives of more Americans through accidents than have all of the wars in which we have participated.

This chapter highlights the problem of accidents in our transportation systems and the important programs designed to reduce both the number of accidents and their resulting casualties as well as the enormous property loss. Since the accidents and property losses are many times greater in highway transportation than in railroad, air and water transportation combined, most of the chapter will be devoted to automotive traffic.

Highway Transportation

Motor vehicle transportation is the medium for our mass mobility—an essential factor in the modern economy. Our major source of employment is in the automotive and related industries. In the relatively short span of 70 years traffic has crowded the nation's streets and highways, transformed the methods of public safety and produced extraordinary changes in our culture. In the period since 1939 to the present, economic losses from traffic accidents totaled more than $104 billion, to say nothing of the loss of life and personal injuries (14). The motor vehicle is by far the most relentless accidental killer in modern society. If *all* personal injuries are counted, more persons are disabled by motor vehicle accidents than by any other type. As a destroyer of property the motor vehicle has no equal except warfare.

To the extent that the sheer number of motor vehicles in operation contributes to this condition, there would seem to be little prospect for improvement. There are now more than 85 million privately and publicly owned vehicles operated in the United States, of which three-fourths are passenger cars; the remainder, buses and trucks. More than 7 million new passenger cars are being built each year (2). The annual production of the latter is expected to increase to 12 million by the year 1980 and to 26 million by 2000. The total registration of passenger vehicles may reach 120 million by 1980 and will probably rise to 244 million by the year 2000 (15).

The motor vehicle itself is an inanimate object; it has no power to perform without guidance from a human being. It is not so much the vehicle, or the congestion, or the street and highway environment which creates the traffic accident problem. It is primarily the poor judgment and deficiencies of the driver which are responsible.

Although nothing can minimize the tragedy of accidental death and injury, all other forms of transportation in the United States are minor in their accident toll as compared with motor vehicles.

The Traffic Accident Record

Traffic accident records help in measuring what is happening and, from their study and analysis we can determine the steps to be taken for effecting a safer, smoother flow of traffic. Violation records provide the basis for reviewing human failures, such as inattention or nonconformity to traffic requirements, which result in unsafe operation of a motor vehicle. Accidents and the laws are closely related—some experts claim that 90 per cent of the accidents involve one or more violations of the traffic laws. So close is this bond that the techniques of traffic law enforcement might be regarded as major techniques of traffic accident prevention.

Traffic Accident Data

A complete record of a traffic accident covers a multiplicity of factors. At the least it must include:

1. Facts of a collision, of what, with what.
2. What happened if there was no collision involved.
3. Location: rural, suburban, urban; specific street or highway and exact location thereon.
4. The highway: classification, surface, condition, surroundings.
5. The time: day, night, the hour.
6. The vehicle or vehicles: direction, speed, condition.
7. The driver: sex, age, residence, license, experience, condition.
8. The pedestrian (if a pedestrian accident): his age, condition, actions.
9. All other contributing circumstances, including actions of driver or drivers involved.
10. The record of death, injury, property damage.

Other facts are also needed. As an accident is generally the result of a human failure, any study of the accident is also a study in human behavior. Why did this individual act as he did? What was the background —physical, mental and emotional—which led up to the accident?

In a recent year for which complete data are available:

19 million drivers were involved in
11 million traffic accidents and
40,900 deaths resulted;
3,345,000 persons were injured, and
there was an economic loss of over $8 billion.

Causes of Highway Accidents

Every effort at the reduction or prevention of traffic accidents is complicated by the fact that for any given accident there are apt to be multiple causes. It is almost impossible to point at one single event in the circumstances surrounding an accident and say, "this was *the* cause." There may be two, five, ten or more components, the elimination of any one of which *might* have prevented the accident.

Over the years certain facts regarding the conditions under which traffic accidents take place have remained fairly constant. Most accidents occur:

in clear weather, on dry, well-surfaced roads;
on Saturdays and Sundays;
during hours of darkness or semi-darkness;
to drivers operating a vehicle in their own state, relatively near home.

The circumstances contributing to traffic accidents and their frequency are shown in Table 8.

TABLE 8

Contributing factors	*Per cent of accidents*
Following too closely	16.5
Failure to yield right-of-way	15.0
Speed too fast for conditions	13.3
Drove left of center	5.5
Had been drinking	5.4
Made improper turn	4.7
Improper overtaking	4.1
Passed stop sign	3.3
Disregarded signal	2.9
Defective brakes and lights	1.9
Other improper driving	26.7

It is noteworthy that some 65 per cent of these contributing factors are classed by highway safety programs as a part of the "in-a-hurry complex."

State, County, Municipal Relationships

State laws for the control of drivers, vehicles and traffic are basic. Except in rare instances authorized by the state legislature, the laws or ordinances of a lesser jurisdiction (county or municipal) cannot depart from the state provisions. The state, for example, is the *only* source of driver licensing and vehicle registration.

Counties and municipalities enact laws or ordinances in line with state statutes and are responsible for the enforcement of both state and local laws within their respective jurisdictions. The state police force or state highway patrol concentrates upon highways outside municipal boundaries—the so-called major rural highways. Sheriff's highway police, in general, are responsible for law enforcement on secondary rural highways, although in some states, sheriff's police are active on all highways within a county.

Among the best state-county-municipal relationships are those in which the local jurisdictions have technical assistance available from the state. Traffic engineering is a good example. The small community rarely has the services of a traffic engineer. In many states, traffic engineers in the state highway department are available to consult with local jurisdictions and help them work out problems of traffic control. Similarly, in many states the training facilities of the state law enforcement agency are available to counties and municipalities, frequently with assistance from a state college or university.

Standards In every technical field of street and highway safety certain standards have been developed. None of these standards are allowed to remain static—they change, after experience and study, as new conditions arise in traffic control. The fundamental standards in the various fields have been developed through the work of professional groups and organizations of officials as follows:

Traffic Law Enforcement:
- Police—International Association of Chiefs of Police
- Court—Traffic Court Conference of the American Bar Association.

Engineering:
- Highway—American Association of State Highway Officials and U.S. Bureau of Public Roads
- Traffic—Institute of Traffic Engineers
- Signs, Signals, Markings—National Conference on Uniform Traffic Control Devices

Education:
- National Commission on Safety Education of the National Education Association
- National Conference on High School Driver Education
- National Conference on School Transportation

Motor Vehicle Administration (vehicles and drivers):
- American Association of Motor Vehicle Administrators

Laws & Ordinances:
- National Committee on Uniform Traffic Laws and Ordinances

Accident Records:
- National Conference on Uniform Traffic Accident Statistics

Public Support:
- National Safety Council.

The Program of Traffic Accident Prevention

> Traffic accidents can be greatly reduced. But there are no shortcuts, no quick or simple cures. Slogans, gimmicks and "drives" yield no lasting benefit. The remedy lies in a balanced program, fully used by public officials and fully supported by the public, on a continuing basis.
>
> *The President's Committee for Traffic Safety, "Highway Safety—Action Program," 1960.*

Legal responsibility for safety on the streets and highways is vested in government—state, county and municipal. Except for such specialized matters as the transportation of passengers and property in interstate commerce, where the Interstate Commerce Commission is the regulatory authority, the federal government has had no jurisdiction and only evinces a cooperative concern in highway safety. In the early days, states viewed drivers of motor vehicles as a source of tax revenue and laws were enacted for purposes of identification and income rather than control. The early control measures related, for the most part, to rules of operation which restricted speed or prevented the frightening of horses. The concept of driver licensing, driver control and traffic control is more recent and, typically, state legislatures gave the powers of control to the department which has been responsible for the revenue-gathering procedures.

But the motor vehicle—the leading symbol and means of a mobile civilization—forced the issue of control. Today, at the very least, each state has some combination of departments and agencies with responsibility for highways, vehicles, drivers, traffic and safety. Ordinarily these are:

1. Motor Vehicle Department: driver licensing, vehicle registration, central accidents and violations records.
2. State Police or Highway Patrol: in which from 80 to 100 per cent of the duties relate to highway traffic.
3. Highway Department: construction and maintenance of highways to standards of safe design, adequacy of width and surface and similar engineering features; the function of traffic engineering.
4. State Department of Education; teaching and supervision of safety education, mainly high-school driver education, adult driver education and work in the elementary schools.
5. Courts: the judicial power of the state in the operation of traffic courts.
6. Public Service/Utilities Commission: regulation of carriers of passengers and property for hire in intrastate commerce.
7. Special authorities: for turnpikes, toll roads, parkways, tunnels, toll bridges.
8. A wide variety of additional departments and agencies with minor jurisdictions.

The Action Program

In substance the foregoing tabulation includes most of the areas covered in *The Action Program* (15) of the President's Committee for Traffic Safety. This *Program* is our nearest approach to a statement of national traffic safety goals to which states, counties and municipalities subscribe. Originally drawn up in 1946 at the President's first Highway Safety Conference, it has been revised periodically to keep abreast of the times. *The*

Action Program is a summary of the experience and recommendations of the nation's leadership in the traffic safety field. It is *not* a federal program to which the states are invited or directed to adhere. It is a statement of our traffic safety needs based on tested experience. It does not tell us *how* to achieve these objectives. And herein lies one of the difficulties in attaining a concerted, unified highway safety effort.

> I am confident that Americans everywhere, if they have some personal contact with someone who is affected by automobile accidents would realize how dangerous it is to speed on the highway—to risk as many lives as we do—to kill as many people as we do—to handicap physically as many people as we do by indifferent and speedy driving. This is something all of us can do. Federal government can do its part, all of you ladies and gentlemen of the state and local levels can do your part but in the final analysis depends upon understanding what a wonderful machine the automobile is but how dangerous it can be when it is not under control.
>
> *Excerpt from a statement by the late President Kennedy to the President's Committee for Traffic Safety.*

We are composed of 50 states, the District of Columbia, the Commonwealth of Puerto Rico and some small dependencies. In these areas there are thousands of counties and communities—all separate entities of government. Each recognizes that it shares a common problem in highway safety, but each is certain, all too often, that there is something unique or peculiar about that problem within the boundaries of one state, county, or municipality. This psychology of "our problem is different" has been perhaps, the barrier to progress in highway safety. As many safety technicians have expressed it, "We have the 'know how'—the problem is to apply it!"

Often supplemental to the official highway safety activity of governments, but as frequently in a position of leadership with new program ideas, are some extensive national traffic safety programs of a wide variety of business and industry groups. Some of them are "direct action" programs which operate at the state and local level. Business and industry also provide grants of funds and staff assistance to technical or educational groups and to institutions and organizations of officials for the furtherance of the highway safety program. Typical are the work of the automotive industry (automobiles, tires, petroleum, etc.), the property and liability insurance companies, automobile clubs and highway user organizations.

All of these had a hand in the development of *The Action Program,* as did the forces of organized public support represented by safety councils, civic, service, religious, fraternal, farm, labor, youth, women's, professional and other organizations. *The Action Program* is, therefore, the common link for the many groups interested in highway safety along with the expressed desire of all of them to reduce and prevent traffic accidents. To describe, even briefly, the traffic safety activity of all the official and nonofficial organizations would require a volume in itself.

The complaint is frequently heard that no one seems able to state simply:

What needs to be done in highway safety;
What is being done;
Who is doing it.

The situation is understandable. Probably no one knows the entire scope. The problem is too complex, the efforts too varied, the responsibilities too widely scattered to obtain a single national pattern. The generalizations of highway safety are readily expressed. The specifics of doing something about it are much more difficult!

Traffic Control Measures

Much of the highway safety program centers around the effort to control the three basic factors in the traffic situation: the highway, the vehicle and the driver. Each of these could be the subject matter of a complete text—but the essentials can be expressed rather briefly.

The Driver The effort directed toward this factor is known as "The Driver Control Chain." The ultimate purpose of driver control is to keep as many good drivers on the road as possible. Drivers who become involved with traffic law enforcement and with the driver license suspension process of motor vehicle departments would probably challenge this statement, as would those who approach highway safety from the negative side and contend that the purpose of driver control is to get the bad drivers off the road. In reality, it adds up to the same thing. If the attempt to educate drivers to perform safely and to assure their compliance with traffic laws, and the application of corrective measures are unable to keep them on the road as "good" drivers, there is no alternative but to remove them from the highways.

The "Driver Control Chain" is, therefore, the sum of the influences on the driver from predriver years through his entire experience as a driver. It is the influence of his parents when he is a preschool passenger in the family car—the influence of the schools on his behavior as a pedestrian and bicycle rider—the influence of youth organizations on his social behavior—his high school driver education course—his study for a driver license examination—the driver license examination—the contacts with the motor vehicle department when renewing the license or registering his vehicle—the impact of the court in case of a traffic violation—the impact of safety programs. The list is almost endless.

The Vehicle The modern motor vehicle has been engineered to a high level of efficiency. And while it is a powerful object capable of high speeds, it has been engineered to a high level of safety for those who use it properly. Body, frame, brakes, steering, glass, visibility, tires, the elements which make up so-called "roadability," have been steadily improved over the years.

At one time it was believed that approximately 5 per cent of accidents were in part due to mechanical failure and another 5 per cent to highway and weather conditions. The former cause includes tire failure and faulty brakes, headlights, steering mechanisms, windshield wipers and other conditions. It is probable that this percentage is actually higher. At any rate, a good state traffic safety program will include periodic official inspections of vehicles, as well as an educational program to influence drivers to keep their cars in good mechanical condition.

The Highway The driver and the vehicle are placed together on the third factor—the highway. On the new roads a high degree of safety has been engineered. Road surfaces and sight distances have been improved, many curves and hills removed, lanes marked, traffic control signs and signals made more readable, and many dangerous railroad grade crossings eliminated. The limited-access highway, reaching the apex of current safety knowledge in the Interstate System, has removed accident-producing highway situations. Of course, there are still narrow, secondary roads, and there always will be. But, generally speaking, the highway environment is safer today than at any time in our history.

Why then, does the traffic accident experience not improve? There is no simple answer. With the most highway safety effort since the movement began, recent years do not show improvement. The fault lies largely with the driver. While it is possible to produce safer vehicles and safer highways, we have not yet produced many safer drivers. This is an objective of driver education and of programs of traffic accident prevention and highway safety.

Traffic Safety Management

In recent years, one new professional approach has evolved in traffic safety programming which may bring official highway safety activity to a much more efficient level and result in a much more effective performance in reducing accidents. This fresh approach applies the management principles of business and industry to the official highway safety program of a state, county or municipality on the basic premise that from 5 to 15 program segments conducted by 5 to 15 departments or agencies, each with statutory jurisdictions and responsibilities and each with its own objectives, are wasteful and confusing.

Traffic safety management does not propose the creation of a "super-agency" to take over the legal responsibilities of state police, motor vehicle, highway, law, education or other departments. Rather, it proposes a businesslike structure of coordination for a state, county, metropolitan area of municipality where:

1. The total problem of highway traffic and transportation is studied and analyzed, using all available inventory resources, to determine where the program stands and what needs to be done.
2. Priorities are established through the joint agreement of all agencies concerned.
3. Official agencies, while continuing the "everyday things to be done" of their normal functions, concentrate on the priorities as the items of major importance to the total highway safety program.
4. Public announcement is made of these major priorities in order that the people may know what constitutes the official objectives for safer highways and safer highway transportation, why they have priority and how the public officials propose to reach the goals.

One result of the program is that of giving new professional stature to those officials responsible for the administration of a coordinated traffic safety program, as directed by the departments and agencies with statutory jurisdictions in the many related highway, traffic and safety fields.

Commercial Vehicle Transportation

According to *Automobile Facts and Figures* (2), there are over 13 million trucks and buses in the United States. This is about 40 per cent of the total in the world. Nearly 3 million of these are on farms. Special taxes on trucks provide a revenue of $3.6 billion to the states and the federal government. These commercial vehicles are subject to the laws and regulations of state motor vehicle departments that have been discussed in this chapter. In addition, many trucks operate under the regulations of the Interstate Commerce Commission.

Trucks Today trucks rank second to railroads in the tonnage of freight transported; they carry nearly 25 per cent of the intercity volume. One of the great advantages of truck transportation is the facility with which products can be delivered, even to small towns and villages—a door-to-door service. Trucks supply the only freight service for over 25,000 United States communities.

The accident rate for trucks has steadily declined from the period after World War II when it was 47 per 100 million miles. Now it is about 12—a striking reduction. Even with increased congestion, a greater number of trucks on the road, and more miles travelled, the truck safety record is steadily improving.

There are, nevertheless, serious safety problems in trucking. According to state police, two serious dangers are speeding and "tailgating." The big tractor-trailers, holding almost as much cargo as a freight car, have far too many accidents from these and other causes. Even though they are under Interstate Commerce Commission regulations as well as those of state motor vehicle departments, enforcement is often lax, especially at night. On many truck highways it has been found necessary to confine trucks to one lane, especially near metropolitan areas. While this may reduce speed, it may increase "tailgating."

Despite many problems, there is every reason to believe that truck transportation will continue to grow rapidly; it is essential in our economy.

Trucking companies realize the value of selecting superior drivers and providing good training programs, and the importance of the proper maintenance of equipment. For illustration, the standard training course recommended by the American Trucking Association (1) consists of well over 50 hours of instruction—four times as much time as is given to practice driving as in the typical high school course in driver education.

Buses There are over 300,000 motor buses registered in the United States. Of this number, over 200,000 are school buses. Pupil transportation is a highly important part of the school program and is discussed in a later chapter.

As might be expected, while passenger travel by rail has been decreasing, bus transportation has shown a rapid growth. This is especially true in metropolitan areas.

The safety record of buses has been generally good, much better than that for passenger cars. This is largely due to the careful selection and training of operators and to organized safety programs. Obviously, improved construction and maintenance of buses and better highways have also aided in establishing better safety records. As new roads are built under federal and state highway building programs, bus travel between cities is steadily increasing. Buses have also taken the place of street cars in community transit systems and are also widely used for commuter services.

Other Forms of Transportation

Motor vehicle accidents, as has been stated, result in far more deaths than the total for all other forms of transportation. During a recent year, while there were 42,500 accidental deaths on highways, the number in railroad accidents was only 700; aircraft, 1,000; and water transport, approximately 1,000. The total for the three forms of transportation was only 6 per cent of the number of deaths from motor vehicles. There were 1,347 deaths from grade-crossing accidents involving motor vehicles and trains, which are included under highway fatalities.

It is of interest to note the relative safety of the various forms of transportation. This is measured in terms of the death rate per 100 million passenger miles (14) as shown in the following table:

TABLE 9

TRANSPORTATION ACCIDENT DEATH RATES

Form of transportation	*Passenger death rate*
Passenger automobiles & taxis	2.2
Passenger automobiles on turnpikes	1.1
Scheduled air transport (domestic)	0.57
Buses	0.16
Railroads	0.10
Street cars and trolley buses	0.04

Not too much confidence can be placed in this table in drawing conclusions as to the relative safety of the various means of travel. Several bad aircraft or railroad accidents in other years have resulted in great increases in rates. For illustration, 10 years ago the rate for railroads was 0.58; and for aircraft, 1.15, because of several bad accidents. However, it is of interest to note that theoretically, on the basis of the statistics in the table above, it would be 14 times safer to cross the United States in a bus as in a passenger car.

It will be noted that the table does not include passeger deaths on inland waterways. No facts are available as to what per cent of the 1,000 deaths were passengers on public carriers.

Railroads The railroads have made a highly important contribution to the growth of our country. In 1915, the total railroad miles of track was over 264,000 but since then has steadily declined, until today there are hardly more than 150,000 miles. Some once-important main railroads have gone out of existence. Passenger and freight traffic have steadily decreased and many of the railroads are in bankruptcy. The chief reason for this has been the growth in the use of passenger cars, buses and air transport. From 1959 to 1962 passengers using air transport greatly increased. During this same period, the number of passengers carried by buses (city and inter-urban) doubled—at the expense of the railroads. Many rail lines are kept solvent only because of income from freight. With the decline of railroad traffic, passenger deaths since 1940 (as would be expected) have decreased 30 per cent; deaths of employees on duty, 50 per cent; and deaths of trespassers, 50 per cent. Total accidental deaths have declined from 1,200 to 700.

Causes and Prevention of Accidents Accident causes vary from year to year. For accidents in which passengers were killed the following causes were found: failure of engineer to see signals; mechanical failure of equipment such as air-brakes; floods and washouts; high speed on curves; lack of block signals; and lack of protection at grade crossings.

The Interstate Commerce Commission has had a strong influence on railroad safety. It has insisted upon the installation of many safeguards such as automatic couplers, air brakes, automatic controls, and all-metal cars. It has stipulated the maximum number of hours that an employee can be on duty. It has required railroads to install an inspection system for trains and for the right-of-way. The railroads themselves have also become leaders in the safety movement. The Harriman Safety Awards, given by the American Museum of Safety and the Association of American Railroads each year, are greatly prized.

Combating grade-crossing accidents has been a difficult problem. Many overhead crossings are being built, but they are expensive. Automatic signals have been installed to warn drivers. In spite of all safety measures, statistics show that in 50 per cent of the night accidents, the motor vehicle actually ran into the side of the train or the locomotive.

Trespasser accidents are being reduced by erecting fences along the right-of-way, constructing bridges for pedestrians, and by safety instruction in the schools.

Air Transport The growth of civil aviation in the decade following World War II exceeded all forecasts. In 1945 the airlines flew 3.4 billion passenger miles; in a recent year the number had jumped to 39 billion, about ten times greater. In addition, according to the *FAA Statistical Handbook of Aviation* (8):

1. Private aircraft increased since 1945 from 38,000 to 75,000.
2. The number of airports and airfields has doubled.
3. In ten years passengers carried on domestic airlines increased from 21 to 55 million.
4. Overseas passengers increased from 1.3 to 5.3 million.
5. The number of employees of airlines increased from 35,000 (not including military installations).
6. The number of employees in the aircraft industry is over 670,000.
7. The number of civil transport planes increased to 1,854, of which 319 were turbojets, 215 turboprops, and the remainder piston planes.

Causes and Prevention of Accidents The Civil Aeronautics Board reported that in a recent year, 10 per cent of the accidents were chargeable to weather, 10 per cent to power plant failure, and 23 per cent to pilot error. The balance (i.e. 57 per cent) were due to structural failure, fires, collisions and other causes. In some accidents the causes could not be determined.

Aviation Safety

No phase of airline operation gets greater concentration than safety. Not only are there federal safety regulations, but the airlines, also, have their own rigid safety standards. The progress made in making flying safer over the years bears this out.

Federal Aviation Agency Statistical Handbook

Many types of accidents can be and are being reduced. Attention to design and quality of material, together with better knowledge of structural stresses, are decreasing the number of accidents. Better weather reporting, better lighting of airports, and improved instruments for "blind" flying and landing are reducing accidents due to weather. Failures due to personnel are more difficult to control, but improved training and physical examinations provide some help. More frequent and better inspections of aircraft also tend to improve the safety record.

In the past ten years there has been a decrease in the death rate for passengers. Unfortunately, with the advent of the high-speed jet with a pay load of 100 or more, a bad accident usually means the death of all passengers and crew, and is front-page news. On the other hand, every day in the year traffic accidents kill over 100 persons. It is a matter of interest that theoretically, on the basis of the accident rate, a passenger could travel constantly for over 9,000 days or approximately 26 years before being killed. No passenger should be unduly concerned about his safety when travelling by scheduled air transport.

Figure 10:2,
A Great Airport Like Kennedy International Has To Combine Both Air and Motor Vehicle Traffic

The Federal Aviation Agency has the authority over safety in civil aviation (7). It prescribes standards for the construction, inspection, and maintenance of aircraft, rules concerning aircraft flight, and regulations of the hours of service of employees. It also certifies employees and aircraft and approves airport design. It insures that civil aircraft are designed and manufactured according to the highest safety standards, operates air traffic controllers day and night, and makes use of radar and radio to aid pilots. Another agency, the Civil Aeronautics Board, is chiefly concerned with investigating accidents and conducting studies in matters pertaining to accident prevention. In addition, state agencies also exert certain controls over the construction of airports, and the airlines themselves are active in the training of pilots and crews and in the maintenance of aircraft.

In recent years there has been a remarkable development of high-speed jet transportation. Nearly all of the aircraft operating between New York, Chicago and Miami are jets. The same is true for overseas travel. The safety record of these aircraft has been unusually good.

Non-transport Accidents It is of interest to note that in a recent year the number of deaths in private aircraft used for pleasure, instruction and business was 864, six times that of the scheduled air carriers and six times that of the nonscheduled operations, both domestic and international.

Inland and Coastal Waterways Passenger service by public carriers on inland and coastal waterways has all but disappeared. There are still a few steamers and ferries on lakes, bays and rivers but the number of passengers carried is small. On the other hand, while freight tonnage has declined, it is still important, especially on the Mississippi and other rivers and on the Great Lakes and coastal waterways.

National Safety Council statistics for a recent year show 1,000 fatalities in water transportation accidents but no facts are available as to the number of passengers (14). It is probable that many of the victims were employees on freight boats, barges, tugs and ferries.

Regulations for Motor Boats There is a lack of control of motor boating. Only a few states have regulations, there is but little enforcement, although more states are developing regulations, and the training of operators is limited to instruction given by the United States Coast Guard and the Power Squadrons. An accident prevention program would include the following (16):

1. Licensing of operators.
2. Inspection of power boats.
3. A state manual of regulations.
4. Enforcement.
5. Instruction for all operators.
6. Equipment on boats.
7. Swimming and water safety.

Ocean Transportation Accidents to American ships resulting in the death of passengers are rare. There are many reason for this. In the first place, ocean liners are made of steel construction and have double bottoms and compartments. They are all equipped with life boats, rafts, life preservers and elaborate fire prevention and fire-fighting apparatus. Many other kinds of safety equipment are in use such as radio and radar, echo depth finders, stabilizers, direction finders and fog horns.

Ships are inspected by the United States Coast Guard. There are strict regulations regarding the kind of cargo that can be carried and other considerations of safety. Lighthouses, buoys marking obstructions and weather bureaus provide additional safety, especially near the shore. The iceberg patrol of the Coast Guard keeps ships informed about dangerous conditions and the weather bureaus warn of hurricanes and other storms. The Coast and Geodetic Survey prepares charts as aids to navigation.

While no reliable facts are available, it is probable that over a ten-year period the relative safety in ocean travel would rival that of the railroads. An ocean voyage today is undoubtedly as safe as staying at home.

summary

Five decades ago, railroads were the most important form of transportation for both passengers and freight. Today motor vehicles, including passenger cars, buses and trucks, are by far the most important. In a relatively short period of time, motor vehicles have increased to over 85 million, congesting the nation's streets and highways, transforming the methods of public protection and producing extraordinary changes in our culture. Each year, well over 40,000 persons are killed in highway accidents, several million are injured and the economic losses total several billion dollars.

Highway safety has had some 40 years of organized program effort. In recent years, this effort has become much more effective because of the organized activities of private and public agencies. This is centered in the *Action Program* of the President's Committee for Traffic Safety. It includes programs on (1) enforcement, (2) engineering, (3) education, (4) motor vehicle administration, (5) laws and ordinances, (6) accident records, (7) and public support.

National, state and municipal government agencies have extensive safety programs. Private organizations such as the automobile and insurance industries are also active. Bus and truck companies have improved their accident records.

However, in spite of these activities, highway accidents have been steadily increasing. Obviously, the chief reason for this is the striking increase in the use of motor vehicles. While the *death rate* has decreased, fatalities have steadily increased in number. We have been able to produce safer vehicles and highways, but have not had much success in producing safer drivers. It is evident that most of the work of the *Action Program* should be directed toward improving the behavior of drivers and pedestrians.

Passenger transportation by railroads has steadily declined in the last decade. In some instances, important railroads have gone out of existence; other lines are kept solvent because of the income from freight. The safety record for railroads has been unusually good; they are one of the safest forms of transportation.

Air transport has shown a remarkable increase during the last two decades; in fact, it is about 10 times greater than it was in 1945. No phase of airline operation gets greater attention than safety. Not only are there federal safety regulations, but also the airlines have their own rigid safety standards. The accident rate for air transport has shown a steady improvement.

Passenger traffic on inland waterways has all but disappeared. However, private motor boating has greatly increased. While freight tonnage on the waterways has declined, it is still important on the Great Lakes and on coastal waterways. Ocean travel is very safe because of the many improvements that have been made in ship safety.

suggested projects and activities

1. How can you account for the fact that while there are national and state programs for preventing traffic accidents, fatalities continue to rise?
2. What could be done in your community to coordinate the traffic safety activities through better management?
3. Prepare a chart that will show how official traffic safety agencies in a state could be coordinated into a state program.
4. What methods could be used by railroads to regain lost business and remain solvent?
5. Prepare a report to be used for a short talk on how railroads have improved safety.
6. List some of the facts that have resulted in the decline of traffic on inland waterways.
7. Make a list of the methods that have been used by the Federal Aviation Agency and by the airlines to improve passenger safety.
8. What is being done by the United States Coast Guard to improve water safety?

selected references

1. American Trucking Association, *Truck Driver Training*. Washington: The Association, 1959.
2. Automobile Manufacturers Association, *Automobile Facts and Figures*. Detroit: The Association, 1964. Published annually.
3. Ballard, F. A., "Federal Regulation of Aviation," *Harvard Law Review*, October, 1947.

4. Brody, Leon and H. J. Stack, *Highway Safety and Driver Education.* Englewood Cliffs, N.J.: Prentice-Hall, Inc., 1962.
5. Daggert, Stuart, *Principles of Inland Transportation.* New York: Harper & Row, Publishers, 1955.
6. Federal Aviation Agency, *A Picture Story of the F.A.A.* Washington, D.C.: The Agency. (n.d.)
7. ________, *The Federal Aviation Agency.* Washington, D.C.: The Agency, 1964.
8. ________, *F.A.A. Statistical Handbook of Aviation.* Washington, D.C.: The Agency, 1964.
9. Frederick, John H., *Commercial Air Transportation.* Homewood, Ill.: Richard D. Irwin, Inc., 1946.
10. Insurance Information Institute, *Insurance Facts.* New York: The Institute, 1964.
11. Interstate Commerce Commission. *Revised Safety Regulations, (Motor Carrier).* Washington, D.C.: The Commission.
12. Lansky, Hans A., *Resources in America's Future.* Baltimore, Md.: Johns Hopkins Press, 1963.
13. National Safety Council, *Annual Traffic Inventory.* Chicago: The Council.
14. ________, *Accident Facts,* Chicago: The Council.
15. President's Committee for Traffic Safety, *Highway Safety—Action Program.* Washington, D.C.: The Committee, 1960.
16. U. S. Coast Guard, *Laws Governing Marine Inspection.* Washington, D.C.: The Treasury Department, 1963.
17. ________, *Rules and Regulations for Passenger Vessels.* Washington, D.C.: The Treasury Department, 1964.

11

meeting disasters

The word "disaster" in the minds of people is synonymous with calamity. Recorded history presents numerous examples of disaster such as the Biblical flood that inundated the earth, the destruction of Carthage, the San Francisco earthquake and the Coconut Grove fire in Boston. From these lessons man has sought to find a means of control which would reduce loss of life and property damage.

Studies of disasters by social psychologists have dealt with the reactions of people and with finding means to control them so that rescue work and rehabilitation can proceed efficiently. Individual panic (blind flight) does not occur as often as people would assume. Nevertheless, its contagiousness gives it an importance far out of proportion to its individual frequency. It is important, therefore, that communities be organized so that those who would attempt to be calm and helpful have intelligent direction to channel their energies into constructive efforts.

Moving to the disaster area necessary equipment such as fire apparatus, ambulances, heavy construction equipment, and food and clothing demands that access roads be kept clear of other vehicles and curious people. The lives of many survivors would be jeopardized by bottlenecks there. It is essential that this reaction to a disaster be anticipated and more damage prevented through prompt action to control traffic by police or other agencies. It is important that those assigned this responsibility should immediately set up road blocks to keep the access roads open.

Recognition must be given to some of the people who seek entry into the area. They fall into various groups; therefore, different control techniques are needed. Following the rush of rescue equipment, there is a convergence of workers concerned with disaster relief. The American National Red Cross, Civil Defense, the Salvation Army, ambulance squads, and other organizations enter the area with personnel and materiel to alleviate the suffering of the survivors. It is imperative that these be identified by arm bands or uniforms.

The nonofficial convergers present the principal problem to traffic control agencies. They are the anxious, the curious, those who want to assist but are unorganized, the exploiters (looters, souvenir hunters, profiteers and relief stealers), and the politician who seeks publicity for his efforts. These nonofficial entrants may be controlled by the following methods (1):

1. Organization of an information corps to disseminate information to the mass media so that people will remain at home and listen to radio or television.
2. Cease and desist appeals.
3. Setting up of emergency registration and automatic notification procedures.
4. Centralization of records of survivors.
5. Control of population movements:
   a. Use of road blocks or traffic barriers,
   b. Pass or identification system.
6. When the area has been brought under control, it may be feasible to set up guided bus tours so that people can satisfy their curiosity in safety. In this way the continuing efforts to clear away remaining debris or to demolish unsafe structures are not impeded.

Kinds of Disasters

Disasters may be divided into two classes: those caused by nature, and those that are the result of man's activities. In both types man plays an important role either through his actions or his inaction. The civil defense organizations and the American Red Cross have proved to be of value in the many disasters which have struck our nation. People of our coastal areas learned this when they were hit by floods and fires. As a result of their training, members of rescue organizations have been able to save lives, alleviate suffering and reduce property damage. These organizations are characteristically American in the tradition of the early pioneer days—neighbors volunteering to help neighbors who have met with misfortune. Within the past five years, more than one hundred areas were declared disaster areas by our Presidents and were given federal assistance. Statistics show that no part of the country is immune to disaster.

Natural Disasters

Nature is often unpredictable and capricious. Disasters frequently result in heavy damage to property and, sometimes, loss of life. Usually, knowledge of possible damage can allow people to take precautions that will minimize losses, but the event itself cannot be deterred.

Hurricanes Hurricanes originate near the equator. They are known in some areas of the world as typhoons or cyclones and are powerful storms, with winds often exceeding 100 miles per hour. Technically, a storm is not a hurricane until the wind velocity reaches 74 miles an hour. The hurricane's diameter is usually large, sometimes exceeding 500 miles, and its path of destruction may stretch for thousands of miles. Fortunately, the Hurricane Forecasting Service of the U.S. Weather Bureau tracks these storms from their inception and releases advisory bulletins through the mass media as to location, direction and rate of movement and wind velocity.

Damage as a result of hurricanes is brought about by high winds, heavy rainfall within a relatively short period or high waves and tides. Although they originate over a large water area, they often move inland causing heavy damage hundreds of miles from the coast. The following safety measures should be stressed:

1. Keep your radio on and listen to advisory warnings from the weather bureau.
2. If you are in the path of the storm, board up windows or close storm shutters. Have flashlight and batteries, candles, drinking water and prepared food available.
3. Stay off roads and, if driving after the storm subsides, be alert for washouts and debris.
4. Evacuate shore areas when warned. Delay may cause you to be marooned or drowned.
5. See that loose objects around the lawn and yard are secured for they can become flying projectiles. Take all necessary fire precautions in the home for assistance may not be available for a few days.

Tornadoes Tornadoes, also called "twisters," are violent weather phenomena that are usually most prevalent in the spring and early summer. While they may strike anywhere in the continental United States, they occur most often in the central states. Tornadoes are usually produced when two masses of air of sharply contrasting temperatures

Figure 11:1,
HURRICANES, FOLLOWED BY TIDAL WAVES, CAUSE ENORMOUS PROPERTY DAMAGE AND FREQUENTLY RESULT IN MANY DEATHS AND INJURIES. (WHILE MOST HOMES WERE DAMAGED IN CAMERON, LOUISIANA, BY HURRICANE AUDREY, RESIDENTS TOOK SHELTER IN THE REINFORCED CONCRETE COURTHOUSE AND WERE SAVED.)

come together. In the whirlpools of air that result, the wind velocity may go as high as 500 miles per hour. A tornado's diameter is small, but its length may reach one-fourth of a mile, and it moves forward at from 25 to 40 miles per hour.

Ordinarily, a tornado lasts a short time but its path of destruction is generally 15 to 20 miles long. There is a sudden lowering of the atmospheric pressure and a violent uprush of air near the center of the storm which is powerful enough to lift automobiles and demolish buildings.

One method of protection against tornadoes is through underground shelters. In addition, there are certain things one may do to enhance his chances of survival (11):

1. If caught outside in open country, it is best to move at right angles to

Figure 11:2,
A TORNADO DESTROYS NEARLY EVERYTHING IN ITS PATH. SEVERAL HUNDRED OCCUR EACH YEAR AND CAUSE HEAVY LOSSES.

the tornado's path. If there is no time, lie flat in the nearest depression, such as a ditch or ravine.

2. In a city or a town, seek shelter in a strongly reinforced building, but stay away from windows.
3. At home, the corner of the basement toward the tornado usually offers greatest safety. If there is no basement, take cover under heavy furniture against inside walls.
4. In schools, stay away from windows and utilize the lower floors. Avoid auditoriums and gymnasiums with large, poorly supported roofs.
5. Keep calm, because the chance of the tornado reaching you is slight.
6. In areas where these storms are frequent, or in any area when a storm is approaching, keep tuned to the weather news of your local radio station.

Blizzards A blizzard is a winter storm characterized by strong winds, blowing snow and extremely cold weather. People caught in such a storm may experience difficulty in breathing. Other dangers are frostbite, heart attack from the extreme effort of travel, losing one's way and death from freezing. It is best to seek shelter when warned by radio or television.

Floods Lowland areas in the United States are subject to floods but these do not constitute serious threats to life because their occurrence is usually forecast sufficiently in advance. In hilly or mountainous areas, flash floods may strike without warning. Safety measures include avoiding valleys and climbing to higher elevations.

Earthquakes Many earthquakes originate beneath the sea and cause little concern. Strong and destructive earthquakes are rare; they result from cracking or dislocation of great masses of rock far beneath the surface of the earth. While seismologists are well aware of the areas where earthquakes are likely to strike, they are unable to predict when they will occur. The most useful protection in an area that has a history of tremors is to live in an earthquake-proof structure. The earthquake is over in a matter of seconds or minutes; the essential things that can be done are to avoid panic and, if indoors, stand in an inside corner or beneath a solidly arched doorway..

The Alaska earthquake of 1964 and tidal waves that followed were one of the worst natural disasters to occur in modern times. This disaster practically destroyed the thriving city of Anchorage and many other Alaskan towns and villages such as Valdez and Kodiak. Fortunately, the loss of life was not as great as might have been expected, but the property loss in Alaska and along the Pacific coastline in Canada and the United States exceeded $800 million, most of which was not covered by insurance.

While the damage from the earthquake was tremendous, it is probable that the loss from the tidal waves was even greater. As a matter of fact, these waves should be called seismic rather than tidal; walls of water as high as 50 feet swept through some coastal communities causing complete devastation. Even 1,800 miles away at Crescent City, California, the damage was very heavy. Effects of the earthquake were felt as far away as Los Angeles and Japan. Alaska and other West Coast sections were declared disaster areas.

If this earthquake had occured along the eastern coastal area of the United States, the loss of life and property would have been many times greater. Fortunately, the East Coast is not in the earthquake zone.

Conflagrations Fires have already been discussed in chapter 9. When a fire gets out of control and sweeps over a large area, we may have a real disaster resulting in a loss of life and valuable property. Few communities are immune from a disaster due to fire.

In such a case, all of the fire apparatus available is called out. Sometimes it is necessary to dynamite buildings to stop the spread of the flames. Often this can be accomplished by drenching adjoining buildings.

Fighting a great forest fire becames a real problem for the forest services and local fire departments. Some burn for days, and destroy thousands of acres of valuable timber. Fortunately, fire control measures are tending to reduce the dangers.

Wartime Disaster: Nuclear Attack

The development of atomic and hydrogen bombs and the threat of their use in war presents one of the greatest menaces to mankind. To

Figure 11:3, FOREST FIRES BURN MILLIONS OF ACRES EACH YEAR.

successfully survive a nuclear attack the public must become aware of the nature of radiation and the means to prevent it from becoming a threat to existence.

The detonation of a nuclear weapon causes a tremendous explosion which produces heat, blast and radiation. The heat waves spread out from the point of detonation at 186,000 miles per second and start fires, cause explosions and produce burns on exposed surfaces. The destructiveness of this heat wave falls off rapidly with the distance from its point of origin. Air blasts or shock waves travel at 720 miles per hour. These are responsible for smashing glass, demolishing frame houses and inflicting physical damage to living things. A burst of radiation from a nuclear bomb lasts up to one minute.

Shelters

The importance of the shelter program is related to delayed fallout. A ground explosion throws millions of tons of earth and other materials up into the air. These materials become radioactive and are carried by winds in the high atmosphere to far-away areas where they settle down to earth as fallout. It is true that a fallout shelter would afford no protection in the immediate area of detonation but anyone in a suitable shelter 12 miles away would have an excellent chance of escaping unharmed. This estimate of the Office of Civil Defense is based upon the fact that the 5-megaton bomb (5 million tons of TNT) would be the best tactical weapon because of its weight and the fact that the destructive power of a nuclear detonation does not increase in direct proportion to the size of the weapon.

Protection Against Nuclear Detonation

Areas such as New York City, Chicago and other large cities have a natural protection against fallout. The interior halls on the third to the ninth floors of a twelve-story reinforced concrete building would provide a protection factor of 50. In the subbasement of a building the radiation would be cut to a 1000th. Suburban homes can have dirt piled around basement windows and be reasonably good shelters except during intense radiation. Schools make ideal shelters because they are usually the most substantial buildings in the community and are distributed in proportion to the density of the population. Measuring devices such as personal dosimeters and survey meters with Geiger tubes have been developed to tell us the roentgen rate per hour. A person can remain in a shelter a few days or weeks until the Office of Civil Defense monitoring teams determine that radiation has dropped to levels where it no longer is lethal.

Education for survival is the primary problem of the civil defense program today. The following are pertinent facts about radiation that should be known by all adults and children (14, 15):

1. In the general bomb area, fall out radiation intensity decays 90 per cent in the first seven hours. In two weeks it is down to a 1000th. The radiation problem decreases as distance from the blast area increases.
2. One may be exposed to an accumulated dose of as much as 450 roentgens within two to twelve weeks and still have a 50-50 chance of survival. Less than 200 roentgens would probably produce no fatalities.
3. Radiation sickness is neither contagious nor infectious.
4. Fallout cannot make anything radioactive. Food and water that have been exposed to fallout radiation are contaminated only to the extent that they contain fallout particles. Washing, peeling, or brushing foods removes these particles. Water supplies can be decontaminated by sedimentation and filtering. Brushing one's clothes and taking a shower help decontaminate the human body.
5. Fallout cannot blanket the entire world because of the nature of hemispheric air movements. Nor will large areas of the world become uninhabitable for centuries.

The Role of the School

The American people subscribe to a wide variety of beliefs as to the proper functions of their schools. Many communities have developed plans for protection and survival in which the school building plays a prominent part. The school itself, however, has the obligation to make its own plans for the protection of its children in disaster and for the training of its personnel so that pupils and teachers will respond automatically and effectively in disaster situations. It is generally agreed that training children to face emergency situations should be a part of the regular school program. Indeed, many subject areas offer opportunity to discuss natural disasters and radiation hazards.

Administrative Responsibility By virtue of his office, the school administrator is the responsible authority who sets up school programs to protect lives and property. From the time pupils start for school until they return home, schools stand *in loco parentis*. The superintendent of schools, as chief administrator, is responsible for the development, implementation and administration of a disaster protection program in the schools.

Many school superintendents may feel that an over-all civil defense program is a part of his job which should be delegated to an assistant. The defense director may wish to form a defense council made up of school administrators, the medical director and other key school personnel. Such a council may set up the policies which will govern all schools following the approval of the school board.

The School Program The principal, as the key person in his school, must assume the responsibility of working with his staff to develop a program that will offer maximum protection to the staff and the student body. Each principal should select a civil defense coordinator who will be assisted by people such as the custodial staff, administrative assistants, community law enforcement agencies, fire protection agencies, student and faculty representatives, and civil defense authorities. Disaster planning is readily adaptable to instruction because many of the subject areas lend themselves directly to discussion of natural events and radiation hazards. Through students it is often possible to send information into the homes. Many school systems have instituted adult education courses in civil defense and medical self-aid.

Basic to planning an adequate protection program is an awareness of the types of disasters that can strike a community. A survey should be carried out to determine:

1. The natural disasters likely to occur in the area.
2. The man-made hazards in the vicinity of the school, such as airports, oil tanks, etc.
3. The most probable types of enemy attacks and the degrees of danger (target critical or noncritical).

A second type of survey would identify community resources:

1. Human resources—people willing to serve in the protection program and the special skills they possess or may develop.
2. Physical resources—buildings available for shelter, evacuation facilities and areas, hospitals, and communication media.

The education of our children to the hazards of the twentieth century is vital to their proper growth and development into emotionally stable adults. All of us, in the course of living, must face danger of one kind or another. It is an important part of education to learn to face danger realistically. The school has a dual role to play in preparation for disasters. First, it must assume the responsibility for the children and staff when the school is struck by disaster; second, it must do all that it can to inform the general public so that they too can act intelligently when disaster threatens or strikes.

Guidelines for Teaching and Planning for Disasters

1. Civil defense must be taught, not only as preparation for disaster caused by war, but for its value in times of natural disasters such as floods, fires, hurricanes and blizzards.
2. It is important that we try to maintain in the minds of pupils a correct balance between fear and confidence. This is best done by indicating to them the devastating power of the atomic and hydrogen bombs. On the other hand, we should stress the strength of our country's defenses in Nikes, Conelrad, and interballistic missiles, and the Strategic Air Command.
3. We must develop confidence in our pupils to cope with survial problems if they come. We must not encourage defeatism.
4. Confidence and understanding on the part of pupils will avoid confusion and panic should an emergency arise. This is best accomplished by imparting information on disaster survival at different grade levels:
   a. In the classroom.
   b. Through school assemblies.
   c. Through special subject areas.
   d. By conducting civil defense drills and fire drills as is required by law.
5. We must not assume that disasters cannot strike us. No school in the United States can be certain that it is entirely free from the threat of disaster. When these are preventable, prevention must be the first stop in a protection program. For example, fire can be curbed by fireproof construction, fire control systems, and the reduction of combustibles. Natural gas seepage into a school building transforms a natural hazard into a man-made catastrophe when someone strikes a match. The danger to pupils from all types of disaster, natural or man-made, can be reduced by proper planning.

Warning Most predisaster programs assume that some time will elapse between warning and disaster. It is important that an adequate warning system be developed. Warning may come by telephone, radio or television, the civil defense direct voice warning system, or from the community air raid sirens.

It is important that each school develop a quick, positive and accurate warning system to carry the message to staff and pupils so that they may take proper predetermined action to protect themselves. Schools use a variety of warning systems: bells, whistles, hand- or motor-driven sirens, public address systems, telephones. Speed and accuracy are important. Pupils should be prepared to respond automatically, promptly and correctly upon hearing the various signals.

BE PREPARED CHECKLIST

USE THIS CHECKLIST TO MAKE SURE YOUR FAMILY IS PREPARED FOR DISASTER.

	YES	NO
Every member of the family knows what to do in case of fire, flood, hurricane, or tornado.	______	______
Our house, garage, and yard are clear of burnable rubbish.	______	______
Our electrical and heating systems have been checked for safety.	______	______
All fuels and flammable fluids are stored in safe containers, outside the house.	______	______
We have fire extinguishers, a hand water pump, and/or garden hose properly located for fire-fighting purposes........	______	______
Every member of the family knows general first aid rules.	______	______
At least one adult in our family has first aid training.	______	______
We have the necessary first aid supplies in our home.........	______	______
We have an emergency shelter stocked with ample food, water, and equipment.	______	______
We know the attack warning signals and what to do if they sound.	______	______
We know how to use our radio for emergency information.	______	______
We know protective measures against fallout.	______	______
Our car is in good running condition. Gas tank is kept more than half full at all times.	______	______

EVERY ANSWER WILL BE "YES"
IF YOUR FAMILY IS PREPARED

Figure 11:4, CHECKLIST FOR FAMILY SAFETY.

Organizing Civil Defense

In an address before Congress the late President Kennedy, describing "urgent national needs," emphasized that the military strength of the United States and the free world served as a powerful deterrent to enemy attack. Then he stated the philosophy of civil defense:

> But this deterrent concept assumes rational calculations by rational men. And the history of this planet is sufficient to remind us of the possibility of an irrational attack, a miscalculation, an accidental war which cannot be either foreseen or deterred. The nature of modern warfare heightens these possibilities. It is on this basis that civil defense can readily be justified—as insurance for the civilian population in the event of such a miscalculation. It is insurance we trust will never be needed—but insurance which we could never forgive oursleves for foregoing in the event of such a catastrophe (9).

National Organization The national civil defense program is under the jurisdiction of the Department of Defense. Its prime purpose is to provide shelter areas and to provision them with food, water, radiation measuring instruments and medical and sanitation supplies. Trained leadership is essential to effective civil defense. The Office of Civil Defense (OCD) has established schools to train such leaders so that they may in turn train others in their communities. The following courses are given: Civil Defense Management, Shelter Management, Radiological Monitoring, and Radiological Defense Officer.

Panic

There are many disasters in which the loss of life and the number of injuries is greatly increased by panic. Extreme fear and terror cause people to lose self-control in efforts to save their own lives or those of their children. There have been many instances where a cry of fire in a public gathering resulted in panic in the attempt to get out of the exits. According to Cutter in *Panic and Its Control* (6),

> cloudbursts, floods, flash fires, fights and many other happenings of a similarly critical nature, occur with such rapidity that man's ordinary reasoning processes are suspended. Under such circumstances, man's desire is only to ecape.

Many of the 493 deaths in the terrible Cocoanut Grove night club disaster in 1942 were in part due to panic. Fire panic in the St. John's Hotel in Newfoundland resulted in 100 deaths. The same could be said of the Triangle Shirtwaist fire in New York where many of the panic-stricken shop girls jumped to their deaths. On the other hand, there have been many instances of disasters at sea where there has been very little panic.

It would appear that panic would be greatest in the case of terrible fires, tornadoes and hurricanes where people can see terrible dangers approaching, but this is not always true. According to Robinson in *The Face of Disaster* (16) the National Academy of Sciences-National Research Council has established a special Committee on Disaster Studies, now known as the Disaster Research Group to study how people act in disasters. Various reports have been issued, but it will take several years before the group's studies can be completed and evaluated.

Robinson points out that there are several reasons why panic occurs (16):

1. People fail to heed warnings.
2. They wait until it is too late to seek shelter.
3. They are poorly informed—they do not know the serious nature of the danger.
4. When the disaster strikes, they are unprepared and are panic-stricken.

What can be done to reduce the ever-present danger of panic? This is an important problem and is being studied by the Disaster Research Group. Cutter (6) stresses the fact that we can do much by seeing to it that buildings where meetings are being held are fireproof, with no combustible decorations, and with adequate exits and stairways, and doors that always open outward. There should also be emergency lighting and fire fighting equipment.

The Organization and Administration of Disaster Relief

Two books provide useful material on disaster relief. The first of these is the *National Plan for Emergency Preparedness* (15) of the United States government. A second is the *Disaster Manual* (3) of the American National Red Cross. Both of these describe the activities that should be set in motion following a disaster. There is a great similarity between relief procedures in the various kinds of disasters. People need to be rescued, to have medical attention, to be housed and fed following most disasters. Debris and wreckage has to be cleared, transportation must be provided, and emergency repairs made. In Section 3 of Public Law 875, of the 81st Congress, the assistance of Federal agencies is pledged:

> In the interest of providing maximum mobilization of Federal assistance under this act, the President is authorized to coordinate in such manner as he may determine the activities of the Federal agencies in providing disaster assistance.

In many cases this assistance is granted without compensation.

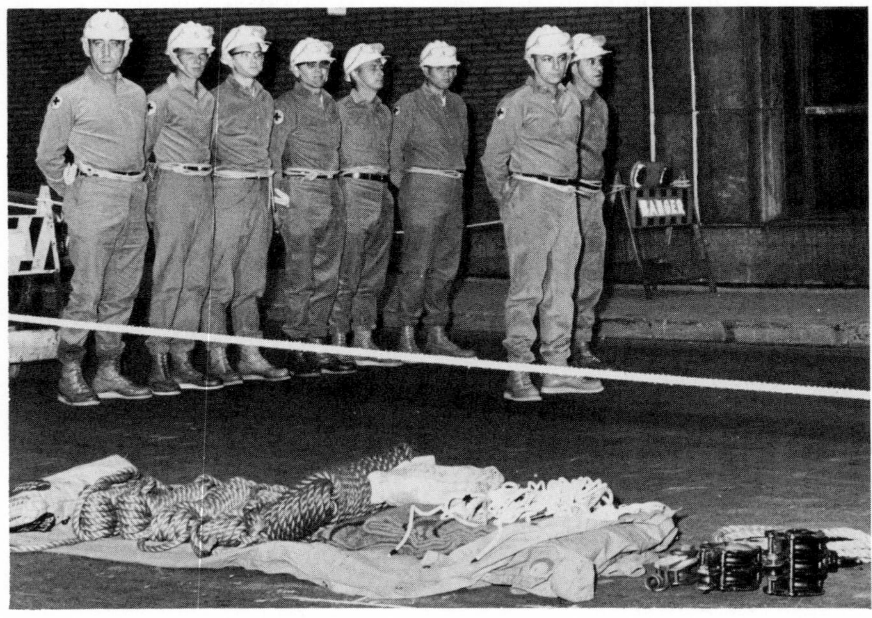

Figure 11:5,
A RESCUE SQUAD READY FOR AID WHEN DISASTER STRIKES.

The following is a brief analysis of the procedures in the case of many disasters:

A. If it is small, rescue is provided by local agencies—the police and fire departments, civil defense, ambulance squads, local hospitals, the American Red Cross, military services and others.

B. If it is a major disaster such as a hurricane, a flood or a big earthquake, the district is designated as a major disaster area and the federal government steps in with a variety of services such as:
   1. Giving or lending supplies, facilities, personnel, and other resources.
   2. Distributing food supplies and medicine through the American National Red Cross.
   3. Donating equipment and supplies that may be surplus. (This includes a wide variety of materials.)
   4. Providing protective services.
   5. Erecting temporary housing or emergency shelter.
   6. Clearing debris and wreckage.
   7. Reimbursing local governments for certain expenditures.

In a major disaster a wide variety of services can be utilized. For example, the U.S. Department of Agriculture (Rural Electrification Administration) can assist in the restoration of electric power, for supplies and other technical assistance. The Department of Commerce can aid in the rebuilding of roads and bridges. The Department of Defense can become the directing force in the entire operation, providing manpower, trucks and bases, field sanitation, removal of debris and many other forms of assistance. The U.S. Army Corps of Engineers is especially equipped for rescue and repair. Other agencies of the federal government can be called upon for services.

The American National Red Cross is charted by the Federal government but can make a major contribution. The Red Cross can provide a wide variety of supplies and services including food, shelter, clothing, medical and nursing aid, family services, survey, communications, transportation, supply, warning, rescue, evacuation, fund raising and police information. The various chapters of the Red Cross have disaster plans and after local police, fire department and civil defense are apt to be first on the scene.

It can readily be seen that outstanding work in disaster relief can be done by federal agencies and the Red Cross.

Local schools and colleges can do useful work. Members of the faculties of colleges and schools can be called into service by rescue authorities. Many schools stockpile food, water and clothing for use should a disaster occur. Many universities have engineers, doctors, nurses, chemists and other technicians on their staff. They also have buildings that can be used for repairs. Students can also be assigned to rescue and repair squads while cafeterias can be used for feeding refugees.

Each year there are a number of major disasters. There are few nations that have such a variety of services available as the United States.

summary

Communities need to be prepared to meet natural disasters, such as tornadoes, fires, floods, earthquakes, hurricanes and blizzards. It is surprising to note the large number of deaths and the tremendous losses of property that have resulted from these disasters. It appears that no part of the country is immune from disaster. Forest fires and conflagrations occur in almost every state. While tornadoes are most common in the central and southern states, there are occasions when they strike the New England and Middle Atlantic states. Earthquakes are more common on the Pacific Coast, disastrous floods occur in almost every state, while hurricanes strike the Gulf and Atlantic coasts, often extending to the Middle Atlantic and New England states.

Schools have a dual role to play in the protection of children. First, they must assume responsibility for the children and staff when the schools are struck by disaster. Second, they must do all they can to inform children and their parent so that they will act intelligently when disaster strikes. Many communities have developed plans for the education and protection of people in which the schools have a part to play. Training children to face emergencies should be a part of the school program.

There are many disasters in which the loss of life and the number of injuries is greatly increased by panic. Extreme fear and terror cause people to lose self-control and their only desire is to escape. While panic is difficult to control there are methods being used which have been found to be valuable. School fire drills have undoubtedly been helpful in reducing panic among children in case of fires or explosions. Lifeboat drills have aided in reducing the loss of life from marine disasters. Warning systems have been helpful in the control of panic. Schools and colleges aid in providing information that will help prepare for disasters.

The federal government has taken action in the organization and administration of disaster relief. A part of this work is being done by civil defense workers. The American National Red Cross also has a wide-spread program for aiding victims of disasters. There are few countries that have better programs and facilities for aiding in disaster relief than the United States.

suggested projects and activities

1. Make a list of the kinds of disasters that have occurred in your area.
2. What organizations could be called upon for help in case of a disaster in your community?
3. Make a list of the disasters that have occurred in the United States during the last year.
4. List the steps to be taken to reduce panic among people in case of a disaster.
5. Consult your local hospital and determine the medical planning for disaster aid.
6. Prepare an organizational chart of the chain of command for civil defense in a city.
7. Organize and set forth a plan for the development and training of a rescue squad for your school.
8. Construct a model of an air raid fallout shelter for the home.
9. Make a large map of your community. Indicate the following on it:
   a. your school
   b. other schools
   c. the civil defense center
   d. the principal highways for evacuation or over which people may come to your community for shelter
   e. shelter areas
   f. reservoirs, if within town limits
   g. electric power stations and substations
   h. water pumping stations
   i. telephone exchanges
   j. hospitals or areas designated as first aid centers for an emergency
   k. fire stations
   l. key people
   m. agency addresses essential to know in a disaster.

selected references

1. American Association of School Administrators, *Disaster Protection Handbook for School Administrators*. Washington, D.C.: The Association, 1959.
2. American Council on Education, *Civil Defense and Higher Education*. Washington, D.C.: The Council, 1954.
3. American National Red Cross, *Disaster Manual*. Washington, D.C.: The Red Cross, 1955.
4. Byrne, Charles T., "Lead the Way," *Nations Schools,* Vol. 17: May, 1963, 43-46.
5. Connecticut State Department of Education, *Education for Natural and Wartime Emergencies, a Handbook for Teachers*. Hartford: The Department. 1960.
6. Cutter, Walter, *Panic and Its Control*. New York: Association of Casualty and Surety Companies, 1957.
7. Department of Health, Education and Welfare, Office of Education. *Education for National Survial*. Washington, D.C.: The Department, 1956.
8. George Peabody College for Teachers, *Disaster Readiness in Undergraduate Education*. Nashville, Tenn.: The College, 1960.
9. Kennedy, John F., "Urgent National Needs." Address to the Congress of the United States, May 25, 1961.
10. MacKaye, William, "Black Warning of the Tornadoes," *Saturday Evening Post,* November 14, 1953.
11. National Commission on Safety Education, National Education Association, *Schools and Civil Defense*. Washington, D.C.: The Commission, 1964.
12. National Safety Council, "Preparing for Disaster," *Safety Education*, April, 1962.
13. New York State Civil Defense Commission, *Civil Defense and the Schools*. Albany, N.Y.: The Commission, 1953.
14. ________, *Survival in a Nuclear Attack*. Albany, N.Y.: The Commission, 1960.
15. Office of Emergency Planning, *National Plan for Emergency Preparedness*. Washington, D.C.: Government Printing Office, 1964.
16. Robinson, Donald, *The Face of Disaster*. Garden City, N.Y.: Doubleday & Company, Inc., 1959.
17. Strasser, Marland K. *et al., Fundamentals of Safety Education*. New York: The Macmillan Company, 1964.
18. The University of The State of New York, State Education Department, Bureau of Elementary Curriculum Development, *Fire Prevention Education*. Albany, N.Y.: The Department. 1958.

12

first aid

It is essential that every school system develop policies and practices for providing first aid to the injured. While safety programs are concerned with the prevention of accidents it is inevitable that even under the best practices some injuries will occur. When they do, first aid must be given. When sudden illnesses arise, first aid must be available. Beyond the administration of first aid to the injured and the ill it is known that the instruction of school youth and adults in first aid procedures lessens accidental injury to persons who have had such training. Education in first aid contributes to safe living.

First Aid Procedures

The school must be responsible for handling injuries and sudden illnesses that occur to pupils, staff and visitors in any area of the school's jurisdiction. Adequate facilities and properly trained personnel must be provided by the school to treat emergency cases and to establish—with the aid of legal advice, the local medical profession, the hospitals in the area and parent-teachers organizations—a plan for consistent and uniform handling of all such cases in order to protect the pupils and others against possible inadvertent neglect and the school against unjustified criticism. School policy should govern the nature of first aid to be given; the notification of parents of the injured child, or a responsible individual in the event someone other than a school youth is involved; transportation of the injured person to his home, or to a hospital; guidance given, whenever necessary, to sources of further treatment; maintaining accident reports and submitting records to appropriate agencies.

When a doctor is readily available, only that assistance necessary to preserve life and prevent aggravation of the injury should be provided until he arrives. Special types of assistance exclusive of practicing medicine may be given by capable nurses, teachers and administrators who have had training for such activity. School board policy should spell out quite clearly what they may or may not do. Because legal decisions have held that the school is responsible for providing first aid care to those injured in school areas, many cities now require that teachers and select staff members be prepared and certificated to administer first aid.

All school personnel must be informed about the procedures established for their areas in the event of an accident or emergency. Instructions and written policy should make clear the following requirements:

To whom immediate notice should be given if someone is injured or taken ill suddenly.

Who shall be notified if accidents occur, with or without injury, and if a capability of further harm exists, as well as a specified time limit for notification.

Where cases requiring minor first aid shall be treated.

How qualified persons may be reached and directed to the injured who are not to be moved.

What records are to be made of injuries, illnesses, accidents; where, and by whom. (Person in charge of activity area, statement by the injured, statements of witnesses, statements of inspectors where necessary)

The telephone number or call signal of each person having emergency duties or assignments is to be posted in properly designated areas, at all telephone locations, and, if advisable, in teachers' roll books. Emergency directions may be also placed on wall placards in all schoolrooms, giving emergency directions to persons using the facilities.

Care must be taken that substitute teachers are given written instructions for their temporary periods of service.

School officials and first aiders must be ready to act with dispatch when an emergency occurs. They will need information of this type:

Parents' full names, addresses, telephone number, and place of work or contact.

Names of persons who are authorized to act on behalf of the injured or ill if parents or responsible persons cannot be reached.

Name(s), address(es) and telephone number(s) of physicians who are designated to act on behalf of persons needing care.

Name and address of hospital to which person(s) should be taken in case of serious emergency.

Complete health and injury record of the pupil, including records of any hospital or medical insurance plan that would aid the youth in receiving proper care.

Basic First Aid

First aid is the immediate temporary treatment given in an emergency illness or injury before the services of a physician can be secured. Its purposes are to preserve life, prevent the aggravation of injuries or illness, and alleviate suffering. The basic directions that apply at the scene of any accident or emergency situation are divided into two groups: standard operating procedures, and admonitions that pertain to some special situations or types of emergencies.

The following are operational directions for giving first aid:

Keep the victim in a comfortable position, lying down preferably, and covered.

Examine him thoroughly for all injuries, not just those immediately apparent.

Look for:
- a. serious bleeding
- b. stoppage of breathing
- c. evidence of poisoning
- d. fractures, dislocations, burns, minor wounds, symptoms of concussion or other possible cause of unconciouness.

Send for medical assistance, and provide the following information:
- a. who is calling, where the patient is
- b. describe the injuries, symptoms, accident or emergency, and supplies available
- c. state the first aid that has been rendered
- d. receive further instructions for care until qualified help arrives.

The admonitory group of directions includes:

Do not move an injured or ill person unless there is a strong probability that the emergency would be aggravated by not moving him.

Do not give the unconscious person anything to drink.

Keep onlookers back and away from victims.

Keep the victim calm and comfortable by reassuring him. It is desirable to keep him from seeing or learning the extent of his injury.

All apparently severely injured persons must receive preventive care for shock as quickly as possible. Do not wait for shock to develop.

First Aid for Common Occurrences

A few situations that occur from time to time in the schools are considered here. Full details on first aid will be found in the references listed on page 217.

Shock Some degree of shock follows all injuries, large or small. A major injury may result in little shock or no apparent reaction. Shock may not appear immediately after an accident. Its manifestation may be delayed and if so, the shock is often more severe than it would have been if it occurred immediately. More people die from shock that accompanies an injury than from the injury itself.

Among the old and the very young, shock is greater than in the other age brackets because of contributary factors such as fear, lack of understanding, stress and susceptibility to injury. Among the aged, falls frequently are the indirect cause of accidental deaths, since a fractured hip or pelvis usually produces severe stock, which may be fatal. Among the very young, pain from a severe injury coupled with fear and anxiety often causes panic or hysteria along with severe shock.

Shock symptoms vary considerably from person to person. At times, only a few symptoms appear; at other times, nearly all may be present. The common symptoms include: pale face, weak and rapid pulse, cold, clammy skin, and cold perspiration on the sides of the forehead, upper lip, and palms. As shock progresses, breathing becomes shallow and an occasional sighing breath is taken by the victim; nausea, dizziness, restlessness and anxiety may develop. As shock progresses more deeply, the victim is less responsive, is unable to react well, loses anxiety and the dizziness may disappear. Finally, he lapses into unconsciousness, at which point he is in great danger.

To treat for shock, *keep the victim covered* and raise his feet above the level of his head.

Bleeding The easiest way to control bleeding is to apply pressure to the bleeding part. Any clean material may be held on the wound. Usually, the application of a sterile pad and a tightly wound bandage around the pad and the body part will stop the flow. In severe cases, digital pressure or a tourniquet may be used. The tourniquet should only be used if it means saving a life. Advanced study of first aid is recommended before one becomes involved in using the latter procedure, since it could itself cause serious injury.

Cuts, Scratches and Abrasions Minor wounds should receive prompt attention for the danger of infection is ever present. The first-aider will wash his hands before washing the wound. The wound should be washed with soap and water, dried, and then treated with an approved antiseptic. If a minor wound shows evidence of irritation, or fails to heal promptly, medical treatment is required. Puncture wounds must receive medical treatment to guard against tetanus.

Burns and Scalds The pain from burns is due to the exposure and injury of nerve endings. Relief from pain may be obtained by immersing the area in tepid water or by applying a paste of baking soda. Ice is used very generally for burns and works well in preventing blistering. Exposure to air intensifies pain. Pain may be lessened by applying several layers of sterile gauze to form a thick dressing and then enclosing the part with a snug bandage. Greasy ointments or salves, antiseptics, absorbent cotton, and flannel, should not be used on blistered or destructive burns for they complicate subsequent treatment. Any serious or extensive burn or scald should receive immediate medical attention. Acid, caustic and other chemical burns should be washed thoroughly with running water to remove all traces of the chemical and then treated as other burns.

The important principle with burns is to treat for shock, relieve pain and prevent contamination.

Fainting Fainting is a reaction of the nervous system that results from a temporary diminution of blood in the brain. Usually psychic factors initiate fainting. It is a temporary condition from which one recovers quickly when placed on his back. The patient should be kept reclining for ten minutes. An ammonia ampule may be helpful in reviving the individual who has fainted. If fainting is prolonged, a doctor should be summoned for it is no longer a case of simple fainting.

Fractures, Skeletal Injuries Fractures, dislocations, sprains, strains and bone bruises require special care. If a bone is broken, the patient should be kept quiet until the arrival of a doctor; any attempt to move him may aggravate the injury. If doctors are not readily available, a fractured limb must be immobilized by a qualified first-aider. In case of a dislocation, prompt and proper treatment by a physician is necessary to prevent further injury to the ligaments, blood vessels, and nerves that are injured. No unnecessary movement should be permitted. Severe injuries to bones, joints and muscles should be treated by a physician. In all cases of injury to the skeletal system and its supporting tissues, shock care should be provided while the injured part is properly supported and rested.

Animal Bites All victims of animal bites should receive shock care and be seen by a physician so that proper care may be advised and notification to the health authorities be made officially. Regardless of the kind of animal, the bite area should be thoroughly washed with soap and water for several minutes, dried, and a sterile dressing applied. An antiseptic will be applied by a physician as follow-up treatment.

Poisoning The widespread incidence of poisonings of all kinds and

Figure 12:1, PATROL RESCUES AN INJURED SKIER.

the need for very prompt and effective action has resulted in the setting up of poison control centers near all major population areas. The telephone number of the nearest poison control center should be immediately available in any home, office or school. (In addition, all emergency telephone numbers should be kept next to all telephones.)

When poisoning occurs, a doctor should be called immediately. Read the label on the poison container for the antidote and treatment. In most cases the patient should be induced to vomit by being given quantities of water. Continue to administer water and induce vomiting until the fluid raised from the stomach has become clear. No emetic should be used in cases of acid or alkaline poisoning: antidotes are diluted milk of magnesia for acids, vinegar for alkalis. If a caustic substance has been swallowed do not induce vomiting. Do not give an unconscious person any liquid to drink. In all cases of poison, the victim should be treated for shock. It may be necessary to administer artificial respiration in some types of poisoning and continue it for hours or even days although not by the first-aider.

A basic principle in poison control is to bring antidotes to any poisons into the home whenever a poison is purchased. Each home should also have a universal antidote available. Furthermore, careful storage and proper supervision of all poisons must be provided.

Foreign Bodies in the Eye Foreign bodies of all kinds can become lodged in an eye. A speck of soot in the eye is very common and can usually be easily removed. Because of the danger of injury the patient must not rub the eye when an irritant is in it. If a gentle closing of the eyelid does not remove the object, the eye should be washed with clean water introduced by a medicine dropper. The eyelid may be turned back and the object removed by a bit of moistened sterile gauze or a wisp of wet cotton. If an object is on the cornea or iris it may not be easily seen. Furthermore, the danger of injuring the cornea exists. In such cases, have a doctor treat the patient. The eye should be covered with a light sterile compress to avoid painful movements of the eye and the patient taken immediately to the physician. Chemicals should be removed by washing the eye with large quantities of water for 10 to 15 minutes.

Unconsciousness Unconsciousness with breathing or without breathing is usually divided into three categories—red, white or blue—flushed, pale or cyanotic. *Red* unconsciousness is associated with a stroke due to sunstroke or high blood pressure, or less frequently with chronic alcoholism or diabetes. It is treated by the application of cold compresses to the head, raising the shoulders and head while the patient is recumbent, and attention by a physician. *White* unconsciousness indicates shock as a result of hemorrhage, injury, fainting or heat exhaustion. Treatment for shock is administered. *Blue* unconsciousness usually indicates respiratory obstruction, drowning, acute heart attack, or poisoning. Artificial respiration is essential if the victim's breathing is insufficient to sustain him.

Unconsciousness of any form can be dangerous. Suspect injury to the brain; this is especially true if it is prolonged, intermittent, or if the victim has had head injuires. In any of these cases, the victim may be red, white, or blue and must be attended by a physician. Unconsicous victims should be transported in a recumbent position.

Artificial Respiration Certain types of accidents—the most frequent of which are immersion in water, electrical shock, gas poisoning, and respiratory obstruction—cause stoppage of breathing, and death may occur as a result. First aid can prevent this by producing forced breathing in the victim through any one of the accepted means of resuscitation. Among them are the use of the mechanical resuscitator, the mouth-to-mouth technique, the Holger-Nielson (back pressure-arm lift) manual method and the Silvester method (chest pressure-arm lift). In addition to the mouth-to-mouth resusciation technique, persons who are qualified may use the closed chest heart massage measure if the victim's heart is in arrest. A full discussion of resuscitation techniques is available in standard texts on first aid listed at the end of this chapter.

Since the mouth-to-mouth method is generally preferred, the procedure for carrying it out is described. Turn the victim on his back and:

1. *Wipe out victim's mouth quickly.* Turn his head to the side. Use your fingers to get rid of mucus, food, sand, and other matter.
2. *Straighten victim's head and tilt back so that chin points up. Push or pull his jaw up into jutting out position* to keep his tongue from blocking air passage. This position is essential for keeping the air passage open throughout the procedure.
3. *Place your mouth tightly over victim's mouth* and pinch nostrils closed to prevent air leakage. For a child, cover both nose and mouth tightly with your mouth. (Breathing through handkerchief or cloth placed over victim's mouth or nose will not greatly affect the exchange of air.)
4. *Breathe into victim's mouth or nose* until you see his chest rise. (Air may be blown through victim's teeth, even though they may be clenched.)
5. *Remove your mouth and listen* for the sound of returning air. If there is no exchange, recheck jaw and head position. If you still do not get air exchange, turn victim on side and slap him on back between shoulder blades to dislodge matter that may be in throat. Again, wipe out his mouth to remove foreign matter.
6. *Repeat breathing,* removing mouth each time to allow for escape of air. For an adult, breathe about 20 times per minute. For a child, take relatively shallow breaths, about 25 per minute. Continue until victim breathes for himself.

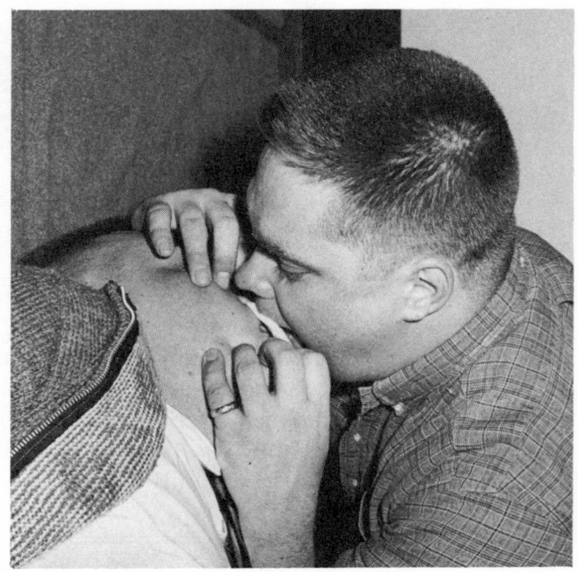

Figure 12:2, PRACTICE IN MOUTH TO MOUTH RESUSCITATION. THIS METHOD IS WIDELY USED TODAY. ONE SHOULD STUDY THE STEPS CAREFULLY. NOTE THAT THIN PLASTIC TISSUE IS USED TO PREVENT INFECTION.

The Holger-Nielson or back pressure-arm lift method is briefly described:

1. Quickly place the victim in a prone position hands under head, elbows outward, and check his mouth to clear it of obstruction, if necessary. Kneel at his head and place your hands on his back below his shoulder blades, with thumbs parallel to the backbone.
2. Rock forward gently so that about 35 pounds of your weight forces air

from the victim's lungs. Your elbows are to be straight and the pressure is to be applied smoothly.

3. Release pressure by rocking backwards and at the same time slide your hands along the victim's back, past his armpits, and down near his elbows.
4. Carry the victim's arms upwards as you rock backwards. At this point a third person may hold the head to maintain an airway. When you have reached a kneeling position with a straight back, his chest will be at a maximum lift for taking in air. Now lower the arms and slide your hands to the original position while rocking forward and apply pressure on the shoulder blades with a forward and downward movement to coincide with the rocking movement. Each cycle should take five to six seconds—12 per minute.

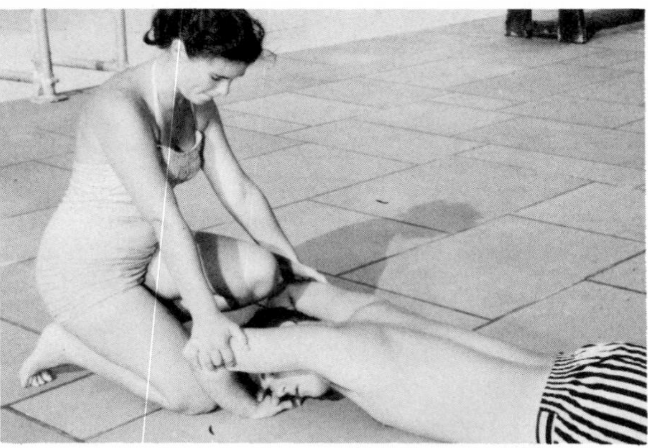

Figure 12:3, BACK PRESSURE-ARM LIFT: REACHING MAXIMUM LIFT.

Whenever artificial respiration is initiated, it is to be continued until the victim has recovered or medical examination reveals that continued action is useless.

Emergency Medical Identification A new universal symbol of emergency medical identification is now receiving widespread recognition. Developed by the American Medical Association, it is intended to identify and give health information about any person needing first aid. The figure is illustrated below. Essential information is given on the card. For special medical problems a plastic or metal disk should be worn at all times stating precisely the kinds of special care the person requires.

Figure 12:4.

First Aid Instruction

At a meeting of school administrators the problem of teaching first aid to elementary and secondary school pupils was discussed. The consensus was that in times of stress any person might be called upon to administer first aid, especially if officially recognized persons were not immediately available. Similarly, it was believed possible that high school pupils and many upper elementary grade pupils, if properly trained, would be capable of administering such aid for the more common and less serious injuries, serving as assistants to the persons actually in charge.

Figure 12:5,
THOUSANDS OF CLASSES OF FIRST AID HAVE BEEN HELD IN SCHOOLS, COLLEGES, INDUSTRIES AND IN POLICE DEPARTMENTS. THIS ILLUSTRATION SHOWS A CONTEST CONDUCTED BY THE INTERNATIONAL FIRST AID AND RESCUE ASSOCIATION WHICH COOPERATES WITH THE AMERICAN RED CROSS IN TRAINING PROGRAMS.

The American National Red Cross gives a series of first aid courses that are designed to meet the needs of all phases of industrial, school and community life. The prescribed course of training that would enable school teachers to be certificated as first aid instructors is relatively short, and can be taken by any interested teacher who contacts the local chapter of the Red Cross.

The direct responsibility of the teacher of first aid is to translate course materials into actual practice, but because of the nature of first aid and because "a little learning is a dangerous thing," certain precautions must be taken:

1. Pupils, both children and adults, must have ample time in which to learn first aid skills such as bandaging, treatment and the like.
2. There must be effective management of the class to insure proper attitudes toward the seriousness of the work; the potential dangers and values, the life-or-death phases of the treatment, must be made clear.
3. Throughout the instruction emphasis must be placed on the fact that the first-aider should not try to take the place of a doctor. A doctor should be called to tend any injury especially if it occurs on school property, during school hours or during a school activity.
4. It is as essential for a trainee to know what not to do as it is for him to know what to do.
5. There is a tendency to overemphasize some phases of instruction, for example, fractures and dislocations. In school courses there is little need of considering the more specialized phases of first aid. The discussion of elaborate tables of antidotes is usually a waste of time, since few homes have the antidotes listed. An analysis of accidents to school children shows that the following injuries are common and can therefore be made the basis of first aid instruction:
   Cuts, abrasions, punctures and lacerations
   Bruises
   Sprains and strains
   Burns, scalds, bad sunburn
   Bleeding
   Shock and fainting
   Fractures and dislocations
   Electric shock, gas poisoning, drowning
   Bites of animals
   Internal and external poisoning
   Foreign bodies in the eyes and ears
   Frostbite
6. In addition to the areas suggested above, instruction should be given in (a) methods of bandaging, (b) materials needed in first air kits, (c) lifting and carrying patients, and (d) making patients comfortable.
7. First aid supplies should be available in the offices of the nurse or school doctor, the physical educator, principal, and teacher of shop and laboratories.

The First Aid Program

First aid care must be given to students, staff and visitors whenever the need arises. The responsibility for administering a first aid program rests with the head of the school. An effective program should provide for: the proper care of the injured; effective notification of designated parent or person, physician, and school administrator; transportation when needed; guidance for further treatment; accident reports as required; and an instruction program to develop first aid skills and concepts among students and staff. While school boards should establish policies and procedures for the first aid program, each individual should attempt to gain competencies that would enable him to aid the injured, knowing what to do and what not to do. Furthermore, first aid training tends to lessen accident experience among trainees.

suggested projects and activities

1. Prepare an objective test on first aid essentials for either elementary or secondary school pupils.
2. Outline a series of first aid demonstrations, including the floor plan, number of performers, order of events, and materials needed.
3. Prepare for a quiz program a series of 30 questions on first aid essentials, on either the elementary, the secondary, or the adult level.
4. Write a dramatization of a first aid situation for a particular school level.
5. Prepare a series of slides illustrating first aid procedures in several situations such as boating, life saving, bandaging.
6. Arrange for a demonstration of mouth-to-mouth resuscitation and closed chest heart massage for students in a safety course. Have a physician present to answer questions.
7. Develop an exhibit of new devices for first aid treatment.
8. Attempt to identify the ten leading misconceptions about activities requiring first aid for students in a neighboring school or college.

selected references

1. American National Red Cross, *First Aid Instructor's Manual.* Washington, D.C.: The Red Cross, 1957.
2. ________, *First Aid Textbook* (4th ed.). Garden City, N.Y.: Doubleday and Company, Inc., 1957.
3. Bureau of Naval Personnel, *Standard First Aid Training Course* (NAVPERS 10081). Washington, D.C.: U.S. Government Printing Office, 1955.
4. Department of the Army, *First Aid for Soldiers* (FM 21-11). Washington, D.C.: U.S. Government Printing Office, 1954.
5. Elkow, J. Duke, "Action on Accidents," *Safety Education Digest.* New York: The Center, 1955.
6. Equitable Life Assurance Society of the United States, *Home Health Emergencies.* New York: The Society (out of print).
7. Henderson, John, *Emergency Medical Guide.* New York: McGraw-Hill Book Company, 1963.
8. U.S. Department of Health, Education, and Welfare, Public Health Service, *Artificial Respiration, Mouth-to-Mouth or Mouth-to-Nose Rescue Breathing.* Washington, D.C.: The Department (n.d.).

13

the role of safety education

What is the role of safety education? This question may be answered in a number of different ways. The first answer to come to mind is that safety education saves lives. Another is that it saves time and money due to the fact that it reduces the waste caused by accidents. Still another answer might be that the role of safety education is to enable people to interact with each other and with their environment more efficiently and with greater satisfaction. It is not enough just to live; it is also important to have a good life. When appropriately incorporated into the total school program with due concern for the responsibilities in instruction, administration and protective areas, safety education contributes to the enrichment of other phases of the school program. The role of safety education is to improve the conditions for learning and practicing safe behavior and, in this role, it harmonizes with and strengthens the total school program. It involves a group of educators with special preparation whose purpose it is to improve safety education. Furthermore, it involves *all* educators to the extent that accident prevention, as a part of administrative, protective and instructional responsibilities, may be incorporated into their daily work.* During a relatively short history, safety education has progressed from presentations of accident statistics and the memorizing of safety rules to comprehensive programs of instruction and protection.

A Discipline in American Education

A discipline may be defined as a body of knowledge organized around basic concepts and theories. Educators and other specialists have defined a comprehensive body of knowledge in safety education and have developed programs for treating it integrally with general education. In its concern with the administrative, protective and instructional phases of safety education, the profession is constantly coming to grips with more intricate problems in accident prevention efforts with the increasing knowledge and effective applications of new facts. In the words of Sarah C. Caldwell, "A profession is based on, and is custodian of, a body of specialized knowledge which it is pledged to enlarge and improve (3)."

Within this discipline there is professional concern about how to create a greater public awareness of the fact that people must learn to select low-risk action rather than high-risk action; and, further, to extend the awareness that the best place to learn this safe behavior is in the nation's schools. There is concern about the thousands of lives lost and the millions of injuries annually on our streets and highways, on farms, in homes, in business and industry and in governmental occupations. As pointed out by Arnold B. Barach in the recent publication, *1975 and the Changes to Come* (1), the influx of raw youth arriving at industry's door almost concurrently with the flowering of automation, presents a crisis which must be met by revised industrial and school training programs. Barach made no specific reference to the problem of accidents, but it takes no stretch of the imagination to extend the meaning of the above statement to include accident prevention education as being essential for our survival. Teaching for survival cannot be viewed apart from the school's responsibility for general education.

Professional Quality in Teaching Safe Living

What are the elements needed to assure top-quality teaching of safe living? It is impossible here to develop all of the areas that this question

* The terms "safety education," and "accident prevention," are used interchangeably to refer to the over-all program of administration, instruction, and protection for safe living in schools and colleges.

suggests, but some ideas which are based on the principles of learning and of human growth and development should illustrate the importance of quality in safety education. In safety education, as in other areas of learning, we deal with growth and we need to see the urge to grow, both in the pupil and in ourselves as educators. Usually we can see in the learner this urge to grow merely by listening to him and by observing his behavior. This is true no matter what we teach, but it is neither quite as true nor nearly as important in other subjects as it is in teaching people to survive. When the teacher senses this growth dynamism, he can better inspire the learner to learn. It has been said that an inspiring teacher is one who can help the learner believe that his subject matter can live within him. This can be paraphrased, "an inspiring teacher is one who can help the learner believe that he *must* learn how to avoid accidents." In this field we must help the pupil to see that learning safe living is a practical thing. Then, we must inspire him to believe that subject matter, in this case safety subject matter, can live within him—can give him insight for selecting low-risk behavior.

Now, as we focus our attention more closely upon quality in teaching safe living, we need to recognize the significant process of decision-making. In order to teach sound decision-making in maintaining safe behavior it is necessary for us to look at ourselves as educators.

Since teaching rests on a person-to-person relationship and since maintaining safe behavior involves dynamic relationships of people in their environment, it is highly important that the safety educator make every effort to understand the learner. A teacher once said, "I don't need to understand the child, only how to teach reading." If this is a naïve statement about the teaching of reading, as it obviously is, then one only needs to substitute the word "safety" for "reading" at the end of the sentence to appreciate the absurdity of such an attitude about the child and accident prevention education. Particularly in teaching safe behavior, we need to know how the learner feels about himself, about people and about things around him, in order to help him relate himself to them in safe ways. His learning and his safe conduct depend largely upon his feeling of comfortableness about himself, and from his history the safety educator must take cues and find guides for creating situations out of which he can evolve safe behavior. But, understanding an individual learner, as important as it is, is not enough.

We need further insight into human behavior to help us use this understanding. In teaching for safe living, our goal must be to teach everyone, not just those who wish to specialize in one field or another. For what does it profit society to prepare scientists who are unable to live with reasonable safety? This does not mean merely tapping this "well of quality" the first period on Monday morning. Rather, we must share this quality widely day-by-day. The safety educator's conduct should consistently demonstrate his understanding of and his dedication to principles of safety.

More and more we must perceive and utilize scientific methods in safety education. We need to become expert in putting together accumulated facts about the learner to derive guidelines for stimulating and teaching him how to assess and deal safely with the risk in a situation. Also, we need the facts that science gives us about the learning process to help inspire and guide the child's urge to grow, to grow in citizenship and in safe conduct. We should be keenly aware of the scientifically proved fact that every human wants to learn provided that he can realize what the learning holds for him. No matter how much we drill the student on safe use of tools, or use of seat belts in automobiles, for example, he will adopt the practice only to the extent that he comes to accept it as being important to living. In this connection, we must be ever aware of the fact that the teacher cannot motivate. This happens within the learner. But, we can help him capture what he needs for motivation and learning. So, in a larger sense, the learner teaches himself—he teaches himself safe behavior. But this does not mean that what the teacher does is unimportant; for it is the teacher who creates the situations, the climate for this self-directed, self-valued learning for safe living.

Learning is further enhanced when differences among learners in the group are accepted, first by the teacher, then by the pupils themselves. To be an accepted member of the group may very well keep an individual from risk-taking conduct which he otherwise might have chosen just to get attention. Thus, it is important to emphasize group learning and, at the same time, to guide the group in establishing sets of values which are conducive to safe living (2). The values held by the learner and his peers are important in the teacher's efforts to create conditions for effective learning. If the accepted norm within the group is represented by using the railroad tracks as a route to and from school, stealing hubcaps, or playing the game of "chicken" on the highways, then the task of the teacher is to arrange experiences whereby the group can evolve a more acceptable and safer behavioral norm.

In dealing with individual differences among learners, the safety educator will do well to remember that the rate at which the learner utilizes his energy has much to do with his learning pace, how readily he adjusts to safe practices in a school environment which is new to him, or how readily he adjusts to the progressively more complex traffic situations in freeway driving, or even space travel (5). For the safety of individuals it is often important to minimize as much as possible the degree of threat which different situations hold for them. One way to keep such threat at a minimum for pupils in the school environment is to see to it that they are not expected to venture into situations before they have gained experience enough to adjust safely in them. The pupils' physical and emotional differences will determine the differences in the rates at which they can adjust.

Figure 13:1,

Disabled Persons Learn to Drive. Orthopedic Disabilities do not Necessarily Keep One from Gainful Employment or Driving. Hundreds of Thousands of Disabled Persons Have Learned to Drive Specially Equipped Cars.

Innovation in Education and Responsibility for Accident Prevention

Change in our society has wrought great change upon education in America. One of the important changes which has come in response to the demands of society has been the development of safety education. Now, with the exploration of space is coming a great reshaping of programs in American education and, because of these dramatic changes, the role of safety education is being tested on many fronts. If safety education is to keep its place in this melting pot of educational change it, too, will have to change. Obsolete safety education concepts and methods will not meet the requirements which society sets for programs of American education. With intensified scientific efforts and the resultant acceleration of technological change, the hazards of daily living will be further increased. Thus, we may expect that society will require more efficient and more effective life-saving education in the future than has been required in the past. With this in mind, let us look at some of the significant innovations which are said to be evolving in American education generally, and consider the role of safety education in relation to them (6).

1. *Efforts in education to produce fuller and more effective utilization of human talents.*

The talents of both teachers and learners, and of other professional and lay personnel are seen to be highly important. Team teaching, employment of students as teacher aides, and independent study, among other things, illustrate advances in the utilization of human talent. In safety education, particularly driver education, these practices have been quite common for a number of years. For example, teachers who give classroom and practice driving instruction cooperatively demonstrate this team approach. Today there is much to be learned by the safety educator from research done in other areas of education in the interest of fuller utilization of human talent. As social science researchers and educators conduct important rsearch to "learn more about learning" in general, those of us who specialize in accident prevention education must be alert to opportunities for making application of their findings. We must also concern ourselves more with research expressly designed to shed greater light upon the task of teaching safe behavior in schools and colleges.

2. *Efforts to gain fuller and more effective utilization of time.*

Changes in length of instructional periods, length of courses, length of school day, and the introduction of flexible scheduling and summer programs illustrate the growing concern in American education for better utilization of time. Safety education has been extended in all of these ways. The safety educator must continue to search for other changes which will help to extend safety education to all people. The time is already here when administrators and teachers concerned with the instruction in this area must implement further change in present school programs. As conditions in the school and community change, it may well become necessary to schedule definite blocks of time for safety education emphasis in order to keep the accident rate of both youth and adults from getting entirely out of hand. Surveys of conditions in schools and communities can reveal conditions which signal the dangers created by the addition of new and unfamiliar facilities such as new recreational areas, new industry and new freeways, or the shifting of employment from one industry to another. Then schools can work with the community and with industry in providing specialized safety preparation to cope with such new conditions in appropriate blocks of school time, and in harmony with the school's general education program. This innovation is offered as an addition to the traditional integration of safety content, the safety instructional units, and separate courses. While these traditional programs will surely need to be modified in keeping with changes in general education, it is not likely that these established processes will be replaced.

3. Efforts to gain fuller and more effective utilization of technology.

Safety education employs, in one way or another, most of the technological resources now employed in other fields of instruction, such as teaching machines, television, films, magnetic tapes and other electronic devices. As research and experimentation go forward in education generally, safety education specialists must keep pace with these developments and adapt and extend them in every way possible in the interest of more effective education for safe living. Administrative and protective measures, as well as instruction, will be increasingly important. Experimentation and research can provide better understandings for school plant inspections and for sound administrative policy regarding inspection. What could be more important among efforts for a greater utilization of technology in education than to safeguard school plants and equipment through more effective inspection for fire prevention?

4. Efforts to improve the curriculum.

Curriculum development centers are examples of efforts to keep in step with the demands of our society and to meet the challenge of world pressures. With innovations in procedures for content selection and sequence, and in materials development and instructional methodology for other fields of instruction, must come changes in programs of safety education as well.

There is today an urgent need for research-based optimum placement of safety content in the total school program. As the curriculum in schools may be organized on a vertical continuum to provide learning experiences on the basis of individual student differences and rates of learning, it will be essential to incorporate safety learning experiences to harmonize with these newer curriculum patterns. Otherwise, the safety educator will be left behind in the outmoded curriculum rubble and the role of safety education will be something far less than will be needed. More effective leadership for safety instruction in connection with curriculum planning and action will be necessary in the years ahead.

Accident prevention leadership by administrators as well as safety education specialists will be more important than ever in an age of rapid change. School boards should select administrators from applicants who have background preparation and who have demonstrated dedication to accident prevention and safety education as a part of the total school program. Administrators, in turn, will need to select teaching and supervisory staff who have had preparation in this field, and who have a zeal to teach for safe living. Competent supervisory personnel will be needed in greater numbers to assist other professional staff in furthering safety instruction throughout the curriculum, and to provide the leadership necessary to assure that emphasis will be given to different phases of accident prevention in special blocks of school time as school and community conditions may require.

5. *Efforts to improve teaching and the education of teachers.*

Greater emphasis is being placed on the *general education* of teachers, on *simplification of the theoretical content* of professional preparation, and on the improvement of clinical experience for the preservice teacher. What does this mean to the professional safety educator and to the role of safety education? Without going into all the implications for safety education, it seems sufficient to suggest only two or three. Greater emphasis on general education for teachers will mean that the preservice teacher must either extend the amount of college preparation before entering the teaching field, or he must compromise, with fewer number of credit hours in his area of specialization. This is likely to mean stiffer competition for safety education subject matter in the over-all program of general education of preservice teachers. This is likely to mean that teachers specializing in safety education will have to select their program of courses from a wider range of related fields as part of his preparation. It also suggests the need for greater attention to the incorporation of more safety education subject matter in courses for teacher preparation. The role of the safety education specialist will be even more important in seeing to it that the substance of safety education is effectively incorporated into the over-all teacher education program. Furthermore, safety education offerings in teacher preparation will need to be more carefully harmonized with the trend toward broader patterns of teacher certification by state agencies.

These changes in general teacher education are coming about at a time when the need for thorough preparation of college safety education personnel and school system supervisory personnel, and for teacher specialization in safety education is greater than ever before. A program of safety education limited by the lack of qualified professional staff can never enable the schools to prepare the more than 60 million school and college enrollees for safe living.

6. *Efforts to change the design and arrangement of the physical facilities for education.*

Changes which are coming about in educational plants and other facilities are perhaps the most dramatic indications of the influence of technology and the demands of our society on American education. Architectural designs such as an entire school "in the round," school buildings under ground, and windowless buildings above ground, were undreamed of a few years ago. Such innovations impose changes in school curriculums and school administration in general. They represent a tremendous challenge to the safety education profession and stand as warnings to reassess and regroup for an extended and more effective role for safety education.

Importance of Professional Organization

We have discussed the urge to grow, on the part of both the learner and the safety educator. The elements of teaching quality, outlined in this chapter, suggest the need for continuous teacher growth. It is easier to satisfy our urge to grow professionally if we are active in the program of the professional organization in our chosen field. There is a place for both the preservice teacher and the in-service teacher in such an organization. Active participation in the work of the professional organization helps the safety educator in sound decision-making in the classroom, in administration, and in his total responsibilities for fostering accident prevention. The professional organization needs the safety educator and the profession serves the safety educator by helping him increase his competence in teaching safe living. Since ours is a discipline based on a body of specialized knowledge, and since this body of specialized knowledge is bound to change rapidly, we need to maintain close contact with our profession in order to grow with this constantly changing field.

The profession has ethical standards and we need the profession to help maintain the high standards of integrity in the teaching and administration of safety education. Since the profession influences public policies, the safety educator has an obligation to participate in the development of sound policies. He will benefit from the group solidarity found in the profession and will be a more effective representative of his discipline as he assumes responsibility to strengthen it.

Because democracy places high value on each life, many elements of quality are required of the safety educator, not the least of which are qualities of moral and spiritual values. These provide the best setting in which the learner may develop an ever-evolving process of learning safe living. Upon the role of the professional as a representative of the profession depends the role of safety education and thus the well-being of our society.

summary

Safety education has clearly demonstrated its value and has become a definite responsibility of the schools. It saves lives and reduces injuries and the waste caused by accident. Instruction in safe living should be given to all pupils—either through the direct method or through integration or correlation with other subjects. Driver education, for example, should be available to all eligible students.

Changes in our society, the development of new products, technological advances and the increased mobility of our people will result in a further increase in the hazards of daily living. Children must be prepared to meet these hazards. The facts that research and science give us must be used to guide the child's urge to grow in citizenship and safe conduct. For no matter what he knows about the safe use of tools, machinery and automobiles, students will adopt safe practices only as they accept them as being important to living.

The content and methods of teaching will change as a result of research and the needs as shown by accidents. There will undoubtedly be a greater use of team teaching, the utilization of students as teacher aids and independent study. More attention will be paid to a fuller and more effective use of time. There will be a greater use of audio-visual aids, radio and television in the teaching of safety education. The curriculum should not remain static but must change to meet new problems and new hazards. Most of all there will be improvements in the preparation of teachers. This may mean the introduction of safety education courses for undergraduates. On the other hand, greater attention will be paid to the incorporation of safety subject matter in other courses—the sciences, physical education, the social sciences, psychology and industrial arts.

In the critical days ahead, safety education, which has so clearly demonstrated its value in saving lives and reducing injuries, should be maintained and extended. Education for safe living should be a basic responsibility of the schools.

suggested projects and activities

1. Make a list of the professional characteristics that would make a person a superior teacher of safety education.
2. What are some of the technological developments since World War II which have resulted in greater hazards?
3. What illustrations can you give of efforts to improve the curriculum in safety education?
4. What methods are being used to improve the standards of teachers of safety and driver education in your state?

selected references

1. Barach, Arnold B., and the Kiplinger Washington Editors, *1975 and the Changes to Come*. New York: Harper & Row, Publishers, 1962.
2. Brody, Leon, *Basic Aspects and Applications of The Psychology of Safety,* pp. 13-14. New York: New York University, 1959.
3. Caldwell, Sarah C., "A Decision Not Lightly Made," *ADEA News and Views,* March, 1963, pp. 1-2.
4. Murphy, Lois Barclay, "Self-Management Capacities in Children," in *New Insights and the Curriculum* (1963 Yearbook), pp. 107-120. Washington, D.C.: Association for Supervision and Curriculum Development, a department of the National Education Association, 1963.
5. National Commission on Safety Education, National Education Association. "Safety Education in the Space Age." Washington, D.C.: The Commission, January, 1960. A single mimeographed page.
6. Nelson, Lester W., "A Perspective on Innovation in Education." Unpublished address before the professional staff of the National Education Association, October 31, 1962.

14

the elementary schools

In the last two decades much of the success in reducing the death rate for child accidents has been due to the work of the elementary schools. While in recent years the trend in the death rate for secondary school pupils has gone upward, that for the elementary schools is still downward. Since 1922, the rate of this age group has dropped more than 50 per cent. It could be shown that this downward trend in the death rate over a period of years has resulted in the "saving" of many thousands of lives. Safety education is certainly producing results. Many cities with good all-around safety programs have shown a striking reduction in child accidents.

> Saving Lives
>
> The death rate from accidents of children of school age declined from 30.0 in 1933 to 18.8 in 1963. Theoretically, this means that there has been a "saving" of over 30,000 child lives in the 30-year span.
>
> *Prepared from data in "Accident Facts," National Safety Council.*

How can the needs of safety education be determined? First, through an analysis of accidents. In a sense, an accident can be

OUR CHILDREN'S WORLD

AGE AND INTERESTS	HAZARDS	SUGGESTIONS
The "Hand to Mouth" Age ***UP TO 2 YEARS***	Avoid small toys which may be swallowed . . . flammable objects . . . toys with small removable parts . . . poisonous paint on any object . . . stuffed animals with glass or button eyes.	Sturdy rattles . . . brightly colored objects hung in view . . . rubber or washable squeak toys and stuffed dolls or animals . . . large, soft colored balls . . . blocks with rounded corners . . . push-and-pull toys with strings or rounded handles . . . nests of objects.
The Explorative Age ***2 TO 3 YEARS***	Avoid anything with sharp or rough edges which will cut or scratch . . . objects with small removable parts . . . poisonous paint or decoration . . . marbles . . . beads . . . coins . . . flammable toys.	Sand box with bucket, shovel and spoon . . . large peg boards . . . wooden animals . . . cars and wagons to push around . . . tip-proof kiddie cars and tricycles . . . large crayons . . . low rocking horse . . . small chair and table.
The "Let's Pretend" Age ***3 TO 4 YEARS***	Avoid toys which are too heavy for child's strength . . . poorly made objects which may come apart, break or splinter . . . sharp or cutting toys . . . highly flammable costumes . . . electrical toys.	Small broom and carpet sweeper . . . toy telephone . . . dolls with simple wrap-around clothing . . . doll buggies and furniture . . . dishes . . . miniature garden tools . . . trucks and tractors . . . non-electrical train . . . drum . . . costume clothes . . . building blocks.
Beginning of Creative Age ***4 TO 6 YEARS***	Avoid shooting or target toys which will endanger eyes . . . ill-balanced mobile toys (tricycles, wagons, etc.) which may topple easily . . . poisonous painting sets . . . pinching or cutting objects.	Blackboard and dustless chalk . . . simple construction sets . . . paints and paint books . . . doll house and furniture . . . small sports equipment . . . skipping rope . . . wash tub and board . . . paper doll sets with blunt end scissors . . . costumes . . . modelling clay.
Beginning of Dexterity Age ***6 TO 8 YEARS***	Avoid non-approved electrical toys . . . anything too large or complicated for child's strength and ability . . . sharp edged tools . . . poorly made skates . . . conductible kites . . . shooting toys.	Carpenter bench and well-constructed, lightweight tools . . . sled . . . construction sets . . . roller skates . . . approved electrical toys . . . kites . . . equipment for playing store, bank, filling station, etc. . . . playground equipment . . . kites . . . puzzles and games . . . sewing materials . . . dolls and doll equipment.
Specialization of Tastes and Skills ***8 AND OLDER***	Avoid air rifles, chemistry sets, dart games, bows and arrows, dangerous tools and electrical toys UNLESS used under parental supervision . . . motor scooters . . . non-approved electrical toys.	Hobby materials, arts and crafts, photography, coin and stamp collections, puppet shows . . . musical instruments . . . gym and sports equipment . . . model and construction building sets . . . electric train with Underwriters' Laboratories approval . . . bicycle . . . science sets . . .

NATIONAL SAFETY COUNCIL

considered an indication of an educational shortage. Most accidents are due to errors or failures to follow safe practices. Thus the accident facts of the school system can be used to show where special stress should be placed. This means that all school systems should have established procedures for accident reporting. The records should be analyzed and the results made available to the schools as well as to other organizations in the community. Some types of accidents tend to be most common during certain months; for example, burns and scalds in October, home accidents in November. For this reason, schools generally organize their instruction on a seasonal or monthly basis.

Evidence of need also comes from a study of the hazards in the environment of the children. Are there unusually dangerous street crossings? Are there dumps where children play or streets on which the sledding in winter is hazardous?

A third indication of need can be developed from an analysis of child activities in which there are elements of danger. Some children play on dangerous streets; they go on hikes and camping trips; they compete in athletic sports; they learn to swim and use boats and canoes; they use various kinds of sharp tools in and about the home—in all of these activities there may be an element of danger. As a matter of fact, according to *Accident Facts* (13), accidents for both boys and girls are much more common in out-of-school activities than in those under the jurisdiction of the school. They should have instruction to prepare them to meet the dangers involved in these activities.

Figure 14:2,
SAFETY LESSONS BEGIN IN THE KINDERGARTEN.

These three areas of need should be considered in organizing the school safety program. There will be differences between the safety content in Texas and Maine because of the differences in climate and environment. Likewise, there will be differences between rural and urban schools. As a matter of fact, there can be differences between the programs in one school and another in the same city. Even children differ from one community to another.

Organizing for Instruction

The most commonly used method for teaching safety education is integration with other school subjects and activities. There are several subjects in which safety can be integrated, such as elementary science, reading, the social studies, and health and physical education—subjects in which there is a direct relationship to safety education. There is one weakness in this method in that teachers sometimes forget or neglect to emphasize safety when it is most needed. It is best to see that it is included in the course of study or the lesson plans. The lesson outlines provided by the National Safety Council and the American Automobile Association are helpful in providing materials for monthly emphasis.

Some schools organize a separate course in safety, giving it the same status as any other course or subject in the curriculum. This provides for a more comprehensive treatment of the content and gives safety a definite time allotment. Correlation with other subjects is carried on as the necessity presents itself, frequently as a unit of work that is used in language, composition, dramatics and other subjects.

A combination of several methods is used in many schools and results in greater emphasis on the subject. This includes direct classroom instruction, integration, pupil organization, teaching through routine activities, and special programs. Ideally, safety education is under the direction of a city supervisor who coordinate's the safety work of the school system. In some cities, school buildings also have safety coordinators who aid in organizing programs.

Pupil Activities

Since safety education involves knowledge, skills and attitudes, the pivotal point in safety instruction is "learning by doing." As in the scouting programs, the schools need to emphasize the various activities in which the pupils learn by doing. These are school safety patrols, junior safety councils, bicycle inspections, field days, school assemblies, excursions and field trips, exhibits and other activities in which the children participate. Following is a discussion of some of the more important activities.

Excursions and Field Trips

Any excursion, field trip or tour of inspection requires certain safety precautions. These involve planning the trip, and taking precautions going to and from the place of visit. The success of the trip depends to a great extent on the degree to which pupils are prepared.

The following are examples of field trips that teachers have found useful. In many cases school buses are used for transportation.

1. A trip to a nearby fire station to observe apparatus, fire prevention methods and fire-fighting techniques.
2. A visit to a traffic intersection to see how pedestrian and vehicle movement is regulated.
3. A visit to an airfield to study how air traffic is made safe.
4. A visit to an ocean liner or river steamer to observe safety precautions (upper grades).

These can be used as a basis for compositions, dramatizations and oral reports.

Surveys and Inspections

In the upper grades, surveys and inspections can be used. There are several types that have been used to advantage.

1. A survey of the playground and its equipment to determine hazards that might cause serious accidents and that should be eliminated.
2. A study of how playground hazards may be corrected.
3. A survey of local traffic conditions to determine the number of pedestrians and motor vehicles passing at certain intersections. This can be used to determine safe routes to school.
4. An inspection trip through the school building to determine the provisions taken to protect pupils (fire protection, directional signs, safety conditions).
5. In cooperation with parents, an inspection to ascertain the safety conditions in the home.

Programs and Campaigns

Many schools organize safety campaigns, sometimes including assembly programs. In other instances, most of the project is conducted in the homerooms. The following are examples of campaigns that have been used effectively:

1. Fire prevention home inspections. These are usually conducted in October. Inspection blanks may often be secured from the local fire department.

In addition to working with parents in conducting the inspection, efforts should be made to correct the hazards.

2. Clean-up campaigns are used in many schools. Sometimes these are confined to the school and the grounds. In other cases, the homes are included.
3. Learn-to-swim campaigns are often conducted, usually in connection with the local American Red Cross. Much depends upon the facilities available. Schools are fortunate when they are located near bathing facilities or have their own pools.
4. Some schools conduct courtesy campaigns. Such campaigns have been found to be useful in reducing accidents. Courtesy and safety go hand in hand.

Exhibits, Demonstrations and Field Days

Many schools have at least one safety exhibit each year. Others include demonstrations and field days in their programs. The following are illustrations of these types of activities:

1. Bulletin board displays of posters, pictures and items of current interest. These should be changed regularly. Posters can be secured from the National Safety Council, the American Automobile Association, and some insurance companies.
2. Demonstrations of bicycle safety often make interesting assembly programs.
3. Fire departments often arrange for visits to schools in order to demonstrate apparatus together with fire prevention and fire-fighting methods.
4. Exhibits are often arranged for holiday seasons such as Christmas and Halloween.

Suggestions for School Assemblies The following are illustrations of types of assembly programs for the elementary schools:

September: Installation of school safety patrol. Pedestrian safety.

October: Fire prevention. This might be an outdoor demonstration by the fire department or a talk by a fireman in the auditorium followed by a motion picture.

November: Home safety. A skit or demonstration showing the types of home accidents and their prevention. Courtesy campaign.

December: Holiday safety.

January-February: Skit on sledding and skating. Safe practices in archery or industrial arts.

March: First aid demonstration.

April: Practices on playgrounds. Bicycle safety.

May: Camping, swimming, boats and canoes.

June: Skit on vacation hazards.

A variety of films is available in most of these areas. Dramatization by pupils usually has greater appeal than talks. For information on playlets and skits, consult the National Safety Council.

School assemblies offer excellent opportunities to involve the entire community in safety activities. Frequently, it is possible to build an assembly program on a theme that may be receiving national or local emphasis. Monthly safety projects are often valuable. For example, each October, nation-wide safety programs stress fire prevention. The school, through its assembly, may schedule dramatic presentations on fire safety. Later the classroom teacher may build upon the work that was highlighted and provide further knowledge, skills and attitudes about the effective use of fire.

Junior Safety Councils These are found in some elementary schools, but more often on the secondary level. For further information, see Chapter 15 on secondary schools or secure the booklet on *Junior Safety Councils* from the National Safety Council.

National Safety Council Honor Roll Many schools belong to the National Safety Council Honor Roll. This is designed to help schools upgrade their programs and to gain recognition for their achievement in safety activities. Schools are required to fill out a checklist which indicates the safety activities they have carried on during the year. Copies of this evaluation checklist and further information on this program can be secured from the National Safety Council. To qualify for Honor Roll recognition, a school's safety education program must be evaluated by a local committee of five consisting of the principal, the president of a parent group, a student, a civic leader and the president of the local safety organization.

Methods of Instruction

The School Administrator and the Safety Program (4) emphasizes the following points:

> Since living safely involves knowledge, skills and attitudes, lessons should be given that will aid in developing all of these.
>
> Learning by doing should be emphasized at all grade levels.
>
> Practice lessons, demonstrations, dramatizations, visual aids and field trips have been found to be particularly valuable.
>
> Activities involving the preparation of safety posters, projects and compositions are plentiful and useful.
>
> Many helpful tools of safety instruction, such as readers, visual aids, reference books and lesson leaflets are available.

Not all of these methods are equally effective. Consider the problem of teaching primary children how to cross the street at an intersection. While motion pictures could be used to show this, or the teacher could talk about safe methods, undoubtedly the best method would be to have the children actually practice crossing the street under the supervision of a police officer or a safety patrol. Another method would be to practice crossing in a classroom situation or on the playground under simulated conditions. Still another would be to have some pupils demonstrate correct procedures. But in the long run, actual practice is undoubtedly the best method, especially if it is followed up by group discussion, which could assist in influencing attitudes.

The same methods could be applied to other situations to teach children:

How to escape from a smoke-filled room.
How to extinguish a clothing fire.
How to use a knife.
How to swim.

Learning by doing Actual practice in safety procedures is an effective method because it results in the improvement of skills. This method is featured in the Boy and Girl Scout programs; they learn by doing. There are many activities that can be taught by the practice method.

Demonstrations and dramatizations Plays, dialogues, games, radio or television skits, and demonstrations are especially valuable with elementary school pupils. Children are usually ready for self-expression through dramatics. Safety playlets are especially effective if well done. Pupils can use playlets written by others or, what is still better, they can prepare the playlets themselves and give them in a classroom, in the auditorium, or on local television stations. Copies of playlets can be secured from the National Safety Council.

Audio-visual methods Motion pictures, slides, posters, radio and television are also useful. Unfortunately, not too many good elementary school motion pictures are available in the field of traffic safety. Visual aids should show the safe way rather than the unsafe way. Showing the latter is called negative teaching, and if it is used, it should be followed up by positive lessons showing the safe way.

Radio and television have been used for several years in teaching safety. It is expected that in the future educational television will come into more general use and include more safety education programs.

Safety Units

The National Commission on Safety Education has issued two publications for elementary schools: *Safety Guides for You—in the Primary Grades* (9) and *Safety Guides for You—in the Intermediate Grades* (10). Both of these show the organization of safety units.

The following samples show the method used in developing the units and suggest the content.

In the Primary Grades

Unit—No Place Like Home for Potential Accidents

This unit on "Home Safety" highlights hazards and ways to avoid them. It indicates when to "keep off," and when to handle with care. It seeks to develop the child's responsibility for safe use and care of his own things.

Since home is a center of interest for elementary school beginners, there is a natural setting for learning home safety rules. This unit also treats the schoolroom "home" in a similar manner.

There is a page on "Why be concerned about home safety?" and several pages of rules or points of emphasis for youngsters, headed

What—To know and do.

The following are typical items selected from well over 100. For a complete listing, secure a copy of the Guide itself.

All through the house

Waxed floors are slippery. Watch your step.

Windows are to see out of—not to lean out of.

If you lean against a screen, it may break. Screens are not built for leaning purposes.

Kitchen and bathroom

The kitchen is the most dangerous place in the home.

Turn gas on or off only in the presence of grownups.

Basement and steps

Keep the basement neat and orderly and clean.

Stay away from the axe, sharp tools and pointed rods. Use saws and hammers that are your size.

Halls and stairways at home and at school

Use the handrail. The steps may be worn or slippery, and the rail will help support you.

Walk downstairs, one step at a time.

Schoolroom

Doors should be opened slowly and closed carefully.

Stay away from the hot radiators and steam pipes.

How To Develop The Unit

Each teacher will find his own method of introducing the unit. A conversation, an accident, a story, a question may introduce a problem which can be used for an approach. Center a conversation around the home in order to become acquainted with the children's own homes and families. The following activities are suggested:

Tell or read stories about home life.
Dramatize home activities or parts of the stories about home life.

Explore and Experience

Plan and build a playhouse.

Have the children tell about accidents that have occurred in their homes.

Find stories in readers about home life. Identify those that tell about safety in home activities.

Leave a Lasting Impression

The accumulation of material and the progress of activities may lead to some natural culmination. Something which the children think is fun can be planned to bring home all the information in this unit.

The following are suggested: a "Home Safety Exhibit", a "Parents' Party", safety games and skits, check-lists on *Be Safe at Home.*

The items under "What to Know and Do" are important; these can be converted into a check test.

Other Guides for the Primary Grades

The following units have been developed for primary grades:

You Act as You Think and Feel.
Put an Accent on Safety in Your School Curriculum.
Insure a Round Trip to School and Home Again.
Play Safe to Have More Fun.
Eat, Drink and Be Safe.
"Clothes Make the Man," Safe and Comfortable.
You and the Burning Facts.
You and the Animals You Meet.
You and Civil Defense.
Every Day in Every Way You Are Taking a Test in Safety Practices.

Intermediate Grades

A similar publication has been prepared for the intermediate grades. The units are more advanced but are similar in organization. The following are the units included:

Figure 14:3, PLAYGROUND EQUIPMENT MUST BE DESIGNED FOR DURABILITY AND SAFE USE.

You Act As You Think and Feel.
Put an Accent on Safety in Your School Curriculum.
You Can Be Safe in a Crowd.
You in the Driver's Seat.
Safety and Highways and Railways.
Skyway Safety in the Air—on the Ground.
All Aboard for Safety.
Be a Live Wire Concerning Electricity.
Forest Fires Are Everybody's Business.
You and Civil Defense.
Do As I Do—For Safety at School.

Material for these units can be found in *Safety Guides for You—in the Intermediate Grades.* It will be noted that in this method safety is being taught through language, art, elementary science, dramatics, visual aids, reading and other subjects. It appears that pupils would learn a great deal about safety in this method.

OTHER PUBLICATIONS FOR THE ELEMENTARY SCHOOLS

Two of the best sources of lesson outlines are the National Safety Council and the American Automobile Association. Also valuable are the "Data Sheets" that appear in the magazine, *Safety Education,* published by the Council and *School and College Safety—Congress Transactions*. *Saftety Education* ceased publication in May, 1965; a new quarterly magazine *School Safety* is now available from the Council.

The National Commission on Safety Education has several publications for the elementary schools, in addition to those that have already been mentioned. These include: *Safety Education in the Rural Schools; Our Schools Plan Safe Living; Fire Safety: For Teachers of Primary Grades; Fire Safety: For Teachers of Intermediate Grades*. Several textbooks and readers are also available. The chief weakness lies in the lack of visual aids for the elementary schools.

summary

The safety program of the elementary schools is highly important. Over a period of years, it has resulted in the "saving" of thousands of lives and injuries. The habits and attitudes which children develop in the early grades tend to be continued into adult life.

However, there are many schools that do not have well-organized programs. This is unfortunate because it has been clearly demonstrated that such programs tend to reduce child accidents. A well-organized program will consist of a number of important activities including (1) accident reporting (2) safety instruction in all of the grades, (3) pupil organizations and special programs such as surveys and inspections, (4) the use of audio-visual aids, (5) monthly or seasonal stress on various safety problems, (6) continuing evaluation of over-all effectiveness of the program, and (7) published safety policies.

Safety education may be taught through integration, by the direct method or by a combination of both methods. It is important that the teachers have courses of study, lesson plans or safety units to follow in order to cover the more important aspects of safety education.

MATERIALS FOR THE LOWER ELEMENTARY GRADES: SAFETY LESSON (15)

People who will help us to be safe

This is the first month of school.
We will learn many things.
We will learn to be safe.
Do you know who will help us?

The policeman will help us

He will teach us how to use the traffic lights safely.
He will help us cross streets safely.

Do you see our friend, the policeman?
Tell how he will help us.
To do this write in the spaces in the sentence.

The policeman will help us _______ _____________ safely.

The patrols will help us to be safe

They will tell us where to cross the street.
They will tell us when to cross the street.
We should always obey the patrol.

Do you see our friend, the patrol?
Look at the sentence under his picture.
Write a word in the space.
The right word will tell us what to do to be safe.

We should always _______ the patrol.

The bus driver will help us to be safe

He will ask us to sit down and be quiet in the bus.
He will tell us to keep our heads and arms inside the window.
He will tell us how to get on and off the bus safely.
He will show us how to cross the street at the bus stop.
He will help us to be safe.

Do you see our friend, the bus driver?
Write a word in the space in the sentence.
This will tell how the bus driver helps us.

The bus driver will help us to be ________ on his bus.

Our teacher will help us to be safe at school

She will teach us to act safely in the classroom.
She will teach us to use pencils and scissors safely.
She will show us how tŏ use the drinking fountain safely.
She will show us how to walk up and down stairs carefully.
We are glad that she will help us to be safe at school.

See the picture of our teacher.
Write a word in the space in the sentence.
This will tell what our teacher does for us.

Our teacher will help us to be safe at ___________.

Our parents help us to be safe

Our parents do not want us to be hurt.
They try hard to keep us safe.
They tell us many ways to be careful.
They tell us what not to do.
We should listen carefully to what they say.

Here is a picture of a father and mother.
They are telling us how to be safe.
Write a word in the space in the sentence.
This will make a story about parents and safety.

We should ________ __________ when our parents talk about being safe.

Following our safety leaders

- Policeman
- Patrol
- Bus Driver
- Teacher
- Parents

We should follow our safety leaders.
They help us to act safely.
We should follow their suggestions.

• ● •

Choose a safety leader.
Draw a picture of this person.
Under the picture write MY FAVORITE SAFETY LEADER.
Put your pictures on the bulletin board.
Ask other classes to come and see them.

UPPER ELEMENTARY SAFETY LESSON

Follow the leaders—to safety

In every community there are people who help others to be safe.
In every school there are people who help children to be safe.
In this safety lesson we will learn about these people.
We will learn who they are and how they help us.
We will also learn how we may work with them for safety.

Safety leaders: Policemen . Crossing Guards . School Patrols
Teachers . Bus Drivers . Custodians

What should we know about them?
Following are some paragraphs.
If we write the correct words in the spaces, we will see how they can help us.
Words are supplied for each paragraph, but be sure each work is in the correct space.

The policeman
(words to use: crosswalk, automobiles, signals)

1. He will halt ________ so we can cross safely.
2. He will teach us how to use traffic ________.
3. He will tell us to cross only at the ________.

The crossing guard
(words to use: lead, directions, cross, policeman)

1. The crossing guard is not a ________.
2. He (or she) will tell us when to ________ the street.
3. He (or she) may ________ us across.
4. We should always follow his (or her) ________.

The school patrol
(words to use: when, stop, wait, gap, obey)

1. The patrol should not ________ cars.
2. He should watch for a ________ in traffic.
3. He will tell us ________ to cross.
4. We should always ________ for his directions.
5. We should ________ the patrol.

The bus driver
(words to use: seated, heads and arms, in and out, street)

The bus driver feels very responsible for our safety. He will ask us to—

1. stay s________ when the bus is moving.
2. keep our h________ and a________ inside the window.
3. hold onto the hand rails when getting i________ and o________ of the bus.
4. cross the s________ very carefully after we get off the bus.

The teacher
(words to use: walk, fountain, pens, pencils, scissors, knives, floor, wiping, climbing, ladder)

Your teacher will teach you many things about safety. She will—

1. tell you how to w________ safely in the corridors.
2. explain the dangers of playing at the drinking f________.
3. show you how to use safely such things as p________, p________, sc________, kn________. (Can you name four things?)
4. help you get the habit of picking things up off the f________ and w________ up spilled liquids.
5. point out the danger of cl________ on boxes or chairs to reach for things instead of using a l________.

The custodian
(words to use: report, hazards)

The custodian keeps the building in a safe condition.

1. He will help us to remove h________ from the school.
2. If we know of a hazard, we should r________ it to him.

Make a list of possible hazards in school.
Do any of them actually exist? What should be done about them?

Follow the leaders—to safety

You have discussed how different people help you to be safe.

1. What can you do about this?
2. How can you follow these leaders and really be safe?
3. Can you make some poster cartoons to illustrate this? Call them "Follow our safety leaders." Put them where other groups can see and discuss them.

GENERAL SAFETY TEST FOR ELEMENTARY SCHOOLS

		YES	NO
1.	Is it safer to cross the street at the intersection rather than in the middle of the block?	Y	N
2.	Should pedestrians walk on the right side of highways when there are no sidewalks?	Y	N
3.	Should bicycles be used on the right side of streets?	Y	N
4.	Are school safety patrols useful in reducing accidents?	Y	N
5.	At intersections, is it better to run across the street rather than walk?	Y	N
6.	Should bicycles stop at Stop signs?	Y	N
7.	Is it a good practice to use roller skates on busy streets?	Y	N
8.	Should school safety patrols stop automobile traffic?	Y	N
9.	Should tricycles be ridden on sidewalks?	Y	N
10.	Are matches and smoking the principal causes of fires in the home?	Y	N
11.	Does fire require air in order to burn?	Y	N
12.	Is Fire Prevention Week in November?	Y	N
13.	Is a poisonous gas formed when fires burn?	Y	N
14.	Should gasoline be used for dry cleaning in the home?	Y	N
15.	Is carbon monoxide gas used in extinguishing fires?	Y	N
16.	If one's clothes catch on fire, is it best to run?	Y	N
17.	Does spontaneous combustion occur when metals are stored?	Y	N
18.	Are sparks from railroad engines the principal cause of forest fires?	Y	N
19.	Is lightning one of the most important causes of home fires?	Y	N
20.	Is water the best extinguisher for an oil or grease fire?	Y	N

suggested projects and activities

1. Prepare a kit of free or low-cost materials that could be used by teachers in the elementary schools.
2. Prepare a survey blank that could be used by pupils in studying safety conditions in their school.
3. Draw up plans for a school assembly program that would feature bicycle safety.
4. Two elementary schools out of ten in your city do not have patrols. Prepare an outline of the value of patrols that you could discuss with the principals.
5. Three officers have been designated by the police department to give 15-minute talks on traffic safety in elementary schools. Prepare an outline of a talk they could use in assemblies attended by grades 1 to 6.
6. You have been asked to prepare an outline of a 30-minute talk to be given before the Parent-Teacher Association of an elementary school. Use for your subject, "Teaching Safety in the Elementary Schools."
7. Which safety organizations would you include at the elementary school level? Prepare an outline showing the procedure you would follow in organizing two of these.
8. Prepare an annotated bibliography of safety education materials for the elementary school teacher.

selected references

1. American Automobile Association, *Monthly Lesson Plans*. Washington, D.C.: The Association.
2. American National Red Cross, *First Aid Handbook*. Washington, D.C.: The Red Cross (n.d.).
3. Boy Scouts of America, *Handbook for Boys*. New Brunswick, N.J.: The Boy Scouts. See publications on *Cycling, Automobiling* and *Swimming* (n.d.).
4. Center for Safety Education, New York University. *The School Administrator and the Safety Program*. New York: The Center, 1956.
5. ________, *Family Recreation and Safety*. New York: The Center, 1961.
6. National Commission on Safety Education, *Bicycle Safety*. Washington, D.C.: The Commission, 1950.
7. ________, *Fire Safety for Teachers in the Primary Grades*. Washington, D.C.: The Commission, 1950.
8. ________, *Fire Safety for Teachers in the Intermediate Grades*. Washington, D.C.: The Commission, 1950.
9. ________, *Safety Guides for You—in the Primary Grades*. Washington, D.C.: The Commission, 1961.
10. ________, *Safety Guides for You—in the Intermediate Grades*. Washington, D.C.: The Commission, 1961.

11. ________, *Safety in the Rural Schools*. Washington, D.C.: The Commission, 1948.
12. ________, *The Elementary School Principal Plans for Safe Living*. Washington, D.C.: The Commission, 1956.
13. National Safety Council, *Accident Facts*. Chicago: The Council (annual).
14. ________, *Foundations for Safe Living*. Chicago: The Council, 1948.
15. ________, *Safety Education*, Chicago: The Council.
16. ________, *Safety Education Data Sheets*. Chicago: The Council.
17. ________, *Safety Education Safety Lessons*. Chicago: The Council.
18. National Rifle Association, *Junior Rifle Handbook*. Washington, D.C.: The Association, 1957.
19. Office of the Superintendent of Public Instruction, Illinois, *The Challenge of Safety Education*. Springfield, Ill.: Office of the Superintendent, 1959.
20. Texas Education Agency, *The Elementary Teacher and Safety Education*. Austin, Texas: The Agency, 1952.

15

the secondary schools

Adolescence is a period in life when individuals seek new adventures. In increasing numbers young people are fishing and hunting, swimming and camping, motor boating and water skiing, and competing in athletics and other physical education activities. Each year over a million youngsters are learning to drive in high school driver education courses. Some work for the junior and senior Red Cross Life Saving and first aid certificates. Many are interested in scouting, or in amateur rocketry, aviation or chemical experiments. Farm youngsters frequently work on tractors, combines and other power machinery. Some youth participate in such strenuous activities as ski jumping, skin and scuba diving, and mountain climbing. Others will seek adventure in undesirable activities.

Almost every youngster wants to live adventurously. He likes activities which provide a thrill. He generally likes television programs, motion pictures and books on adventure. He is at an age when he is increasingly "on his own." In addition, there is a tendency to look at safety as something that is negative, restricting his freedom. But as Albert W. Whitney pointed out many years ago, *safety leads to greater adventure* (12). We learn safe practices in driving so that we can have the great adventure of a month's vacation trip in the mountains. We learn safe practices in swimming so that we can become a water sports counselor in a camp. In following safe practices we eliminate irresponsible acts that tend to end good adventures.

The Accident Problem

As might be expected, because there is an element of danger in many of the activities that have been mentioned, accidents are on the increase among secondary school students. While there has been a steady decrease in the death of pupils in the elementary schools, this is not true for the secondary schools.

The secondary-school years are a period in the life span in which several kinds of accidents reach a peak. Deaths from drowning are highest during this period while the death rate from motor vehicle accidents is also high, although below that of the 20 to 25 age group. An examination of accident records will reveal that nonfatal accidents in athletics, physical education and recreation are also numerous. In most high schools at least one-half of the accidents in the school program take place in these activities. Hunting and fishing accidents are also common among boys.

How can this be explained? In the first place there is greater exposure. More and more youngsters are learning to drive, to swim and to take part in competitive sports. More are fishing and hunting, camping and mountain climbing, using motor boats and sail boats. Farm youth are operating power machinery. There is an element of possible danger in all of these activities. As the exposure increases, accidents tend to do likewise, in spite of the fact that many kinds of activities have been made safer.

School-Age Accidents

The death rate for accidents among those in the 15-19 age group is 2.6 times that of the 10-14 age group. This is chiefly due to the incidence of motor vehicle accidents.

National Safety Council, "Accident Facts"

With their physical abilities—coordination, agility, vision and skill—young people should have the best accident record of all of the age groups. But these abilities are not enough. Many youngsters have not developed the proper judgment, experience, and attitudes that contribute to safe living, and these cannot be acquired in a short period.

Also, there are certain psychological characteristics common in adolescence which tend to encourage accidents. The adolescent has feelings which are easily hurt, he is overenthusiastic about relatively unimportant things and he loses his temper for seemingly trivial reasons. He tends to give way to his feelings and gets upset and angry easily. He likes to belong to groups and tends to follow the ideas of these groups or clubs. He likes to be a leader and to have attention drawn to his abilities.

There is also a lack of safety instruction in the high schools. Many schools have an adequate driver education program, but are doing little in other phases of safety. Yet the accident record shows that more stress should be placed on general safety—especially in certain subjects. Accidents are caused by what might be called an educational shortage. A youngster may *know* of the dangers of an activity, but he may not have the *skills* and the *attitudes* to meet these dangers. Developing skills and attitudes is one of the functions of the secondary schools. Research has shown that faulty attitudes are highly important as a cause of motor vehicle accidents (3). It is probable that the same is true for accidents in other activities, such as swimming, skiing and athletics.

The safety program covers not only the student's school activities but also his experiences in the home and in the community. Other agencies in the community are concerned with preventing accidents and fires, such as the police and fire departments, the playground and recreation departments, the Red Cross and local safety councils. Each of these organizations can do much to aid in the work of the schools.

In this chapter we will discuss the various safety services the school can render, safety instruction, methods of teaching, organizing the curriculum, cocurricular activities, and audio-visual aids. Because of its importance, driver education is discussed in Chapter 4.

Safety Services

When we consider the broad program of safety education, we see many responsibilities that can be given to members of the faculty, the principal, the custodian and the students. The safety services which the schools might offer are the following:

1. Establishment of a student accident-reporting system (see Chapter 17).
2. Periodic surveys of buildings and grounds to assure protection to students on school property.
3. Provision for efficient and safe school bus transportation.
4. Organization of a student bus patrol.
5. Student or teacher monitors in halls, cafeteria and gymnasium.
6. Supervision by teachers for all school-sponsored activities, whether on or off the campus.
7. Physical examinations by a competent physician.
8. Facilities and trained personnel for first aid.
9. Reference books and periodicals on safety in a central library.
10. Facilities and equipment for the use of visual aids.
11. Psychophysical testing equipment for driver education.
12. Student disaster teams.

Methods of Organizing Safety Instruction

Several methods may be used in teaching safety education. Each of these methods has its values; each its weaknesses. It is frequently said that the secondary school curriculum is already so overburdened that no additional work can be taken on. But if it is agreed that one of the primary purposes of education is to prepare students to *live safely,* there can be no question that safety instruction should be included in the curriculum. The question is how this instruction can best be provided. The following are the five methods most commonly used:

1. Integrating safety with existing subjects and activities.
2. Teaching safety as a separate and distinct unit in existing subjects.
3. Organizing safety education as a separate subject.
4. Centering safety instruction around pupil organizations and activities.
5. A combination of two or more of these methods.

Integration The method or methods used will depend on the general organization of the school. If integration is used, there should be careful planning to avoid much duplication. Integration is one of the better methods because safety is taught when it is needed and is related to the particular subject. For example, the dangers of carbon monoxide would be stressed in chemistry when the characteristics of the gas were being discussed. The dangers of using benzine as a dry cleaner could be included both in general science and in home economics. There are hundreds of examples of integration that could be applied in high school subjects. There is one weakness in integration. Only too often the teacher neglects to stress the safety element. It may not be included in the textbook, and therefore is not considered. The following newspaper clipping is a good indication of the lack of instruction:

> John Burns of Washington Junior High School was badly shocked by an electric wire on December 14th. He and Frank Smith were running an electric wire from one house to the other in order to install a telephone system. The wire came in contact with a 110-volt A.C. power line and John was badly burned. It was fortunate that this was not the high tension line with 2200 volts or he might have been killed. This is the third accident of this type that has occurred in the city in the last three months.

Somewhere along the line, in general science, physics or electrical shop, some teacher had failed to give adequate instruction to these boys. Instruction that keeps young people from being killed or seriously injured is certainly important. There are many ways in which safety can be integrated with other school subjects. The following are illustrations:

Water safety is properly included in health and physical education courses.
Fire prevention can be stressed in general science, physics and chemistry.
Home safety instruction naturally belongs in home economics.

Recreational and athletic safety should be covered in physical education.

All shop teachers should stress safe shop practices.

The safe use of firearms can be included in physical education.

Figure 15:1, RIFLE PRACTICE UNDER CONTROL. (RANGE AT MUNFORD HIGH SCHOOL, DETROIT.)

Safe practices in farming can be taught in agriculture.

First aid can be included in both health education and homemaking.

The safe use of gas and electricity should be emphasized in science, home economics and industrial arts.

The dangers of contaminated food, poisons, injurious plants and animals, medicines, alcohol and narcotics can be stressed in the sciences and in home economics or health education.

Teaching safety as a separate unit in existing subjects This method of correlation is preferred by many schools. Safety units are included in health education or physical education. The method has one weakness. Only too often the health textbook or course of study that is used devotes altogether too little space and time to safety education. Some health textbooks may have as many as 25 chapters with only two or three devoted to accident prevention. Obviously, safety education should be allocated much more space and time than just part of a health education program.

Teaching safety education as a separate subject A number of schools prefer this method. Some offer driver education during one term and general safety the other. They have prepared courses of study in which all phases of safety education are included except driver education. They

Figure 15:2, PROPER SHIELD OF AREA AND EYES OFFERS PROTECTION TO THE STUDENT USING A KILN.

feel that integration leaves too much to chance and the whims of the teacher. In the direct method, they can be sure that all materials are covered.

There is, however, a weakness in this method. Critics say that it tends to be too academic. They feel that shop safety should be taught where it is needed—in the shop. Chemistry safety belongs in the chemistry laboratory. Football safety should be taught by the coaches on the playing field. Certainly the ideal place to stress accident prevention is where it comes up naturally in an activity.

Centering safety instruction around pupil organizations and activities This method is also widely used, especially in junior high schools. There are many activities involving clubs, patrols, junior safety councils, hall monitors, assembly programs, and the like that can be used for safety instruction. Those cocurricular activities are important and will be discussed later in this chapter.

A combination of two or more of these methods As a matter of fact, combining methods is the general practice in many schools. Sometimes all of the methods that have been discussed are used. Because of the serious nature of many accidents, safety must be given special stress.

Methods of Teaching

What methods should we use in teaching safety? This is an important question. We are trying to improve the practices of students and are concerned not only with their knowledge about safety, but also with their skills and attitudes. A safe person *knows* of the dangers of the water; he has certain swimming and life-saving *skills;* and most important of all, he has good *attitudes.* The kinds of lessons that might be satisfactory in teaching history or geometry will not apply as well to safety. We want to develop safe behavior; we should use types of lessons that improve knowledge, skills and attitudes. Applying this to hunting, where over 50 per cent of the accidents involve teen-agers, a student may be well-informed about shotguns and rifles, but unless he has developed the proper skills and attitudes in the use of firearms, he will not be a good companion on a hunting trip. These three essentials can be applied to all phases of safety. Unfortunately, only too often there is not enough time available, and instructors stress knowledge and pay little attention to skills or attitudes. Naturally, much depends upon the quality of the lesson. A top-notch motion picture on driving might be far more useful than a dramatization. Likewise, a good discussion on motor boat safety might be more effective than a demonstration in changing attitudes. So much depends upon the quality of the lesson as well as the amount of time devoted to it. Following is a list of types of lessons:

Practice exercises.
Demonstrations.
Dramatizations.
Discussions.
Problem solving.
Audio-visual aids.
Question and answer.
Lectures.

Practice Exercises This is considered one of the better methods of teaching safety—actually having the student practice the steps involved. To teach the steps in life saving, the instructor uses land drills followed by actual practice in the water. Likewise, to teach safe use of the band-saw in the shop, the instructor would demonstrate proper procedures and then have the students practice the steps. Unfortunately, because of limitations of time and equipment, the use of the practice lesson is limited.

Demonstrations This is also one of the more effective methods of teaching—the teacher or student demonstrating the safe practice. In most instances, this type of lesson would precede a practice lesson. The following are examples of useful demonstrations:

Showing safe practices in the use of machinery in a school shop.
Demonstrating stopping distances of an automobile.
Showing proper methods of locating a blown fuse and installing a new one.
Showing techniques in first aid.
Showing proper methods of sliding in baseball.
Demonstrating the use of the various types of fire extinguishers.
Extinguishing a clothing fire.
Showing methods of breaking holds in life saving.
Showing how carbon dioxide extinguishes a flame.

Dramatizations These are especially valuable for assembly programs in both junior and senior high schools. They will be discussed later in this chapter under cocurricular activities. Because of the time required to prepare playlets, they are used rarely in the classroom. Debates and discussions are easier to arrange and prepare.

Problem Solving One of the best methods of teaching in the high schools is through problem solving. Thinking is primarily problem solving and problem solving appears to be one of the most meaningful kinds of learning. This method has many applications in the field of safety. Much instruction could be organized around a series of problems. In fact, there is a close relationship between steps in the thought process as identified by Dewey and problem solving: (1) the difficulty is felt; (2) the problem is clarified and defined; (3) there is a search for clues to the answer; (4) suggestions for the solution are tried out; and (5) the solution is accepted or rejected.

The following are illustrations of problems suitable for junior high classes:

What methods could be used to reduce accidents in school playgrounds?

What safety activities are carried on by the police and fire departments?

Problems for senior high school classes might include the following:

What methods could be used to prevent accidents in boys' or girls' camps?

What methods can be used to reduce home fires in our community?

Discussion The discussion method has been in wide use for many years. More recently, new interest has appeared in *group discussion.* It is a technique in which a leader, in this particular case an instructor, outlines relevant problems for the consideration of the group. From this point he proceeds to function as a catalyst or agent of progress while the group strives to reach a solution, usually under a student chairman. The instructor or the leader does not participate in the discussion by expressing his own opinions. According to Brody,

> . . . the purposes of group discussion are to stimulate group analysis of situations and to enable the members of the group to profit from their pooled experience or thinking (3).

In addition, according to Sawers,

> Ideally, the traditional methods of lecture and recitation, though valuable to effect certain purposes, should generally be avoided in a group discussion setting. . . . It is often better to allow adolescents to reach conclusions by themselves in a conducive atmosphere rather than "preach" to them (11).

Sawers has developed a pamphlet, *Group Discussion Techniques for Driver Education* (11). In it he includes several pages of discussion "starters"—guides for the teacher in organizing a plan. These consist of a number of situations, problems and questions that could be used in a high school driver education course.

While the Sawers pamphlet is on driver education, there is no reason why the ideas proposed could not be applied to other phases of safety. For illustration, the following might be good group discussion questions:

What causes the most water accidents at beaches—inadequate swimming skills or poor practices?

What do you consider to be most important in a summer camp—a well-constructed swimming area on the lake, or a well-defined program of safe practices and controls of swimming?

Should state laws be passed that would eliminate professional boxing?

Audio-visual Aids This method is so important and so widely used that it will be given special attention in a section in this chapter following cocurricular activities.

Question and Answer It is probable that this method is one of the most widely used types of classroom activity. It has been subject to the same sort of criticism as the lecture. Nevertheless, this type of activity can be very fruitful. It has certain advantages if used intelligently. What are some requirements of the method?

The questions should be directed first to the class.

They should be directly relevant to the material under consideration.

They should be thought-provoking—provocative and meaningful.

In a subject like driver education where only 30 periods are available for the course, the question-and-answer method enables one to cover more subject-matter. But it is best to combine this with other methods such as problem solving and demonstrations.

Lectures The very nature of teaching involves "telling," "explaining," "demonstrating" and "talking to" the class. These could be considered forms of the lecture. Some lecturing is necessary, but it tends to be used too much. It centers the learning process on the teacher rather than the student. It tends to provide a passive learning experience. It is best to use this method only when necessary. Much of the material in lectures will be found in textbooks and supplementary materials.

Organizing the Safety Curriculum

According to *Education for Safety,* a publication of the California State Department of Education (1),

> The program of safety education in junior high school and high school includes experiences in many aspects of education. In the fields of agricultural education, business education, health education, physical education, recreation, homemaking education, and industrial arts education, there are certain hazards peculiar to each field; these can be identified, and information concerning them can be provided in a very meaningful way.

Various methods can be used in organizing the safety curriculum. One method is to set up a committee of teachers in the various related departments and have them prepare the materials to be covered in each subject. Another, is to have one committee prepare the outline of a single course in general safety, and another, the course in driver education. Texas has adopted a plan of bringing together leaders in the field, including teachers and principals, in a summer course and having them work on the secondary school course of study. Florida used a similar method, although their manual was confined to driver education. It is of interest to note that while many states have developed courses of study in driver education, few have courses in general safety.

The method used will depend upon the general organization of the schools. If safety education is offered as a separate course, it should be of equal status with other school subjects in order to command respect from both teachers and pupils. If it is to be taught as a unit in existing subjects, it should have a definite time allotment and be included as a part of the subject requirement. If the safety program is centered in cocurricular activities and special projects, adequate guidance and supervision must be exercised. Such a program, however, does not fulfill the obligation of the secondary schools; it should be augmented by classroom instruction somewhere in the curriculum. It should be emphasized that careful preparation and planning must be followed in order to avoid impromptu or purely extemporaneous presentations by subject-minded teachers.

The Texas Education Agency recommends that safety topics be integrated as follows (13):

Agriculture: use of gas and electricity; home lighting and heating; safety in garage, yard and garden; safe practices in agricultural employment; using hand tools on farm and ranch; maintaining personal safety in agricultural pursuits.

Aeronautics: rail, water and air travel; the pilot and his plane; safe practices in commercial employment; safe practices in industrial employment.

Band: classrooms and auditoriums; school bus safety.

Biology: wounds; control of bleeding; asphyxia; fractures; poisoning; snakes; lunch rooms.

Chemistry: causes of fire; fire extinguishers; gas and electricity; cleaning materials; lighting and heating; use of science laboratories; handling fireworks; industrial employment.

Commercial subjects: safety on the job; handling electrical equipment; cost of accidents in terms of insurance.

English and journalism: identifying poisonous snakes and plants; seashore recreation and enjoyment; fishing, hunting and hiking as year-round sports; courtesy in the classroom or auditorium; community responsibility in fire prevention.

General mathematics: use of accident figures from local hospitals or officials; cost of accidents to individuals; comparison of the cost of accidents to amount spent for their prevention.

General Science: fire prevention; sanitation; electricity; gas; bicycling; transportation by rail, water, and air; school bus safety; the pilot and his plane.

Health education: first aid for wounds; common emergencies; participation in public recreation.

Homemaking: use and care of household equipment; electrical appliances; first aid; handling gas; poisons; use of the family car.

Homeroom: halls and stairs; classrooms and auditoriums; cafeteria and lunchroom; restrooms; fire prevention; fishing, hunting, and hiking; public recreation.

Physical education: physical education activities; swimming and life saving; public recreation in parks and playgrounds; first aid.

Physics: electricity; explosives; small crafts.

Social studies: handling fireworks; public transportation; industrial safety; safe practices in commercial employment; safe practices in agricultural employment.

Producing the Course of Study

Since very few states have developed courses of study in general safety for the secondary schools, city or county school systems may wish to develop their own courses.

Using a committee of teachers and principals appointed by the superintendent is considered the best approach; it directly involves faculty members, and it leads to greater professional awareness. Moreover, when the course finally reaches the classroom, it is more readily used by teachers because they are familiar with it.

In the production of the course of study or syllabus, a detailed plan should be followed. The following are the steps briefly outlined for a large city with a number of high schools:

1. The superintendent appoints a committee consisting of representatives from each school.
2. The departments represented on the committe include: science, social studies, physical education, industrial education, health education, home economics, English and driver education.
3. The superintendent or his representative meets with the committee on the first day, and explains the purpose of the project. A general chairman is elected and the group is divided into subcommittess for the subject areas.
4. Subcommittee chairmen and secretaries are elected at the first meeting of the subcommittees. Members of the subcommittees represent the various schools.
5. Members of the committees are supplied with all of the accident facts that are available, together with publications in the field.
6. There are two procedures that can be used in organizing materials:
   a. The general committee decides where the following are to be taught:

Safety in—	Safety in—
Physical education	School
Athletics	Traffic
Recreation	Health education
Water sports	Home economics
Boating and sailing	Industrial education
Transportation	Fire prevention
Motor boating	School bus
Home	Firearms
Farm	Electricity

These areas are then assigned to the various subcommittees—science, social science, etc.

b. The material is developed in principal areas—recreation, physical education, fire prevention and fire fighting, etc. The subject in which it is to be taught is specified in the introduction to the report of the subcommittee.

The first method (a) is probably more specific. The second (b) allows for more freedom; for illustration, parts of fire prevention can be taught in general science, chemistry, industrial education and home economics.

7. Organization of materials in the course according to procedure (b) above:
   a. A short overview (importance of the area)
   b. Objectives of the unit
   c. Materials to be covered in the units
   d. Activities to cover these materials (the parallel column format is recommended for this)
   e. Evaluation (tests and measurements)
   f. Visual aids
   g. Selected references
8. The general committee meets regularly so that reports can be given on progress, style and format. It is important that the course of study have uniformity.
9. As far as possible the visual aids and selected references should have been reviewed by members of the subcommittees.
10. Editorial work is done—preparation of introduction, acknowledgments, methods of teaching and administrative details.
11. The course is mimeographed and distributed to schools for tryout before publication in final form. Rather than having the course sent out by the superintendent with a covering letter, it is better to have a meeting of teachers or department chairmen at the school at which the new course is discussed.

The Instructional Unit The plan for the type (b) course of study has been described in detail for it is most generally used. In type (a) a different plan is followed:

1. The general committee is divided into subcommittees by subject areas—the sciences, social sciences, etc.
2. These subcommittees include representatives of the various subjects; for example, the science committee would include teachers of general science, biology, physics and chemistry.
3. Each committee would then allocate certain phases of safety to the subjects; for example, most of fire prevention would go into general science. More advanced materials would be included in chemistry.
4. The subcommittees would then report back to the general committee, showing the allocation of materials to be covered.
5. The materials might be divided into a series of units; for example, in homemaking there might be units on: (1) use and care of household equipment, (2) electrical appliances, (3) poisons, and (4) "do-it-yourself."
6. The units would then be organized using the following plan:
   a. Title the unit through the use of a challenging problem
   b. Indicate the specific objectives for teachers and for students
   c. Break down the unit into subject-matter content
   d. List the sources the pupils will consult
   e. List the activities in which the students will engage

f. Prepare materials needed to supplement the textbook
g. Plan culminating activities in which the students may summarize their accomplishment
h. Devise a test for the unit

7. There should be a tie-in with out-of-school activities, utilizing the experiences in the home and community.
8. A well-prepared unit will allow students freedom to work, go to the library, visit shops or recreational centers, and the like.
9. Time limits should be set after which students should make reports as to their progress.

In the hands of an alert and skillful teacher the unit plan becomes an effective tool through which learning may be made more meaningful. Investigation of traffic hazards at intersections, trips to industrial shops, visits to fire departments and other places to see safety at work are but a few of the activities that might well be carried out through this method of teaching.

Cocurricular Activities

An important objective in safety education is the development of safe practices. Cocurricular activities are of unusual value because they provide opportunities for application of safe practices—serving on the safety patrol, working on the safety council, acting as a hall monitor, arranging for a school assembly, and aiding in supervision in the school gymnasium or on the playground. This is especially true in the junior high school. Students can learn *about* safety in the classroom, but the cocurricular activities provide opportunities for *actual practice*—learning by doing.

Accident prevention programs of schools can take on added life and significance if administrators, supervisors, teachers, pupils and parents plan and work together to achieve the objectives of the school safety education program. Student safety organizations can originate and develop many safety plans. Such cocurricular activities, properly planned, wisely guided and supervised, have definite values:

1. They provide training and experience in safely handling hazardous situations that are commonly encountered in life.
2. They represent a high type of individual and community service and thus provide an excellent form of civic training.
3. They teach the meaning of justice and the importance of law observance.
4. They develop qualities of leadership and ability to follow.
5. They improve morale and raise standards of safe conduct throughout the school.

Kinds of Cocurricular Organizations

The success of cocurricular organizations depends in large measure on the type of faculty leadership provided. Activities should be started in a small way and developed gradually and naturally. The program should be meaningful and realistic to all participants, for maintaining pupil interest is of primary importance.

Two kinds of organizations will be discussed: (1) those in which the primary purpose is safety, and (2) those in which safety is not the prime purpose but plays an important part. The student safety council is an example of the first; the hunting club and the water safety club, the second.

Student Safety Councils The student safety council is composed of representatives of the various homerooms and delegates from other groups. It may assume leadership with respect to safe conduct in the school building, on the grounds, and in the entire neighborhood. The student body is kept informed of the work in safety through the representatives who report back to their groups after each council meeting. Thus the whole student body can be united in the cause of safety, and projects set in motion can become the responsibility of each student. Councils of this type have developed more in the junior than the senior high school. Copies of the handbook, *The Junior Safety Council* (8) can be secured from the National Safety Council.

The functioning and useful council considers every aspect of accident prevention. To do this, regularly scheduled meetings must be held, weekly, semi-monthly, or monthly, with provisions for special meetings as necessary. A long-term program to be sponsored by the council will be determined by the conditions in each school, with emphasis on time of year or on special activities; the outline below considers both.

September A get-acquainted meeting to introduce members, explain what each group represents and what it is doing to help prevent accidents.

October A committee is appointed to draw up plans and post rules for a safe Halloween from a fire prevention standpoint.

November The inspection committee reports on school building hazards, and the indoor patrol on pupil traffic. Plans are made for a safe Christmas.

December Home safety during the Christmas festivities is discussed, and rules for selection of toys are drawn up.

January Safety in winter is studied, reinforced with talks by experts on first aid and ice rescue.

February A report on school accidents during the first six months of school with emphasis on the individual pupil in the school safety program.

March Home safety; emphasis on how the parents and council may cooperate.

April Safety in play. The accident prevention committee reports on the number and type of accidents on playgrounds. Plans are laid to prevent such accidents.

May Street safety. The safety patrol captain reviews the work of the patrol; short talks are given on bicycle and roller skating hazards.

June Safety during the summer vacation, with reports on swimming and camping safety.

School Safety Patrols These are found in most junior high schools. However, the work of patrols has been covered in the chapter on elementary schools.

Bicycle Safety This has been covered in the chapter on elementary schools.

School Safety Court The school safety court is used frequently as an auxiliary to the general student safety organization. It is primarily a secondary school group because greater maturity and experience are required of those called upon to pass judgment upon violators of safety rules. It cannot succeed until every pupil realizes that the safety court exists for the good of the student as well as for the school as a whole. This makes it necessary for every pupil to understand the function of the court, to be in sympathy with its purpose, and to be willing to give wholehearted support to its achievement. The school principal or sponsor must take special pains to develop in his students the ability to distinguish between needless tale-bearing and reporting the act of a student that may lead to danger.

School Assemblies Assembly programs should be timely, brief, and based on current student needs. Each year four or five assemblies might well be devoted to various areas of safety education. A variety of good motion pictures and sound film slides are available for showing. Dramatizations and demonstrations are especially valuable. If talks are given they should be short and preferably accompanied by visual aids. The following are illustrations of possible assembly programs:

Demonstration by driver education students of activities of the class.
Home safety demonstration or playlet by home economics students.
Fire prevention playlet or demonstration by science students.
Safe practices in athletics, showing safety in major sports.
Land drills for Red Cross Life Saving course.
Farm safety demonstration.
Motion picture on water skiing combined with a short talk on safe practices.
Talk and motion picture on safe boating practices.

Other Activities

Safety demonstrations, exhibits and displays Demonstrations can be staged as a part of an assembly program, in the gymnasium, on school grounds, in the cafeteria or other rooms. Exhibits and displays of posters, driver testing apparatus, and materials developed in club activities will reveal the work being done.

Teen-age conferences Many states hold teen-age conferences. Some of these are held in regional centers with representatives of high schools participating; others are state conferences held at the state capital. In most states, these feature driver education and traffic safety. These conferences are organized and run by the students. Following an opening session, the group is divided into workshops which conduct discussions, and which usually make recommendations regarding problems they have been considering. These are summarized at a final meeting of the conference. The delegates are expected to report the highlights and recommendations of the conference at an assembly in their high schools.

Road-e-o's For over ten years junior chamber of commerce, in cooperation with various industries, have been conducting Road-e-o's for teen-agers. This is an attempt to prove that young drivers can be safe drivers. The program consists of personal interviews, knowledge tests, skill tests, psychophysical tests and attitude scales. Local winners go to a state contest; state winners to a national contest which is held in Washington. Prizes are awarded in the form of scholarships. It is a real honor to be judged a winner in the state and national contests.

Radio and television A number of schools are using radio in safety instruction. A few are using closed-circuit television. In a number of cities, television is being used to teach a part of the driver education course. As educational television expands, there will be opportunities to give instruction to a large audience of students with interesting safety programs. Open-circuit television through regular channels can also be used to reach adults. Television programs in high school driver education are working out satisfactorily in the Dade County Schools in Florida, Cincinnati, Ohio, and other cities.

Publications A weekly or monthly column in the school paper or local press is a means of encouraging safety activities in the school and the country. The school paper can also be used to give out news regarding school safety organizations.

Excursions and trips Students should be familiar with the safety activities of public agencies in the city as well as of private organizations such as industries. Trips can be arranged to visit them. These trips should be followed up by discussions of practices observed.

Drives and campaigns The school safety council can organize drives or campaigns which will tend to focus the attention of the entire school on the problem, and will develop a sense of group responsibility. The following are examples of useful campaigns:

Vehicle check
Bicycle safety
Pedestrian protection
Clean up week
Courtesy
Fire prevention inspection
Home safety
Safe driving

Other Safety Groups

There are many other clubs and other activities that are directly or indirectly related to safe practices. The following is a list of the more common:

Parking monitors They can also aid in the control of traffic within the school building.

Shop safety engineers These assist the instructor in checking wearing apparel and the use of goggles, watching out for dangerous practices, and inspecting machines, tools and storage space. They also report hazards, take charge of the bulletin board, and assist the instructor in other ways.

Student leaders in physical education Since many of the accidents in the school occur in physical education activities, it is recommended that student leaders be appointed to assist instructors. In some schools they form a group known as the *leaders corps*. Among the responsibilities of student leaders are the following:

1. To assist in the daily inspection of play areas and apparatus.
2. To instruct students in the use of apparatus and facilities.
3. To assist in safe and correct performance of activities.
4. To assist in setting up and storing equipment and supplies.
5. To assist as game officials at school athletic events.
6. To act to promote safety in interschool athletic contests.

Aiding in Community Safety In some cities, local safety organizations request the help of schools in making, (1) surveys of playground facilities, (2) surveys of fire prevention facilities in amusement places, (3) traffic surveys at intersections, and (4) studies of pedestrian violations. Other schools conduct home accident surveys, using survey blanks provided by the local safety council or the fire department. In some cases activities of this kind are assigned by the classroom teacher. Students should have practice in studying various community problems and setting up programs on the basis of findings.

Other Club Activities A study of secondary schools would show a large number of clubs in which safety plays a part. This is especially true in the junior high school. Among those that are found in schools are the following:

Swimming and water safety
Rifle
Hunting
Scouting
Archery
Motor boating
Science
Radio
Hiking
Chemistry
Skiing
Sailing
Sports Leaders
Future farmers
Safe driving
Rocketry
Electricity
Scuba and skin diving

Audio-visual Aids

Educational experiences may be divided into two types: real, and contrived or simulated. In safety, as in other fields, real experience is to be desired, but frequently it is impossible. It follows that the next best choice is to use situations that resemble reality as closely as possible. Most audio-visual aids are for this purpose.

As an illustration of the above, consider the following situation. Teachers of driver education have been urged to include "action in driving emergencies" in their programs—what to do when a tire blows out, when a car is forced off the road, or in other situations. Because of the dangers involved and the time required it would not be feasible to put high school students into hazardous situations. The next best thing would be to have demonstrations, but these might be difficult to arrange. However, motion pictures are available which show many of these situations. Even better than seeing a film on emergencies is reacting to them on a simulator.

Motion Pictures One of the outstanding features of films is that they can bring into the classroom scenes of action and behavior drawn from all phases of living—working, driving, traveling and recreation. These films can depict hazardous conditions and give vicarious experiences. They can be shown entire, or in part, and on some projectors, can be shown in slow motion.

It must be kept in mind that a visual aid is an *aid* to instruction. Some teachers use them too much. This is especially true in driver education where there is such a wide variety of films available. There are three primary objectives in the use of motion pictures:

1. To develop and/or modify attitudes.
2. To show technical aspects of developing skills and concepts.
3. To provide vicarious experience of dangerous situations so that students may learn safe behavior.

There is always a danger of overuse of films, especially those that are inappropriate. Films do not take the place of the teacher. When used they should be introduced and followed up by discussion.

Slides and Film Strips These two types of aids are extremely adaptable when shown with commentary by the teacher or a student. One big advantage is that they can be spaced and sprinkled through the discussion period to illustrate specific points. While they do lack motion, they are good to illustrate the discussion or lecture. The following are their principal uses:

1. To illustrate specific topics, devices and equipment.
2. To stimulate discussion.

3. To summarize or clarify a unit of work.
4. To add interest to class discussions.

Since film strips and slides are easy to make and inexpensive, many teachers are producing their own. The 35 mm. color slides have come into general use. A series of good slides concerned with local conditions, provides one of the best ways of teaching safety.

Demonstrations Mock-ups, real objects, cut-aways and models are used in demonstrations, which have already been mentioned under methods of teaching. Demonstrations closely approximate real situations and frequently can be among the most effective of all audio-visual aids. They are especially useful in teaching the mechanics of the car, rules of the road, and traffic problems. The magnetic traffic board and the flannel board are widely used in the high schools.

Figure 15:3, FLANNEL BOARD DEMONSTRATION.

Live shows, radio and television These media have perhaps the greatest potential of all the avenues of safety education. They can reach a very large audience; in fact, one television program can be seen by millions of people. Educational television shows great promise and has been growing rapidly. When producers of television shows are persuaded to make safety a matter of real concern, accident prevention will receive an enormous stimulus. As an illustration of this, consider the matter of automobile seat belts. Several kinds of media have been employed to encourage their use, and it is probable that radio and television programs have had much to do with their acceptance by the motoring public.

Much more use should be made of both radio and television. The chief difficulty is the cost. Industries and other sponsors must be persuaded that safety is worth more than spot announcements and brief references. There is plenty of drama and human interest in life saving and accident prevention.

Graphic Displays Charts, graphs, posters and bulletin board announcements serve a useful purpose. If well done, they concentrate much safety information of various types. They are widely used in industries. Posters can be secured from the National Safety Council and from some insurance companies. When used on bulletin boards they should be changed regularly. These aids are also useful for illustrating talks and demonstrations.

Other Aids Contests, award programs and field trips, when used, each should be well planned. A top-flight guest speaker at an assembly can do much to reenforce the safety program; a poor speaker can do more harm than good.

Industries make more use of contests and award programs than schools. In fact, many schools do not like contests such as the Road-e-os. But they do stimulate interest and attention.

summary

In increasing numbers, young people are participating in activities which can be hazardous—driving, boating and canoeing, swimming, hunting and fishing, competitive sports, skiing, camping and even mountain climbing. There are also dangers of fire, experimenting with chemicals and "do-it-yourself" activities.

The secondary schools have the responsibility of preparing young people to meet the dangers involved in these activities. In general, most of this instruction will be given as a part of existing subjects such as physical education, the sciences, social sciences, industrial education and home economics. Driver education, however, is offered as a separate subject. Some schools center safety instruction around pupil organizations and activities. There are many kinds of cocurricular activities in which safety can be emphasized. Other schools give courses in general safety education.

It has been found that the best methods of teaching including practice exercises, demonstrations, dramatizations, the use of visual aids and discussion. Discussions are especially valuable in improving attitudes.

There are relatively few state courses of study in safety education. It is therefore recommended that the schools develop safety programs by organizing courses of study and assigning certain phases of safety to existing subjects. They should also stress safety in a number of cocurricular activities. It is important that instruction emphasize attitudes and skills as well as knowledge.

suggested projects and activities

1. Find out what phases of safety are being taught in the local high schools.

2. Prepare a radio or television script on one or more aspects of safety.
3. Find out what methods are being used to teach (a) motor boat safety, (b) hunter safety.
4. Conduct a survey of the hazardous situations that exist in your community.
5. What evidence can you find that general safety is being given inadequate emphasis in high schools?
6. Prepare a program for a school assembly to stress fire prevention.
7. If you were appointed a safety coordinator in a high school and were given half time off, what would you do to organize a program?
8. Make a list of five kinds of safety programs that could be included in assembly periods.
9. Make a list of the types of safety instruction that could be integrated with existing school subjects.
10. Report on your use of an audio-visual aid to convey a safety idea, concept or knowledge item before a specific audience. Indicate success or failure in teaching with this aid.

selected references

1. California State Department of Education, *Education for Safety.* Sacramento: The Department, 1963.
2. Dale, Edgar, *Audio-Visual Methods in Teaching.* New York: Dryden Press, 1954.
3. Dunbar, Flanders, and Leon Brody, *The Psychology of Safety.* Center for Safety Education, New York University, 1959.
4. Florio, A. E. and G. T. Stafford, *Safety Education* (2nd ed.). New York: McGraw-Hill Book Company, 1962.
5. Goodman, David J., "Comparative Effectiveness of Pictorial Aids." Unpublished doctor's thesis, New York University, 1943.
6. National Safety Council, *Accident Facts.* Chicago: The Council (annual).
7. ________, *Safety Education in the Secondary Schools.* Chicago: The Council, 1949.
8. ________, *The Junior Safety Council.* Chicago: The Council, 1945.
9. ________, *Student Safety Activities.* Chicago: The Council, 1945.
10. ________, *Secondary School Outlines.* Chicago: The Council (monthly).
11. Sawers, Kenneth, *Group Discussion Techniques for Driver Education.* New York: Center for Safety Education, New York University, 1961.
12. Stack, Herbert J., ed., *Safety for Greater Adventures.* New York: Center for Safety Education, New York University, 1953.
13. Texas Education Agency, *Safety Education in Secondary Schools,* Bulletin 533. Austin: The Agency, 1952.
14. Wiles, Kimball, *Supervision for Better Schools.* Englewood Cliffs, N. J.: Prentice-Hall, Inc., 1961.

16

colleges and universities

Today many colleges and universities are as large as small cities. It is to be expected that they will have many of the safety problems of a typical small city. They need police officers to control traffic and provide protection, and a fire department to fight fires; their shops and laboratories have safety problems such as are found in industries; they may operate a fleet of trucks, buses and passenger cars. In addition, new buildings are being constructed and old ones repaired; dozens of miles of streets and sidewalks are being built and maintained—in fact, the university is a city in itself, with many other safety problems similar to those found in a community.

Accidents and Fires

Accidents are far more common in colleges than might be expected. One reason for this is the large percentage of students who participate in organized athletics, intramural sports and other physical education and recreation activities. In a study conducted by the University of Minnesota Health Service (11) it was found that in one year 2,600 injuries were reported out of a student body of 23,740, about half of which were on the campus, the remainder off-campus. Thus, one out of every eleven students was involved in an accident. A study conducted by the American College Health Association and the National Safety Council (1) showed that in eleven colleges there were 8,500 injuries in one year; one-half of these occurred in recreational activities. It is therefore clear that more students are injured on and off the campus than has been realized.

Fatal accidents on the campus are rare, but a surprising number of students are killed or seriously injured off the campus. Many accidents occur to students driving to games, going home for vacations, or taking pleasure trips. In a recent year one college reported six fatalities, another three, while many had at least one. Motor vehicle accidents and drowning were the chief causes of death.

Studies of nonathletic injuries on the campus show that the five most common locations of accidents are the laboratories, other buildings, streets (involving pedestrians and cyclists), dormitories, and automobiles. As would be expected, these vary widely in the various types of colleges.

Employee Accidents

Since all states now have Workmen's Compensation Insurance, accidents involving employees must be reported. According to *Campus Safety News,* published by the State University of New York (10), during one year there were 752 injuries among the more than 11,771 employees in 40 colleges. Thus, one out of each 15 employees was involved in an accident. It can readily be seen that a high accident frequency among employees can result in high insurance costs. This is one of the reasons why many colleges conduct safety courses for employees.

Fire Losses

According to the National Education Association, a study of 1,800 colleges and universities showed an average of 100 residence fires during a school year. The probabilities, therefore, are 1 in 18 that a residence building on a campus will be visited by a fire each year.

Many colleges have "temporary" barracks for housing students and for classrooms. Others have fraternity, sorority and other student housing, (often old wooden buildings) without adequate fire escapes or means of egress. While no facts are available on the annual fire losses in colleges, it is probable that the figure is high. Fire prevention and protection, therefore, become important parts of the campus safety program. The loss of a library, for illustration, is very serious for it may take years to replace the building, the books and other materials.

Campus Safety

In recent years there has been a significant increase in campus safety in colleges. In the last fire years well over 300 colleges have organized some type of program. Their representatives have formed the Campus Safety Association as a part of the National Safety Council, and meet regularly to discuss problems and to improve standards.

One of the reasons for the growth in interest in accident prevention was the increase in accidents among the student body. Another was the mounting costs of public liability, property damage, fire and other kinds of insurance, especially in private institutions. The number of fires in dormitories and other student housing undoubtedly had some influence. Added to these were the problems of traffic control and parking, especially in institutions where there were large numbers of commuters.

Organization of a Program

In many cases, there were several members of the faculty who had had safety experience—in industry, in the armed forces, or in some other activity, who recognized the importance of safety. Committees were formed and took steps to convince the college administrators that a program should be adopted.

There is obviously a great difference between the safety problems of a small college and those of a large university. The diversified activities found in our great variety of institutions preclude the adoption of a single type of safety program. However, there are essential elements for any program that have been suggested to the Campus Safety Association (8).

Elements of the Program

1. A basic safety policy.
2. Safety leadership.
3. Safety organization.
4. Maintenance of a safe environment.
5. Fire prevention and protection.
6. Reporting and follow-up of accidents.
7. Training.
8. Promotion of interest.
9. Education for safe living.
10. Off-campus activities.

The degree to which these elements will develop varies widely among colleges. It has been found that the most progress will be made when there is a full-time safety director and a strong central safety committee or council.

A Safety Policy The first step in the development of a program is to convince the college administrators of the importance of campus safety. After several meetings of a committee, a proposal is prepared, and arrangements are made for a conference with the president or other administrator. He will generally ask the committee to prepare a tentative program, a budget and a general safety policy. This policy might cover such subjects as (a) What is a safety program? (b) Why is it necessary? (c) What are the desired ends? (d) Who is responsible for its direction? (e) What is the role of students, faculty and staff in promoting the success of the program? After the policy statement is approved by the president, it is sent out to deans, directors, members of the faculty, and other employees of the institution. It is also released to college papers and posted on bulletin boards so that it will be read by students. Unless the president and the deans are convinced of the value of campus safety, it will not be too productive. As in industry, management must take the lead in the development of a strong safety program.

Leadership Leadership starts with the president and extends to the deans and department directors, to the faculty, and to those members of the staff who are in charge of the physical plant, the business office, the grounds, and other departments. Added to this is the leadership that comes from the central committee or council and from the safety director himself. Leaders in student government will also provide help in convincing the student body of the value of the program.

Organization All colleges utilize a central safety committee or council. In the smaller institutions there may be but one committee; in the larger universities there may be many subcommittees. Sometimes, the vice-president of the college acts as chairman; in other cases the chairman is a dean or the business manager. The safety director usually serves as secretary. The committee is usually made up of some of the most influential leaders on the staff, for example, the medical officer, the director of health and physical education, the instructor in safety courses, the dean of the engineering school, and the superintendent of buildings and grounds.

Maintaining a Safe Environment Safe environment is an all-inclusive term and refers to all parts of the college campus, including buildings and grounds, roadways and sidewalks, transportation facilities, off-campus housing and recreational areas such as playing fields, parks and playgrounds. All of these should be inspected periodically either by committees of the faculty or by such specialists as safety engineers from insurance companies or the state labor department, fire prevention experts, and public health officers. Some colleges have students aid in these inspections, usually as recorders.

Figure 16:1,
MODERN SCHOOL PROVIDES A SAFE FUNCTIONAL ENVIRONMENT.

These inspections invariably reveal hazardous conditions. The following are some of the most common:

Poor illumination in halls and stairways.
Unguarded machinery in shops.
Slippery floors in dormitories.
Lack of fire escapes in off-campus housing.
Lack of fire extinguishers in buildings.
Unsafe practices in laboratories.
Lack of stop signs for controlling vehicular traffic.
Lack of supervision of college trucks and passenger cars.

These conditions should be reported to the committee, and appropriate steps taken for corrective action. Some corrective action requires an engineering approach, such as the installation of machine guards in industrial shops. Other requires regulations, such as rules for the use of motor vehicles on the college campus, and safe practices in the shops. Still other action involves an educational approach, such as training drivers, custodians, cafeteria workers, and other employees.

Accidents tend to be most common in the physical education program. In fact, in some colleges more than one-half of the accidents are in physical education and recreation activities. Special attention should be given to the inspection of facilities and to the correction of hazardous conditions.

Fire Prevention and Protection This is a highly important part of the safety program. In some colleges, a large percentage of the safety directors' time is spent on these activities.

The Campus Safety Association, with the National Board of Fire Underwriters and the National Fire Protection Association, has prepared a *Student Residence Fire Check list* (6) which can be secured from the National Safety Council.

The following are some of the recommendations to help reduce losses from fires:

The Standard Check List mentioned above should be used when facilities are inspected. When inspections reveal hazards, corrections should be made.

Fire drills should be conducted in all college buildings where students are housed; civil defense drills, in *all* buildings.

Arrangements should be made with the local fire department to aid in the inspection of buildings and for fighting fires.

All buildings should be equipped with fire extinguishers. Some should have sprinkler systems.

Fire escapes should be installed where needed.

The campus safety program should include fire prevention and protection demonstrations, motion pictures or other visual aids. The local fire department can give help in this.

Special attention to fire prevention should be given in laboratories, farm buildings and storehouses.

Reporting and Follow-up of Accidents Accident reporting and follow-up might be called the keystone of the safety program. This is the best way to get the facts about accidents and take steps to prevent a recurrence.

The investigation of accidents can be carried on by the department chairman or dean with the assistance of the safety director. Follow-up should include recommendations for the removal of the hazard, changes in procedures, or other remedial action. Minor changes can be taken care of by the department itself; major changes may have to go to the central committee and the administration. The following is an example of the latter case:

Temporary bleachers used at a football field collapsed at a game, resulting in the injury of several spectators. An investigation showed that the bleachers were over 12 years old, in bad condition, and unsafe. It was recommended that they be discarded and new bleachers installed. This required the action of the athletic department, the safety committee, the president, and the business manager.

Several types of corrective action may be utilized. The following are illustrations:

Engineering—Several accidents involving pedestrians and motor vehicles occurred at an intersection of two streets on the campus. A traffic count was taken which justified the installation of a traffic light.

Enforcement—Several accidents were reported which resulted in injuries to the eyes from failure to wear goggles in machine shops. Regulations regarding the use of goggles were then enforced and there was no further trouble.

> *Education*—A number of drivers had been involved in minor accidents on the campus. They were required to enroll in a short refresher course.

These three approaches, well known in the traffic field, can be utilized in the attack on all kinds of accidents. Accident report blanks can be secured from the National Safety Council.

Training Training, in this case, refers primarily to instruction given to employees—drivers, custodians, guards, traffic police and others. Many safety directors conduct short training courses for all employees.

Promoting Interest A number of methods are being used to promote interest in safety. These include the use of stories in college newspapers, radio spot announcements, posters, placards, and motion pictures. Contests between fraternities have also been found useful in some colleges. To maintain interest there must be communication between the college administrator, the safety director, and the faculty and student body.

Off-Campus Activities In many institutions off-campus accidents are far more serious than those on the campus. This is especially true where there are large numbers of commuters. Traffic accidents lead as a cause of death and serious injury, followed by drowning and fires.

It is difficult to develop a program to reduce these accidents. However, the following methods have been used by some institutions and have been found valuable:

> Restrict the use of automobiles to those students who are commuters. Require the commuters to have cars inspected. Some colleges also give tests to all drivers. Parking is controlled by parking permits.
>
> Arrange for bus or railroad transportation to games. Some of the worst accidents involve passenger cars on the way to or from athletic contests. Some colleges also arrange for public transportation for vacations and holidays.
>
> Provide faculty supervision for off-campus trips, using college or public carriers.

Safety Instruction

In recent years there has been a significant increase in safety instruction in colleges and universities. This is especially true in teachers colleges, schools of education, engineering colleges and extension or off-campus divisions. Instruction includes not only courses, but also conferences, seminars, workshops and informal discussions. It also includes the integration of safety into existing courses. While there are great differences in what is being offered in the various types of colleges, the prevention of accidents and fires is important in all institutions.

Teachers Colleges and Colleges of Education

A recent study showed that there were well over 400 institutions that were offering courses in safety education. Two courses were most common, Driver Education and General Safety. In addition, most of these colleges give a course on Swimming and Water Safety. In certain states where certification requirements for safety teachers are high, other courses are provided. The following are the most frequently mentioned.

Organization and Administration of Safety Education
Advanced Driver Education
The Psychology of Safety
Prevention and Treatment of Athletic Injuries
Health and Safety Education
First Aid

Some of these colleges offer a minor in safety education.

Engineering Colleges and Extension Departments

A survey of the credit and non-credit offerings shows that the following courses are listed in college catalogs.

Traffic and Transportation Departments

Principles of Traffic Engineering
Highway Engineering
Street and Highway Design
Supervision of Commercial Motor Vehicle Fleets
Traffic Control for Police Departments
Traffic Police Administration
Traffic Court Procedures

Industrial Departments

Industrial Safety Engineering
Industrial Fire Prevention
Engineering Control of Health Hazards
Fire Prevention and Protection

Some colleges also provide short courses or conferences in subjects such as:

School Bus Driver Training
Training for Volunteer Fire Departments
State Traffic Management
Traffic Control for Police Departments.

Education for the Student Body

Even if an institution has all of the courses we have listed, only a small percentage of the student body would be reached. What can be done to provide some instruction to a larger number of students? An analysis of accidents to college personnel shows that the following are most frequent: accidents in physical education, athletics, and recreation; those involving the automobile; burns or scalds from fires; those occurring in shops and laboratories. In some colleges, around one-half of these occur off the campus. An education program should therefore stress these four areas.

Integration There are many subjects in which safety can be integrated, for example:

Athletic safety in all sports.
Water safety in physical education.
Recreational safety in physical education and recreation.
Fire prevention in chemistry and home economics.
Vocational safety in industrial arts and vocational education.
Farm safety in agriculture.
Home safety in home economics.
General safety in orientation courses and in health instruction.
Traffic safety in science, psychology and social studies.

Similarly, industrial safety and fire prevention could be integrated with industrial and management courses in the engineering colleges. Integration is of value for safety learnings will reach a large number of students not enrolled in safety courses.

Informal Instruction

A variety of methods can be used. Among these are stories in newspapers, notices and posters on bulletin boards, fraternity and sorority conferences, motion pictures, and announcements of rules and regulations.

Some colleges require that all students who drive to and from school have their cars inspected and take a series of tests. Others have short refresher courses. Still others penalize drivers for violations and require them to attend a school for violators.

Safety Centers

A number of institutions have organized safety centers. These are variously known as institutes, bureaus or centers. Examples are the Bureau for Highway Traffic at Yale University, which prepares traffic engineers; the Traffic Institute at Northwestern University, which offers courses in traffic control; and the New York University Center for Safety Education, which might be called a multipurpose center, for it offers courses in many fields of safety.

If offering four or more courses in the safety field was all that was necessary to qualify as a safety center, there would be several hundred in the country. But according to a definition proposed to the Campus Safety Association (5):

> A safety center is an organization formed by a college or university dedicated to accident prevention and related fields. It functions as a focal point for the institution's resources, providing a liasion unit that serves college and university personnel, state or local officials, business, industrial and professional interests and the public at large. It makes use of a staff of professional safety specialists and the services of other disciplines and units on or off the campus to provide leadership for and assistance in coordinating and improving accident prevention efforts. Activities related to a safety center may include safety courses, conferences, research projects, production of materials and publications, and public information on safety matters, and make available consultation services on accident prevention problems.

According to this definition, not many colleges have safety centers. However, it is expected that more centers will be organized in the coming years, especially in state universities. A center provides the best way to organize and coordinate a complete safety program.

Adult Education

In recent years there has been a significant growth in safety education for adults. The program in the schools and colleges, important as it is, is only a part of a larger task of providing safety education for the great army of adults. For example, what can be done to improve the practices of adult drivers, most of whom have had no formal instruction? Similarly, what can society do to reach adults with lessons on home safety, fire prevention and recreational safety?

There are two general methods that are being used: (1) courses, institutes and conferences, and (2) the use of educational media—newspapers, radio, television, motion pictures, posters and the like. It will not be possible to discuss these methods in detail; this would require a chapter in itself.

Courses for Adults

Many of the courses listed in this chpater under Engineering Colleges and Extension Departments are for adults. Some of these carry college credit; the majority are a part of the noncredit program. Other courses are offered by industries, commercial fleets, civil defense, police departments, the Red Cross, the Coast Guard, insurance companies and other agencies. Thus a course in Traffic Control for Police may be given by a college or by a state or county police association. Similarly, a college may offer a course for school bus drivers, or it may be given by the state department of education.

The following groups or subject-matter areas are often used as bases for organizing safety instruction for adults:

Traffic

School bus drivers
Supervisors and drivers of commercial motor vehicle fleets
Traffic engineers
Adult drivers:
  Public school courses
  Commercial driving schools
  Driver-improvement schools
Traffic police
Traffic court magistrates
Traffic safety managers

Industrial

Industrial safety supervision
Industrial hygiene
Safe practices for employees
Industrial fire prevention

Water

American Red Cross swimming courses
Red Cross life-saving courses
Red Cross instructors, lifeguards, examiners
Y.M.C.A. and Y.W.C.A. instruction for adults

Recreation

Power-boat safety
Playground instructors
Hunter safety instruction
Instruction at skiing centers
Camp counselors

Fire Prevention and Protection

Volunteer fire departments
Fire prevention engineering
Fire fighting
Forest fire prevention and protection

In addition to the above, several states conduct conferences on home and farm safety. Others have instruction in civil defense. As can be seen, there is a wide variety of courses or conferences in which safe practices are emphasized.

Educational Media

It will be noted that most of the courses listed above are for supervisors or leaders in the field. What can be done to reach adults who will not attend courses or conferences? There are a number of educational media that have been found useful.

The Press Newspapers are one of the most effective instruments for public safety education. It has been said that the press "can make or break a safety campaign." It can run editorials or articles on many phases of safety. Accounts of accidents are educational in themselves, as are stories of seasonal hazards, holiday campaigns, check tests, and records of suspension of licenses. The press wants "live" news of safety activities in actual practice. Stories on work being done by safety patrols, in driver education courses, and by volunteer ambulance squads, or on the arrests of hit-and-run drivers by accident prevention squads provide good news.

An analysis of newspapers during the year will show articles on a variety of subjects—fire prevention, safety in the home, in industry, in swimming and boating, in using firearms, and many others. A community that has a newspaper which is thoroughly sold on safety is indeed fortunate.

Radio and Television In recent years radio and television have come into more general use in accident prevention and fire prevention, broadcasting dramatizations, demonstrations, talks, spot announcements, roundtable conferences, and quizzes. There is little evidence as to the relative values of these methods, but it is felt that dramatizations and demonstrations are especially useful. Radio transcriptions on safety subjects are also coming into wider use.

Programs on safety may be made effective if the following rules are observed:

1. Talks should be brief, dealing with specific subjects rather than with generalities.
2. Interviews should be specific, timely and localized.
3. Dramatizations are recommended because of their high interest value. But if the script, dialogue or presentation is amateurish, the program is likely to be disappointing.
4. Spot announcements should be supplied regularly to radio and television stations and, if possible, should be prepared locally.

Visual Aids Motion pictures provide one of the best visual media used in safety. They include not only films used in motion-picture houses, but also those shown at adult schools, churches, clubs, conferences and the like. During the past few years there has been a rapid growth in the use of 16 mm. sound films for instructional purposes. A number of the films recommended for school use are adaptable to adult groups also. In communities where school projection apparatus is not available, arrangements can usually be made with the state motor vehicle departments or with state police for showing films at meetings.

Millions of posters are put up each year throughout the country, especially in industrial plants and public places and in the schools. Many are furnished without charge by insurance companies and other agencies;

others can be purchased from the National Safety Council. Outdoor posters displayed prominently on bulletin boards in cities have been helpful in focusing public attention on safety.

Exhibits and demonstrations range from small exhibits in store windows, in industries and before small gatherings, to large ones at state and local fairs, conventions and safety council meetings.

Booklets, Leaflets and Tests Millions of copies of various types of safety publications are given to the public each year. In fact, if one made a collection of all the free materials that are distributed, he would have a good safety library. Some of these materials are good and contain some valuable information; others are chiefly for institutional advertising and are of little value.

While most of the materials are in the traffic safety field, there are publications on a variety of other subjects, such as home safety, fire prevention, swimming and water safety, and safety in farming, in recreation and in hunting. Many of these are distributed at schools and carried home to be read by parents. Publications of this kind should be of value in raising the general level of public knowledge.

National, State and Local Conferences Thousands of safety conferences of various types are being held each year. These range from the national conferences called by the President, to the local conferences called by the Mayor. These undoubtedly have some value. To them must be added the safety meetings held by service and civic clubs, parent-teacher organizations, churches, insurance organizations and the like. These also have value in adult education. Not only are they informative, but often they provide an opportunity for discussion.

Does Adult Safety Education Pay?

It is difficult to measure the value of educational activities in reducing accidents to adults. There is clear proof that child safety activities do reduce accidents; the death rate for children of school age has dropped 18 per cent in the last decade (7). And we do know that during this same period the death rate for adults has also been decreasing. But this reduction is due to many different factors of which education is only one. Engineering and enforcement of regulations are also important. However, we know that school-trained drivers have better accident and violations records than the untrained. We know that well-trained bus drivers have better safety records. We also know that schools that introduce sound safety programs are able to reduce accidents materially. We must conclude with the general statement that education directed to the public good—to improve safety and security—eventually pays dividends.

summary

Many colleges and universities have problems similar to those of towns and small cities. They need police protection and traffic control. They should have fire prevention programs and facilities for fire fighting. They need safety programs to prevent accidents in laboratories, shops and other college buildings—including off-campus residences. Since a large percentage of the accidents are in physical education and recreation activities, colleges require a safety program that will tend to reduce such accidents. They will need a traffic safety and parking program, especially if there is a large number of commuters. There are many other ways in which the safety problems of a college resemble those of a community.

To provide for these activities, many colleges have established campus safety programs, usually under the supervision of safety committees and, in most instances, a director. These committees are responsible for the development of accident prevention and fire prevention activities at the college and its off-campus centers. These committees report directly to the president or his representative. Among the more important responsibilities of the committees are (1) establishing an accident-reporting system, (2) inspecting buildings for hazardous conditions and recommending the correction of such conditions, (3) training employees, (4) organizing plans for traffic control and (5) appointing committees to develop an educational program for both students and faculty. Accidents and fires are more common in colleges than might be expected. While fatalities on the campus are rare, there are far too many off-campus traffic accidents.

Many institutions, especially state universities and teachers colleges have organized courses, conferences and workshop for preparing leaders in the safety field. These include teachers, traffic engineers, industrial safety and fire prevention supervisors. Other colleges have courses for police, firemen, school bus drivers and supervisors of commercial fleets. Safety education programs are also organized for members of the college community not enrolled in such courses.

The problem of providing safety education for adults is an important one. Colleges and high schools are organizing courses and conferences that reach a small percentage. Other organizations, such as the Red Cross, the Forest Service, the Coast Guard Auxiliary, health departments, industries and insurance companies have training activities. For the most part, the vast majority of the adult population will have to be reached through various educational media such as newspapers, radio and television, posters, exhibits and motion pictures.

suggested projects and activities

1. Conduct a survey of one of the older buildings at your school and list the conditions that you consider hazardous.
2. If there is no accident-reporting system at your school, how would you convince the administrator that one should be installed?

3. Give some illustrations of how each of the 3 E's could be used to prevent football accidents.
4. Prepare a 10-point checklist that you could use in checking fire hazards in a student residence building.
5. Make a list of subjects taught in your school in which safety could be integrated.
6. What steps would you go through in organizing a campus safety program?

selected references

1. American College Health Association and National Safety Council, *Survey of Accidents to College Students*. Chicago: The Council, 1955.
2. Florio, A. E. and T. Stafford, *Safety Education* (2nd ed.). New York: McGraw-Hill Book Company, 1962.
3. National Commission on Safety Education, *Courses in Highway Safety and Highway Traffic*. Washington: The Commission, 1958.
4. ________, *University Transportation and Accident Prevention Centers*, Washington, D.C.: The Commission, 1962.
5. National Safety Council, "Definitions of a Safety Center," in *Transactions, School and College Conference*. Chicago: The Council, 1960.
6. ________, *Student Residence Fire Checklist*. Chicago: The Council, 1959.
7. ________, *Accident Facts*. Chicago: The Council, 1962.
8. ________, *National Conference on Campus Safety Reports*. Chicago: The Council.
9. Nihan, James, "A Practical Approach to College Safety Programs," in *Seventh National Conference on Campus Safety*. Chicago: National Safety Council, 1960.
10. State University of New York, *Campus Safety News*. Albany: The University, 1962.
11. University of Minnesota, *Employee and Student Accident Experience*. Minneapolis: The University, 1961.

17

organization, administration and supervision

Three important phases of the safety program will be considered in this chapter: organization, administration and supervision. These are overlapping functions, for both administrators and supervisors organize programs and administrators, especially school principals, supervise. In cities where good all-around programs have been organized, this is largely because administrators have been convinced of the value of safety education and are working with supervisors and teachers in carrying out plans. For illustration, there are at least 20 cities in the country that have had well-organized programs for at least 15 years. They have been fortunate over the years to have administrators who are convinced of the value of safety and supervisors to aid in its organization. The accident record of these cities is considerably better than that of the average city.

All administrators should be convinced of the value of safety education for the 18th Yearbook of the American Association of School Administrators, *Safety Education,* was formally approved by them. Its value was further emphasized in the various national safety conferences called by Presidents of the United States. *Planning Functional School Buildings* (11:231) includes an excellent statement of its importance:

> The welfare of pupils should take precedence over all other considerations. Of the factors of welfare, safety is perhaps the most vital. Granted that the future of society is based on the youth of today, our first concern is with the physical safety of youth so that they may attain able-bodied adulthood. . . . There can be no compromising where safety is concerned; to do so would be to betray the trust and welfare of parents, community and the nation.

Administration

There are seven major elements in administration: (1) Planning, (2) Organizing, (3) Staffing, (4) Directing, (5) Coordinating, (6) Reporting, and (7) Budgeting. These elements would also apply to safety. These elements were developed by Gulick and are reported in Bucher's Text (2).

1. *Planning* is the process of outlining the work that is to be done. The superintendent of schools must see to it that plans are organized for the various phases of the safety program.

2. *Organizing* is establishing the structure of and relationships between the various activities with clearly defined lines of authority. Thus, it is a good idea to have an organization chart prepared that will show lines of activity and responsibility. In larger school systems, safety may be assigned to an assistant superintendent or to a safety supervisor.

3. *Staffing* is the selection, assignment, and training of the personnel. Some school systems will have a personnel department, but in the great majority of cases, the superintendent working with school principals will assume this important responsibility himself.

4. *Directing* is providing the leadership that must be given to the program by the administrator. For illustration, the quality of the safety activities in a school building will depend to a large extent on the leadership given by the principal. He must be courageous, determined and persistent in seeing to it that the program is carried out.

5. *Coordinating* is interrelating the various parts of the program within an organization. This aids in the elimination of duplication, and in the development of standards and competent leadership. For illustration, in a school system in which the six high schools teach driver education, there should be coordination through standardization of programs, acquisition of visual aids and evaluation. However, this does not mean that standards should be hard and fast; they should provide for experimentation. Some schools would use range plans; others, simulators.

6. *Reporting* is supplying information to administrators regarding various phases of the safety program. Obviously, this also includes accident reporting. In addition, the school personnel must be kept informed by the administrator. The principal, for example, must keep teachers informed about important developments in the program, using various

media such as mimeographed bulletins and reports at teachers meetings.

7. *Budgeting* is financial planning and accounting. The superintendent must see to it that a budget is prepared for the various elements of the safety program. He must be ready to justify it.

Administration should be democratic and not autocratic. Goals should be developed through the group process. The superintendent should consult with members of his staff before undertaking a major change in program. It is important to good morale that in a conference each member's contribution should be encouraged and respected. This is especially important at meetings of the board of education.

In this chapter we will discuss the responsibilities of administrators and school boards in the selection of school sites, and safety in the construction and maintenance of school bulidings. This will be followed by a discussion on the standard accident reporting system. The organization of an instruction program in accident prevention will next be discussed. This will include such subjects as safety in school buildings and on school grounds, in vocational shops, laboratories and in physical education activities, and seasonal and neighborhood hazards. Community relations will also be discussed. Finally, this chapter will discuss the techniques of supervision, what supervisors can do to evaluate and strengthen a safety program, and the responsibilities for supervision by administrators, supervisors and teachers.

Organizing the Program

Responsibility for the Program The board of education, working through the superintendent of schools, is responsible for the development of the safety program. Certain phases of the responsibility may be delegated to assistants or to the supervisory staff. The principals are primarily responsible for the safety activities in their buildings and may assign certain duties to members of the staff. The board of education, through the superintendent, should prepare and issue regulations having to do with responsibilities for the protection of school children and property. These normally cover such subjects as: responsibilities of principals and teachers, duties of custodians, inspection of buildings and grounds, fire and civil defense drills, accident reporting, first aid procedures, pupil transportation, and equipment used in shops, gymnasium and playgrounds.

The School Environment

Administrators and teachers working for the safety of children should give special consideration to the school environment. To be sure, we

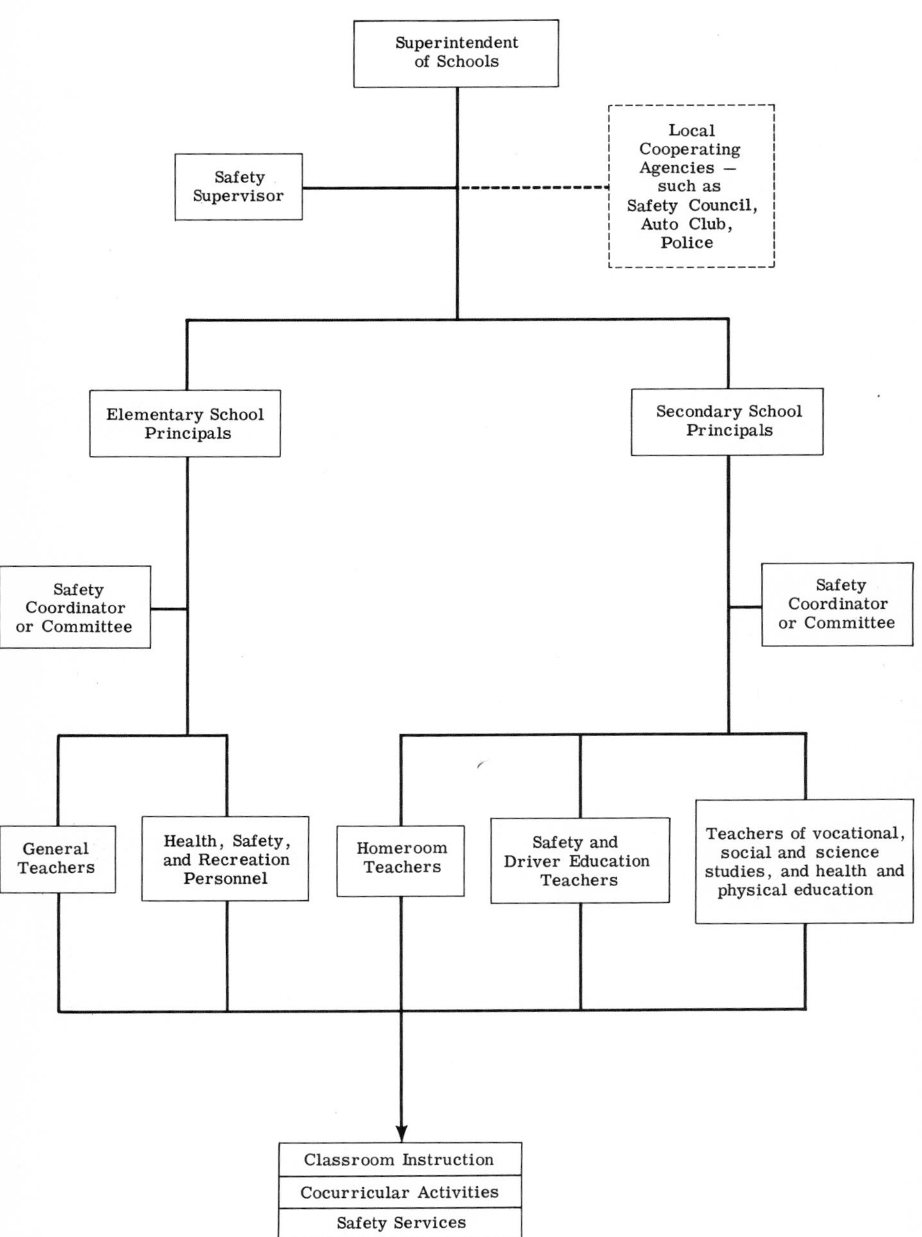
Superintendent
of Schools
Safety
Supervisor
Local
Cooperating
Agencies —
such as
Safety Council,
Auto Club,
Police
Elementary School
Principals
Secondary School
Principals
Safety
Coordinator
or Committee
Safety
Coordinator
or Committee
General
Teachers
Health, Safety,
and Recreation
Personnel
Homeroom
Teachers
Safety and
Driver Education
Teachers
Teachers of vocational,
social and science
studies, and health and
physical education
Classroom Instruction
Cocurricular Activities
Safety Services

Figure 17:1.

endeavor to provide a reasonably safe school plant and we strive to maintain some degree of supervision to prevent injury to pupils and damage to school property. Yet, we sometimes neglect to consider the total environment factors in day-by-day activities when planning for the safety of our children.

School environment, as the term is used here, includes every phase of the school's and the community's influence upon the safety of children. It includes the school plant and grounds, parent and pupil relationships, and administrative phases.

A Safe School Community

What would a survey of the community around the school show? Are there railroad tracks which children sometimes cross? Are there lakes where there is little or no supervision of bathing? Is there a lack of controls for ice skating and sledding in the winter months? Are there dumps, junk yards, or abandoned houses in which children play? Is there little police protection at certain corners on the way to and from school? Is there overcrowding on school buses? Is there a lack of school safety patrols at important crossings near the school buildings? Is there a lack of supervision on the playgrounds when they are open?

These are all situations which can give rise to accidents. While the schools have no jurisdiction over many of these areas, they know that they can contribute to accidents if they are not controlled. In many cases this is where police protection is needed. It follows, therefore, that both administrators and teachers must concern themselves over the community's total safety scene. Not only do more accidents take place in out-of-school activities than within the school building, but they are more serious accidents.

The School Site and Plant

Factors to be considered in the evaluation of a safe school environment include the selection of a school site, proper construction of school buildings, and the control of school situations in which the pupils daily spend their school hours. Unfortunately, teachers and administrators too often have little to say about school sites and plants. The following are safeguards that should be established for the protection of pupils:

1. The school and playground should be in clear view when approached from any direction on the highway. Standard school signs should be used.
2. Schools should be located away from heavily travelled business or industrial districts. Single floors, or not more than two floors are recommended.
3. Schools should not be located next to or near industries or railroads which disturb the schools by offensive odors or noise.

4. The school grounds should be as level as possible.
5. School sites should be adequate in size with plenty of room for playgrounds or athletic fields—5 acres for elementary, 8 to 10 acres for junior high schools and 10 to 15 acres for senior high schools.
6. Playground areas should be surrounded by fencing not less than eight feet in height.
7. Provision should be made for loading and unloading children from school buses.
8. A parking area should be set aside for teachers in the elementary schools and for students and teachers in the high schools.
9. A service driveway should extend to the street or an alley. All trade and other service vehicles should use this driveway.
10. Parking areas should be marked and parking permits required for students using facilities.

Teachers' and Pupils' Responsibilities in Plant Maintenance The care and maintenance of the plant are important factors in providing a safe school environment. Untidy, unclean, neglected school buildings and grounds breed carelessness and indifference in both teachers and pupils. In the school safety program particular attention should be given to all parts of the school: toilets, lunchrooms, locker rooms, gymnasiums, shower rooms, swimming pools, shops and laboratories, and auditoriums, as well as corridors, hallways and classrooms. As in industry, good housekeeping is essential.

Planning Safe School Buildings When planning and constructing buildings it is important to bear in mind the most serious hazard to the safety of occupants—fire. According to the National Board of Fire Underwriters in *Fire Safe Schools* (4), it is estimated that 4300 school fires occur annually that endanger the lives of pupils and teachers. In view of these and other facts it is to be expected that state and local school authorities, and safety and fire prevention organizations will have established standards regulating the construction of school buildings. The more important standards include the following:

1. *Buildings must be fire-resistive,* and, in areas subject to earth tremors, earthquake-resistive.
2. Ideally, school buildings should *not exceed two stories* in height even if fire-resistive. Unless special means of evacuation are used, the problem of emptying the building in case of emergency is aggravated by the height of the building.
3. *If not fire-resistive,* buildings should be provided with special stops of fireproof materials in the walls, partitions, and concealed recesses to serve as checks in case of fire.
4. *Large floor areas* should be divided into smaller areas by fire walls, with approved fire doors where fire walls extend across the corridor.
5. *Corridors* and *stairways* should be fire-resistive and should meet local and state standards as to number, location, width, size of risers, treads, railings, and landings.

6. There should be at least two exits and fire escapes from multiple-story buildings; these should be the regular enclosed stairway connecting directly with the corridor, and a smokeproof tower built on the outside wall of the building. The number, size and location of exits should meet the specifications set forth by local and state building codes, usually issued by the state department of education.
7. All *exit doors,* from classrooms as well as from the building, must swing outward. Outside doors should be equipped with self-closing devices and panic bolts that operate easily.
8. The *heating plant* and *fuel storage rooms* should be located outside the school building proper. If located within the building, they should be completely enclosed by fireproof walls and ceiling, the fuel room opening only to the furnace room.
9. Adequate *fire protection equipment* should be provided. Automatic sprinklers should be used in rooms where fires are most likely to start or spread quickly (boiler rooms, laboratories, cafeteria kitchens, shops and auditoriums); chemical extinguishers of the proper type, placed in convenient locations in corridors, laboratories, shops, cafeteria kitchens and on auditorium stages, should be used to check fires in their early stages. Every school building should be equipped with a fire-alarm system reaching into every part of the building, but separate from the regular signal system and designed to take its place in case of damage by fire.
10. Rooms in which large groups gather, such as the *auditorium* and the *gymnasium,* should be placed on the first floor to permit quick evacuation in case of need. These rooms should be constructed according to local and state codes, and should be provided with adequate fire protection equipment, including storage space for stage properties.
11. The provision for *sanitary facilities* is an important consideration in the health and safety of pupils. *Toilets for each sex, washing facilities,* and *drinking fountains* should be conveniently located on each floor of the building, sufficient to meet the needs of pupils as well as the standards set by school authorities as to installation and quality.
12. Whether the *ventilation* system is of the positive (mechanical pressure) or the open-window type, it should be sufficient to provide adequate circulation of fresh air in the classrooms. Special or individual air exhausts should be provided in toilets, laboratories, cafeteria kitchens, and all shops in which fumes and dust are produced. The introduction of air-conditioning systems should be accompanied by a study of the possible new fire hazards involved. Smoke detectors, dampers, and automatic shut-off power are essential in mechanically operated ventilating systems.
13. The *lighting* in all parts of the school building should be sufficient at all times. In classrooms, maximum daylight means a solid battery of windows on one side of the room. In terms of artificial or electric light sufficient and proper lighting ranges from 10 to 15 foot-candles.
14. *School furniture* and *equipment* must be adequate and safe. Furniture which fits the child should be provided in every room. Machines and equipment used in shops, laboratories and school cafeterias should be supplied with approved safety appliances. Gymnasium and playground apparatus should meet the most rigid standards to assure their adequacy for the safety of pupils at all times.

Providing Safety in Existing Buildings One of the great problems confronting school authorities is how to increase the safety features of existing buildings. Some buildings no longer suitable for school purposes because of age must be modified as best they can until the district is financially able to replace them. According to one report, the most serious dangers in old buildings are likely to be furnace and coal rooms without fire-resistant dividing walls, faulty wiring, unsafe stairways and exits, loose plaster ceilings and splintering floors. For the elimination of these hazards, the report recommends the following obvious procedures:

1. Rebuild furnace and coal rooms outside the building, or if this is impossible, enclose them within fire-resistive ceilings and walls with kalamein doors with fusible links that automatically close the doors when heated.
2. Check all wiring for defects and enclose exposed wires in conduits.
3. Rebuild wooden stairways with fire-resistive materials, and enclose with fire doors, and partitions, making a firewell leading to the outside. Many older buildings have stair landings in the middle of the building instead of near an exit. Such stairways should be replaced with stairwells as described above, or the building should be provided with an outside fire tower.
4. Check ceiling plaster frequently. Ceilings in old buildings often are finished with heavy plaster that sooner or later may become loose and fall. Replace these ceilings with lighter materials that are fire-resistive and sound-deadening.
5. Splintering pine floors are dangerous and should be replaced with new hardwood or manufactured flooring.
6. Install an automatic sprinkler system to protect basement, stairways, and corridors.

It is highly recommended that potential accident hazards be eliminated. Many are violations of Board of Underwriters standards, and their removal may favorably affect insurance costs. Projections and obstructions in corridors, on stairways, and in gymnasiums; slippery floors and stairs; the absence of handrails on stairways; heavy swinging doors with hard-working hinges and panic bolts—these are but a few of the many hazards that need careful attention periodically if the safety of the pupils is to be assured.

Accident Reporting

The accident reporting system recommended to school authorities is the result of studies by school administrators, safety supervisors, teachers and leaders in safe school practices. It is called "The National Safety Council Standard Student Accident Reporting System (7)," and meets the objectives of a well-planned operation of this nature. Its primary purposes are as follows:

1. It is a preventive device, indicating focal points of trouble and providing clues to danger points that need correction.
2. It is a defensive device. In case of lawsuits resulting from an accident or injury, the basic questions of negligence and liability revolve about the facts of the accident contained in the report.
3. It is a protective device in the sense that teachers and school boards are provided with a basis for an effective defense if a suit is brought.
4. It is a constructive device in that it can be used as a guide for curriculum planning.

Administering the Program The following steps are fundamental to the program:

1. *All* injuries, no matter how slight and no matter who the victim, are to be reported, provided the incident occurred on property over which the school has jurisdiction, or occurred in connection with any school activity, or affected any right of the school. Frequently what may seem to to be a minor injury develops into something of major proportions.
2. Every employee, regardless of rank, should be required to submit a report of every accident to which he was a witness, or of which he was immediately cognizant.
3. Reports should be submitted only to the reporting employee's superior, unless other officers are specifically designated by the superintendent or the school board.
4. Reports should be prepared and submitted immediately; under ordinary circumstances a reasonable period of time should not extend beyond 24 hours.
5. All legal papers served upon school officials or employees in connection with school matters should be forwarded immediately to the proper officials, who should be designated in advance for the receipt of all such legal documents.
6. Copies of accident report blanks should be strategically distributed in key points throughout the school system, and employees should be apprised of their availability.
7. All pupils should be immediately informed of a definite procedure to be followed in the event of any accident. This is necessary in case an injury occurs when no teacher or school employee is present. Part of an assembly program early in the term may well be devoted to a short discussion of this pupil responsibility.
8. If no nurse or doctor is assigned regularly to the school, at least one person on the faculty should be trained and qualified to render first aid treatment.
9. *Advance* arrangements should be made with hospitals or clinics or other medical dispensaries to handle emergency cases. If this is impossible, arrangements should be made *in advance* for emergency use of neighborhood doctors.
10. Parents or guardians of an injured pupil should be notified in case of serious injury. The principal should have on file the parental home and business address and telephone number for every student in the school, as well as the address and telephone number of the personal or family

physician of every student in the school. Such lists must be kept up to date.

The Accident Report

First of all it is necessary to have an accepted definition of an accident. The following are definitions; it will be noted that they are quite different.

Definitions of an Accident

One that is widely accepted is "an accident is an unplanned and uncontrolled event in which the action or reaction of an object, substance, person, or radiation results in personal injury." This definition is one which schools could use in reporting accidents. However, damage to property is not included.

The American Standards Association states briefly: "An accident is an event which results in physical harm to a person." It is further explained that physical harm includes traumatic injury and disease as well as adverse mental, neurological, or systemic effects resulting from an exposure or circumstances encountered in the course of employment.

William E. Tarrants of the American Society of Safety Engineers has urged a more complete definition:

> *An Accident*—An unplanned, not necessarily injurious or damaging event, which interrupts the completion of an activity, and is invariably preceded by an unsafe act and/or an unsafe condition or some combination of unsafe acts and/or unsafe conditions.

Routine Procedures

The following are routine procedures for accident reports:

1. The report should be forwarded to the agency designated in advance to receive it: the board's legal department, the superintendent of schools, the business manager or other stated official.
2. Copies of the report should be sent to all department heads.
3. A routine should be provided for rectifying defects disclosed in the report, whether they are matters of personnel administration, equipment, or buildings and grounds. Inaccurate and unsafe practices should be modified, and structural defects should be corrected by the responsible officials.
4. Periodic summaries of the accident reports should be made to isolate recurrent types of accidents and accident trends. Intelligent handling of carefully prepared accident reports, coupled with a continuous analysis of accident causes and a systematic attempt to eradicate them, is a most efficacious weapon in the hands of safety educators and school board officials.
5. Monthly summaries of accidents should be made available to school administrators and supervisors.

STANDARD STUDENT ACCIDENT REPORT FORM
Part A. Information on ALL Accidents

1. Name: ______ Home Address: ______
2. School: ______ Sex: M ☐; F ☐. Age: ____ Grade or classification: ____
3. Time accident occurred: Hour ______ A.M.; ______ P.M. Date: ______
4. Place of Accident: School Building ☐ School Grounds ☐ To or from School ☐ Home ☐ Elsewhere ☐

5. **NATURE OF INJURY**

Abrasion	____	Fracture	____
Amputation	____	Laceration	____
Asphyxiation	____	Poisoning	____
Bite	____	Puncture	____
Bruise	____	Scalds	____
Burn	____	Scratches	____
Concussion	____	Shock (el.)	____
Cut	____	Sprain	____
Dislocation	____		
Other (specify)	______		

PART OF BODY INJURED

Abdomen	____	Foot	____
Ankle	____	Hand	____
Arm	____	Head	____
Back	____	Knee	____
Chest	____	Leg	____
Ear	____	Mouth	____
Elbow	____	Nose	____
Eye	____	Scalp	____
Face	____	Tooth	____
Finger	____	Wrist	____
Other (specify)	______		

DESCRIPTION OF THE ACCIDENT

How did accident happen? What was student doing? Where was student? List specifically unsafe acts and unsafe conditions existing. Specify any tool, machine or equipment involved. ______

6. Degree of Injury: Death ☐ Permanent Impairment ☐ Temporary Disability ☐ Nondisabling ☐
7. Total number of days lost from school: ______ (To be filled in when student returns to school)

Part B. Additional Information on School Jurisdiction Accidents

8. Teacher in charge when accident occurred (Enter name): ______
   Present at scene of accident: No: ______ Yes: ______

9. **IMMEDIATE ACTION TAKEN**

First-aid treatment	____	By (Name): ______
Sent to school nurse	____	By (Name): ______
Sent home	____	By (Name): ______
Sent to physician	____	By (Name): ______
		Physician's Name: ______
Sent to hospital	____	By (Name): ______
		Name of hospital: ______

10. Was a parent or other individual notified? No: ___ Yes: ___ When: ______ How: ______
    Name of individual notified: ______
    By whom? (Enter name): ______
11. Witnesses: 1. Name: ______ Address: ______
    2. Name: ______ Address: ______

12. **LOCATION**

	Specify Activity		Specify Activity
Athletic field	______	Locker	______
Auditorium	______	Pool	______
Cafeteria	______	Sch. grounds	______
Classroom	______	______ shop	______
Corridor	______	Showers	______
Dressing room	______	Stairs	______
Gymnasium	______	Toilets and washrooms	______
Home Econ.	______		
Laboratories	______	Other (specify)	______

Remarks

What recommendations do you have for preventing other accidents of this type? ______

Signed: Principal: ______ Teacher: ______

Organizing the Instruction Program

The superintendent of schools is responsible for the inclusion of safety education in the school curriculum. The implementation of the program may be delegated to an assistant superintendent, to a supervisor of health and physical education, or to a safety supervisor. However, the superintendent is directly responsible to the board of education. The principal of the individual school should be the person charged with making sure that he has on his staff at least one qualified person in the field of safety education.

Whenever possible, it is a wise move to organize a school safety council in each school district. In fact, in many cities there is a community-wide safety organization. Safety extends into mamny areas and a local safety council, made up of representatives of the police and fire departments, the Red Cross, the P.T.A., insurance underwriters, automobile clubs and others, can do much to aid in the work of the schools. This is especially true since more than one-half of the accidents and practically all of the fatalities take place off the school grounds. The school has the responsibility of protecting the lives of children both on and off the school grounds.

In the organization and administration of safety education programs, two problems must be considered: (1) securing faculty cooperation; (2) the nature, scope, and organization of safety education.

Securing Faculty Cooperation The success of the program will depend to a large extent on faculty cooperation. This becames the responsibility of the administrators and the supervisors. Most teachers have had but little formal instruction in safety education. It will therefore be desirable to arrange for in-service courses, conferences or institutes, the distribution of safety education literature, the showing of visual aids, and faculty meetings for development of a positive philosophy toward safety education.

Scope and Organization of the Program Three criteria will determine the nature and scope of the program: (1) the activities in which students participate, (2) the hazards to which they are exposed, both in school and out of school, and (3) an analysis of the accident experience of the schools. Thus, in the elementary school a study should be made of pupil activities during various months of the year, both in school and out of school, and an analysis made of the accident records for the various months and of the various grade levels. From this, a month by month program can be prepared for the various grade levels. According to *The Administrator and the School Safety Program* (3) certain types of accidents tend to pre-

Figure 17:2,
SEVERAL HUNDRED COLLEGES PROVIDE TRAINING FOR HIGH SCHOOL TEACHERS.

dominate in certain seasons or months of the year. The emphasis on safety education in many cities is as follows:

Sept.—Traffic Safety
Oct.—Fire Prevention
Nov.—School Safety
Dec.—Home Safety
Jan.—Winter Safety
Feb.—First Aid
Mar.—Public Safety
Apr.—Play and Recreation
May, June—Vacation

This is not a hard and fast outline. Ideally, every phase of safety should be stressed *before as well as when it is needed.*

In the primary grades instructional content should be concerned principally with everyday practices—going to and from school, roller skating, using scooters and bicycles and safe practices in the school. Consideration should also be given to recognizing hazards in the home that lead to burns, poisoning, falls and other common accidents.

In the intermediate grades the individual's personal safety will be considered further, and his responsibility for the safety and welfare of the group should be stressed. New areas that might be introduced at this level include fire prevention, water safety, first aid, safety in athletics and recreation, and on playgrounds. The growing interest of pupils in group and club activities should be used to develop a greater sense of responsibility for the welfare of the group. This can be encouraged through patrols, bicycle clubs, safety councils, school assemblies and other co-curricular activities.

On the high school level both personal as well as group safety should be emphasized. Instructional materials should be more advanced. Safety in sports, in the school shop and in home economics, in recreation, and in boating and canoeing, should receive attention. To prepare students for safe practices in traffic situations, a course in driver education is most important.

School Jurisdiction According to *Accident Facts* (8) approximately 40 per cent of school accidents take place in organized games; 15 per cent in unorganized games. Of the remainder, 10 per cent are in auditoriums and classrooms, 10 per cent on stairs and in corridors, 5 per cent in shops and laboratories, 5 per cent on the way to and from school, and 10 per cent in miscellaneous places. While there is considerable variation between the elementary and the secondary schools, these distributions indicate in a general way those aspects of the school environment that should be given attention. Some specific instructional items for these phases are suggested below:

School Grounds

Athletics and unorganized activities. The distribution of playground accidents indicates a need for careful supervision if accidents resulting in injuries are to be reduced materially. It is therefore necessary that pupils be taught the skills essential to safe participation in the various activities—organized and unorganized, supervised and unsupervised. They should appreciate the value of consideration and good sportsmanship for safe participation. Furthermore, the playgrounds should be laid out to separate players according to ability and interest, the more vigorous games being played in the outer areas of the grounds. The grounds should be kept free of obstructions, bicycles, stones, broken glass and the like. Strenuous games should not be played during the hottest part of the day or when the player is tired and fatigued. Overexertion may cause illness or injury.

School ground apparatus. Unless pupils are taught the correct way to perform on playground apparatus, many accidents may result, some of them quite serious. Children should be taught to wait until *swings* have stopped before getting off. They should not swing too high nor play too near to the swing areas. Neither should they run under the swings when pushing another child. They should swing only when seated, never standing up.

When playing on *slides,* children should carefully climb the ladder, wait until the slide is clear, then slide down feet first, in a sitting position. On *teeter-totters,* they should face each other, keep their feet out from under the board as it approaches the ground, and should warn their partner when they are about to get off or on. When using the *bars* and *rings,* children should be instructed to travel only in one direction, taking firm grip on the apparatus before traveling. They should refrain from taking hold of another child who is using the apparatus, and from doing tricks unless a high degree of skill has been developed.

Whatever the type of apparatus, careful instruction in its use as well as in matters of courtesy, caution, and consideration for others will reduce playground accidents. Close supervision also will help to keep accidents at a low rate.

School Buildings

The following are suggestions for reducing accidents in various parts of the school building:

Corridors and stairs. Pupils should always walk in corridors and on the stairs to avoid crowding and colliding with others. They should walk up or down steps one at a time and hold on to the rail. At the drinking fountain they should await their turns, avoiding pushing and crowding. To reduce the possibility of accidents, the floor around the fountain should be kept dry, and corridors and stairways should be kept free of obstructions. Respect for safety rules and obedience to them should be observed by both pupils and teachers. Unsafe conditions in corridors and hallways and on stairs should be brought to the immediate attention of the proper authorities.

Classrooms and auditorium. Safe practices in classrooms are an absolute essential. Pupils should early be taught good housekeeping procedures and habits of safe behavior. They should know where to keep school equipment and personal belongings, how to handle pointed objects correctly, and why not to play near radiators or electric light fixtures or on chairs or ladders. Sufficient place for storage should be provided. Pencils, crayons, pins, needles and beads should not be placed in one's mouth, ears or nostrils, wobbly chairs, boxes or tables should not be used in place of a ladder.

Because of its use by large numbers of persons at one time, the auditorium merits special consideration. Preferably located on the ground floor, the auditorium should be equipped with approved fire-fighting apparatus, safety doors, and lighting facilities. Stage equipment and scenery should be of fireproof materials, securely fastened when used, and stored in fireproof cases when not in use. Dressing rooms should be in order at all times. To assure maximum safety, pupils should be orderly in passing to and from the auditorium, frequent fire drills should be held, and periodic inspections should be made.

Gymnasium, swimming pool, and locker rooms. The gymnasium accounts for the largest percentage of all school building accidents. Reduction of these accidents is possible only under the most careful supervision. Pupils should be properly dressed before being permitted to engage in gymnasium activities. The equipment should be in good condition and should be used by pupils only after they have acquired the necessary skills—and then under the supervision of the instructor or a designated supervisor. Under no circumstances should pupils be permitted to disregard the safety rules and regulations that have been set up. "Horseplay" and "roughhousing" should not be tolerated. In addition, all exposed equipment and projections should be covered with protective materials.

Vocational shops, laboratories and home economics rooms. Eighteen per cent of school building accidents happen in the school shops, laboratories, and home economics rooms. To prevent these accidents, pupils should be thoroughly instructed in the proper use of tools, equipment, supplies, and protective equipment. They should also develop good housekeeping practices and suitable habits in the use of materials and the disposal of waste, rubbish and unused materials. They should be led to appreciate the need for giving their undivided attention to their work, especially when they are operating power machinery or using hot equipment, dangerous chemicals, and the like. Machinery should be stopped before it is oiled, adjusted, or repaired. Operators should not stand in line with swiftly moving or revolving parts. Hot materials or chemicals should be handled with protective gloves or pads, and where there is danger of splashing, the face should be protected. Proper illumination and ventilation, careful observance of rules and regulations, and the development of safe personal habits will do much toward increasing safety in these areas.

Seasonal and Neighborhood Hazards There are other possible hazards in the environment that should be controlled. Coasting and ice skating, for illustration, will be common to most of the northern states. Many communities have a program for safe coasting. Streets are set aside by the police department and stanchions or wooden horses placed on both ends. Red lanterns are put on stanchions at night. The schools are notified as to the designated streets, and parents are requested to see to it that children use these streets and no others. The schools also teach safe practices in coasting. In some communities it is the responsibility of the police department to control the use of ponds and lakes for ice skating. In others, the park or recreation department takes over this responsibility.

Swimming in unsupervised places, such as rivers, lakes, or abandoned mines or quarries also presents a problem. Signs can be erected forbidding trespassing, but such signs may have little influence on children on a hot summer day. Whenever possible, mines and quarries should be drained and filled in, or fences should be erected. Both the schools and the homes should emphasize safe swimming places and condemn the unsafe. In recent years, more and more communities are building swimming pools and providing supervised areas on rivers and lakes. They are also exercising control of the safety at commercial swimming pools in their areas. Approved sanitation methods and protection of bathers by trained lifeguards are essential controls.

Establishing Community Relationships The school is one of many agencies in the community interested in the problem of safety. The safety of school children is a single but inseparable phase of this problem. As the community is rendered safer for all, so will it be safer for school children. For this reason—as well as for the broader reason that education is maintained by society to serve society—the school administrator should view himself as a community leader in safety and accept the responsibility of assisting in appropriate safety projects of other community agencies. In this connection, he may be guided by the following considerations:

1. The supporting activities contemplated for the school must be sound from an educational point of view.
2. Such activities as provide for pupil participation should be welcomed, because through them pupils have the opportunity to participate in worthwhile community projects.
3. There is a reciprocal value in having school staff representation at safety council meetings, parent-teacher meetings on community safety, and other programs of public import in this field.
4. A program of exceptional potential for community safety is the utilization of school children to make their parents aware of home and traffic hazards and of the need for correction and control of these hazards.
5. Through the use of newspapers, radio, and television, as well as special evening courses and meetings for adults, the school administrator can conduct a broad program of adult safety education which will not only serve the community well but also strengthen its primary program of education (3).

The Teacher One of the best measures of the quality of the safety program is what goes on in the classroom. For the teacher is *in loco parentis,* and is responsible for the supervision, protection, and instruction of the pupil. In general, accidents in school buildings are not numerous; schools are one of the safest places in the world for children. But there are certain responsibilities of teachers that are very important:

1. Seeing to it that children do not expose themselves to dangers in and about the school.
2. Insisting that safe practices be followed in fire drills, in the corridors, and in shops and laboratories.
3. Insisting on safe practices in the gymnasium, on playgrounds and athletic fields, for the majority of school accidents take place in activities here.
4. Seeing to it that in case of accident the pupil is given first aid and that the accident is reported.
5. Watching out for special dangers in the environment outside the school, and stressing safe practices to meet these dangers.

Supervision

Lack of supervision might well be called one of the weaknesses of the safety education program. There are only several hundred part-time or full-time safety supervisors in the country where, according to the National Safety Council, there should be several thousand. It is of interest to note that over the years the cities that have had outstanding programs and low child accident rates have been those with qualified safety supervisors.

There are several reasons why states and cities should have supervisors or directors of safety education:

1. Many teachers have had little or no formal preparation in college courses for the teaching of safety education; they need help.
2. Hazards in the environment of children have been increasing rather than decreasing.
3. Many school systems have important problems in pupil transportation, which can be assigned to the safety supervisor for solution.
4. It has been clearly demonstrated that a well-organized child safety program will reduce accidents.
5. One of the best ways to insure a sound program is through adequate supervision.

The Nature of Supervision According to Kimball Wiles in *Supervision for Better Schools* (13):

> Supervision is assistance in the development of better teaching-learning situations. Certain members of the staff are labeled supervisors. Although they do not do all of the supervising, they have a great part in determining whether supervision is good. They help establish communication. They help people hear each other. They serve as liaison agents to get persons into contact with others who have similar problems or with resource people who can help. They stimulate staff members to look at the extent to which ideas and resources are being shared, and the degree to which persons are encouraged and supported as they try new things. . . . They bring to individual teachers, whose confidence they possess, appropriate suggestions and materials. . . . The supervisor's role has become supporting, assisting and sharing rather than directing.

In general, Wiles' concepts of the functions of supervision apply to safety education. However, there are some differences. As will be noted in the following abstract of a *Job Analysis of the Safety Supervisor* (9), prepared by the School and College Conference of the National Safety Council in 1958, a number of the activities of the safety supervisor are administrative. He may direct pupil transportation; he may represent the superintendent and the schools at conferences of community organizations. He may have other administrative duties.

In order to provide assistance to a school system preparing to select a safety supervisor, an abstract of the job analysis is given below.

1. *Determination and coordination of administrative policy in safety.* Unless someone is charged directly with developing an administrative policy regarding safety, important educational elements may be neglected. Safety is unique in that it cuts across all areas of instruction and reaches into exceptionally important administrative fields. The supervisor assumes some responsibility in administration. To illustrate:
   a. The collection, analysis and use of data from accident reports are essential to the school safety program.

The supervisor develops a method of collecting these reports, preparing monthly summaries which are furnished to the National Safety Council, the school administrators, local safety councils, and to other organizations. An annual report is prepared and, with the monthly summaries, is used as a basis for curriculum development.

b. Safety programs also operate outside the school building, thereby involving additional public relations aspects.
The supervisor develops all activities and procedures in cooperation with the policies of the local administration. He helps interpret the safety program to the public, secures the cooperation of community leaders and organizations, and aids classroom teachers in selecting safety materials from outside agencies. He also secures the cooperation of administrators in correcting existing school hazards. In addition, he secures publicity about safety activities through newspapers, radio and television programs, and other educational media.

c. Safety instruction for beginners confronts the child all at once, thus involving unusually important instructional and control demands.
The supervisor helps bring to the attention of teachers and parents the need for precautions, and protection for young children. He works with teachers to improve safety instruction, and develops adequate instructional guides and aids for teachers. He cooperates with community agencies to secure protection for children.

d. The exit drill and other emergency situations outrank most administrative necessities in legal, instructional and control imbalance.
The supervisor assists each building in setting up adequate fire drills and civil defense drills. He makes certain that provisions are made for handicapped children, and that special drills are included involving blocked exits, staircases, and corridors.

e. Safety must be an integral part of all curriculum areas, such as shop, home economics, science, physical education and social studies.
The supervisor cooperates with these departments in furnishing related materials, accident reports, and guidance in developing programs.

f. Safety must be built into all school buildings.
The supervisor aids in the inspection of buildings, and recommends correction of hazards. He also cooperates in the construction of new buildings through conferences with the architect and administrators.

g. The community must share responsibility for the development of safety practices and attitudes.
The supervisor cooperates with community agencies in furnishing materials, aiding in local programs, and providing school activities for these agencies.

2. *Development of safety curricula.* The supervisor serves as the safety education consultant for the curriculum committee of the school system. In this capacity, he works with teachers and principals to improve safety programs.

3. *Improvement of instruction in safety.* The supervisor keeps informed about the latest developments in local state and national safety programs, research, and information. He works with teachers and principals to improve safety instruction and encourages research, the use of visual aids and the like.

4. *Development of improved community coordination in safety.* The supervisor works with all useful outside agencies, often as a member of a local safety council. These community agencies all play a vital part in the development of improved public relations and safety practices of the schools.
5. *Evaluation of the effectiveness of the safety program.* The supervisor reviews the goals and objectives of safety education, and studies accident summaries and other accident data. He also assists principals and teachers in developing evaluation instruments. He encourages schools to participate in the National School Safety Honor Roll.

Obviously, the nature of this program depends to a large extent on the size of the school system and the general policies regarding safety education.

summary

Much of the success of the safety program depends upon its organization, administration and supervision. These three functions overlap; a superintendent and a principal can be an organizer, an administrator and a supervisor.

Administration has seven main elements—(1) planning, (2) organizing, (3) staffing, (4) directing, (5) coordinating, (6) reporting, and (7) budgeting. It is primarily a function of the superintendent and the principal although in actual practice much of the work is done by a supervisor.

Organization refers to the structure of the various safety activities providing clearly defined lines of authority. It involved those factors that have to do with the total school program, such as safe environment, accident reporting, safety instruction, community relationships, pupil transportation and cocurricular activities. The board of education, working through the superintendent of schools, is responsible for the development of the safety program. However, certain phases of the program will be delegated to assistants, safety supervisors and principals.

Supervision refers to the operation of the program. The supervisor's role has become supporting, assisting and sharing rather than directing. He works with teachers and administrators to organize the program and then cooperates with them to see that it is carried out. There are several hundred full time safety supervisors in the country but there should be several thousand. Most of the cities that have had outstanding child safety records over the years have been those with supervisors or directors of safety education. This is also true in state driver education activities; states with the best programs have one or more supervisors. The supervisor normally assumes some responsibility in administration, often representing the superintendent. He works to set up accident reporting systems, to develop safety curricula, improve instruction, secure better community relationships and evaluate the effectiveness of the safety program.

TEACHER'S EVALUATION CHART

1. Did you have participation of pupils and teacher in selection of subject matter and in planning of activities?

2. Has there been centralization of the program around the needs and interests of the individuals and group?

3. Has there been modification of classroom instruction by conference, excursion, research, dramatization, construction, sharing, interpreting and evaluating activities?

4. Has there been provision of opportunity for intelligent self-direction?

5. Has there been concern of safety program for all phases of safe living for all groups in the community?

6. Has there been an emphasis on development of desirable attitudes?

7. Have student surveys of safety hazards been carried out, such as: in school buildings, on playground, at street crossings, in recreational activities, control of bicycle and automobile traffic around school building and proximate areas?

8. Have assembly programs been utilized to stress safe living?

9. Have bulletin boards and similar types of displays been utilized to better inform the school as to safety problems?

10. Has there been a notable improvement in attitude of pupils toward safe living?

11. Has provision been made for reporting of accidents? Are they classified for the purpose of study and revision of program?

12. Has there been an increase in cooperative planning on the part of pupils and teacher?

13. Have you made greater use of available agencies stressing accident prevention activities?

14. Have you provided a reference shelf for the collection and use of safety materials?

15. Have you made frequent use of select visual aids in safety?

16. Has the administration given full co-operation in the planning of your program?

suggested projects and activities

1. As a newly appointed safety supervisor, what steps would you take to inform yourself as to the status of accident reporting in the schools?
2. Make a list of at least 10 community agencies that might be represented on a city safety education committee.
3. As a supervisor you have been requested to organize a bicycle testing program for the 30 schools in your city. How will you organize this program?
4. Prepare a chart illustrating the responsibilities of various school personnel in promoting and conducting an adequate safety education program.
5. Make a list of 10 community agencies. Indicate what each of these agencies could do to aid in the school safety program.
6. Prepare an outline of a short talk (15 minutes) explaining the values of an accident reporting system.

selected references

1. Aaron, James E., "A Study of Supervisory Practices in Safety Education in Selected Areas in the United States." Unpublished doctor's thesis, New York University, 1960.
2. Bucher, Charles A., *Administration of School Health and Physical Education Programs.* New York: The C. V. Mosby Company, 1958.
3. Center for Safety Education, New York University, *The Administrator and the School Safety Program.* The Center, 1951.
4. National Board of Fire Underwriters, *Fire Safe Schools.* New York: The Board, 1954.
5. National Commission on Safety Education, *Checklist on Safety and Safety Education in Your School.* Washington, D.C.: The National Education Association, 1953.
6. ________, *The Elementary School Principal Plans for Safe Living.* Washington; National Education Association, 1945.
7. National Safety Council, *Standard Student Accident Reporting System.* Chicago: The Council.
8. ________, *Accident Facts.* Chicago: The Council (annual).
9. ________, *Job Analysis of the Safety Supervisor.* Chicago: The Council, 1958.
10. Silverwood, George P., "Safety in the School Environment", *Journal of Health, Physical Education, and Recreation,* March, 1960.
11. Sumption, Merle R. and Jack L. Landes, *Planning Functional School Buildings.* New York: Harper & Row, Publishers, 1957.
12. Tead, Ordway, *The Art of Administration.* New York: McGraw-Hill Book Company, 1951.
13. Wiles, Kimball, *Supervision for Better Schools.* Englewood Cliffs, N.J.: Prentice-Hall, Inc., 1961.

18

safety in pupil transportation

Pupil transportation in the United States today is big business. It is big in size, big in cost, and a big operation to administer. Over 12 million students, one out of every four, depend on school buses; in some states it is one out of two. There are well over 190,000 buses in the country that travel over 1.3 billion miles each year at an approximate cost of $410 million. The accident, injury and fatality rates, while not high, still are in need of further reduction. While accident statistics are not too accurate, in a recent year 43 states reported 54 students killed and 2,978 injured. This record can be improved upon.

While the National Safety Council has always been interested in pupil transportation, the death of seven children and injury to 19 others in school bus-train collision in Oakland, Maryland, prompted the Council to list a three-point program to safeguard school bus passengers.

The Council said, "above all, schools should have a person with direct authority for establishing and administering a safety program for school bus drivers." The three-point program included:

1. Selection and training of school bus drivers.
2. Inspection and preventive maintenance of school buses.
3. Establishment of legal standards for the behind-the-wheel performance of drivers through driver licensing.

It has also been recommended by some groups that each school bus have a patrol to keep discipline among students, thereby allowing the driver to concentrate on his number one job—driving.

Three more objectives could be added:

Education of the pupil in safe transportation practices.

Use of efficient business methods in organizing and operating the program.

Establishing state regulations requiring vehicles to come to a stop when school buses are taking on or discharging passengers.

Selection, Education, and Placement of the Driver

In the preparation of this chapter, the recommendations of the Report of the President's Committee for Traffic Safety on *Education* (16) have been used as a guide. The following recommendations are emphasized in this section:

Establish or adopt standards and procedures for selection of reliable and qualified bus drivers, utilizing the recommendations of the National Conference on School Transportation as a guide.

Require applicants to pass medical examinations and tests of knowledge and driving ability as they relate to school bus operation. Experience should be considered, but more important are the applicant's physical, mental and emotional qualifications.

The responsibility of driving a school bus and the importance attached to this task by certain school administrators is expressed well by Kearney when he states (4):

> The man who drives a bus load of children to school every day, in all kinds of hazardous highway and weather conditions, is charged with grave responsibility. Together with a ship's captain, or an airline pilot, precious human lives depend upon his experience, skill, and judgment. Yet, despite the increasing dangers of highway travel, many communities pay minimum attention to the dependability of their school bus drivers.

A trend decidedly in evidence is the use of younger persons as drivers of school buses. Some 20 states currently assign some secondary school students for this purpose, and reportedly other states are considering doing so. It would appear that this practice warrants further investigation, especially by those school systems where difficulties are being encountered in procuring and retaining the services of qualified adults. According to Murray, of the U.S. Office of Education (6:7):

> Driving a school bus is more often than not a low paying, part-time job requiring only a few hours' work each day. In the majority of cases it represents a side job; and as a result school bus drivers are usually recruited from a variety of local sources; farmers or ranchers, garage mechanics, gasoline station operators, store clerks, truck drivers, school teachers, barbers, housewives, ministers, and in some states high school students, represent in many cases, the local groups from which many of our school bus drivers are recruited.

Hyde, formerly of the North Carolina State Department of Motor Vehicles has this to say (3):

> Is it a safe practice to use students as school bus drivers? . . . North Carolina, with students holding more than 90 per cent of her some 7,700 school bus driving positions, has made the most extensive use of this practice, although students drive school buses in twenty-three states.

Hyde is strongly in favor of the use of student drivers. They are carefully selected, are given 12 hours of classroom instruction and six hours of practice driving before they are certified. They are supervised by state and local supervisors and are inspected by the highway patrol.

In selecting drivers for school bus operations, consideration should be given to physical condition, prior record of driving experience (accidents and/or violations), knowledge of recommended driving practices, ability to demonstrate adequate manipulative skills on a series of road tests as well as on a controlled course, teacher ratings (where student drivers are used), and psychosocial factors (marital status, siblings, educational level, job history, hospitalization record, civil and federal offense record, and general social behavior).

Once a driver has been employed, he should be familiarized with his equipment, the areas he will serve, the routes over which he will operate, the schools he will service, the school officials with whom he will work, and the pupils he will transport as well as procedures to be followed in the event of accidents, road failure, inclement weather, emergency situations and the like. Naturally, matters of salary, benefits, incentives, retirement plans and other policies which affect him should be outlined and explained in full.

According to Murray (6), "state requirements specify that individuals employed as school bus drivers are to be of good moral character and reputation, and abstain from the use of profanity, narcotics and alcoholic beverages."

Supervision of Instruction

Many states now have supervisors or directors of pupil transportation. Larger cities and many counties also have supervisors devoting either full time or part time to pupil transportation. Among the standards and activities recommended in the report of the President's Committee for Traffic Safety (16) that was cited earlier in this chapter, there are several that have to do with supervision of pupil transportation. Some of them were taken from the National Commission of Safety Education publication, *Selection, Instruction, and Supervision of School Bus Drivers* (8):

> Cooperate with official agencies, such as the motor vehicle department and the highway patrol or police, in the enforcement of pupil transportation standards.
>
> Sponsor institutes and courses of instruction for school bus drivers and maintenance personnel, coordinated by the state education agency to assure consistency in training; and assist local administrators in setting up their own instructional programs.
>
> Encourage research to insure continual development of sound safety practices and programs in pupil transportation.
>
> Encourage colleges and universities to include in school administration courses instruction in the administration and operation of pupil transportation programs.
>
> Vest in one staff person definite responsibility for instructional programs for drivers and maintenance personnel.
>
> Enforce the requirements of the state education authority regarding pupil transportation.
>
> Provide continuous supervision of operating and maintenance personnel.
>
> Provide the state supervisor of transportation with pertinent data on school transportation, including data on accidents to pupils being transported, so that safer and more effective programs of pupil transportation may be developed.
>
> Seek the cooperation of community and parent groups in assuring safe pupil transportation.

A great variety of training programs are now in use in the states. In some, the state supervisor, in cooperation with the state police or patrol, conducts one-day institutes for bus drivers prior to the opening of school. In others, the instructors are given intensive, approved courses offered at regional centers or at colleges. North Carolina has a staff of 30 highway safety personnel who devote 80 per cent of their time to the instruction of student bus drivers. Maryland has a preservice course for drivers, followed by a final performance test conducted by state police. Pinellas County, Florida, and other school districts, have regular classes in school transportation headquarters and conduct classes for all drivers. Many of the states make use of safety engineers from insurance companies and supervisors of commercial fleets in their instructional program. Others use driver education teachers from high schools adn colleges as part-time instructors.

Several college courses for supervisors of pupil transportation have been offered. In addition, supervisors of pupil transportation have been meeting annually at the National Safety Congress and at conferences called by the National Commission on Safety Education of the National Education Association.

Selection, Inspection, and Maintenance of Buses

Two of the important recommendations of the President's Committee for Traffic Safety (16) follow:

> Adopt uniform state standards for school buses which meet or surpass the national minimum as recommended by the National Conference on School Transportation. Standards adopted should be so enforced that no substandard or unsafe vehicles are permitted to operate. New vehicles should be required to meet these standards, and periodic inspection should be part of a state-sponsored program to keep vehicles in safe operating condition.
>
> Since recognized national agencies have established standards for equipment in cooperation with manufacturers, school officials and safety specialists, there is every reason for a state, county, or municipality to be guided by them. Once the equipment has been purchased, it must be maintained at optimal efficiency. A properly organized preventive maintenance program will ensure a minimum of road failures and accidents traceable to mechanical failures.

Figure 18:1,
School Bus Fleet in Pinellas County, Florida.

Maintenance Buses are expensive. "It is of the utmost importance, due to increasing operational cost and capital outlay, for a district to establish a safe, efficient and economical maintenance program that will insure maximum longevity for their school bus fleet," according to the

Supervisor of Transportation in the Ohio Department of Education (14). When fleets were small, local garages could take care of maintenance, but now that the number of buses in a district may be large, it has become necessary to establish shops or garages for maintenance. This includes (a) a repair and replacement program, (b) a summer maintenance program in which the vehicle is thoroughly inspected and parts replaced, (c) preventive maintenance, in which all vehicles are inspected and repairs and replacements are made before there is a serious breakdown, and (d) developing a dedicated maintenance staff. The last is highly important and only the best mechanics should be used.

Inspection Periodic inspection is the heart of an effective preventive maintenance program; it is also one of the greatest factors in a safe pupil transportation operation. It should not be left to the various departments of motor vehicles or state police; the driver, the shop foreman, the supervisor or director of the operation should also participate. Drivers can be especially helpful in spotting mechanical troubles. They can report them to the shop foreman who can see to their correction before there is a serious breakdown. In addition to the regular inspections, drivers must start each day's work with an inspection of their vehicles. Courses for the maintenance staff as well as for drivers should be organized.

Teaching School Bus Safety to Children We can have safe, well-equipped buses and highly reliable drivers, but if our children do not practice safety we will continue to have many bus accidents. One recent study showed that out of 31 bus fatalities, 24 occurred before boarding or after alighting from the bus. Another national study reported by Mangum (5) showed that of 54 pupils killed, 19 were off the bus, usually crossing the street. We need not only to teach safe practices on the bus, but also to emphasize those off the bus.

Safety for School Bus Passengers Roy Martinez of the staff of the National Safety Council has prepared some good instructions for school bus passengers:

> *Walking to the bus stop.* Leave home early enough to arrive at the bus stop on time. Walk facing traffic, if you are walking where there are no sidewalks. Do not accept rides from strangers.
>
> *Waiting for the bus.* Wait off the road. Don't horseplay. Respect people's property. Stay back until bus comes to a complete stop.
>
> *Boarding.* Wait for bus driver's signal before crossing a street. Stay at least ten feet in front of bus. Board in an orderly fashion, always use the handrail. Greet your driver. Get to your seat as quickly and quietly as possible without running.
>
> *Riding on the bus.* Obey the driver cheerfully. Conduct yourself aboard the bus the same way you do in the classroom. Stay in your seat while the bus is in motion. If, however, there are not enough seats, stand facing the front, one foot forward to brace for a sudden stop, and grasping a handhold. When seated, make sure that your feet and other objects are out of the aisle. Get

permission from the driver before opening any window. If windows are open, do not put anything outside, arms, legs, books, or pencils. Do not write on bus panels or windows. Do not eat on the bus, as spilled food or food in the mouth can be dangerous. Keep your voice down, so the driver can listen for other vehicles. You must be quiet at railroad crossings to allow the driver to hear the signal of an approaching train. Warn the driver if you spot a danger he may not have seen.

Inform the driver when you expect to be absent from school, so that he will not be looking for you at the stop. Report to him any damage that you see has been done to the bus. Keep the bus clean and neat. There shouldn't be any trash or garbage on the bus at any time. Get rid of it before you enter. Do not bring animals or insects on the bus. If your teacher should request that you take an animal or insect to school for display, arrange another means of taking it there.

Take musical instruments, dinner buckets, brief cases, and other large parcels to your seat with you. Place them under the seat. Do not put them at the front of the bus where other students may trip on them or they may distract the driver. Do not tamper with any part of the bus or its equipment. The first aid kit, fire extinguisher, flares and fuses are for emergency use only. You can hurt yourself and others by playing with them. You may make them unuseable for some future emergency.

Unloading. Get off the bus quickly and quietly, without crowding, shoving or pushing. Walk straight to your assigned area. Do not linger around the bus loading and unloading zones.

Stay seated until the bus comes to a complete stop. If you need to cross the street in front of the bus, go at least ten feet from the front. Make sure that the driver can see you, before you cross. Wait until the driver gives you a signal before crossing. Walk out as far as the side of the bus away from the curb and look both ways before continuing to cross. If there are no sidewalks, walk facing traffic. Get off only at your assigned stop, unless you have permission to get off at another stop. If there is a school bus patrol, help him by obeying his instructions.

In addition to classroom instruction, it is recommended that bus patrols be used. Many supervisors also recommend bus evacuation drills. They feel that the bus driver himself can do much to teach safe practices to children.

Transportation Areas, Routes and Stops

Walking distances, traffic and other hazards, physical condition of individuals, and availability of commercial transit facilities should be considered before bus routes and stops are determined. Once the service area has been selected, it is necessary to survey it thoroughly to check on road conditions, railroad crossings and other factors that might affect the operation. Other data should include the locations of houses and the number of children of school age at each. Many school districts have set 1.5 miles as the distance above which transportation will be provided. After the routes are established, changes should be made only when a thorough evaluation reveals that they will improve the health and safety of pupils or increase the efficiency of the operation.

Periodic surveys by a qualified individual will pinpoint dangerous aspects. Poor driver performance, pupil behavior and vehicle condition, as well as hazards along the road, should be referred immediately to the appropriate agency for remedial action. The driver too should be encouraged to report such conditions accurately and promptly upon the completion of each trip. The traffic engineering section or the state or country roads department should be consulted when there is a question as to the use of a particular road or highway and its environs. Similarly, the local enforcement agency should be advised when frequent violations of laws and ordinances affecting school bus operation are observed.

The National Safety Council has a School Bus Accident Prevention Service that is used by many school districts. It provides posters, films, film strips, tests and other materials. The Safe Driver Award is provided for an operator who drives one year without a preventable accident. There are also awards for each year of safe driving. It is felt that these awards are helpful in improving the morale of drivers. They become the badges of an expert driver.

At the school plant a great deal can be done to ensure safe loading and unloading operations. First, one or more teacher-sponsors should be assigned to supervise these operations. Second, vehicles of administrators, faculty and staff members, personnel, students, and visitors should be controlled so that they do not interfere with bus arrivals and departures. Third, an interior road network with one or more loading docks or areas should be considered at larger schools where adequate grounds are available. Finally, the arrival and departure times of buses should be staggered to avoid the traffic congestion that results when too many buses arrive or depart within a short period of time.

Use of Efficient Business Methods

In selecting, maintaining and inspecting equipment, efficient business methods are a necessity. If buses are to be purchased, specifications should be rigid and should be complied with strictly. Drivers of vehicles, as well as owners of privately-owned vehicles, should be under contract. Records on drivers should be kept—accidents, violations, complaints and the like. Some districts use a point system to record violations and accidents. Others utilize the state point system. A poor record may show the need of a refresher course; a good record merits commendations and awards.

A pupil transportation system that runs itself may soon develop into a costly venture. It is essential to have someone who has the training, the responsibility, the ability and time to be in charge of the operation.

State and Local Regulations

There are several of the recommendations of the President's Committee for Highway Safety that apply to state and local regulations:

> Provide leadership in the development of a comprehensive safety program in pupil transportation.
>
> Where necessary, promote the enactment of uniform state laws that require special caution when passing school buses, such as those recommended in the *Uniform Vehicle Code* (10).
>
> Provide facilities for handicapped children whose condition makes special transportation necessary.
>
> Provide sufficient vehicles to avoid overloading and to limit the time that children spend on buses.
>
> Develop, in line with state rules and regulations, detailed operating practices for the guidance of school bus drivers, including such items as: routing of buses to promote safe and economical transportation; establishment of a maximum speed limit to meet local conditions, and designation of safe loading and unloading zones.
>
> Encourage the organization and operation of school bus patrols, using national recommendations as a guide.

These recommendations need but little explanation. Certainly the school administrator must take the leadership in the development of a program. This includes the state and local superintendents and the supervisors of pupil transportation.

The *Uniform Vehicle Code* devotes several pages to regulations for school buses (10:182). It is not possible to include all of these regulations; the following is a brief digest:

> *Signals.* Every school bus shall be equipped with two flashing red lights in front and in the rear.
>
> *Signs.* Bus shall carry in the front and rear signs—SCHOOL BUS—in letters not less than 8 inches in height.
>
> *Stopping.* Buses shall come to a full stop at railroad grade crossings.
>
> *Overtaking and Passing.* The driver of a vehicle shall come to a full stop when a school bus is taking on or discharging passengers, and not proceed until the bus has moved ahead. When there are separate roadways, or highways separated by a medial strip which pedestrians are not allowed to cross, it is not necessary to stop.

While these regulations are in the *Uniform Vehicle Code,* they have not been adopted in all states.

There is no question about the value of having local rules and regulations which are in line with state practices. This is especially true in a large school district. Nor is there any question about the need for vehicles for handicapped children. It is, of course, ideal if all passengers can have seats, but unfortunately, this is not always possible. There are some strong arguments for seat belts, but up until now very few have been installed, except in station wagons. All school buses should be painted the standard yellow color.

Insurance

Most school districts purchase insurance on buses or are self-insured. Insurance should cover the occupants of the bus and the driver for public liability and property damage.

summary

Pupil transportation in the United States is an important responsibility of the schools, for one out of every four pupils depends upon school bus transportation. The number of buses in use exceeds 190,000 and the annual cost of operation is more than $410 million dollars.

The accident rate for pupil transportation is not high but can be improved upon. States with good safety records have found that one of the best ways to maintain safety is by careful selection and training of qualified bus drivers. Most states have state supervisors of pupil transportation and have developed training programs. Obviously, the selection, inspection and maintenance of school buses is an important feature in the safety program. National standards for buses have been recommended and adopted by most states. Since buses are expensive and carry a priceless cargo, they should be inspected regularly, and repairs and replacements should be made before there is a serious breakdown. It is also essential to teach school bus safety to pupils. This especially true since a surprising number of accidents result from their bad practices. Many school districts also use school bus patrols.

The Uniform Vehicle Code devotes several pages to regulations for school buses. These have been recommended by the President's Committee for Highway Safety and adopted by most of the states. All of these regulations, together with the other features of the Council safety program, have tended to improve the accident record of pupil transportation.

suggested projects and activities

1. Prepare a checklist that could be used in your city to determine the status of pupil transportation.
2. Make a list of some of the weaknesses in pupil transportation in your area.
3. Outline the organization of a school bus safety patrol in your city. Include such items as objectives, selection, relationships with the driver, pupil control and the like.
4. Design a school parking area which will include space for: a) loading

and unloading of school buses, b) faculty and staff cars, c) student cars, d) delivery vehicles, bicycles and power cycles, e) visitors, parents and other users of the school.

5. Prepare a list of standards that could be used in the selection of bus drivers.
6. What are the components of an effective bus maintenance program? What standards should be used in a procurement program?
7. What regulations are in effect in your school system as regards pupil transportation—its financing, administration and its supervision?

selected references

1. Belknap, Burton H., *The School Bus: A Handbook for Safe and Economical Transportation*. Minneapolis: Educational Publishers, 1951.
2. Federal Security Agency, U.S. Office of Education, *School Bus Drivers: Current Practices in Selection and Training,* Pamphlet No. 100. Washington, D.C.: The Agency, 1946.
3. Hyde, Wallace N., "Use of Student Drivers for School Buses," *School and College Safety,* Vol. 24, Chicago: National Safety Council, 1959.
4. Kearney, Paul W., "Who Drives Your School Bus?" *Safety Education,* March, 1954.
5. Mangum, William J., "School Bus Accident Summary," *School and College Safety,* Vol. 23, Chicago: National Safety Council, 1961.
6. Murray, John B., "Driver Selection is Important." *School and College Safety,* Vol. 23, Chicago: National Safety Council, 1961.
7. National Commission on Safety Education, National Education Association, *Minimum Standards for School Buses* (rev. ed.). Washington, D.C.: The Commission, 1954.
8. ________, *Selection, Instruction, and Supervision of School Bus Drivers.* Washington, D.C.: The Commission, 1960.
9. ________, *Tentative Standards for Transit and Metropolitan Types of School Buses.* Washington, D.C.: The Commission, 1952.
10. National Committee on Uniform Traffic Laws and Ordinances, *Uniform Vehicle Code.* Washington, D.C.: The Committee, 1962.
11. National Education Association, Department of Rural Education, *Pupil Transportation.* Washington, D.C.: The Association, 1953.
12. ________, Research Division, *Safety in Pupil Transportation.* Washington, D.C.: The Association, 1936.
13. Nelson, Benjamin W., "Encompassing Contract Bus Operators in the Training Program." *School and College Safety,* Vol. 23, Chicago: National Safety Council, 1961.
14. Parsons, John M., "The Apex in School Bus Maintenance," *School and College Safety,* Vol. 23, Chicago: National Safety Council, 1961.
15. Patterson, Ronald D., "Recommended Practices and Procedures for the Improvement of Programs for the Selection and Education of School Bus Drivers." Unpublished doctor's thesis, New York University, 1959.
16. President's Committee for Traffic Safety, *Education: A Section of the Action Program for Highway Safety,* Washington, D.C.: The Committee, 1960.

19

liability and insurance

In the society in which we live some method has to be provided to cushion us against serious personal financial loss. People engaged in professional activities are most vulnerable to being sued because of errors of commission or omission. This situation is especially noted among doctors and first aid workers who hesitate to render service in accident situations for fear of an action in malpractice being instituted against them. The seriousness of this situation has caused many states to pass legislation protecting doctors from suits arising from their treatments in emergency situations. The teacher also faces the possibility of being sued, and like the doctor, must protect himself against the possibility of financial disaster resulting from actions in negligence being brought against him. The greater part of wisdom comes from experience; in the experience of accidents, lawsuits and insurance policies is a wealth of information for teachers and administrators. By learning what we must do to avoid the consequences of liability, we can prevent future accidents. By providing ourselves and our schools with adequate insurance, we can secure protection against serious losses.

The following discussion of liability and insurance should be helpful to teachers and administrators in preparing themselves to give proper guidance to their students.

Liability

When a teacher is held liable for an accident, he may have to pay out of his own pocket the person whom his negligence has injured. Liability is a legal conclusion dependent upon a state of facts; when this state of facts spells negligence, liability follows, with certain exceptions to be discussed below. Conversely, no matter how serious the injury, or how lamentable the accident, if the facts absolve the teacher of negligence, he will not be held liable. *Negligence,* then, is the key to liability.

Negligence The law has evolved a formula for the determination of negligence, which is easier to state than to apply. *A person is negligent when he has failed to act as a reasonably prudent person would act under the circumstances.* Either action or inaction may constitute negligence if, under the circumstances involved in the particular situation, that action or inaction was not what a reasonably prudent person would have done.

The reasonably prudent person. It will be noted that the standard of care by which one's actions are judged is the action of a reasonably prudent person under the identical circumstances. Reasonable prudence consists of the ability to foresee or anticipate difficulties from a given set of circumstances. If a reasonably prudent person could or should anticipate some danger under the circumstances (and it need not be the actual injury which did occur (5), the failure to take precautionary measures in terms of such foreseeable dangers constitutes negligence. The ability to gauge dangers in terms of anticipation is the basic element of the negligence formula. Lengthy citation of cases is not in point here (21), but it is clear that certain obvious neglects will brand a teacher as negligent. Where he permits the use of defective equipment, or allows untrained students to make use of inherently dangerous tools, or fails to make adequate safety preparations, or ignores clear and obvious danger signals such, for example, as the illness of a child about to partake in strenuous physical activity, he subjects himself to the possibility of negligence judgments in court. Any alert teacher would anticipate, for example, that some pupil might hurt himself if dangerous chemicals were left easily accessible, or if students were permitted to use a baseball bat without a knobbed handle (8). If a reasonably prudent teacher, with knowledge, experience, and responsibility, would have foreseen some accident and acted accordingly, the failure to act accordingly results in negligence (26).

The attendant circumstances. Since negligence is a factual question, the specific facts surrounding the incident are of greatest importance. Though it would probably be negligent to fail to provide a referee for a competitive basketball game, nonprovision of a referee for a free-play game is not negligence (11). Furthermore, since the scope of the teacher's duties in great measure conditions the limit of what may be expected of him, it also circumscribes the reasonable limits of his negligence. The more extensive duties and responsibilities of principals and superintendents clearly imply that more extensive activities are necessary on the part of principals or other supervisors; a principal may well be liable under circumstances that would clear a teacher of all blame. However, a teacher is not responsible for every accident that occurs in a school; some accidents are not due to anyone's fault and are simply unavoidable. Since negligence is gauged by the ability to anticipate danger, when accidents occur under circumstances where danger was not within the realm of reasonable expectation, the teacher is not legally responsible.

There are a few words or expressions in legal terminology with which teachers and administrators should be familiar. *Liability* and *negligence* have already been defined.

In loco parentis, meaning "in place of the parent," describes one who acts as a parent or a guardian.

Contributory negligence is failure by a person to exercise reasonable caution in his own behalf to prevent an injury that he sustains through the negligence of another.

Tort is a civil wrong entitling a person injured to sue the person responsible for the wrong.

Plaintiff is the person who initiates legal action against another, called the *defendant.*

Definitions of other terms will be found in *Who is Liable for Pupil Injuries* (15) and *Liability for Accidents in Physical Education, Athletics and Recreation* (13).

Defenses to Liability The law sets up a series of defense for those charged with negligence as a result of which even a negligent person may escape liability for his negligence. First, to result in liability, the negligence must have some substantial connection with the injury complained of. So, for example, a principal's negligence in permitting a school race to be conducted out on the sidewalk was too remote from the injury due to a collision between a racing student and a pedestrian for the principal to be held liable. Second, just as it is true that a teacher must refrain from being negligent with respect to her pupils, so must the pupils refrain from being negligent with respect to their own welfare. In other words, contributory negligence on the part of the injured party cancels out the teacher's negligence except in a few states which have adopted the comparative negligence doctrine. It is, therefore, a question of fact, dependent upon all the surrounding circumstances, whether a fifteen-year-old student who was racing, head down, across a road, as a result of which she ran into a truck, was guilty of contributory negligence (25). Third, a person cannot sue a teacher to recover for damages for a risk voluntarily assumed through participation in an activity of which the risk was a normal and necessary concomitant. For example, spectators at baseball games assume the normal risk attendant upon the foul tips. And fourth, no one can be held liable for an injury caused by an act of God, such as the unexpected slamming of a glass transom due to a sudden gust of wind.

Determination of Negligence Whether a teacher or a school board has been negligent is not determined by professional educators but by juries and courts composed of laymen. Teachers or school boards sued for negligence must persuade these laymen that their professional conduct measures up to those standards of care which laymen think school people should apply in schools. The significance of this factor of legal procedure upon the ultimate control of curriculum, methods of teaching, and pedagogy is obvious, but somewhat beyond the scope of this chapter.

School District Responsibility According to *Who is Liable for Pupil Injuries* (15):

> In the absence of a statute to the contrary, it is the commonplace rule that school districts, as government entities, are immune from tort liability for injuries suffered by pupils. This immunity applies to their own negligent acts, as well as to the negligent acts of their officers, agents, or employees; or for injuries arising from dangerous or improper care and maintenance of school buildings and grounds, defective appliances, or unsafe operation of the school transportation system. The common-law governmental immunity doctrine has been challenged in the courts time and again. However, there is a developing trend toward abrogation of governmental immunity by judicial decision. . . .
>
> Statutes in several other states have seemed to point to the abandonment of the doctrine (governmental immunity) by the legislatures, but strict court interpretations of the statutes have held otherwise. . . .
>
> The common-law immunity doctrine protecting governmental entities from tort liability suits stems from the English case law. Its theoretical basis evolved from the medieval concept of the "divine right of kings" from which came the maxim that "the King can do no wrong."

This sovereignty extends to the school district, the school administrator, and to employees of the board of education. Thus, in most states, a boy injured in a school shop would not be able to collect damages, but if he were working part-time in an industry, he would be covered by Workmen's Compensation Insurance.

Recent Developments. "The trend away from the governmental immunity rule, has, until recently, been almost wholly dependent upon statute. Although the King-can-do-no-wrong doctrine was originally judge-made, it was considered to be thoroughly imbedded in our law that what the courts could do would not undo what they had already done," according to Rosenfield.* The following is a summary of his remarks regarding this problem:

* From an address by Harry Rosenfield at the National Conference on Accident Prevention in Physical Education, Athletics and Recreation.

1. The community pays for the school building, for light, heat, school contracts, salaries and the like. Why should the injured pupil or teacher pay out of his own pocket for an item that is an operating cost of the school budget—in fact, if not in law?
2. In 1959, the Illinois Supreme Court changed this policy of judicial decision and ruled that school boards will hereafter be liable for negligence.
3. More recently, Wisconsin and Minnesota followed Illinois, although Pennsylvania ruled the other way.
4. Moreover, Alaska and Arizona appear to be moving in the same direction as Illinois.

The Administrator's Responsibilities Court cases involving the school administrator are rare. Usually, lawsuits brought by injured pupils are brought against teachers. However, the principal, like the teacher, can be liable under certain conditions, especially if an accident has resulted from his failure to provide proper supervision.

The Teachers' Responsibilities Since teachers are more closely related to the activities of pupils, they are most often involved in negligence cases. Every teacher should, therefore, be familiar with laws of negligence in his state and take proper precautions to prevent accidents. For various reasons, it is a bad practice to leave a classroom unattended for a length of time. It is important that good supervision be provided.

Statutory Imposition of Responsibility on School Districts According to *Who is Liable for Pupil Injuries* (15):

> Thus far, the courts in three states, Illinois, Wisconsin, and New York, have placed on school districts legal responsibility for torts without prior statutory imposition of liability. By judicial determination, the school districts in Illinois and Wisconsin are no longer protected by the common-law governmental immunity rule, and are liable to pupils, negligently injured in school accidents. Before the enactment of the save harmless statute in 1938, New York courts had held school boards liable in their corporate capacity for injuries resulting from their negligent performance of duties imposed on them by law. . . .
>
> Two other states, New Jersey in 1938 and Connecticut in 1945, enacted save harmless laws practically identical to the New York law. These two laws also require the school boards to pay legal expenses of teachers when pupil-injury suits are brought against them; but this does not apply to New Jersey teachers sued for damages because of corporal punishment, which is prohibited by statute. . . .
>
> In three states, Wyoming, Oregon, and Massachusetts, school districts may assume the liability imposed on a teacher because of negligence. In 1955, Wyoming passed a permissive save harmless statute with provisions similar to New York's mandatory law.

Some Basic Considerations Certain crucial considerations stand out in our discussion up to this point. Since our activities have to pass muster with laymen (who determine whether we have been guilty of negligence), it behooves us all to make sure that our actions bear the sign of plain common sense. It is not necessary that we lag behind public understanding of advanced pedagogical techniques, but it is well to realize that some of our procedures have never met the scrutiny of people not bedeviled by our professional jargon, who might think some of our actions little short of foolish. It may be psychologically expedient to make the school "bad boy" a member of the safety patrol; but it is of highly doubtful legality, since we have no right to subject the other pupils to his irresponsibilities. Our public school system must be responsive to and appreciative of the general mores of our people. And whether or not we wish it, such is the effect of a court trial on negligence.

Most basic of all lessons to be garnered from a legal study is the safety education precept that we should be more actively eager to avoid troubles than to conduct post mortems upon them. Prevention can best be achieved by careful attention to the focal points of trouble. The school's safety committee or safety supervisor should prepare for the staff suggestions growing out of close study of the monthly accident summaries. A wise principal will insist upon receiving some form of inspection reports; if he cannot get them through engineers or specially trained observers, he will seek to encourage in his teaching body a habit of watchful alertness to defects observable even by nonprofessional inspectors. Perhaps he will want to use the special checklist prepared for just such a purpose by the National Education Association (14) or materials prepared by responsible agencies such as the National Safety Council (18), the Center for Safety Education (4), or the National Fire Protection Association (17). However he decides to do it, the administrator will do well to have periodic reports and thorough examinations of every school building with reference to safety devices; the condition of structures, equipment, and ground; and safety education procedures. The very fact that a supervisor has taken the trouble to require such inspection reports will show, in any lawsuit, that he has acted with some degree of reasonable prudence in an effort to prevent accidents.

Recommendations The field of school activities is far too broad for any listing of specific safety recommendations that grow out of a study of legal cases. Certain special fields of activities, however, recur so frequently in professional problem clinics that perhaps a short discussion would not be out of order.

Field trips. Any activity that takes the students away from the school premises subjects them to a greater variety of risks than those normally present in the ordinary school routine. Consequently it is wise to insist upon parental consent for all such field trips, although it must be borne in mind that any parental waivers or releases are of no avail to protect the teacher or school board from suit for negligence on the part of the injured child. The school should make adequate advance preparation covering all the aspects of the trip, including time schedules, training of guides, special attention to transportation facilities, complete instructions to the students coming on the trip as to their behavior at various parts of the trip, and other similar precautions.

Physical education, athletics and recreation. A large percentage of accidents, sometimes more than 50 per cent, take place in physical education and athletics. Therefore, the supervision of these activities must be close so that the teacher may not be held negligent in case of an accident.

The following are requirements of good supervision:

> *Facilities and equipment.* Teachers should inspect equipment and facilities before allowing students to use them, for example, apparatus used in the gymnasium. Unsafe equipment should be locked up or chained.
>
> *Difficult activities.* Care must be used in allowing youngsters to attempt difficult feats for which they are not trained or those that are beyond their abilities.
>
> *Certified teachers.* In many states it is especially important to have physical education activities supervised by teachers who hold physical education certificates. The use of a noncertified substitute to supervise activities is unwise.
>
> *Athletics.* Coaches should take special care through training, supervision and proper equipment to reduce the hazards of sports.
>
> *Physical examinations.* These are recommended not only for athletic teams but for all students who take part in physical education and recreation activities. It is also advisable to have a doctor at games.

Pupil Transportation. The importance of safe practices in pupil transportation has been discussed in Chapter 17. Since well over 12 million students are transported daily in 190,000 buses, problems of safety are highly important. Many states allow boards of education to take out school bus insurance. Buses should be inspected regularly, drivers should be trained, bus safety patrols organized, and safety instruction should be given to all pupils. School buses or public carriers should be used to transport athletic teams, bands or other groups of pupils.

Safety Patrols. Although only a few states have adopted laws specifically authorizing the organization of school safety patrols (and in some cases exempting teachers and principals from liability in connection therewith), it would seem that at this date no one could successfully question the propriety of such activity as a legitimate school function, if properly administered. The importance of proper operation of the program cannot be overemphasized. The board of education should formally adopt the plan as a school function. The scope, operation and limitations of the plan should be clearly outlined and explained to all concerned. Parental consent should be obtained for students to act as patrols. Only responsible pupils should be chosen and they should be adequately trained in their duties. The entire scheme should be organized in advance, the whole school notified of its operation and of the duties of the various components of the school population in relation to the patrol plan as a whole. The supervisor who leaves delineation of details to the future is taking an unwise and unnecessary risk. It should be kept in mind that while some of the work in training members of the patrol may be given to the police, responsibility for the operation and supervision of the patrol is a function of the schools. In their organization of patrols schools should follow the *Standard Rules for the Operation of School Safety Patrols* (18).

Vocational Shops. Needless to say, adequate safety instruction is of paramount importance in any shop where dangerous equipment is used by pupils. Only properly equipped students should be permitted to handle such equipment. It would also be of great assistance to all concerned, as well to the teacher in self-analysis and to his attorney in litigation, if the vocational shop teacher were to keep a dated checklist of all pupils who receive instruction on each type of dangerous operation and of each step in the various safety lessons.

Driver Education. Driver education, comprising classroom and practice driving, has become an integral part of the secondary school curriculum. Many states have enacted statutes authorizing and describing procedures. As a general practice, it is recommended that vehicles used for driver education be covered by insurance, including public liability, property damage, collision, and fire and theft insurance.

Unsafe Buildings and Grounds. Unlighted and poorly lighted stairs, especially those without hand-rails, have been dangersous parts of school buildings. Injuries from accidents are compensable by the school board only if the district can be held liable for negligence or there is a safe place statute applicable. Buildings should be inspected regularly for hazardous conditions and such conditions should be removed or corrected.

Playground and Recess Games. Playgrounds should be supervised during both organized and unorganized play and such supervision should be adequate. School districts should make rules and regulations for pupils' conduct on playgrounds so as to minimize dangers.

General. It is wise for school boards to have published rules and regulations covering school activities. Such manuals may be of great value to school attorneys in case of liability suits against the school district or its employees.

Accident Reports. The importance of accident reporting has been discussed in Chapter 17. Every school district should have an accident reporting system. Such reports have several uses, but they are of special value in case of questions about legal liability.

School Facilities. A school gymnasium measured 80′ x 43′ and eight overlapping basketball courts were crowded into that space. Someone was hurt and the court held this to be negligence because the school should have anticipated injury in so overcrowded a space (2).

An applicant for a teaching job was required to take a physical examination in the course of which she was directed to bat a softball and run to first base in a gymnasium. The sack used as a base was not anchored; it slipped, and she was injured. Negligence was held. In Michigan a spectator at a football game was injured when she fell into an unlighted ramp at the school parking lot. Negligence was held (26). A North Carolina decision was rendered that a school bus driver was negligent when he gave children an open bucket of gasoline, as a result of which, children on the school grounds were burned when the bucket ignited.

Insurance

Insurance may be described as a device for reducing or eliminating the most of certain risks. It is a promise by the insurance company to an insured of service and protection. The company agrees to render aid of various types in its services and make good financial loss up to the terms of the contract.

There are several different types of insurance, such as life, accident and health, Workman's Compensation, automobile, fire and marine, and liability insurance. This chapter is concerned primarily with two of these, liability and automobile insurance.

Liability Insurance

This type of insurance is closely related to accident reporting and liability. It can have many different applications. For example, the teacher can have liability insurance on his car; he can purchase it on his home; he can have it in connection with his work in the schools. Briefly defined, it is an attempt to protect oneself or one's organization against the need for paying liability judgments growing out of negligence. A person may assert that he has been injured in person or property by another and may claim damages as compensation for the injury. Therefore, protection in the form of liability insurance is needed to protect the individual or organization against suits for damages.

Where there is no statutory authorization for such purpose by the school board, or where the doctrine of government immunity prevails, the general rule seems to be that insurance may not be legally purchased by school boards to cover either their own liability or that of the school staff. School boards, except in the few but growing number of states that have been listed in this chapter, are not liable for any negligence. Consequently, except where authorized by statute, they may not legally purchase protection against a risk to which they are not subject. This prohibition frequently causes great hardship, since it may leave the injured person without means with which to pay his medical and other expenses. Curiously enough, when the school custodian or cafeteria worker is injured, the state Workman's Compensation Insurance steps in and the injured worker is compensated. But this does not apply to the injured teacher. However, in New York State, while coverage of school personnel in non-manual occupations is not mandatory, many school districts have voluntarily included their teaching personnel in their Workmen's Compensation Insurance program. There is no question of the right of a teacher to purchase liability and accident insurance out of his own funds, and there is an increasing tendency, especially among teachers of physical education, driver education and vocational education, to do so. In the few states that have been previously listed, the school board will protect the teacher against liability suits.

When the purchase of liability insurance is being considered, careful reading of the policy is important to insure that the precise limits of coverage and protection are clearly defined. Certain clauses should be provided to include coverage of pupils, teachers, substitutes, and teachers in training. The types of activities protected should also be stipulated—field trips, school camps, gymnasia, athletics and other aspects of the school program. Unless all of these problems are dealt with in advance, there may be inadequate coverage in the policy. One cannot be too careful when purchasing liability insurance.

School Bus Insurance

A substantial number of states allow school districts to carry school bus liability insurance. This is as it should be. Suppose an accident occurs involving a school bus which carries no insurance. The medical and other costs to the families of injured pupils might be very high. Why should pupils be penalized by having to ride on buses not covered by insurance? In this same state all other public carriers are required to carry insurance. It is probable that within a few years all school buses will carry insurance.

Automobiles Used in Driver Education

A number of states allow school districts to purchase insurance for vehicles used in driver education. This might include (a) fire and theft, (b) public liability, (c) property damage, (d) collision and (f) comprehensive coverage. When driver education is to be offered by a school, state liability laws or interpretations by state law departments should be examined to determine the most appropriate types and amounts of coverage and to secure protection of the teachers from damage suits. In states where it is not permissible to purchase insurance with public funds, some other means should be devised to secure funds to provide this protection. As a matter of interest, in recent years there has been a tendency for schools to purchase insurance with much higher liability limits—$100,000 or even more.

It is also advisable for teachers to set up some type of records system for practice driving. Such records would be of value for educational purposes, and in addition, would be useful in case of liability suits against the school district or the instructor.

There is no common-law immunity in California, Connecticut, Illinois, Minnesota, New Jersey, New York, and Wisconsin, and it exists only to some extent in Washington, which means that damages sustained by students in driver education courses in those states could be paid for by the school district or by their insurance carrier.

Insurance for Teachers

Unless a state has provisions to protect teachers in case of liability suits, it is advisable that instructors consult with state or local lawyers regarding insurance. Policies are not expensive, and will protect the insured against damage suits involving injury of pupils attributed to negligence. Since accidents tend to be more common in activities such as physical education, driver education and industrial arts, teachers of these subjects should be the first to get insurance coverage.

One important point must be mentioned for teachers purchasing liability insurance. All policies require that the insured notify the company promptly of any accident and give all necessary information and cooperation. It is just possible that such provision may conflict with the bylaws of the board of education, which are part of the teacher's contract. Some boards specifically prohibit teachers from making such information available except to school officials. In that case, some reconciliation between these conflicting provisions must be made, either by eliminating the clause in the policy or through a suspension of the bylaw.

Athletic Benefit Insurance

Wisconsin was the first state to initiate a form of athletic benefit insurance. It was established as a voluntary athletic benefit or quasi-insurance plan by the State Interscholastic Athletic Association. At the present time all states have some optional or permissive plan of benefit insurance. However, the plan has gone far beyond activities in athletics in many states. Some include compensation for pupils injured in any school-sponsored activity, either on or off the school premises.

These benefit plans, similar in a way to Workman's Compensation Insurance, provide payments for injuries to cover the estimated cost of medical treatment according to a schedule. The plans are usually associated with the state athletic association. Two methods are used to pay the cost of this insurance. Some states permit the use of school funds; in others the cost must be paid by the student or his parents. Some policies cover all sports; some, all school activities; and still others cover all sports with the exception of boxing, football and wrestling. Accidents and injuries must be reported to the state association which makes the payments, usually according to a schedule. The rates may vary from year to year on the basis of experience.

There has been a diminution of liability suits in school districts where student accident protection plans have been put into effect. Policy limits for injury or death usually approximate $3,000 and the annual cost is just a few dollars. The parent of an injured student tends to be less suit-conscious when medical expenses are taken care of by such insurance.

Athletic benefit insurance has two distinct advantages. First, it enables injured students to secure adequate medical diagnosis and necessary treatment, usually by specialists in the medical field. Second, it does provide teachers with some protection from liability suits; parents of injured students who have received medical care are not likely to initiate suits. Since this type of insurance is relatively inexpensive, it is urged that all schools take steps to provide pupils with this form of protection.

summary

At one time in the various states, school boards could not be held liable for injuries sustained by pupils; they could not be sued. However, an increasing number of states have passed legislation abolishing the doctrine of governmental immunity.

When a teacher is held liable for an accident he may be sued and, if found negligent, he may be forced to pay the costs. He is negligent if he has failed to act as a reasonably prudent person would act under the same circumstances.

There are certain activities of the schools that should be closely supervised, for they entail important risks. They include field trips, physical education activities, pupil transportation, safety patrols, vocational shops, driver education and recreation. Schools should see to it that these activities are closely supervised and controlled by competent teachers. If a school district or a teacher can show that the activity was properly supervised, there is less danger of being found negligent in case of an accident.

In the society in which we live, some method has to be provided to cushion us against serious financial losses. This is the function of insurance.

There are many types of insurance, but those with which the teacher should be most familiar are liability and personal accident insurance. Administrators should also be familiar with automobile and fire insurance, for most school districts and colleges carry insurance on buses and school buildings.

All states now have some type of athletic benefit insurance, usually administered by a state principals association. It is somewhat like Workman's Compensation Insurance, for the payments for injuries are intended to cover the cost of medical treatment but are limited to the amount of the policy. Many current policies provide compensation for pupils injured in all school-sponsored activities.

suggested projects and activities

1. Prepare an objective test covering all of the definitions used in connection with negligence and liability. Administer this test to the class.
2. Consult an insurance agent or broker and make a list of the suggestions he makes for reducing accidents in the schools.
3. Conduct a survey of a school building and list hazardous conditions that need correction.
4. Prepare a list of reasons why all states should allow their school districts to purchase insurance for school buses.
5. Make a list of the kinds of insurance that should be purchased by a teacher of physical education who owns his home and has a car. He is married and has four children.
6. What types of insurance should be purchased on the car which is being used for practice driving on city streets?
7. Prepare an outline of a report to be given in class on the athletic benefit insurance plan used in your state.
8. Prepare an outline of the pros and cons of abolition of the doctrine of governmental immunity for negligence.

selected references

1. *American Law Reports,* Vol. 86, "Tort Liability in Public Schools and Institutions of Higher Learning," pp. 489-601, 1962.
2. Bard V B E, 285 App. Div. 1148, 140 N.Y. Supp. 2d. 167 (1955).
3. Bard V B E, 140 N. Y. Supp. 2d 850 (N.Y. 1955).
4. Center for Safety Education, New York University, *The Administrator and the School Safety Program.* New York: The Center, 1952.
5. *Drum v. Miller.* 135 N.C. 204,47 S.E. 421 (1904); *Olson v. Cushman,* 224 Iowa 974, 276 N.W.77 (1937).
6. Drury, R. L., ed., *Law and the School Superintendent,* Chap. 15. Cincinnati, Ohio: W. H. Anderson Co., 1958.

7. Edwards, N., *The Courts and the Public Schools,* Chap. 15. Chicago: University of Chicago Press, 1955.
8. Garber, L. O., "The Case of the Negligent Coach," *The Nations Schools,* May, 1937, p. 77.
9. ________, *Student Accident Reporting.* Chicago: The Council, 1958.
10. Hetlel, W. L., "Legal Basis for the School Safety Patrol," *Proceedings—National Safety Congress,* 1960, p. 23.
11. *Kerby v. Grove Union High School District,* 1 Cal. App. 2d. 246, 36 Pac. 2d. 431 (1934).
12. Kigin, D. J., "Who Pays for Shop Accidents," *School Safety,* Dec., 1961, p. 10.
13. Leibee, Howard Clinton, *Liability for Accidents in Physical Education, Athletics and Recreation.* Ann Arbor: Ann Arbor Publishers, 1952.
14. National Commission on Safety Education, *Checklist of Safety and Safety Education in Your School.* Washington: The Commission, 1960.
15. ________, *Who is Liable for Pupil Injuries?* Washington: The Commission, 1963.
16. National Education Association, *The Teacher and the Law.* p. 76. Washington, D.C.: The Association, 1959.
17. National Fire Protection Association, *Building Exits Code.* Boston: The Association, 1959.
18. National Safety Council, *Standard Rules for the Operation of Schoolboy Patrols.* Chicago: The Council.
19. *Rapisardi v. Board of Education of New York City,* 242 App. Div. 647, 273 N. Y. Supp. 360 (1934).
20. Remmlein, M. K., *School Law* (2nd ed.), Chap. 16. Danville, Ill.: Interstate Printers and Publishers, Inc., 1962.
21. Rosenfield, H. N., *Liability for School Accidents,* p. 5. New York: Harper & Row, Publishers, 1940.
22. ________, "Legal Liability and the Cost of Accidents," *Safety Education,* April, 1957, Chicago: National Safety Council.
23. ________, "Guilty: The Law and School Accidents," *Safety Education,* April, 1963, p. 12.
24. *Streicher v. N.Y.,* 15 App. 2d 927, 225 N.Y. Sapp. 2d 602 1962.
25. *Taylor v. Oakland Scavenger Co.,* 110 Pac. 2d. 1044 (California, March 1941).
26. *Watson v. School District,* 324 March 1, 1936 N.W. 2d 195 (1949).

20

safety agencies and the community

It has been found that in the long run communities with an active safety organization have the best accident record. It is not difficult to distinguish communities with sound, effective programs of community action from those which are doing little or nothing to provide needed service and support. In some cities there are local safety councils affiliated with the National Safety Council which cover all phases of safety. In others, the program is entirely devoted to traffic safety; in still others the local group is a part of a state safety council.

The Role of Official Community Agencies

Every community, large or small, has a number of elected public officials who are given legal responsibility for the health and welfare of the community. These officials are members of the common council or other governing body. In some instances, county, state or federal agencies have been designated by law to provide safety services. To carry these out effectively in a given area in a community, sound laws and ordinances, adequate, well-prepared personnel, and adequate budget resources are needed. This is certainly true in the safety services provided by the police, fire, health, medical, public works, building, recreation and parks departments.

Organizing for Community Safety

Local organizations are referred to as safety councils, safety boards or citizens' safety committees. These organizations include representation from civic and business leaders, public officials, safety personnel, and from civic, service, religious, patriotic, professional and other groups. The number of agencies depends largely upon the size of the community. Many of the agencies listed below have safety activities that can be coordinated by the community organization.

Agencies that could be represented in a community safety organization include:

Municipal and County Departments—Police, fire, health, school, park, playground, public works, hospitals.

Civic and Service—Chamber of Commerce, Board of Trade, service and luncheon clubs, veterans organizations.

Social Service—Fraternal clubs, parents organizations, womens clubs, mens clubs.

Education and Welfare—Colleges, parochial schools, Boy Scouts, Girl Scouts, Y.M.C.A., Y.M.H.A., Y.W.C.A., Red Cross, Grange and other farm organizations.

Industrial and Commercial—Industries, insurance companies and associations, automobile dealers, automobile clubs, trade unions, safety engineers.

Many of these groups may be carrying on their own accident prevention projects and activities and should be urged to continue. They come together in the community-wide organization and coordinate their plans to gain maximum effectiveness and avoid duplication.

Each safety organization mobilizes the citizens for accident prevention, carries on a public information program to help individuals become informed and safety-minded, and encourages support of measures for safe living. It should work closely with public officials who have legal responsibility for safety. It will be more successful if all groups interested in accident prevention are represented and its program aims at resolving local problems.

The humanitarian aspect of saving lives is the primary reason for accident prevention. However, accidents and fires result in a direct economic loss. First, the public pays for accidents through taxes, insurance premiums, doctors' bills and the like. In addition, there are the indirect losses, such as the cost of maintaining police and fire departments, hospitals and sanitation departments. Thus, a community will be paying a far greater bill for accidents than for accident prevention.

There are several ways of attacking the accident problem: citizens and public officials may work together at periodic meetings; clubs and organizations may work through their safety committees; newspaper articles may be published calling attention to a safety problem; and radio and television may be used. In some instances these methods work satisfactorily. However, a citizen safety organization combines the best elements of these and strengthens the attack with the vitally needed qualities of continuity, unity and thoroughness. Such an organization must first get the facts; it must appraise the local accident situation and determine what groups are conducting safety programs. It should then identify the groups available to help: service clubs, women's organizations, parent-teacher associations and the like. A plan should be developed to mobilize these agencies.

Although public officials have major responsibility for accident prevention, they cannot do the job alone. Citizens must assume their responsibility by becoming informed and by cooperating with the official safety program. United efforts are needed to get the best results.

Leadership A citizen safety organization should be sparked and guided by community leaders who have records of getting things done. These should be well-known citizens, such as the official of a bank or a service club, well-known and respected doctors or lawyers, or an official of a store, telephone, electric, insurance or gas company. In some cases the mayor or city manager takes the initial step of calling the leaders of the proposed organization together. However, in spite of superior leadership, it should be stressed that seldom does an effective organization exist without strong public support from community agencies.

State and Federal Agencies and Organizations and the Community

State and federal agency services to a community vary widely. Many states have long been recognized for a number of services in the field of highway maintenance and construction, law enforcement, education, health, recreation and fire control. In most states and at the federal level there are rules and regulations laid down to assure integrity and uniformity in statewide control measures important to the general health and welfare. Civil defense, potential area-wide disasters and atmospheric control, along with numerous other special needs have been given priority attention. All community or county governmental agencies and citizens groups will find it to their benefit to explore available expert assistance and program guidance from appropriate state and federal agencies that are concerned with accident prevention and health.

Numerous service organizations, some of them wholly, or primarily dedicated to accident prevention, are available in your state. Some are staffed and budgeted to provide consultation, technical assistance and, to limited degrees, program resources. These organizations can be divided into three groups. First, there are the safety-oriented groups professionally staffed for the purpose of giving assistance in one or more phases of accident control. Second, there are professional groups which have accident prevention as one of their key interests. Third, there are numerous service organizations which participate in a given segment of programming as it touches on one of their group's goals or objectives. A few of the more common services these organizations render are conducting education campaigns, promoting uniform practices, conducting and promoting technical studies, cooperating in a promotional effort, and assisting in developing necessary public support programs.

An inventory of all available state and national organization services should be made in cooperation with appropriate public officials, to determine just how active these groups are, and the type of service they are in a position to render.

Organization Steps The following steps are recommended in forming the organization (4):

1. Organize a steering committee of from five to nine leaders, possibly including the mayor.
2. Secure needed advisory and consultation services from heads of departments.
3. Officials must be assured that the organization does not intend to "meddle" in their affairs.
4. Secure information on the local accident situation from department officials. A lack of such information indicates a basic need of an accident records system.
5. Some information can be obtained from the county coroner's office, the city health officer and the police.
6. Prepare digests of the accident situation in the community.
7. Get the advice of the National Safety Council or other, local councils in the area.
8. Arrange for a meeting of city officials and community leaders to discuss the need for a local safety organization.

Common practices There are certain general practices that should be followed after it has been decided to form a local safety organization:

1. A decision should be made as to whether the organization will cover all phases of safety, or particular phases.
2. Volunteer leadership determines the strength of any community effort. Its discovery, selection and motivation are of paramount importance.
3. The board of directors sets over-all policies and maintains necessary communications with public officials.
4. An executive committee consisting of the officers and committee chairmen should handle the operation of the organization. This committee usually meets once a month.

5. A statement of objectives should be prepared to inform the community of the proposed activities.
6. Bylaws and an organization chart should be prepared.
7. Membership should include all individuals and groups who can contribute to accident prevention.
8. Even the simplest organization needs a paid manager.
9. Officers should be elected to establish committees and set up proper communications.

Financing Any successful organization requires operational capital. It is a case of paying for accidents or paying for prevention. The amount needed will depend on the scope of activities. One suggestion sometimes advanced is that a membership fee of a dollar or two for all who join should be established. In a few cases, this provides the necessary funds, but usually it proves unworkable because of the cost and the time spent in collecting these small amounts. When financial needs have been determined by the committee, a plan can be prepared for securing the necessary funds.

Committees The steering committee has laid the foundation for the new organization and guided it through the first meeting. The officers, directors and chairmen now take on the jobs of establishing committees and setting up proper communications. The five general areas of activities—traffic, home, school, public and occupational safety—provide the starting point for committee organization, but others may be added to take care of special needs. Each committee should proceed as follows (5):

1. Get all of the facts available regarding past and present accident experience.
2. Set up objectives.
3. List the various steps required to attain the objectives.
4. Select a top-priority activities program for the work of the committee.
5. Assign work to members.
6. Enlist the cooperation of groups that can assist.
7. Report activities to the executive committee and the board of directors.
8. Promote the activity by preparing reports, letters and other materials for all public information media.
9. A committee should not be tempted to tackle too many projects at one time. Select a few and after these are completed, plans can be initiated for others.
10. The organization as a whole should maintain an inventory or evaluation of its program and activities. This continuing process will indicate both its strong and weak points and will suggest remedial action.

When every community in the United States has been successful in developing public education and a sound program of public support, the toll of deaths and injuries and the economic loss will be drastically reduced. Community safety organizations have proven to be the most effective way of providing a coordinated attack on accidents in a community.

According to *The Fight for Life* (7), "The total accident situation is a problem of national scope, but solutions must be found at the local, regional and state levels."

Pinpointing and attacking the specific immediate problems are some 200 citizen safety organizations operated by volunteers, and an additional 80 organizations manned by full-time professional staffs. Most citizens councils work in all areas of accident prevention as does the National Safety Council. Accredited organizations, which are subject to annual evaluation of their activities, serve the safety needs of more than 60 per cent of the population of the nation.

summary

It has been found that the best way to combat accidents in a community is through activities developed by a community safety organization—often called a safety council. These organizations coordinate and activate accident prevention programs. Included in the organization are representatives of official agencies, such as the police, fire, health and other departments, community organizations, and agencies with the support of the general public.

To insure a successful organization, several important steps should be taken. A study should first be made of the accident situation to determine the need. At the same time, another study should be conducted among community leaders to determine whether or not there is real interest in supporting such an organization. A steering committee consisting of well-known local leaders should be appointed and, after consultation with representatives of the National Safety Council or local councils, a meeting should be held, with invitations extended to representatives of official agencies, local organizations and citizens support groups.

If a decision is made to go ahead with the organization, two committees should be appointed, one on finance and another on constitution and by-laws. Following this a board of directors, trustees and officers should be elected and a manager appointed. Activity committees should then be selected, normally one for each of the following areas: traffic and transportation, home, school, public, and occupational or industrial safety. These committees establish objectives and plan activities. It has been found best to have them concentrate on a few activities; after these are completed, others can be initiated.

suggested projects and activities

1. Prepare a list of community officials with legal responsibility for some phase of accident prevention.

2. Prepare a list of civic, service, professional, fraternal, women's and other organizations in the community.
3. Make a chart covering a five-year period showing deaths and injuries from various types of accidents.
4. Make a chart covering a five-year period showing economic loss from various types of accidents.
5. List common causes of accidents at work, in traffic, at home and in public.
6. Conduct an inventory of what is now being done in the community to prevent accidents.
7. Arrange for speakers and programs to cover major accident problem areas at public meetings.
8. Develop a scrapbook with newspaper articles on accidents.

selected references

1. Halsey, Maxwell, ed., *Accident Prevention: The Role of Physicians and Public Health Workers*. New York: McGraw-Hill Book Company, 1961.
2. Hebden, Norman, and Wilbur S. Smith, *State-City Relationships in Highway Affairs*. New Haven: Yale University Press, 1950.
3. Ladd, Walter D., *Organizing for Traffic Safety in Your Community*. Springfield, Ill.: Charles C. Thomas, Publisher, 1959.
4. National Safety Council, *Community Safety Organization, Principles, Policies, Programs*. Chicago: The Council, 1961.
5. ________, *Let's Have a Safe Community*. Chicago: The Council, 1963.
6. ________, *Safety in the 60's*. Chicago: The Council, 1959.
7. ________, *The Fight for Life*. Chicago: The Council, 1963.
8. President's Committee for Traffic Safety, *Organize Your Community for Traffic Safety*. Washington, D.C.: U.S. Government Printing Office, 1954.
9. ________, *Workbook—Regional Traffic Safety Conferences*. Washington, D.C.: U.S. Government Printing Office, 1956.

21

measurement and evaluation

Teachers and administrators want to know how well their safety programs meet existing standards; schools and local safety organizations are concerned with accident trends which indicate the extent to which safety education is producing results in reducing accidents. Teachers need to measure the results of instruction through various kinds of tests and scales. These and other problems will be discussed in this chapter.

It should be pointed out that safety education differs from history and certain other school subjects. In those subjects we are primarily interested in the pupil's knowledge and information. However, in safety education, while we test for knowledge, we are primarily interested in behavior resulting from attitudes, skills and knowledge. A safe driver, for example, is not only well-informed; he is skillful and has good attitudes. Thus, an evaluation of a safety program would involve the measurement of knowledge, skills and attitudes.

Evaluation Media

Several methods may be used to evaluate safety programs. One of these is an analysis of safety activities of individuals, groups or communities; a second makes use of accident records to observe accident causes and trends; a third provides for the utilization of tests, scales and other measuring instruments.

Activity Analysis

What kinds of activities tend to make school children safe? For illustration, safety patrols are a part of school programs; therefore, the National Safety Council inventory of safety education includes items that have to do with the operation of patrols. Checklists such as those are prepared by the National Commission on Safety Education (15) and the National Safety Council (18) can be used by administrators to evaluate the safety activities of individuals and of the school district.

In addition, there are many other inventories or standards that can be used: the American Red Cross standards for swimming pools and water safety; the National Board of Fire Underwriters checklists on fire prevention for schools, homes and communities (13, 14).

Another inventory that has been useful in the area of traffic safety is the National High School Driver Education Achievement Program for states (10), which is administered by the Insurance Institute for Highway Safety. Still another is the basis of the National Pedestrian Protection Contest organized by the American Automobile Association. Other inventories are used by the National Safety Council to evaluate city and state activities in traffic engineering, enforcement, traffic courts, accident records, public information, education and other areas. There are also inventories or standards for school building construction, school shops, swimming pools and playground construction, several of which are published by the American Standards Association. In fact, inventories or standards can be found for almost every type of school program.

Inventories which measure the *quantity* of activities in school and college programs are relatively easy to prepare. For example, quantitative items in a school driver education inventory would include such questions as: What percentage of your high schools are teaching driver education? What percentage of eligible students in your school have completed driver education courses?

It is much more difficult to measure the *quality* of a program. The committee that administers the National High School Driver Education Achievement Program has been working for many years to get satisfactory measures of quality. The same is true of the Traffic Safety Inventories of the National Safety Council. They have taken years to perfect. Quality in safety education programs is especially difficult to measure.

Some checklists or inventories, while relatively easy to prepare, could be made more valuable. Many cities, for example, are using home fire-inspection checklists, distributing these to all pupils. It is relatively easy for the child working with his parent to inspect the home. It is possible to organize the program so that pupils report on the inventory form the steps taken to correct hazardous conditions.

Inventories have some value in that they call to one's attention the elements that make for safety, but their greatest value comes when unsafe conditions are corrected, hazards removed and dangerous practices changed.

City and State Surveys

In some instances school boards, at the request of local safety councils, authorize surveys of safety activities. Various techniques can be used, depending upon the time and the manpower available. The National Safety Council inventory can be used for a study of traffic safety education. Checklists can be prepared from *The Administrator and the School Safety Program* (3) or from the *Checklist on Safety and Safety Education in Your School* (15). The latter is comprehensive and includes several hundred items.

Among the subjects that could be included in such a survey are the following:

General administration.
Accident records.
Hazards in and about school buildings.
Daily school routine and maintenance.
Instruction.
Fire and civil defense drills.
Pupil transportation.
Driver education.
Provisions for first aid.

When the survey is completed, a report with recommendations should be prepared. Such a report should point out the strong points of the program as well as those that need improvement. In making recommendations, comparisons with existing standards should be made. Many safety standards are now available from national organizations. Many state departments of education have divisions which establish standards for school buildings. Architects and builders are expected to make use of these standards.

Accident Records

Every school system should have an accident reporting system. Reports should be periodically analyzed by the staff to determine trends in types and causes of accidents. This information should be distributed to the schools, to the press and to other community agencies. The use of these records is discussed in Chapter 17.

It is of interest to note that the cities in the United States that have had

superior child accident records year after year have been those that have good safety programs, including accident reporting, and in a majority of instances that have a safety supervisor.

School districts can compare their accident rates with those of other cities. They can also compare their district's distribution of accidents by cause and place of occurrence with the summary records for all communities that appear in the National Safety Council's publication *Accident Facts* (19).

As in the case of accident records in industry and in transportation, the total of accidents is a far better measure of school programs than the number of fatalities. There are innumerable instances of complete distortion of the accident trend curve for a community by a single bad accident resulting in the death or injury of several people. For example, a single bad school bus accident will sharply increase the pupil transportation accident rate for a community.

School administrators can compare the accident rates of the schools with the national rate. The following National Safety Council list is based on reports from 57,000 school districts with an enrollment of 3.2 million pupils. While this is a small percentage of enrollment in all schools it does provide a good sampling. Rates are based on the number of accidents per 100,000 days.

Accident rate by grades–school jurisdiction

All grades—	Kgn.	1	2	3	4	5	6	7	8	9	10	11	12
10.1	5.0	5.4	5.7	6.6	7.2	8.2	10.1	12.6	14.7	17.9	20.6	20.6	19.2

It will be observed that there is a steady increase in the rate from the kindergarten to the junior and senior high schools. This is largely due to increased physical education, recreation and sports.

Testing in Safety Education

Testing is an important evaluation tool, but for the most part teachers will have to depend on developing their own safety tests or using those prepared by supervisors. To date but few suitable standardized tests of safety education have been prepared. Moreover, the few tests that are on the market are measures of knowledge and information. Standardized scales for measuring attitudes and performance skills are for the most part confined to driver education (4,5,6). Fortunately, most teachers have taken courses in tests and measurement and are familiar with the various types of objective tests.

There are several types for measuring knowledge or information. Among these are multiple-choice, matching, completion, alternate-

MULTIPLE-CHOICE

Each of the following statements has several possible answers; one of these best completes the statement. Indicate your answer to each statement by placing the letter indicating your choice within the parenthesis.

( ) 1. The most common cause of fires in the home is (a) electric short circuits (b) lightning (c) matches and smoking (d) spontaneous combustion.

( ) 2. The most common causes of home injuries is (a) explosions (b) elec- (b) electric shocks (c) falls (d) poisons

Complete the following statements with the most appropriate word or phrase.

1. Most accidents in high schools take place in ________.
2. The poisonous substance present in natural gas used in cooking and heating is ____________________________.

MATCHING

Indicate in the parentheses the numbers of items in the second column that corresponds best to the items in the first column.

( ) a.	Principal cause of home accidents	1.	spontaneous combustion
		2.	physical education
( ) b.	Principal cause of home fires	3.	matches and smoking
		4.	falls
( ) c.	Activity where most school accidents occur	5.	electricity
		6.	industrial arts

Note that the second column has more items than the first. What is the reason for this?

TRUE-FALSE

Some of the following statements are true; others are false. If you think that a statement is true, circle the letter T; if it is false, circle the letter F.

1. Most traffic accidents are caused by faulty brakes. T F
2. If the rear wheels of a car start to skid to the right, turn the steering wheel to the right. T F
3. Lack of knowledge is the chief weakness of drivers that contributes to accidents. T F

JUDGMENT SITUATIONS

In this type, real-life situations are introduced in which pupils are directed to indicate what they would do. The following are illustrations:

1. You are walking along the street and see a wire dangling from an electric light pole. What would you do?
2. While on a canoe trip with another boy, your canoe capsizes 100 yards from the shore. Your friend, who is a strong swimmer, suggests that he swim ashore to get help. How do you feel about this?

response (true-false), and judgment. Some are constructed using one type of item such as multiple-choice; others use several types, for not all questions lend themselves to one. The following are illustrations of the various types:

Other Tests

The following organizations have tests available for general distribution. However, few have been standardized.

Traffic Safety

Aetna Casualty and Surety Co., Hartford, Connecticut
American Automobile Association, 1712 G Street, NW, Washington, D.C.
Bicycle Institute of America, 122 East 42nd Street, New York, N.Y.
Center for Safety Education, New York University, 6 Washington Square-North, New York, N.Y.
Ford Motor Company, Dearborn, Michigan
Humble Oil and Refining Co., Houston, Texas
Iowa State College, Ames, Iowa
National Commission on Safety Education, 1201 Sixteenth Street, NW, Washington, D.C.

Other Safety Subjects

American Red Cross, Washington, D.C. (or local chapters). Water safety, first aid.
National Safety Council, 425 North Michigan Avenue, Chicago, Illinois. Short tests appear regularly in the magazines, *Safety Education* and *School Safety.*
School textbooks. School textbooks in driver education include many tests.

Subjective Tests Many teachers prefer to use subjective tests. They feel that these show the ability of the student to organize programs, to describe activities, and to think through a problem. Many of the items that appear at the end of chapters in this text could be used as subjective questions. Objective tests, however, enable the instructor to cover more ground. A combination of both kinds of tests is often used.

Standard Tests and Scales Standard tests take considerable time to prepare. For illustration, Siebrecht spent several years in developing his *Attitude Scale for Drivers* (4) as part of his doctoral thesis. McGlade's *Road Test* (5) was also an outcome of his doctoral thesis. The Center for Safety Education, which published both of these, required over a year to standardize the *National Test in Driver Education* (7). These three now provide teachers with instruments for measuring the skills, knowledge and attitudes of drivers. There is great need for additional standard tests in various fields of safety especially for use in the elementary schools.

The *Siebrecht Attitude Scale* is made up of 40 items and the individual is asked to indicate his reaction to each item by checking one of the five responses. The following are examples:

1. Drivers convicted of hit-and-run accidents should have their licenses revoked.
   ___Strongly disagree ___Disagree ___Undecided ___Agree ___Strongly agree
2. A person should pass a physical examination before being issued a driver's license.
   ___Strongly disagree ___Disagree ___Undecided ___Agree ___Strongly agree

The Hannaford *Industrial Safety Attitude Scale for Male Employees* (6) consists of 20 items. These are the subject circles "A" for "agree" or "D" for "disagree". The following are examples:

1. Working conditions in any factory are much better if safety rules are lived up to. A D
2. Each employee needs his own personal rules so safety is only partly effective. A D

Performance or Rating Scales

The driver's license examination is one form of performance scale. Several other scales for drivers have been prepared, including one by Neyhart and another by McGlade. The McGlade *Road Test* is made up of 28 items, such as making right turns, changing lanes and stopping at stop signs. The total possible score for a perfect performance is 244 points. Ten points are deducted for poor performance on most of the items, five points for fair. Since the scale has good reliability and validity, it is useful in research studies involving driver testing.

Evaluation of Driver Education

Well over 30 studies of the value of driver education have been reported. Most of these are concerned with studies of the comparative accident record of "trained" in comparison with "untrained" drivers.

There are fundamentally three types of measurement and evaluation studies conducted in driver education:

1. Pretest driver education students with respect to knowledge, attitudes and skills and retest at the end of the course.
   Several studies of this kind have been reported showing that there is an improvement in knowledge, skills and attitudes as a result of instruction.
2. Pretest two generally comparable groups of students, one of which takes a course in driver education while the other does not. Follow by a post-test and compare results.
3. Compare the accident and violations records of two groups that are similar with respect to certain major variables (control factors). One group should have had driver education; the other, not. This is the most common type of evaluation although it is very difficult to conduct. The real problem in 2 and 3 above is how to match the groups. What factors should be matched? Some studies have confined equating to sex and

> age; others have included intelligence, school marks, past driving experience and initial interest. Unless the groups are really matched, the studies will not be of much value.

In all but four of the 30 studies mentioned above, the "trained" group showed a decided superiority over the "untrained" in both accident and violations records. The most important state evaluation study was reported by the Office of the Secretary of State in Illinois. Both the "trained" and "untrained" groups included several hundred thousand drivers. The results confirmed earlier studies, for the "trained" group has a decidedly better record.

Since it is difficult to match groups on the most important factors, the results of many of these studies can be questioned. However, it is generally conceded that drivers that have had instruction have better records than those that have not. New methods of evaluation using other criteria need to be developed. In the meantime, teachers should continue to measure and evaluate, using standard tests that have been mentioned or other tests included in courses of study and textbooks.

There are five basic objectives of driver education that have been discussed in Chapter 4.

Thus far, most evaluation has been concerned with one objective—driving performance, as measured by accident and violations records. Evaluations to cover the four other *main objectives* should also be conducted.

Status of Tests for Safe Behavior in Driving According to Ojemann in *Testing for Safe Behavior* (21):

> A few studies of drivers have shown significant differences in knowledge test scores between high-accident and low-accident groups, but such differences have not appeared consistently.
>
> Speed of movement, skill in manipulation, ability to observe moving objects, perception of depth, judging of distance, and acuity of vision are among the so-called psychophysical factors. It has been found that test results in this area do not correlate highly with actual behavior.
>
> Since knowledge shows a low correlation with actual behavior, other determinants have been studied in recent years and attitude have been a focal point in connection with the search. . . .
>
> The Seibrecht and Iowa State College instruments have proved reliable to a satisfactory extent. Their correlation with actual behavior, however, has not been clearly established.

Personality and Adjustment Tests Many research studies have been conducted in attempts to determine the personal characteristics that contribute to accidents. The tests or scales used include the Minnesota Multiphasic, the Sacks Sentence Completion, the Thurstone Personality Inventory, the Cornell Word Form, the Kuder Preference, the Bernreauter and at least a dozen others. Most of these have been used with two groups of drivers, the accident-free and repeaters. In general, these studies have shown that no single test or scale has much value in differentiating between individuals in these two groups. In some cases, combinations of tests and scales appear to have some value. One comprehensive study of U. S. Air Force drivers was conducted at the University of Colorado Medical School. The instrument that showed the best results in differentiating between accident-repeaters and accident-free was a special adaptation of the *Allport-Vernon Study of Values.*

It is evident that the personality characteristics that tend to make a person susceptible to accidents are deep-seated. There are undoubtedly combinations of characteristics that make up the accident syndrome, a group of concurrent symptoms. However, it is probable that eventually some test or scale will be developed to measure the characteristics that cause accidents. If man can measure the chemical components of the sun and certain fixed stars, the speed of light, a millionth of a second in time, eventually, as the need increases, he will find measurements of accident susceptibility.

Observation of Behavior There is another type of evaluation in which comparatively little has been done. This is the observation and recording of unsafe practices. This technique involves much more time and manpower than giving tests and scales. The latter, however, have not shown much value in measurement of safe practices. The following are illustrations of observation:

1. A principal wishes to know how his patrols are functioning. One measure of this is to observe the number of unsafe acts (violations) by pupils at patrolled intersections and compare this with the number of pupils who cross intersections properly.

2. The number of unsafe acts in industrial arts and vocational education shops can be recorded.

3. Forms of unsafe behavior—running in the corridors and on stairs, unsafe practices in the gymnasium and the cafeteria—could be observed and recorded.

Similarly, behavior in other activities could be evaluated by:

1. Recording unsafe acts at a swimming pool.
2. Recording unsafe acts of youngsters at a camp.
3. A foreman observing bad practices in an industrial shop.
4. A supervisor following trucks in a passenger car and recording unsafe practices. This is already being done in many large fleets and in some cases includes taking motion pictures of bad practices.

There are other activities in which safe practices can be evaluated by the techniques discussed. It is apparent that these techniques are apt to get more useful results than the use of paper and pencil tests and scales. In all these studies individuals should not know that they are being observed.

summary

Teachers and administrators want to know how well their safety program meets existing standards. Boards of education and local safety organizations are concerned with accident trends, which reveal to some extent whether safety education is actually reducing accidents. Administrators also want to know how well buildings and other school facilities meet national safety standards. Therefore, there is a need for measurement and evaluation of the safety program.

There are several methods of measurement and evaluation that schools can use. One method includes surveys and analyses of the safety activities in the schools. This requires the use of checklists or inventories. It also includes surveys of school building and other facilities for hazardous conditions. A second method makes use of the record of accidents and accident trends. This requires a complete accident reporting system. The acid test of a safety program is "Does it reduce accidents?" However, it is best when comparing accidents to use trends over a period of years rather than to do it on a year-to-year basis. Another method is the use of tests, scales and other measuring instruments. Unfortunately, there are few suitable standardized tests in safety education.

It will be necessary for teachers and supervisors to prepare their own tests. The types of objective tests that are used most are: (1) multiple choice, (2) completion, (3) matching, (4) true-false and (5) judgment. While *psycho-physical* tests for drivers are used in many high schools to measure certain personal characteristics, research has shown that the individual characteristics they measure are not of great importance in driving, unless scores are very poor. However, these tests do have educational value and should be continued.

A good measure of the safety of a pupil is his own behavior in day-by-day activities and in hazardous situations. The accident and violations record of a driver is one measure of his behavior on the streets and highways. Similarly, the number of accidents in a school shop is one measure of the value of the safety program. It is expected that in the future more work will be done in the preparation and standardization of new tests and scales.

suggested projects and activities

1. Prepare a short survey form and conduct a study of one of the school buildings to show unsafe conditions that should be corrected. Develop recommendations to correct these unsafe conditions.
2. What methods are being used to correct hazards in your school building?
3. Keep a record of the accidents that occur in your building for one semester. What suggestions could you make for changes in the safety program to prevent recurrence of these accidents?
4. List the advantages and disadvantages of objective and subjective tests.
5. Prepare a 30-item general safety test to be used in the sixth grade before students move on to the junior high school.
6. Prepare a survey form which you could use in a two-day study of an elementary school safety program.

selected references

1. American Automobile Association, *Pedestrian Protection.* Washington, D.C.: The Association (annual).
2. Brody, Leon, "Methods and Patterns of Research in Industrial Accidents," *Annals of the New York Academy of Sciences,* May, 1963, pp. 635-695.
3. Center for Safety Education, New York University, *The Administrator and the School Safety Program.* New York: The Center, 1954.
4. ________, *Siebrecht Attitude Scales.* New York: The Center, 1941.
5. ________, *New Road Test.* New York: The Center, 1963.
6. ________, *Industrial Safety Attitude Scales for Male Employees.* New York: The Center, 1962.
7. ________, *National Test in Driver Education.* New York: The Center, 1963.
8. Gulliken, J. P., *Theory of Mental Tests.* New York: John Wiley & Sons, Inc., 1950.
9. Humble Oil and Refining Co., *You and Your Driving.* Houston, Texas: The Company (n.d.).
10. Insurance Institute for Highway Safety, *Annual Report of the National High School Driver Education Achievement Award.* Washington, D.C.: The Institute, 1963.
11. Iowa State College, *Conover Attitude Scales for Drivers.* Ames, Iowa: The College (n.d.).
12. Mathews, D. K., *Measurement in Physical Education,* Philadelphia: W. B. Saunders Co., 1963.
13. National Board of Fire Underwriters, *Fire Prevention and Protection as Applied to the Public and Parochial Schools.* New York: The Board, 1954.
14. ________, *How Safe is Your Home?* New York: The Board, 1954.
15. National Commission on Safety Education, *Checklist on Safety and Safety Education in Your School.* Washington, D.C.: The Commission, 1953.
16. ________, *Criteria for Driver Education.* Washington, D.C.: The Commission, 1954.
17. ________, *Policies and Practices for Driver Education.* Washington, D.C.: The Commission, 1963.
18. National Safety Council, *Traffic Safety Inventory.* Chicago: The Council (annual).
19. ________, *Accident Facts.* Chicago: The Council (annual).
20. ________, *Safety Education.* Chicago: The Council.
21. Ojemann, Ralph H., *Tests and Evaluation Methods Used in Driver and Safety Education,* abstracted as *Testing for Safe Behavior.* Washington, D.C.: National Commission on Safety Education, 1959.
22. Strasser, Marland K., *et al., Fundamentals of Safety Education.* New York: The Macmillan Company, 1964.

22

research

It has been said that the psychology of safe behavior is no more and no less than the psychology of human behavior in general. Indeed, safety educators and others concerned with accident prevention must go beyond the traditional limits of psychology if they are to render optimum service. The greatest need in the field today is to pull together relevant knowledge from a variety of sciences. The research findings of many disciplines have a bearing upon accident prevention. But if these are to be used effectively, they must be considered in the light of a reasonable conceptual framework.

A Framework of Reference

Traditionally, cause and effect have been regarded as single, consecutive links in a chain. Gradually the life sciences developed a concept of multiple causality. Now scientists are finding it convenient to abandon the concept of causation per se. Thus a physicist may regard a phenomenon as an event taking place in a field characterized by a complex of forces and conditions, and his objective is not so much to find or manipulate a "cause" as to discover a means of effective intervention.

This concept now seems appropriate to the phenomenon of accidents. In the past, scores of studies were undertaken to correlate accident involvement with single isolated traits such as reaction time, visual acuity and intelligence. The results were overwhelmingly insignificant—except that inevitably they indicated the need to look in other directions. The dynamics of accident involvement now seem to fall into the following framework.

Human factors of one kind or another—physiological, biochemical, psychological—underlie any accident. These factors are meaningless, however, without reference to environmental considerations. The latter include such things as the intrinsic nature of a task or activity, social factors or forces, and sheer physical or chemical aspects of the individual's environment. Essentially, the accident problem appears to be a matter of disharmony or imbalance between man and environment, resulting in a hyperstressing situation. Given the "right" combination of human and environmental factors, an accident may ensue. Because of the role of chance, however, the result may not be injurious or even property-damaging. But such potential is always present. Consequently, studying accidents may be less profitable for research than studying the complex of forces or conditions that prevail during an activity.

Fortunately, most of these conditions, human and environmental, appear to be modifiable, by education, engineering, and other means. In such a context there can hardly be accident-prone people in the fixed, predetermined sense. Rather there are accident-disposing sets of conditions.

Problems in Safety Research

The complex, dynamic interrelationships between man and his environment at any given time tend to explain the difficulties and limitations to be found in much safety research of the past. It also sheds light on the lag of present progress in accident prevention. In the first half of the twentieth century, some elementary safety education, some simple mechanical safeguards, and the like served to correct relatively obvious hazards, or at least to bring them under reasonable control. Now researchers must deal with more subtle aspects of the problem, and these are indeed elusive.

For example, a number of investigators have pointed out that, despite all the work that has been done, the best way to detect an individual with accident tendencies is through a consideration of the accidents he has already been involved in. Much "evidence" along other lines may be questioned because it is based on doubtful assumptions and unacceptable statistical methodology or research design.

In the latter regard, accident occurrence to an individual *is* a relatively rare phenomenon, so that a long, carefully checked period of exposure for large numbers of individuals is necessary in order to obtain true measures of accident tendencies. Here, the still limited dependability of accident records and various psychological tests remains an obstacle in the path of definitive research.

One of the major shortages in accident records is sound identification of *degree* of responsibility for an event. A so-called accident repeater may not really be one in terms of responsibility. Or consider the converse, with this illustration: A golfer struck by lightning may be regarded as a victim of fate—but what if he took the risk of threatening weather in the hope that this would make the fairways less crowded?

With regard to psychological tests, the primary need is for more valid, objective, "global" tests of personal adjustment. Such tests would be particularly appropriate to the conceptual framework outlined at the beginning of this chapter. It is well to bear in mind, however, that even such tests could not serve as a total substitute for human judgment, any more than serological tests, X-rays, and electronic computers may be depended on to supplant the clinical insight of the physician.

Statistically, it is to be emphasized again that accidents are so varied in the circumstances attending them, with so many contributing factors, that no *one* factor can be expected to be invariably prominent. Moreover, in our natural search for objectivity and quantification we seem to have undertaken, in safety as in other fields, to measure or correlate nearly everything. Reason has been too often subordinated to measurement and statistics. The problem is aggravated in the case of social and behavioral phenomena whose underlying characteristics naturally tend to shift and drift in ways that thwart true repetition of experimental trials.

Advances being made in research designs do hold hope for a better understanding of accident behavior. Multivariate statistical techniques—as distinguished from univariate experiments in which only the independent variable is significantly altered—are much more compatible with our new conceptual framework. One of the next steps in safety research will be to formulate more sophisticated designs of this order.

Another problem in accident research concerns laboratory studies and the use of instrumentation. There are authorities who believe that one can generalize little from a laboratory investigation of behavior to the actual behavior of human beings in real life. Even physiologists, a precisely working professional group, have encountered difficulties in proceeding from *in vitro* to *in vivo* conditions. Consequently it is necessary to reaffirm the importance of following up the results of laboratory investigations of accident-type behavior by relevant explorations of the real settings in which accidents may occur.

Research and Teaching

Much can be done in relating *available* knowledge in various disciplines to the problems of accident prevention and control. For example, there is already a wealth of clinical information regarding the personality profiles of children, adolescents and members of other age groups. These suggest, among other things, that childhood is a critical period for the formation of safe attitudes; and that the adolescent and aging eras are normally hyperstressing and therefore not likely to be compatible with the requirements of safe behavior.

In seeking additional knowledge, research procedures such as the following are likely to be fruitful:

1. Depth-interviews of students and others about their accident experiences, including minor accidents and those that may not have been reported.
2. Investigation of near-accidents and critical or unusual behavior of students. They are at least logically significant for the understanding and control of accidents.
3. Study of students and others who have a good safety record, as well as problem youth. When we know what makes the good ones good, we shall have a better basis for positive safety education.

To the teacher this will mean that the classroom is also a laboratory. That is as it should be. The art of scientific investigation needs to be regarded as an intrinsic part of the everyday teaching process. That is to say, teachers must really get to know their students; they must be able to detect and interpret critical behavior of their sudents; and they must design their instructional efforts accordingly.

As for "automated teaching," one cannot ignore the present and future impact of programmed texts, teaching machines, driving simulators, and other devices that have been or are being developed and that will be refined by future research. Nevertheless the teacher still occupies the key spot in the learning process. No device as yet programs itself, does a major job in attitude development (the crucial area of safety education), or evaluates the product of its efforts in relation to the objectives of instruction.

These are some of the things that safety educators must be well equipped to do. And if we accept the conceptual framework that underlies this chapter, then it follows that *every* educator is potentially a safety educator. For research in safety and related areas strongly suggests that no single course of study will do the job of effecting safe behavior. Nor will any single methodological formula. Foundations must be laid in the earliest grades and in the home, and pursued at all educational levels. Research that helps to make children more secure, more responsible, more civic minded, is research that helps to preserve them for wholesome adult life.

Finally, a great gap needs to be closed, the gap between research and practice. The findings of research need to be communicated more effectively to the users of research. Although many questions concerning accident prevention still need to be answered, the American public is not receiving the full benefits of what research has already accomplished, because educators and other users have not sufficiently sought out or been informed of these accomplishments. There is a striking parallel to be found in the 1964 report of the President's Commission on Heart Disease, Cancer and Stroke:

> Every day, men and women are dying who need not die . . . not for lack of scientific knowledge, but for lack of the right care at the right time. Every available fact points to the same conclusion—that the toll of heart disease, cancer and stroke can be sharply reduced now, in this nation, in this time . . . without further scientific advance.

This may well be true of the accident problem.

summary

The psychology of safe behavior is no more and no less than the psychology of human behavior in general. The greatest need in the field today is to pull together relevant knowledge from a variety of sources. The research findings of many disciplines have a bearing upon accident prevention.

The complex, dynamic interrelationships between man and his environment at any given time tend to explain the difficulties and limitations to be found in much safety research in the past. It also sheds light on the lag of present progress in accident prevention. It is to be emphasized again that accidents are so varied in the circumstances attending them, with so many contributing factors, that no one factor can be expected to be invariably prominent.

Much can be done in relating available knowledge in various disciplines to the problem of accident prevention and control. In seeking additional knowledge, research procedures such as the following are likely to be fruitful:

1. Depth-interviews of students and others about their accident experiences.
2. Investigation of near accidents and critical or unusual behavior of students.
3. Study of students and others who have a good safety record, as well as problem youth. When we know what makes the good ones good, we shall have a better basis for positive safety education.

Finally, a great gap needs to be closed, the gap between research and practice. The findings need to be communicated more effectively to the users of research.

selected references

1. Brody, Leon, *Human Factors Research in Occupational Accident Prevention*. Chicago: American Society of Safety Engineers, 1962. Published in cooperation with the Center for Safety Education, New York University.
2. ———, "Methodology and Patterns of Research in Industrial Accidents," *Annals of the New York Academy of Sciences*, 107:635-695, May 1963.
3. Haddon, W., E. Suchman and D. Klein, *Accident Research*. New York: Harper & Row, Publishers, 1964.
4. Selye, H., *The Stress of Life*. New York: McGraw-Hill Book Company, 1956.
5. Stratemeyer, C., *Accident Research for Better Safety Teaching*. Washington, D.C.: National Commission on Safety Education, 1964.

23

the future of safety education

Prediction of the future is always an intriguing, absorbing but precarious business. It is difficult to say exactly how far and in what directions the science and art of safety education will move. The startling and wonderful advances made in the last 20 years in the physical sciences could hardly have been predicted. It is regrettable that our advances in the social sciences have lagged so much behind the achievements in the physical sciences. Unfortunately, not many significant advances have been made in our knowledge of behavior, personality and the arts of persuasion.

Much of safety education depends upon the last named fields. How safe a man is depends to a large extent on his behavior, his personality and the success of efforts that have been made in educating and persuading him.

Safety today is far different from what it was for prehistoric man. The primitive lived or died in accordance with the sensitivity and rapidity of his innate responses to threats and hazards. He avoided dangers by dodging, running or climbing out of the way. But today there are myriad threats to survival, many of them hidden, unseen and unfelt. These have to be anticipated and planned for, with safety education preparing us for the proper response.

According to Whitney,

> the outstanding characteristic of our life today is the marvelous control which we now possess over physical forces and conditions. We have a host of powerful forces at our command. . . . A controlled world is now possible as never before.[9]

We have been able to reduce the losses of life from floods, fires and machines used in industry. While electricity is used in most of our homes, it is under control. The same is true of illuminating gas. But we have not had too much success in the control of one type of machine—the motor vehicle.

Safety at the Crossroads

Safety seems to have reached a kind of plateau; the progress we have been making seems to have leveled off. Up until recent years, deaths from accidents were showing a downward trend. Due largely to the increase in fatal highway accidents, this trend has been reversed. The same is true for children of school age. The downward trend in their death rate was reversed several years ago, largely because of the increase in motor vehicle accidents. These increases should be a challenge to safety educators and all others in the accident prevention field to strengthen their activities. If we redouble our efforts in all fields of safety, we will make further reductions in accidents.

Guidelines to Future Success

What are some of the things which safety education in the future must include? We know that from 85 to 90 per cent of all deaths and injuries have human error or failure as their basic, primary cause. We must do more to educate people for safe living. We must do more to get at the underlying causes of accidents and direct our attack at them. As President Howard Pyle of the National Safety Council so aptly states it, "We can only get so much safety as people want to have." We must find the best possible ways of motivating people—practical ways based upon up-to-date thinking. We must focus our attention on human behavior.

Optimism about future improvement in safety is based upon man's ability to surmount obstacles and pierce barriers. For illustration, it has been difficult for us to activate programs in home safety. The home has been man's castle and not subject to many controls. But in recent years, we have made distinct progress in this field. The public at large is more aware of safety than ever before. There is a flood of mass-communication messages using all types of media. The question will naturally be raised —can this communication be made more effective? Research is needed to determine the value of these materials.

Unified Programs

During the next decade there will be far more unified programming and action in all the fields of safety. Interlocking cooperative action by all of the national safety foundations and organizations, schools and colleges, governmental agencies, business and industry, individuals on farms and in homes is needed. More local safety councils will be organized. State health departments will organize attacks on various types of accidents. The agencies in the states that are concerned with the control of motor vehicles will have a unified program. According to Walter A. Cutter in *Traffic Quarterly* (4):

> It is in connection with projective thinking and planning for the future that one of the major advantages of traffic safety management appears. Not only does it provide a framework for dealing more effectively with present traffic because it emphasizes combined and coordinated activity using all brains available, it becomes an admirable tool for continuously thinking ahead. . . . As yet this new professional approach is in its infancy, but in a world where predictions should be made with the greatest care, we make the confident assertion that traffic safety management is a blueprint for both the present and the future.

Personal Approach

Safety programs and activities must be planned in terms of people's personal needs, drives and motives. Advantage must be taken of the startling advances made in selling methods. Product motivation techniques have made many new approaches available. Promoting safety is like selling any other product. The public must be convinced that a definite need exists for it, that it is necessary to their everyday living—not a frill or passing fancy.

The introduction of new and complex machines and the speeding up in production mean that the need for safety is greater than ever. Scientific and technical advances continue to increase faster than man's ability to cope with the problems they create. Safety education aims at reducing the lag between man's creativeness and his ability to adjust to constant changes. Safety educators thus have the important responsibility of both convincing the public of the need for safety and at the same time developing improved attitudes and practices.

Is it possible to encourage safe practices in our youth and at the same time not suppress the love for adventure? We are doing this with our astronauts. Remarkable safety precautions do not detract from the spirit of adventure. We are doing this with our Boy Scouts. Safety is woven into all of the adventures of scouting activities. We are doing this on our winter ski slopes; safety is a must at all good skiing resorts. It can be done in many other fields.

Closer liaison between schools and colleges, industry, and the community must be established and maintained so that graduates will be properly conditioned to live and work safely. School and college graduates must have good safety attitudes derived from actual education in and practice of safe living in their school and other activities. They must know that they will be expected to be proficient in safety just as in the other skills and attitudes they have acquired in school.

Much more needs to be done to get at the underlying causes of accidents. Industry has made great strides in improving the environment of workers and reducing physical causes of accidents. Traffic engineering and improved highways have aided in the attack on highway accidents, but the traffic toll continues to mount. Off-the-job accidents are especially important and are several times more numerous than those that occur at work. Industries and communities must redouble activities in this field.

Institutions of higher learning have an obligation to the social order. This is especially true of state universities. There are many safety problems in industry, transportation, recreation, conservation, disaster control and education in general that they can help solve. This means more training courses in these fields as well as research.

Much of this research needs to be directed toward studies of behavior. Altogether too little is known as to why there is so much unsafe behavior. At one time it was felt that most accidents were due to simple underlying causes that could be revealed by tests and scales. But research studies, especially in the traffic field, have shown that this is not true. The underlying causes of accidents are various and deep seated in the human personality.

Moreover, the stresses leading to these safety problems place a premium on emotional stability, respect for the rights of others and an appreciation of social controls. If these qualities of citizenship are to be developed, the most capable means are to be found in the schools and colleges. Improved training together with research can do much to improve conditions.

Preparation for Leadership

There is a continuing need for leadership in all fields of safety. Traffic and transportation difficulties and the striking increase in motor vehicle registrations will require more traffic engineers, better-trained enforcement officers and motor vehicle examiners, and more traffic court officials.

In recent years there has been a demand for the preparation of state traffic managers or coordinators. Training courses have been arranged by a national committee and are offered at regional centers. These will be continued and expanded to include city traffic coordinators.

In the industrial field, more safety engineers and supervisors need to be prepared. Training opportunities will continue to be provided for supervisors of commercial fleets, instructors in commercial driving schools, fire prevention specialists, leaders in civil defense and drivers and supervisors of pupil transportation.

Some of this training will be given by the industries themselves, while colleges and universities are taking the lead in the preparation of those who will have supervisory responsibilitity. Much training will be carried on by state colleges. Safety centers, institutes or bureaus will continue to be organized, primarily for training purposes. Some of these will be partly financed by private industries or foundations; others by state appropriations and by income from tuition.

Safety Organizations

Since schools and colleges reach but a small segment of the adult population, a broad program of education should be developed by the various safety organizations and agencies. This should cover all of the more important areas of safety education, each organization preparing materials and carrying on activities according to its special interests. Many organizations have been active in promoting safety among adults. Their work is either through direct action, through public support or both. For illustration, the National Safety Council conducts certain activities by direct action sometimes working with local councils. It also provides public support for various types of activities. The work of the Council will continue to expand and more local councils will be organized.

There are many other organizations and agencies whose safety programs will continue to gain in importance. Among these are the Accident Prevention Division of the U.S. Public Health Service, the American National Red Cross, farm agencies and women's organizations. In addition, there is every reason to believe that the safety activities of insurance companies, the American Insurance Association, the National Fire Protection Association and the Insurance Institute for Highway Safety will increase. As a result of the stimulation of the President's Committee on Traffic Safety, it is probable that traffic safety activities of the organizations that make up this committee will be strengthened. Moreover, the accident prevention programs of the various agencies that make up the Federal Interdepartmental Safety Council will probably continue to expand. Accident prevention and fire prevention programs have clearly demonstrated their value over a period of years; they have proved to be a good investment and will continue to grow in importance.

The American National Red Cross

The Red Cross has exerted strong influence for many years in water safety, first aid, and disaster relief. Millions of copies of its publications on first aid have been distributed and millions of people have completed training courses. Most courses on water safety are conducted in schools, colleges and camps.

Influence of National Conferences

Several national conferences on various phases of safety have been called by Presidents of the United States. One of the first of these, "The White House Conference on Child Health and Protection," was called by President Hoover in 1932. This conference heard a report on safety education. Subsequently, a series of national conferences has been called: in 1946, the President's Conference on Highway Safety; in 1947, the President's Conference on Fire Prevention; and in 1949, the President's Industrial Safety Conference. These conferences had much to do with the development of safety education in the various areas. Since 1949, several follow-up conferences have been held. All of these included recommendations urging safety education in their reports. The Conferences on Highway Safety have resulted in the organization of the President's Committee for Traffic Safety. This is a highly important committee and includes over 35 national organizations.

Other Agencies

This brief historical review has touched mainly on the earlier stages of the safety movement and the work of those agencies most closely associated with this development. However, there are many other organizations that have had a valuable influence on safety education, in some instances extending back over 20 years. For illustration, the fire prevention and protection activities of the National Board of Fire Underwriters and the National Fire Protection Association have had outstanding value. The work of the American Society of Safety Engineers has resulted in important contributions to industrial safety. Farm organizations have helped reduce farm accidents. College safety centers have aided in the preparation of teachers. Various departments of the federal and state government have developed safety programs and issued publications. The American Driver and Traffic Safety Education Association has also exerted leadership in the field.

In Schools and Colleges

One might assume that safety education was due for rapid growth for it has so clearly demonstrated its value in reducing accidents to children. The death rate from accidents is approximately one-half that of twenty years ago. The steady decrease in the rate has been due largely to the work of the elementary schools. There are many other illustrations of the value of safety education. Many cities have found that a well-organized program of safety education can reduce accidents over 50 per cent. Several of the larger cities report a reduction of over 75 per cent during the last two decades. Safety education has paid real dividends in reducing child accidents.

It would be expected that any program that reduces child deaths and injuries would gain the wholehearted support of school administrators. The official endorsement of safety education by administrators was given in 1940 when the American Association of School Administrators published the 18th Yearbook, *Safety Education* (1). This publication discussed in detail the essential features of all phases of safety education. It had a valuable effect on the work of the schools.

Yet, there are many cities that do not have satisfactory safety programs. They do not even have accident reporting systems and such systems are the basis of a good safety organization. Moreover, in spite of the fact that regulations in many states require the teaching of safety education, colleges are graduating teachers who have had little preparation to teach safety. While driver education has been generally accepted as a responsibility of the high schools, there are still many states where not more than 25 per cent of the schools are giving this instruction. Thus, while safety education has clearly demonstrated its value, there are many cities where it is given but little attention—where it is apparently considered unimportant.

Several national conferences have been held on various aspects of accident prevention. Some of these were called by the Presidents, some dealing with highway safety, others with fire prevention and protection, and still others with occupational safety. In each of these conferences, committees on education prepared recommendations having to do with the improvement of the safety programs in schools and colleges. More of these conferences will be held. In some instances the national meetings were followed by state conferences. All of these undoubtedly have had value in the improvement of safety education activities. The National Commission on Safety Education has called four conferences on driver education and several on pupil transportation. The recommendations of the driver education conferences, published in *Policies and Practices for Driver Education* (6) have had much to do with setting standards and improving practices. Similarly, the work of the School and College Conference of the National Safety Council has made a valuable contribution to the work of elementary and secondary schools and the colleges. All of these activities have aided in the improvement of accident prevention programs. *Safety education is gaining in importance; in the future it should show steady growth.*

In the Elementary Schools

The reduction of accidents to children has been largely due to the work of the elementary schools. Many states and cities now require the teaching of safety education; this will be true of other states and cities. More states will prepare courses of study in safety education or include it in general elementary school course outlines.

A generation ago there were but few school systems with supervisors or directors assigned to safety education. The number has been growing steadily so that now there are several hundred members of the Supervisors' Section of the School and College Conference of the National Safety Council. School administrators are recognizing the importance of safety education. There is every reason to believe that supervisors will be appointed in more cities and states. In addition, the trend toward the appointment of teachers as safety coordinators in each school will be continued.

Techniques of teaching will improve in safety education as well as in other school subjects. In the future more stress will be placed on improving the skills and attitudes of children. While some cities will continue to use the direct method, devoting a definite time each week to safety lessons, the general trend will be toward integration and correlation with other school subjects. Moreover, certain cocurricular activities, such as safety patrols, that have clearly demonstrated their worth will become widespread.

In the Secondary Schools

The work of the secondary schools might be divided into two main areas, general safety and driver education. Progress in the former has been slow during the past decade while there have been outstanding developments in the latter. While many good reasons can be given why more stress should be placed on general safety, the outlook is not promising. A few schools will offer courses in general safety, but for the most part it will be taught through integration and correlation with other subjects. These methods have not proved as satisfactory in the secondary as in the elementary schools. This points up the need for a school safety coordinator.

Driver education has gained a strong foothold in the schools. While it has been and will continue to be criticized, its future is secure. According to the report of the National High School Driver Education Achievement Program of the Insurance Institute for Highway Safety, while growth in recent years has been slow, it will be more rapid in the future. This will be chiefly due to financial support legislation which has been adopted in more than 20 states and is being considered in others. In recent years, the greatest increase in the number of schools offering courses has been in those states providing financial support. It would appear that the best method of securing funds for this support is to collect fees for learner's permits or add to the cost of the driver's license. At least, this plan is working out satisfactorily in most of the states that have adopted it.

There are certain other problems that will have to be met. One is in the small schools with enrollments of under 100—too small a number for the full-time use of a car. One method that will be employed is to use one car in several schools; another is to offer the course every two years. Another important problem is what to do in the large high schools with enrollments of over 2,500, where 600 students might be eligible for driver education each year. Using the traditional plan of practice driving, this would require five or six full-time teachers and the same number of cars. Michigan and Florida have made great strides in the development of a so-called range or multiple-car plan. Many cities are also using simulators. Two predictions for the future emerge from these situations:

1. The range plan will be adopted by more and more schools.
2. Simulators will be utilized by more schools—especially those with big enrollments.

Both of these plans, which have been discussed in a previous chapter, enable the schools to prepare a larger number of drivers at a lower cost per pupil. In addition, in line with the recommendations of the National High School Driver Education Achievement Program and *Policies and Practices in Driver and Traffic Safety Education,* there are several other trends that will be continued (6):

1. The percentage of schools offering the complete program of driver education, rather than classroom instruction only, will increase.
2. More attention will be paid to the quality of the program, according to standards that have been developed by the National High School Driver Education Achievement Program.
3. There will be a steady growth in the number of parochial and other private schools offering courses.
4. There is a strong possibility that the standards for the approved course will be raised from 30 classroom hours and 6 of practice driving.

5. The qualifications of teachers will continue to improve with more preparation required for permanent certification.
6. The number of schools teaching driver education will continue to grow as will the percentage of eligible students given instruction each year.
7. More schools will develop public relations programs. Driver education needs to have good public support.

Teacher Education

There are some very good indications of the directions in which teacher education will move. There has been a consistent improvement in state certification requirements. In several states nine or more semester hours (three courses) are required for the permanent certificate. As certification requirements increase, the number of courses offered by colleges shows a corresponding growth. For illustration, Pennsylvania now requires 12 points for the permanent certificate in driver education. Over 20 colleges in that state offer three or more courses. As the number of high schools offering driver education increases, there will be a greater need for teacher preparation. More colleges will offer several courses and have minors in safety education.

There are now well over 400 colleges and universities that offer courses in safety education. This number will increase, especially in those states that have passed legislation for the financial support of driver education. In addition, since most teachers in the elementary schools are expected to teach safety education, it is expected that more colleges will provide instruction to prepare them for this responsibility.

Adult Education for the General Public

There is every reason to believe that there will be a steady growth and improvement in safety education for adults. This growth will undoubtedly be most conspicuous in the traffic safety and driver education fields. For illustration, commercial driving schools train well over a million drivers each year. More states will enact legislation directed to the improvement of the practices of these schools. Standards for the selection and training of instructors will be raised. Moreover, training courses for drivers of commercial vehicles and school buses will be given more attention. The same is true for driving improvement schools usually conducted with the cooperation of traffic courts and motor vehicle departments. It is also probable that more will be done in refresher instruction for adult drivers.

There are also indications of progress in other fields of safety. There will be an expansion of the training program in motor boat safety conducted by the Coast Guard Auxiliary, the Power Squadron and the American Red Cross. The same is true for the "hunter safety" courses. More attention will be paid to the prevention of school and college athletics accidents. There is evidence that there will be more farm safety education conducted by farm organizations. More instruction will also be given in water safety, usually with the cooperation of the American Red Cross. Industrial safety instruction will undoubtedly grow.

On the other hand, there are no indications at present of conspicuous growth in home safety or fire prevention education, but it is entirely possible, because of the interest of city and state health departments, that activities in these areas will be strengthened.

Research

Each of the reports of the various national conferences on safety—highway, fire prevention and protection and occupational safety—has included recommendations for research. In studies conducted by the School and College Conference of the National Safety Council, research has been found to be one of the most important needs. Altogether too little is known about the underlying causes of accidents, how to influence human behavior, and the best methods of teaching. There are many unsolved problems in all fields of safety.

What are the indications as to the future of research? This is difficult to predict, but certain observations can be made:

1. There will be an increasing number of research studies carried on by candidates for the master's and doctor's degrees in colleges and universities.
2. There is a need to consolidate or coordinate the research work of national organizations. At present there is too much overlapping and duplication.
3. In recent years, research grants for safety studies have been made available from federal agencies, national foundations and industries. There is every reason to believe that funds will continue to be available.
4. One important weakness in safety education is the failure to publish and make use of research findings. Many valuable studies are gathering dust on library shelves; they should be published and their findings utilized.

summary

Predictions for the future of any educational movement are always difficult to make. This is especially true of safety education and accident prevention. It would appear that any movement that had contributed so much to the saving of lives and the reduction of nonfatal injuries and property damage would be sure to grow. This is certainly true of industrial safety and the school safety movements. Having proven so successful, they ought to expand.

However, it is possible that safety is at the crossroads; it may be that we have reached a plateau or a turning point. If the movement is to grow, more attention must be paid to what people feel about safety and to finding the best ways of motivating them—practical ways based upon up-to-date thinking. The future will show more unified attacks through official and private organizations. There will also be a closer liaison between the schools, the colleges and industry.

Over the past three decades, school safety has paid rich dividends in reducing child accidents. There is every reason to believe that the work of the elementary schools will continue to grow. Driver education in the high schools will also show a steady growth. This is chiefly due to state financial support.

There are also indications that certain phases of adult education will show improvement. Examples are the commercial driving schools and driver improvement schools.

Safety organizations such as the National Safety Council and local safety councils have proven so valuable that they will continue to expand. In addition, there is every reason to believe, because of the stimulation of the President's Committee on Traffic Safety, that the work of the organizations making up this Committee will increase. This will mean more safety programs, more use of educational media, and more research.

suggested projects and activities

1. What are some of the reasons for feeling that safety is at the crossroads?
2. List and discuss briefly the guidelines to future safety success, supporting them with some corresponding predictions for the future of safety education.
3. Explain why closer liaison between schools and colleges and industry must be established and maintained in the future.
4. Prepare a list of ways of meeting the future needs of safety education in elementary schools and in secondary schools.
5. What illustrations can you give of types of safety education being carried on among adults in your community?
6. What methods can you suggest to increase the number of high school students completing driver education courses?

selected references

1. American Association of School Administrators, *Safety Education* (18th Yearbook). Washington, D.C.: National Education Association, 1940.
2. Brody, Leon and Herbert J. Stack, ed., *Highway Safety and Driver Education*. Englewood Cliffs, N.J.: Prentice-Hall, Inc., 1954.
3. Center for Safety Education, New York University, *Family Recreation and Safety*. New York: The Center, 1960.

4. Cutter, Walter A., "Unified Programming and Improved Traffic Safety," *Traffic Quarterly,* April, 1963. This quarterly is published by the Eno Foundation for Highway Traffic Control, Inc. of Saugatuck, Connecticut.
5. Elkow, J. Duke, "Safe Living, 1959-1969—A Prediction," *Journal of Health, Physical Education and Recreation,* April, 1959.
6. National Commission on Safety Education, *Policies and Practices for Driver and Traffic Safety Education.* Washington, D.C.: The Commission, 1960, 1964.
7. National Safety Council, *Safety in the Sixties.* Chicago, Illinois: The Council, 1959.
8. President's Committee for Traffic Safety, *Education.* Washington, D.C.: The Committee, 1960.
9. Stack, Herbert J., ed., *Safety for Greater Adventures: The Contributions of Albert W. Whitney.* New York: Center for Safety Education, New York University, 1953.
10. Strasser, Marland K. *et. al., Fundamentals of Safety Education.* New York: The Macmillan Company, 1964.

appendices

Appendix A
Sources of Audio-Visual Aids

The first sources that one would consult for safety education films would be the lists available in one's state. While they may not have extensive depositories, the following state departments often have films available—Education, Health, Conservation, and State Police or Highway Patrol. In addition, many universities have depositories. It is best to secure films locally when they are available.

The following are among the best known sources of audio-visual aids. All agencies have film lists. In some cases branch offices of organizations have prints available.

AAA Foundation for Traffic Safety, Washington, D. C. • Aetna Casualty and Surety Company, Hartford, Connecticut • American Association of Motor Vehicle Administrators, Washington, D. C. • American National Red Cross, Washington, D. C. • Association Films Inc., New York, New York • Coronet Films, Chicago, Illinois • Encyclopedia Britannica Films, Wilmette, Illinois • Ford Motor Company, Dearborn, Michigan • General Motors Corporation, Detroit, Michigan • Liberty Mutual Insurance Company, Boston, Massachusetts • Metropolitan Life Insurance Company, New York, New York • Modern Talking Picture Service, Inc., New York, New York • National Association of Automotive Mutual Insurance Companies, Chicago, Illinois • National Board of Fire Underwriters, New York, New York • National Commission on Safety Education, National Education Association, Washington, D. C. • National Film Board of Canada, New York, New York • National Safety Council, Chicago, Illinois • Nationwide Insurance Company, Columbus, Ohio • Travelers Insurance Company, Hartford, Connecticut • U. S. Department of Agriculture, Washington, D. C. • U. S. Department of Labor, Washington, D. C. • U. S. Public Health Service, Washington, D. C. • Walt Disney Productions, 16 mm. Department, Burbank, California • Young America Films, Inc., New York, New York • Zurich American Insurance Companies, Chicago, Illinois.

Appendix B
National Organizations and Agencies Publishing Safety Education Materials

There are many organizations that publish safety education materials. The following includes the best known national organizations:

American Automobile Association, Washington 25, D. C. (Or local club) • American National Red Cross, Washington 16, D. C. • Boy Scouts of America, New Brunswick, New Jersey • Department of Health, Physical

Education and Recreation, National Education Association, Washington 6, D. C. • Insurance Institute for Highway Safety, Washington 25, D. C. • National Board of Fire Underwriters, New York, N. Y. • National Commission on Safety Education, National Education Association, Washington 6, D. C. • National Congress of Parents and Teachers, Washington, D. C. • National Fire Protection Association, Boston, Mass. • National Rifle Association of America, Washington, D. C. • National Safety Council, Chicago, Ill. • Office of Civil Defense, Washington, D. C. • U. S. Department of Agriculture, Washington 25, D. C. • U. S. Coast Guard, Washington 25, D. C. • U. S. Forest Service, Washington 25, D. C. • U. S. Dept. of Health, Education and Welfare, Accident Prevention Division, Washington 25, D. C. • U. S. Dept. of Labor, Washington 25, D. C. In addition, a number of industries and insurance companies also have materials available for distribution.

index